DECISION *of* DESTINY

TO *Maralyn and Karen*
   Alice and Homer

Preface

IN many ways it seems presumptuous to attempt to reconstruct the interrelations among factors which enter the equation of such a complex decision as that to use the atomic bombs in 1945. So much of the evidence is fragmentary, so much is conflicting, and so much is recollection that the effort, of necessity, rests as much on conjecture as on fact.

I have tried to minimize conjecture and to maximize fact. And yet there were so many gaps in the data that it was necessary, at times, to weigh probabilities. Wherever possible, I employed original sources. Among others, the Manhattan Engineer District files were particularly useful. I owe much to General Leslie R. Groves, to McGeorge Bundy, and to Professor John

Donovan for their help in obtaining permission to use the files while they were still classified. Without the files, the margin of error would have been far greater.

I should like to thank all of those who have helped in the research of this manuscript. Particularly to Dr. Ruhl J. Bartlett, Professor of Diplomatic History at The Fletcher School of Law and Diplomacy, I owe a deep debt of gratitude for his guidance and his advice. To Dr. Albert B. Martin, Professor of Political Science at the University of Pittsburgh, my appreciation for his wit, his energy, and his realism in introducing me to the study of international politics.

I have found the writing to be both humiliating and humbling: humiliating, because of the repeated reminders of personal limitations; humbling, because while I have but described the actors and their actions, they have performed in the course of humanity. I have tried, therefore, to understand the magnitude of their problems and to make my judgments fair and reasonable. It is all too easy to prescribe, after the fact, the lines of action that should have been followed.

Despite the many frustrations that arose, there have been rewards. A little has been learned. Whatever merit this may have mostly reflects the persistent efforts of friends and teachers. The flaws that are here are mine alone.

W. S. S.

Orono, Maine
June, 1969

Table of Contents

DECISION *of* DESTINY

WALTER SMITH SCHOENBERGER   *University of Maine*

Ohio University Press/Athens

INTRODUCTION

PRESIDENT Harry S. Truman believed that the decision to use the atomic bombs was his alone. He has stated his conviction in his *Memoirs*: "The final decision of where and when to use the atomic bomb was up to me. Let there be no mistake about it. I regarded the bomb as a military weapon and never had any doubt that it should be used." [1] Obviously in a sense this was true; for as President of the United States and Commander-in-Chief of the Armed Forces, a decision of such importance was necessarily referred to him. He could not escape the ultimate responsibility for it. If the term "decision" is used, however, to include the influences that shaped it, the institutions that developed it, and the milieu that conditioned it, then it is also obvious that

Truman's action resulted from the interplay of a complexity of political forces. The President was new to his position. He had little knowledge of the bombs and little direct control over their production. To some degree, he was the instrument of decision rather than its creator. It might be useful to attempt to review and to analyze the factors that conditioned President Truman's decision.

NOTES TO INTRODUCTION

[1] Harry S. Truman, *Memoirs, Vol. I, Year of Decisions* (Garden City: Doubleday and Company, Inc., 1955), p. 419.

CHAPTER 1

FISSION TO MANHATTAN

THE scientific seed which ultimately grew into the mushroom clouds over Hiroshima and Nagasaki was first nurtured in the Kaiser-Wilhelm Institute at Berlin. It was there, in early December, 1938, that Otto Hahn and Fritz Strassmann (who with the exiled Lise Meitner had been experimentally bombarding the uranium atom since 1932) first discovered that their efforts had resulted not in an anticipated minor transmutation of uranium, but rather in fission of the uranium nucleus. This was a development which indicated the possible release of tremendous energy.[1] On January 7, 1939, Hahn and Strassmann pubilshed an article describing their discovery of fission in *Die Naturwissenschaften*. Although Hahn had at first informed no one at the Institute of his discovery, he wrote to Lise Meitner, vacationing at the small town of Kungelo near Goteborg, Sweden, to describe to her the results of his chemical analysis of the products of fission. At the time, Otto R. Frisch, her nephew and a physicist also exiled from Germany, was visiting her in Kungelo. Both read Hahn's letter with serious questions, for its news violated a basic physical law which asserted the impossibility of splitting the nucleus of an atom. After vigorous discussion, however, Meitner and Frisch came to the conclusion that the law was of doubtful validity. They began their attempt to confirm the chemist's results using the techniques of physics.

On January 6, 1939, in Copenhagen, Frisch told Niels Bohr, the Danish physicist, about Meitner's and his experiments. Bohr had already booked passage for January 7 aboard the Swedish-American ship *Drottningholm* to the United States where he planned to visit Albert Einstein at the Institute for Advanced Study at Princeton, New Jersey. He would use this trip to carry the discovery of fission to the United States. On January 15, the day before Bohr landed in the United States, Frisch physically demonstrated in Copenhagen the validity of fission.[2] Bohr arrived in the United States on schedule. On January 26 he found the opportunity to inform a group of physicists meeting at George Washington University of the discovery of fission. Among those present were Enrico Fermi, a noted Italian physicist just recently arrived in the United States, and an expatriate Hungarian physicist, Leo Szilard, who later were to initiate the effort to interest the United States government in the explosive possibilities of fission.

After the meeting at George Washington University, those who attended quickly spread the word of the new discovery; and many successfully tested its validity. By February 15, 1939, *Physical Review* carried reports of positive experimental confirmation of fission from four laboratories in the United States.[3] On March 3, Leo Szilard and Walter H. Zinn demonstrated experimentally that fission resulted in the emission of surplus neutrons which raised the possibility of creating a self-sustaining nuclear chain reaction, the energy of which might be utilized in a bomb of fantastic power.[4] Now it was known that if sufficiently favorable conditions could be established, and if large enough quantities of fissionable material could be manufactured, an atomic bomb might be created.

During the spring of 1939, many of the foreign-born physicists who had recently fled to the United States from the excesses of authoritarianism in Europe grew concerned over the political implications of the new discovery. Some, like Leo Szilard, had escaped the Nazis' anti-Semitism. Others, like Fermi, had emigrated because of the political repression of their scientific activities. They knew that German knowledge of nuclear physics had paralleled and had, perhaps, progressed beyond that of physicists in the United States. Rumors indicated a growing German interest in atomic energy. They knew that following Hitler's occupation of Czechoslovakia on March 16, 1939, exportation of uranium from the rich Czech deposits had been officially banned. They feared that control of an atomic bomb would enable Fascist states to subjugate the world.

Unlike their colleagues from the United States, they had long been accustomed to governmental support for research efforts. Thus, to offset the developing German threat, it seemed both natural and necessary for them to bring the military possibilities of nuclear fission to the authorities in Washington. Although war was not to break out until September, 1939 and the United States was not to become involved until December, 1941, fear of Axis development of nuclear weapons led these foreign-born scientists during 1939 to try to interest the United States government in the military application of nuclear energy.[5]

Those who were most active in the early attempts were Fermi, Szilard, Eugene Wigner, Edward Teller, and Victor F. Weisskopf. All were fugitives from the Nazi advance in Europe. Despite the fact that all but Fermi were comparatively unknown in the United States, they felt it necessary to seek governmental action. There was, however, little effort in common. Fermi and Szilard were the prime movers; the others cooperated on the periphery of influence.

Their first attempt was inauspicious. Fermi was to lecture before the Philosophical Society in Washington on March 16, 1939. His trip to Washington, he felt, could be used to inform the government of the importance of fission. To this end, he and Szilard prevailed upon the Dean of the Graduate Faculties at Columbia University, George B. Pegram, to write to Rear Admiral S. C. Hooper in the office of the Chief of Naval Operations to introduce Fermi and to emphasize the importance of his visit. Pegram's letter, despite its somewhat negative phrasing, was the first step in the association of science and government which later resulted in the manufacture of the atomic bomb. He wrote:

. . . Experiments in the physics laboratories at Columbia University reveal that conditions may be found under which the chemical element uranium may be able to liberate its large excess of atomic energy, and that this might mean the possibility that uranium might be used as an explosive that would liberate a million times as much energy per pound as any known explosive. My own feeling is that the probabilities are against this, but my colleagues and I think that the bare possibility should not be disregarded, and I therefore telephoned . . . this morning chiefly to arrange a channel through which the results of our experiment might, if the occasion should arise, be transmitted to the proper authorities in the United States Navy. . . .[6]

Pegram went on to introduce Fermi, to point out his competence, and to indicate his intention of becoming a citizen of the United States. Early on the morning of March 17, Fermi, armed with Pegram's letter, visited Admiral Hooper in Washington.[7] Hooper listened politely and dismissed Fermi with the request that the Navy be kept informed of developments. His indifference was not surprising. Pegram's letter had been filled with uncertainties; and Fermi, himself, doubted his own predictions. Although scientists at the Naval Research Laboratory were even then discussing the possibilities of fission, the Navy and its scientists were too far removed from their scientific colleagues in the universities to be fully aware of the awesome potentialities.[8]

As spring lengthened into summer and there was no reaction from the Navy to Fermi's visit, Szilard became convinced that another approach must be made. Someone more well known in the United States, someone who might be expected to reach the highest officials must be enlisted if efforts to interest the government were to be successful. He decided, therefore, to seek the support of Albert Einstein, perhaps the most famous scientist then living in the United States.[9]

In July, 1939, Szilard and Wigner met with Einstein at his rented summer home at Peconic on Long Island to request his support. Although Einstein refused to visit President Franklin D. Roosevelt personally, he agreed to sign a letter bringing the information concerning fission to the President's attention. The now famous letter was drafted during the latter part of July and signed by Einstein on August 2.

Sir:

Some recent work by E. Fermi and L. Szilard, which has been communicated to me in manuscript, leads me to expect the element uranium may be turned into a new and important source of energy in the immediate future. Certain aspects of the situation which has arisen seem to call for watchfulness and, if necessary, quick action on the part of the Administration. I believe therefore that it is my duty to bring to your attention the following facts and recommendations.

In the course of the last four months it has been made probable through the work of Joliot in France as well as Fermi and Szilard in America—that it may become possible to set up a nuclear chain reaction in a large mass of uranium, by which vast amounts of power and large quantities of new radium-like elements would be generated. Now it appears almost certain that this could be achieved in the immediate future.

This new phenomenon would also lead to the construction of bombs, and it is conceivable—though much less certain—that extremely powerful bombs of a new type, carried by boat and exploded in a port, might very well destroy the whole port together with some of the surrounding territory. However, such bombs might very well prove to be too heavy for transportation by air.

The United States has only very poor ores of uranium in moderate quantities. There is some good ore in Canada and the former Czechoslovakia, while the most important source of uranium is the Belgian Congo.

In view of this situation you may think it desirable to have some permanent contact maintained between the Administration and the group of physicists working on chain reactions in America. One possible way of achieving this might be for you to entrust with this task a person who has your confidence and who

could perhaps serve in an unofficial capacity. His task might comprise the
following:

(a) to approach Government Departments, keep them informed of the further
development, and put forward recommendations for Government action, giving
particular attention to the problem of securing a supply of uranium ore for the
United States.

(b) to speed up the experimental work, which is at present being carried on
within the limits of the budgets of University laboratories, by providing funds,
if such funds be required, through his contacts with private persons who are
willing to make contributions for this cause, and perhaps also by obtaining the
cooperation of industrial laboratories which have the necessary equipment.

I understand that Germany has actually stopped the sale of uranium from the
Czechoslovakian mines which she has taken over. That she should have taken
such early action might perhaps be understood on the ground that the son of the
German Under Secretary of State, von Weizsacker [sic], is attached to the Kaiser-
Wilhelm Institute in Berlin, where some of the American work on uranium is
now being repeated.[10]

During July Szilard had also enlisted the help of Dr. Alexander Sachs.
Sachs, a director and special economic advisor of the Lehman Brothers
Corporation, an investment concern in New York City, was an economist who
had been close to Roosevelt since 1933. He had been introduced to Szilard
through Gustav Stolper, the former editor of *Der deutsche Volkswirt* (German
Economist), who was at that time in New York.[11] Sachs, it was decided,
would be the intermediary who would deliver Einstein's letter to the
President.[12]

Sachs welcomed the mission. He had both a well-developed sense of
history and a healthy fear of Germany. He agreed to deliver Einstein's
letter. To clarify for the President the significance and progress of current
scientific research, he prevailed upon Szilard to write a memorandum outlining what had already been done and what might reasonably be anticipated.
By August 15 when Szilard completed his memorandum to the President,
Sachs was ready to make his approach. Out of deference, however, to the
political burdens facing Roosevelt as a result of the outbreak of World War
II on September 1, 1939, and his resultant efforts to amend the Neutrality
Acts later in September, Sachs, who wanted plenty of time for discussion with
the President, delayed approaching him until October 11. It was, thus, ten
months after the news of nuclear fission had spread to the United States
that Roosevelt learned of its significance. Only then did he make the first
of a long number of decisions which were ultimately to lead to President
Truman's use of the atomic bomb.

To this first meeting, Sachs took the Einstein letter, the Szilard Memorandum, and a covering letter of his own which he hoped would place the discovery of fission in its proper strategic perspective. While reading his letter

to the President, he mentioned the concern over German progress in the field of nuclear research, the scarcity of uranium, the importance of deposits in Canada and in the Belgian Congo, and the ". . . construction, as an eventual probability, of bombs of hitherto unenvisaged potency and scope. . . ." [13] The President was impressed as he remarked: "Alex, what you are after is to see that the Nazis don't blow us up." Roosevelt then asked his military aide, Brigadier General Edwin M. Watson, to organize a group as recommended in the Einstein letter.[14]

This first move was small enough and, in fact, was to characterize the slow, fitful approach of the government to the promotion of nuclear weapons during the following two years. After consultation with Sachs on October 11, 1939, General Watson chose Dr. Lyman J. Briggs, Director of the Bureau of Standards, to head an Advisory Committee on Uranium. It included Colonel K. F. Adamson of Army Ordinance and Commander G. C. Hoover of the Navy Bureau of Ordinance. During the evening of October 11, Sachs informed Briggs of his selection. Following a conversation between Sachs and Roosevelt later that night, the President decided to call a meeting of the committee and other interested scientists at the White House on October 21.[15]

There was widespread disagreement among the scientific participants at the White House meeting as to the value of the government's promoting nuclear research. Apparently some of the United States scientists felt little urgency. They anticipated that the possibility of a nuclear chain reaction was very remote. Other lines of research, they thought, were far more likely to succeed in helping an American war effort. They wanted to await developments before they diverted energies to what might be a futile effort. In this opinion, the military representatives on the committee concurred. Such attitudes pervaded the report which the Briggs Committee made to the President on November 1. It pointed out that, if developed, a controlled chain reaction might be used as a ". . . continuous source of power in submarines. . ." and that an explosive reaction ". . . would provide a possible source of bombs with a destructiveness vastly greater than anything now known." These military applications could, however, only be considered as possibilities; for no chain reaction had as yet been demonstrated. Nevertheless, the report ended with a recommendation that ". . . adequate support for a thorough investigation of the subject be provided . . ." and, to that end, suggested that ". . . four metric tons of pure-grade graphite . . ." and ". . . 50 tons of uranium oxide . . ." be supplied to Fermi at Columbia.[16] Here was the first halting suggestion of action.

However, little transpired through the winter of 1939–1940. No governmental committee attempted to coordinate scientific activities. The Advisory Committee on Uranium did not meet again until April, 1940. Supplies of graphite and uranium oxide were difficult to obtain. A lull in the war developed in Europe, and many in the government hoped that negotiations might soon result in its conclusion. Roosevelt was having enough trouble trying to convince the Congress that funds should be appropriated in sizable amounts for military purposes, and any effort to convince it to support the extremely uncertain potentialities of nuclear fission must have seemed futile. Laurence's strong criticism of government inaction, his dismay at the futility of scientific efforts, and his irritation that "Einstein's letter lay gathering dust in some White House pigeonhole," that it ". . . produced hardly any action worth mentioning," is somewhat unrealistic in view of the state of nuclear research at the time, the uncertainties of the scientists themselves, and the domestic and international political situation.[17]

Something *was* done by both the interested scientists and the government. And the fact that more was not attempted reflected not shortsightedness but the inadequacies of communication within the system and the political atmosphere within which the government operated.

On February 20, 1940, Briggs sent a memorandum to General Watson reporting the diversion of $6,000 from Army and Navy funds to purchase the materials recommended for the Columbia project.[18] Thus, the first expenditure made by the government to finance the development of the atomic bomb, a project that was to cost nearly $2,000,000,000 by the end of the war, set the pattern of future financing via undirected appropriations for the military. The amount failed to satisfy Sachs who, during February and March, had been consulting with Einstein over recent developments in France. An Einstein letter of March 7, which outlined hopeful developments in the United States and the disquieting news of increased German interest, was forwarded to the President by Sachs on March 15. In his covering letter Sachs requested through General Watson a meeting with Roosevelt to consider the "practical issues" raised by the experimental progress Einstein had mentioned.[19] Watson's March 27 reply to Sachs stated that the Briggs Committee was waiting for reports on progress from the investigations at Columbia before taking further action.

But Sachs, filled with forebodings of possible German success, would not wait. He anticipated a German attack on Western Europe to control the coast from Norway to France, including Belgium. Thus, he argued, both at a conference with Roosevelt early in April and in an *aide-memoire* of April 20, entitled "Import of War Development for and Application to Natural [sic] [National] Defense of Uranium Atomic Disintegration," that the government should take steps to guarantee access to uranium in the Congo, that it should set up either a government or foundation fund so that research could be planned on a more adequate long-term basis, and that it should attract university scholars to the program before they made their commitments for the following academic year.[20] As a result of Sachs' efforts, Roosevelt suggested a second meeting of the Briggs Committee with greater scientific participation and asked Sachs to work with Watson to choose those who would attend.

The Briggs Committee met for the second time at the Bureau of Standards in Washington on April 27.[21] It had before it a progress report of April 25 signed by Einstein, a memorandum letter of April 22 written by Szilard to describe future programs, and the April 20 *aide-memoire* of Sachs which suggested a revised and enlarged governmental organization to promote better planned and more comprehensive research.[22] Although the committee was impressed with nuclear potentialities and agreed that the program should be pursued more vigorously, it failed to make specific recommendations for changes in the government's approach.[23]

German successes in Western Europe soon brought a renewed sense of urgency. The invasion of Belgium on May 10 created the threat to deposits of uranium in the Congo which Sachs and others had anticipated. Sachs quickly wrote to Roosevelt on May 11 and again to General Watson on May 15 urging larger financial support by the government and a reorganization of the atomic program.[24] He pointed out the possibilities for success indicated by the research going on at Columbia.[25] As a result, Roosevelt, apparently influenced by such reasoning and perhaps more strongly by efforts of Dr. Vannevar Bush, president of the Carnegie Institution of Washington, to convince him that an organization should be established ". . . to coordinate, supervise, and conduct scientific research on the problems underlying the development, production, and use of mechanisms and devices of warfare . . . ," set up the National Defense Research Committee (NDRC) on June 27, 1940.[26] Vannevar Bush was named chairman; and the Advisory Committee on Uranium was reconstituted as the Uranium Committee, a subcommittee of NDRC with Briggs continuing as chairman. From then until June, 1941, the Uranium Committee controlled development of the nuclear fission program which was financed by Army and Navy funds.[27] From then until the end of World War II, Vannevar Bush played a major role in the development of the atomic bomb. Sachs' work was finished; and although as an unofficial advisor to Roosevelt he remained in touch with the program throughout its history, the increasing secrecy demanded during the period of large-scale production precluded his taking any active part in its later development.[28] But the government had been alerted. Roosevelt was definitely interested. The apparatus for financial support and coordination of nuclear research was, if only minimally, at least in operation.

Under the NDRC, research was intensified; and government expenditures were increased. On November 8, 1940, the first contract to provide $40,000 for the support of nuclear research at Columbia University was signed by the NDRC on the recommendation of its Uranium Committee. By the summer of 1941 it had negotiated agreements with Princeton University, the Standard Oil Development Company, Cornell University, the Carnegie Institution of Washington, the University of Minnesota, Iowa State College, Johns Hopkins University, the National Bureau of Standards, the University of Virginia, the University of Chicago, and the University of California. The research program was becoming diversified in substance as well as in location. By November, 1941, when the NDRC had relinquished control of the project, contracts calling for expenditures of nearly $300,000 had been signed.[29]

During the summer of 1941, the program had become so varied that the Uranium Committee in its original form proved to be unsuitable to meet the program's evolving needs. As a result the Uranium Section (S-1 Section) of NDRC consisting of four substantive subcommittees was established. In this organizational form, the S-1 Section continued to supervise the program until the summer of 1942.

It now seemed likely that the United States might soon find itself at war with the Axis Powers. The question involving nuclear research would then resolve itself into one of evaluating the possibility of whether the work on uranium could be successful for military purposes in time to influence the war effort. The NDRC, consequently, requested President F. B. Jewett of the National Academy of Sciences to appoint a committee of impartial scientists to review the general situation and to estimate probabilities of success in terms of military application.[30] Arthur H. Compton accepted the position of chairman and first called his committee together in April.

Compton's committee issued three reports, the first on May 17, the second on July 11, and the third on November 6, 1941. Its first report was hopeful but cautious. Atomic power for submarines was possible but not for years. No definite prediction could be made as to when an atomic bomb could be developed. It was plain that, at the earliest, a bomb could not be manufactured before 1945. The committee, nevertheless, suggested that support for nuclear research be increased and recommended the expenditure of $350,000 during the following six months.[31]

As the program expanded, it was foreseen that engineering problems would increase. As a result, the second report of the committee represented the anticipations of its engineers. They were optimistic concerning development of nuclear power. For rapid progress, they recommended the creation of a central laboratory to work on the nuclear chain reaction. Although the committee failed to promise any positive contribution to the war effort, it felt that the possibility of such an eventuality was sufficient to warrant support for a central laboratory. In considering this report, the NDRC was divided on what its future course should be.

The outcome was watchful waiting. The NDRC continued to support the research recommended by the . . . Uranium Committee but did not . . . establish a central laboratory. They were waiting for more evidence, though they knew that if positive action did not come soon it would be too late. The government's responsible representatives were thus very close to dropping fission studies from the war program.[32]

Into this uncertain situation, a new idea was introduced. In a letter of July 11 to the Compton Committee, Ernest O. Lawrence, head of the Radiation Laboratory of the University of California, suggested the possibility of the plutonium bomb. Study by committee members through the fall of 1941 convinced them that, given time and money, such a bomb could be constructed. The third report of the committee stated, therefore, that:

"The possibility must be seriously considered . . . that within a few years the use of bombs such as described here, or something similar using uranium fission, may determine military superiority.

A fission bomb of superlatively destructive power will result from bringing quickly together a sufficient mass of element U-235 (a type of uranium). This seems to be as sure as any untried prediction based upon theory and experimentation can be. . . ." [33]

The committee unanimously recommended that the safety of the nation demanded the greatest effort by the government to produce such bombs.[34]

The three reports of the Compton Committee reflected the growing certainty of its physicists and engineers that an atomic bomb could be fabricated. They provided impetus to the NDRC's drive for funds to support the nuclear fission program. They came at a crucial time when some on the NDRC staff were uncertain about the value of nuclear research to the war effort.

Vannevar Bush used the committee's reports to increase the government's efforts to build an atomic bomb. He had achieved increased stature the previous July 16 when he had accepted Roosevelt's appointment as Director of the new Office of Scientific Research and Development (OSRD).[35] The new agency included the NDRC now under James B. Conant, president of Harvard University. Although Bush was obliged to report to a newly organized Top Policy Committee (TPC) on matters of general policy he had, in effect, become director of nearly all of the scientific activities of the government including the development of the atomic bomb.[36]

During the summer and fall of 1941, Bush had received optimistic reports from British scientists who assured him that an atomic bomb could be built. An official British report to that effect came to Conant on October 3. The British position was given additional force by a report submitted to Bush by Harold C. Urey and George B. Pegram following their visit to the United Kingdom that fall to investigate the level of British research.[37] Armed with the reports of British optimism and the positive recommendations of the Compton Committee, Bush was ready to approach the President to urge him to initiate a maximum effort to build the atomic bomb.

Bush had already briefed Roosevelt and Vice-President Wallace on progress that had been made in research in the United States and in Great Britain. He now sent the recommendations of the Compton Committee with a covering letter of November 27, 1941, in which he pointed out the greater optimism of the British and urged the President to broaden the program, to reorganize its administration, to provide funds from a separate source, and to exchange information with the British.[38] He strongly urged an all-out effort based on the recommendations of the attached reports.[39] Roosevelt quickly agreed to Bush's suggestions.

The next day, November 28, Bush announced to a meeting of the NDRC that he felt that it should no longer control the uranium program. Its members agreed that the project had reached the stage when there was a need for more direct control by Bush. On December 6, Conant, speaking for Bush, told the S-1 Section of the OSRD that it would be reorganized. Conant was to be Bush's representative and Briggs remained as chairman while Pegram was vice-chairman. The three program chiefs, A. H. Compton, H. C. Urey, and E. O. Lawrence, were to be responsible for scientific development. Eger V. Murphree, director of research for Standard Oil Development Company of New Jersey, was responsible for handling technical and engineering matters. The new S-1 Section of OSRD was to report directly to Bush through Conant.[40] Thus, the last day of peace for the United States marked the start of its full-scale effort to develop a nuclear fission bomb.

Just over a week after the Japanese struck Pearl Harbor, the Top Policy Committee met on December 16, 1941, in Vice-President Wallace's office. Marshall and Conant were absent. Harold L. Smith, Director of the Bureau of the Budget, sat in. The committee approved Bush's reorganization of the S-1 section and ". . . definitely felt . . . that OSRD should press as fast as possible on the fundamental physics and on the engineering planning, and particularly on the construction of pilot plants." [41] It was generally understood that once full-scale production began the project should be administered by the Army. The committee's major present concern was to devise ways to obtain sufficient funds to meet the mushrooming costs anticipated as the project grew and, at the same time, to ensure the secrecy which the project demanded. Smith was responsible for suggesting suitable methods for raising funds to replace those limited amounts from the President's fund which were now largely financing the research.[42]

By the end of 1941, then, the United States government had decided to devote its resources to manufacturing an atomic bomb. Fear that Germany might more quickly do so provided the major stimulus to all of its efforts. The prevailing attitude was expressed by Conant to Secretary of War Stimson's Special Assistant, Harvey H. Bundy, at Conant's house in Cambridge, Massachusetts, shortly after Pearl Harbor. "The Germans," said Conant, "can never win this war, and we shall win it unless they are ahead of us in the development of the atomic bomb." [43] To win the war the United States and its allies had to produce the atomic bomb before the Germans. Of this, those committed to the project were convinced.

Beginning in 1942, direction of the work on nuclear fission centered in the S-1 Section under Bush's general direction. Since none of the methods thought likely to obtain sufficient fissionable material for an explosive device had yet been proved and since there was no assurance that the most likely technique would also be the most efficient and economical, the S-1 Section decided to use four different approaches. To do this would, perhaps, be more time-consuming and costly; but time would not be wasted on a single process which might, in the end, prove futile. Members of the S-1 Section, therefore, assumed responsibility for development of each of the different methods. Laurence, at the Radiation Laboratory at the University of California in Berkeley, worked on the magnetic separation of the uranium isotope U-235. The gaseous diffusion studies at Columbia University were supervised by Urey. Murphree directed research on the centrifuge method at Standard Oil Development Company's laboratory at Bayway, New Jersey, in cooperation with J. W. Beams at the University of Virginia. And Arthur H. Compton was responsible for developing plutonium and the study of the physical characteristics of a possibly explosive nuclear chain reaction at the Metallurgical Laboratory at the University of Chicago.[44]

The work went on on all of these fronts. On March 9, 1942, Bush reported to Roosevelt tentatively expressing hope for ultimate success in 1944. He also suggested that during the summer of 1942 the Army be given responsibility for constructing the large plants that eventually would be needed.[45]

Conant reported to Bush on May 14 that five different production methods for fissionable materials seemed equally likely to succeed.[46] He reaffirmed the decision to explore the possibilities of each method, for to give up prematurely on one might occasion fatal delay if the Germans were ahead in a similar program. The crucial question, he pointed out, was whether nuclear weapons were considered as decisive weapons or whether they were looked on merely as tactical or supplementary ones. If the former, no expense in their building was too much. If the latter, less effort needed to be devoted to their development.

A need for better coordination and exchange of information among the different programs developed during the spring of 1942. In order to discourage members of the S-1 Section from discussing their problems individually with Conant and Briggs it was thought better to set up a conference system where all would sit in periodic committee meetings. Thus, in May the S-1 Section was again reorganized into an S-1 Executive Committee with the same membership. The functions of the committee were ". . . to report on the program and budget for the next eighteen months, for each method . . . , to prepare recommendations as to how many programs should be continued . . . , [and] as to what parts . . . should be eliminated." [47] The way was thus prepared for the assumption of control by the Army's Manhattan Engineer District.

NOTES TO CHAPTER 1

[1] Lise Meitner, an Austrian Jewess, had fled from Germany into the Netherlands and then to Copenhagen after Hitler's *Anschluss* with Austria in 1938. Werner Braunbek, *The Drama of the Atom* (Edinburgh and London: Oliver and Boyd, 1958), pp. 175–77. Robert Jungk, *Brighter Than a Thousand Suns: A Personal History of the Atomic Scientists* (New York: Harcourt, Brace and Company, Inc., 1958), p. 66.

[2] O. R. Frisch, "Physical Evidence for the Division of Heavy Nuclei under Neutron Bombardment," *Nature: Supplement*, CXLIII (February 18, 1939), 276. William L. Laurence, *Men and Atoms: The Discovery, the Uses and the Future of Atomic Energy* (New York: Simon and Schuster, Inc., 1959), pp. 32–33.

[3] Columbia University, Carnegie Institution of Washington, John Hopkins University, University of California. Henry DeWolf Smyth, *Atomic Energy for Military Purposes: The Official Report on the Development of the Atomic Bomb under the Auspices of the United States Government, 1940–1945* (Princeton: Princeton University Press, 1945), p. 25.

[4] Leo Szilard and Walter H. Zinn, "Instantaneous Emission of Fast Neutrons in the Interaction of Slow Neutrons with Uranium," *Physical Review*, LV (April 15, 1939), pp. 799–800.

[5] Many accounts have been written about early developments in the field of nuclear physics and about the scientific progress made in the manufacturing of the atomic bomb during World War II. Since this paper is concerned with the political considerations involved in using the atomic bomb, only such scientific events as conditioned relevant political decisions will be considered. James Phinney Baxter, 3rd, *Scientists Against Time* (Boston: Little, Brown and Company, 1947), pp. 419–50; Braunbek, *The Drama of the Atom*; Arthur H. Compton, *Atomic Quest: A Personal Narrative* (New York: Oxford University Press, Inc., 1956), pp. 3–216; Jungk, *Brighter Than a Thousand Suns*, pp. 3–220; Ralph E. Lapp, *Atoms and People* (New York: Harper and Brothers, 1956); Laurence, *Men and Atoms*, (New York: Simon and Schuster, Inc., 1959), pp. 3–100; Smyth, *Atomic Energy for Military Purposes*. This latter work is the official account of the United States government's development of the atomic bomb and is invaluable for its clear, simplified descriptions of scientific processes which might otherwise be somewhat difficult for the layman to comprehend.

[6] This letter is quoted in greater length from a copy from Fermi's file in Laura Fermi, *Atoms in the Family* (Chicago: The University of Chicago Press, 1954), pp. 162–63.

[7] The various accounts differ as to whether or not Fermi saw the Admiral. Laurence states that he only saw two young Lieutenant Commanders who were somewhat over their heads in trying to evaluate Fermi's information and who merely asked that the Navy be kept informed of further developments. Laurence, *Men and Atoms*, pp. 55–56. On the other hand, Mrs. Fermi states that it was Fermi's recollection that he had seen the Admiral and discussed the matter with him. Fermi, *Atoms in the Family*, pp. 163–65. See also Jungk, *Brighter Than a Thousand Suns*, p. 78. Smyth merely mentions Fermi's conference with ". . . representatives of the Navy Department." Smyth, *Atomic Energy for Military Purposes*, p. 47.

[8] Compton, *Atomic Quest: A Personal Narrative* (New York: Oxford University Press, Inc., 1956), pp. 25–26.

[9] Szilard apparently was at this time most interested in guaranteeing sources of supply of uranium. Following German restrictions on exports of uranium from Czechoslovakia, he realized that the only known supplies free of Axis control were in the Belgian Congo. Szilard, therefore, planned to preserve that supply by soliciting Einstein's intervention with the Belgian Queen Mother with whom he was known to be friendly. Jungk, *Brighter Than a Thousand Suns*, pp. 82–83.

[10] The original of this letter is now on display at the Franklin D. Roosevelt Library at Hyde Park, New York. There is some doubt as to who drafted it. Compton states that Szilard and Wigner wrote it. Compton, *Atomic Quest*, p. 27. Jungk, on the other hand, claims that the original draft was the work of Szilard and Alexander Sachs. A later draft, as Szilard recalled, was dictated by Einstein to Edward Teller on August 2; and that draft was used by Szilard as a basis for two drafts, one long and one short, from which Einstein was to choose. Einstein and Teller recollected that Szilard had the final draft with him when he visited Einstein on August 2. Jungk, *Brighter Than a Thousand Suns*, pp. 84–86. Sachs later testified before a Senate Committee that Einstein had written it. U. S. Congress, Senate, Special Committee on Atomic Energy, *Hearings on Atomic Energy*, 79th Cong., 2nd sess., Senate Resolution 179, Part 5, Appendix, (Washington, 1946), p. 556. Hereafter, "Sachs Statement."

[11] Jungk, *Brighter Than a Thousand Suns*, p. 84.

[12] Some doubt exists as to whether Sachs joined the effort before or after Einstein's letter was signed on August 2. The weight of evidence seems to indicate that he was consulted prior to that time. See "Sachs Statement," p. 556; Jungk, *Brighter Than a Thousand Suns*, pp. 84–85; Compton, *Atomic Quest*, p. 27. On the other hand Laurence indicates Sachs was called in after the letter was written to deliver it. Laurence, *Men and Atoms*, p. 58. And both Fermi and Smyth, although only by inference, seem to concur. Fermi, *Atoms in the Family*, p. 166; Smyth, *Atomic Energy for Military Purposes*, p. 47.

[13] This letter is quoted in "Sachs Statement," p. 557.

[14] "Sachs statement," p. 558.

[15] Much of the following account of governmental activity until the Manhattan Engineer District was established in 1942 relies on Sachs' testimony and the Smyth *Report*. Sachs' testimony is important since Roosevelt apparently asked him to be historian of that period for the President's convenience. "Sachs Statement," p. 559. The Smyth *Report*, of course, is the original official account.

[16] "Sachs Statement," p. 560.

[17] Laurence, *Men and Atoms*, p. 59.

[18] "Sachs Statement," p. 562. Smyth, *Atomic Energy for Military Purposes*, pp. 47–48.

[19] Sachs' letter to Roosevelt is quoted in "Sachs Statement," p. 564.

[20] "Sachs Statement," pp. 564–65.

[21] According to Smyth this meeting was held on April 28. Smyth, *Atomic Energy for Military Purposes*, p. 48.

[22] "Sachs Statement," pp. 567–70.

[23] Smyth, *Atomic Energy for Military Purposes*, p. 48.

[24] Sachs' letter to Roosevelt appears in "Sachs Statement," pp. 566–67; see p. 572 for Sachs' letter to Watson.

[25] Research was also continuing at a number of other universities. But, as yet, only that at Columbia was financed by the government.

[26] This citation is from a May, 1940, draft of an Act of Congress, prepared under Bush's direction, which anticipated Congressional action in establishing such an agency. The rush of events in Europe required, however, more rapid Executive action. Baxter, *Scientists Against Time*, pp. 14–15.

[27] Smyth, *Atomic Energy for Military Purposes*, p. 49.

[28] "Sachs Statement," p. 561.

[29] Smyth, *Atomic Energy for Military Purposes*, p. 50.

[30] Smyth states that Briggs requested Bush to ask Jewett to set up this committee; Smyth, *Atomic Energy for Military Purposes*, p. 51. On the other hand Compton writes that Bush asked Briggs to contact Jewett; Compton, *Atomic Quest*, p. 45.

[31] Compton, *Atomic Quest*, p. 47.

[32] *Ibid.*, p. 49.

[33] Baxter, *Scientists Against Time*, p. 427.

[34] Compton, *Atomic Quest*, p. 58.

[35] *The Papers of Franklin D. Roosevelt, Official Files*, (OF 4482) "Office of Scientific Research and Development," Hyde Park, New York. The Executive order setting up the OSRD on June 28, 1941, Roosevelt's letter of appointment of June 28, 1941, and Bush's acceptance are included in this file.

[36] Members of the Top Policy Committee were Vice President Henry A. Wallace, Secretary of War Henry L. Stimson, General George C. Marshall, Conant, and Bush. U. S. Congress, Senate, Special Committee on Atomic Energy, *Hearings on Atomic Energy*, "Statement of Dr. Vannevar Bush, President, Carnegie Institution of Washington, and Director, Office of Scientific Research and Development," p. 146. Hereafter, "Bush Statement." See also U. S. Congress, House, Committee on Un-American Activities, *Hearings Regarding Shipment of Atomic Material to the Soviet Union During World War II*. "Testimony of Henry A. Wallace," 81st Cong., 1st and 2nd sessions, (Washington, 1950), p. 1073; and see also Smyth, *Atomic Energy for Military Purposes*, pp. 53–54, which indicates that the TPC orginated in the fall of 1941. General Leslie R. Groves, in an unofficial history of the diplomacy of the Manhattan Engineer District, indicated that what he called the "General Policy Group" (TPC) was appointed following a late summer conference with Bush. See *Manhattan Engineer District Files*: Harrison-Bundy Series, "3 [sic] Extra copies of Diplo. [sic] History," Folder #111. Hereafter, *MED Files*.

[37] Smyth, *Atomic Energy for Military Purposes*, pp. 52–53.

[38] *Ibid.*, p. 53.

[39] "Bush Statement," p. 145.

[40] Smyth, *Atomic Energy for Military Purposes*, pp. 76–77. Compton, *Atomic Quest*, pp. 62–71.

[41] Smyth, *Atomic Energy for Military Purposes*, p. 78. Here Smyth quotes a subsequent memorandum from Bush to Conant.

[42] Smith's role is discussed in "Testimony of Henry A. Wallace," p. 1073.

[43] Harvey H. Bundy, "Remembered Words," *The Atlantic Monthly*, CXCIX (March, 1957), 57.

[44] Compton, *Atomic Quest*, p. 78. Smyth, *Atomic Energy for Military Purposes*, pp. 77, 79.

[45] Smyth, *Atomic Energy for Military Purposes*, p. 80.

[46] *Ibid.*, p. 80. These five were the centrifuge, gaseous diffusion, magnetic separation, uranium graphite pile, and uranium heavy water pile methods.

[47] *Ibid.*, p. 81.

CHAPTER **2**

THE MANHATTAN ENGINEER DISTRICT

BY early summer of 1942 the decision was made to initiate full-scale construction of manufacturing plants to produce fissionable materials. Bush and Conant recommended this move to the Top Policy Committee in a report on June 13. Wallace, Stimson, and General Marshall approved the recommendation; and on June 17 the report was sent to Roosevelt who endorsed it. He ordered Major General Wilhelm D. Styer, Chief of Staff of the Army Service Forces, to set up a special unit to take the necessary action.[1] As a result, a special organization named the Manhattan Engineer District (MED) was established by the Army's Corps of Engineers on August 13, 1942. The Army was chosen as the administering agency because it could more easily obtain the immense funds which would be needed and because it had the means to administer such a large project and still preserve secrecy.[2] On September 17, Secretary of War Stimson appointed Brigadier General Leslie R. Groves of the Army Engineers to head the MED. The Top Policy Committee met on September 23 and appointed a new Military Policy Committee (MPC) consisting of Bush as chairman, Conant as his alternate, Styer, and Rear Admiral W. R. Purnell, with Groves sitting with the committee as executive officer.[3] During this period and until the spring of 1943 the OSRD S-1 Executive Committee worked with and gradually turned over its functions to the MED. Its major roles had been to advise Bush and Groves and to function as a liaison agency among the scientific, industrial, and military groups involved in the program. Although never officially deactivated, it no longer exercised a significant part in the later work of building the atomic bomb.

By the end of September, 1943, authority had been concentrated in a small group of officials. General Groves' position was pivotal. He had complete administrative control of MED. His ". . . mission as given to . . . [him] by Secretary Stimson was to produce this (the atomic bomb) at the earliest possible date so as to bring the war to a conclusion."[4] It was his duty to coordinate the various parts of the program as they developed, to provide required raw materials, to fix and assure adherence to production schedules, to maintain adequate security measures, and ". . . to arrange for use of the bombs when the time came. . . ."[5] He was to see to it that atomic bombs were made and used as soon as possible during the war.[6] Groves, however, made major decisions only after consultation and approval from the Military Policy Committee. He met with various members of the committee, or with the whole committee at frequent intervals; and major decisions were only taken with their concurrence. Groves testified in 1946:

. . . general feeling always was this, that while I was responsible for the major decisions, no member of the policy committee (MPC) would ever be in a position where he would say that he did not know that these decisions were being taken and that if he had known he wouldn't have approved them and approved of them in advance, and quite a number of them that were quite important were really taken on the initiative of one of the members of that Committee.[7]

So Bush, Conant, Styer, and Purnell had general supervisory control over Groves. In military matters Groves reported directly to the Chief of Staff, General Marshall, and was, of course, ultimately accountable to Secretary of War Stimson who had overall responsibility for the program. These then were the men who directed the program of building the atomic bomb. Its use was implicit in their instructions to manufacture it. As Bush later asserted, their ". . . assignment [was] to develop a bomb for use. . . ."[8]

From September, 1942, with help from the OSRD S-1 Executive Committee, until May of 1943, the Manhattan Engineer District under General

Groves administered the expanding organization which devoted its energies to production of the atomic bomb.[9] The decision had been made to go ahead under forced draft. Ultimate use of the weapon, military conditions being suitable, was generally assumed. Problems that arose now only involved uncertainties of production and the need for speed. They involved the development of the weapon itself, the acquisition of sufficient funds to finance it, the maintenance of security, and the reconciliation of United States' needs with those of Great Britain in exchanging information on atomic matters, winning the assumed production race with Germany, and planning for the bomb's use.

A. Development from September 1942 to April 1945

All doubts about continuing the project were dispelled by the first controlled nuclear chain reaction which Fermi and his co-workers engineered on a squash court under the West Stands of the Stagg Athletic Field, University of Chicago, on December 2, 1942. Not only was the chain reaction demonstrated experimentally, but plutonium, a fissionable material which behaved much like U-235, was also derived in the process.[10]

General Groves, however, had not awaited this development to begin building the manufacturing plant to produce the bomb materials. He had already begun negotiations with the private industrial organizations which were to construct and operate some of the plants which the MED planned. The speed which characterized the entire effort was obvious in these early manufacturing stages. Frequently there was too little time to move from the laboratory stage, to the pilot-plant stage, and on to final production without temporal overlapping. Under conditions of peace, the progress would have been more deliberate. Now, however, pilot plants were constructed before experimentation was completed, and the operating plants were built while lessons were still being learned in the pilot plants.[11]

From this necessarily rapid procedure there ultimately emerged a gigantic complex of laboratories, pilot plants, and production centers, most of which were located in three major areas of operation: at Oak Ridge, Tennessee; at Hanford, Washington; and at Los Alamos, New Mexico. Soon after his appointment in September, 1942, Groves approved a previously selected site in Tennessee on the Clinch River about eighteen miles from Knoxville as the location of the Clinton Engineer Works, the production center for the entire program. The Stone and Webster Engineering Corporation had previously been selected to engineer and construct the works. By October, it became obvious that the operation would be too large and complicated to be handled by any one corporation; and responsibility for different projects was allocated to different companies. As a result, a number of corporations participated in the research, construction, and operation of the various plants.[12]

At the Clinton Works there were four major operations: an electromagnetic separation plant, a gaseous diffusion plant, a thermal diffusion plant, and a small plutonium plant. Each group of buildings was located in a different valley on the site.

Construction of the electromagnetic plant, based on previous research carried on at the University of California and at Princeton University, was authorized by the MED on November 5, 1942. Five major industrial corporations and one university cooperated in putting it into operation. Research and development fell to the Radiation Laboratory of the University of California. The Westinghouse Electric and Manufacturing Company fabricated the mechanical devices. Electrical equipment and controls were supplied by the General Electric Company, and magnets were developed by the Allis-Chalmers Company. Construction was in the hands of Stone and Webster Engineering Company. And the Tennessee Eastman Company operated the plant after it had been built. Possible inefficiencies resulting from this division of labor were largely overcome by establishing a planning center, which included representatives of each concern, at the Radiation Laboratory at Berkeley.[13] In March, 1943, construction began on the first magnetic units which were ready for operation in November, 1943. The plant was in full operation in the winter of 1944–1945 and produced U-235 for use in the atomic bombs.[14]

Work on the gaseous diffusion plant originated on June 1, 1943; and the project was producing fissionable materials prior to the summer of 1945.[15] Preliminary and continuing research on the gaseous diffusion process was the responsibility of Columbia University where the experimental work was directed by Harold C. Urey and J. R. Dunning. M. W. Kellogg Company, which in 1942 had been employed to develop plans for the process and equipment, set up a special subsidiary, the Kellex Corporation, to design the plant. It was built by the J. A. Construction Company of Charlotte, North Carolina, and, after 1943, operated by the Carbide and Carbon Chemicals Corporation.[16]

Unlike the others, the thermal diffusion plant was started relatively late in the program. Research by P. H. Ableson at the Naval Research Laboratory had pointed out the value of this method in the rapid, partial separation of U-235. A pilot plant was established at the laboratory by the spring of 1943 and another constructed at the Philadelphia Navy Yard. The Navy provided plans for a large-scale plant at the Clinton Works, and it was put into operation in the late summer of 1944. Its major function was to supply enriched uranium material to speed up separation of U-235 at the electromagnetic plant.[17]

The fourth major unit at the Clinton Works was a small-size plutonium pile which was built to provide operating information for the large plutonium works at Hanford, Washington. During the latter part of 1942, General Groves convinced E. I. Du Pont de Nemours and Company to engineer, design, and construct this pile.[18] Construction started early in 1943, and the pile began operating on November 4, 1943.[19] By February 1, 1944, small amounts of plutonium insufficient for the needs of an atomic weapon, were being produced. Because of its experience derived from designing and working the West Stands pile at the University of Chicago, the Metallurgical Laboratory was assigned the job of operating the Clinton plutonium plant.

The Clinton works, then, involved the combined efforts of a variety of corporations, universities, and military groups.[20] Its costs were tremendous.[21] Engineering and construction of the plants came to nearly $907,000,000, and operating expenditures were nearly $18,000,000 a month.[22] The city of Oak Ridge, constructed at government expense and housing some 78,000 workers and their families, required nearly $110,000,000.[23]

The Hanford Engineering Works on the Columbia River above Pasco, Washington, was the second major producing center constructed under the authority of the MED. Fear of possible though unknown dangers from radioactivity which might result from concentrating all production at the Clinton Works, the availability of a large supply of pure, cold water needed for cooling the necessary gigantic piles, and access to sufficient electric power from Bonneville and Grand Coulee Dams, led General Groves at the beginning of 1943 to decide to build the large separation plants for the plutonium process at the Hanford site. The major drawback to this location was the distance between the Hanford Works and the Metallurgical Laboratory, the Argonne Laboratory, the small plutonium plant at the Clinton Works, and the home offices of E. I. Du Pont de Nemours Company which was to engineer, build, and operate the plant. It was also difficult to hire and transport workers to this relatively remote location and to house them nearby.[24]

Nevertheless, by January, 1943, a 200 square mile tract on the west side of the Columbia River was acquired by the MED. On April 6, ground was broken for the Hanford construction camp. Work on the first of these piles started on June 7; and the pile was operating in September, 1944. By the fall of 1944 and early spring of 1945, the second and third piles began to operate. The plant was producing plutonium for use in atomic weapons during the early summer of 1945.[25]

Closely associated with the work at Hanford were the studies conducted at the Argonne Laboratory near Chicago which was built in 1943. Here the original West Stands pile was reconstructed and run experimentally to obtain a better understanding of nuclear processes in producing plutonium and uranium. Operated by the Metallurgical Laboratory, it provided valuable information in solving many of the theoretical problems faced in the Hanford operation.[26]

The cost of the Hanford complex also ran high. Total costs of the Metallurgical and Argonne Laboratories were approximately $17,000,000. Construction costs of the Hanford Works came to nearly $302,000,000, and $48,000,000 was spent on housing to take care of a population which, at times, included as many as 18,000 persons. Operating costs were about $3,500,000 each month.[27]

The final and critical operation of the project involved the design and construction of the bomb itself. This took place at Los Alamos, New Mexico, the third major installation operating under the MED. In November, 1942, General Groves chose the site largely because its remoteness promoted both security against espionage and safety from an unexpected explosion.[28] The laboratory was constructed during the spring of 1943; its director, Dr. J. Robert Oppenheimer, reported in March. Previous theoretical work had been conducted since 1941 at the Metallurgical Laboratory and since 1942 at the University of California under Oppenheimer.

A great sense of urgency characterized the work at Los Alamos as elsewhere throughout the MED. General Groves has stated that the function of the laboratory was ". . . to develop the bomb, all the theory connected with the bomb, the designing and engineering of it, and to take the pieces that were made elsewhere, as well as some that were made right there, and assemble them into the final bomb. . . ." [29] Oppenheimer's orders were ". . . to lose no day in preparing an atomic bomb . . . The deadline never changed. It was as soon as possible." [30]

The ultimate design of the bomb itself reflected the requirements of speed. Beginning in December, 1943, Captain W. S. Parsons, on detached duty from Naval Ordnance since the previous May and as head of the Ordnance Division at Los Alamos responsible for designing the bomb, began working on proposed models intended to fit the B-29, the new long-range bomber already in production. The Ordnance Division realized that if they constructed a weapon that had to be carried in an airplane tailored to fit it, it could probably not be used during the war even if it was developed. They chose, therefore, an existing and successful airplane as the carrying vehicle.[31]

By the middle of 1944, fissionable materials were arriving at Los Alamos from the Clinton and Hanford Works. As they arrived more and more rapidly during the spring of 1945, plans were made both for the advanced base from which the attack could be launched and for the initial test at Alamagordo, New Mexico.[32] But quantities of fissionable materials were so small that they were insufficient for use as an explosive until June, 1945. As soon as sufficient supplies of plutonium were available, they were used in the bombs of Alamagordo, Hiroshima, and Nagasaki.[33]

The urgent work at Los Alamos proved to be expensive. Construction and operation expenditures totaled about $60,000,000. Housing the 3,500 workers and their families who lived on the site required an additional $4,500,000.[34]

By April, 1945, when Truman became President, the development of the nuclear weapon was almost successful. Costs had run high, and many men had devoted years of their lives to the work; but success appeared imminent. The atomic bomb was nearly a reality.

B.   Financing the Bomb

Throughout the development of the MED, a major concern of those at the top level involved obtaining the funds for the undertaking without endangering its security. This, even in time of war, was particularly difficult for any administration faced with a Congress interested not only in economies but also in asserting its prerogatives in controlling appropriations. The need for secrecy created the major difficulty; for although Congressmen might have many laudable characteristics, they are, at times, not famous for their reticence.[35] How then could the MED be financed without informing the Congress?

Until 1944, the solution to the problem had been relatively easy. The first small appropriations for research had come from Army and Navy funds. During the periods when the NDRC and the OSRD administered the programs and during the early stages of the MED, such funds as could not be obtained from the military departments had been provided from a special contingency fund which Congress had appropriated to the President. For large-scale production which began in 1943, however, these sources were no longer sufficient. Some new approach had to be taken. Congress would have to be consulted.

To meet this need, Stimson decided to brief a few influential Congressmen with the hope that their discretion would lead them to remain quiet about the bomb while they were convincing their fellow Congressmen that large, undirected appropriations for the Army should be approved.[36] On February 18, 1944, Stimson, General Marshall, and Bush met with Speaker of the House Sam Rayburn, Majority Floor Leader John W. McCormack, and Minority Floor Leader Joseph W. Martin to describe the atomic program.[37] During this meeting a system was devised to assure passage of the needed appropriations. The Speaker would be informed by Stimson as to the way the MED items would be inserted in the request for appropriations. He would then give the information to the floor leaders who would, in turn, talk to a few men on the Appropriation Committee to explain that they had explored the matter with Stimson and General Marshall and had been convinced that this item should not be questioned.[38] Marshall had already described the technical details and power of the bomb, and Stimson had mentioned the fear of prior German success in building it. The Congressmen were duly impressed. They were told that the project would demand an additional $1,600,000,000. Martin has since described the way in which Rayburn, McCormack, and he later manipulated the measure through Congress:

Since war funds generally were lumped together so they could not be analyzed by the enemy, our problem was to get the sums . . . through the House Appropriations Committee. While Rayburn and McCormack went to work on Representative Clarence Cannon, . . . who was chairman of the committee, I won the assent of John Taber, the ranking minority member. Together we all slid the appropriation through the House without any breach of secrecy.[39]

In June, 1944, Stimson employed the same procedure with a group of Senators. Senators Alben W. Barkley and Albert D. Thomas, Democrats, and Senators Wallace H. White and Styles Bridges, Republicans, were asked to push the appropriations bill through the Senate with the greatest secrecy.[40] Apparently Stimson held other meetings on this matter with influential Senators, but it is difficult to fix their dates. Barkley recalls a meeting in his office with Stimson and eight or ten others for a briefing on an important project. Stimson apparently was not specific, for he did not mention the name ". . . atomic bomb." [41]

As a result of Stimson's maneuvers, Congress passed the required appropriation bills. A few other members of Congress, nevertheless, discovered some evidence to indicate what was taking place. Senator Harry S. Truman, for instance, knew that something large and unusual was being built in Tennessee and in Washington. Truman, while Chairman of the Senate's Special Committee to Investigate the National Defense Program, had sent committee investigators to both states to see what was happening. But Stimson had asked Truman to call off his men. Truman accepted Stimson's assurance that the program was both important and necessarily secret and complied with the Secretary's request. In the spring of 1945, Congressman Claire Engel had threatened to make a speech on the atomic bomb on the floor of the House, if Stimson did not permit Congressmen to visit the installations in Tennessee. After an hour and a half of conversation, Stimson convinced Engle to put off his speech. He then initiated plans which would ultimately allow certain members of Congress to visit the Clinton Works in May, 1945.[43]

Some of the leaders of Congress who knew about the project were concerned that it might be a failure. Such a result might adversely affect their political futures. After two billion dollars had been appropriated, therefore, the House leaders refused to appropriate more funds until Stimson had invited them to the Clinton Works. Representative Clarence Cannon has written:

After visiting Oak Ridge we provided further funds but with great doubt as to the eventual success of the experiment. The news that the bomb had fallen was a great relief to the . . . men on the House Committee who alone were aware of the object of the experiment.[44]

And Joe Martin has since expressed the doubts that plagued him:

This was the greatest gamble of the war. We had to take it in the interest of American safety. Yet if the bomb had fizzled into a huge, grim joke, I would have been answerable to my Republican colleagues for having secretly put through a vast expenditure with absolutely nothing to show for it in return. At least we had the satisfaction, such as it was, of seeing the outcome of our gamble. The President never lived to behold what came of this.[45]

Financing the atomic bomb, thus, had involved a number of key Congressmen. They had convinced their respective Houses to pass large appropriations bills by giving their fellow members their personal assurances that the matter was of gravest consequence and required secrecy. Any failure might have worked to their political disadvantage. They, along with Roosevelt, became deeply involved in the success of the new weapon.

C.   Security

Maintaining the security of the atomic project proved to be a general problem of which secret financing was only a part. It was one of General Groves' major concerns. What was being done in the United States had to be kept from the enemy. It also had to be restricted from certain allies. To this end, Groves administered a rigorous system of compartmentalization of information; a technique of using somewhat colorful aliases for top scientists within the program; and a thorough investigation of the activities, past and present, of those who worked on the program.

These actions irritated many of the scientists concerned. They resented restrictions on the flow of information among the various units of MED which compartmentalization demanded. It created, they felt, an undesirable change from their accustomed scientific freedom.[47] To some, their aliases were ridiculous and superfluous. Personal investigations caused much resentment. And yet the necessary security measures created in them a sense of conspiracy, an *esprit de corps* as they filtered out contacts with those not concerned.

Such security measures also had their impact indirectly on those who worked at the various plants and more directly on their leaders. In 1944, when jurisdictional disputes broke out among labor unions at Oak Ridge, to forestall public hearings before the National Labor Relations Board, Under

Secretary of War Robert Patterson and General Groves requested the personal intervention of Director of War Mobilization James F. Byrnes to ask that the unions waive their rights under the National Labor Relations Act of 1935. Consequently, a White House meeting was arranged on the morning of December 5, 1944, among Joseph P. Clark of the International Brotherhood of Fireman and Oilers, Al Wegener of the International Brotherhood of Electrical Workers, Patterson, Groves, and Byrnes. At that conference, the union officials were told of the project and the need for secrecy; and they willingly agreed to help. They were so impressed with the importance of the job that they sacrificed rights given to them by law.[48] They, too, became part of the team protecting a vital project. They, too, became personally involved in the success of the program.

The search for security also stimulated distrust toward the Russians on the part of certain officials administering the program. Soon after he took charge of MED, General Groves became aware of Soviet espionage. He later stated that:

. . . there was never from about 2 [sic] weeks from the time . . . [he] took charge of the project any illusion on . . .[his] part but that Russia was our enemy and that the project was conducted on that basis. . . [He] didn't go along with the attitude of the country as a whole that Russia was a gallant ally. . . [He] always had suspicions and the project was conducted on that basis.[49]

Stimson, also, was troubled with Russian spying on MED projects. On December 31, 1944, he informed Roosevelt that he knew of Russian espionage and was worried over the possible effect of the policy of keeping information about the MED from the Soviet Government.[50] The Soviet Union was considered by some as a doubtful ally. Such opinions were later reflected in their advice to Truman regarding use of the weapon.

It seems, therefore, that the search for security had a twofold effect. It heightened the feeling of urgency among those engaged in building the bomb. It led to their isolation from the public, their personal devotion to the program over a number of years, and, perhaps, to their psychological need to publicly justify their actions. As a result of their isolation, many who later became advisers to Truman were ignorant of the requirements imposed by the international political position on the United States. Because of their involvement they, understandably, felt the need to demonstrate the worth of their work. Because, perhaps, of their need for justification they saw the reasonableness of using an atomic weapon.

D. Problems with the British

Necessities of security created serious inter-Allied difficulties which threatened the maintenance of previously close United States–British relations during

1942 and 1943. American reluctance to risk security leaks, which might arise from a continuation of the former free interchange of nuclear information between the governments and scientists of the two states, caused considerable resentment from Prime Minister Winston S. Churchill and other interested people in his government. This was especially so since they recalled the early stimulus which British research had provided to the American program.

The British Government had first learned of the potentialities of fission in March, 1940. Faced with the immediate needs of the war with the Axis powers, it concentrated its efforts on developing a weapon from the new discovery.[51] In order to examine the problem more completely and to coordinate existing research, a committee of scientists was organized under the chairmanship of Sir George Thomson in April, 1940.[52] Developments during 1940 and 1941 led the Thomson Committee to issue an optimistic report on nuclear potentialities on July 15, 1941. This report which recommended a large-scale effort to produce an atomic bomb reached United States authorities on October 3, 1941, and was influential in convincing them that an intensive effort should be made.[53] Meanwhile, the British had organized their program under a Directorate of Tube Alloys in their Department of Scientific and Industrial Research.[54] W. A. Akers, released from the Board of Imperial Chemical Industries, Ltd., became director; and Sir John Anderson, Lord President of the Privy Council, exercised policy control.[55] The British were convinced that the atomic bomb could be made for use in the war. To that end they devoted the energies of their government. To hasten their effort they promoted cooperation with the United States.

As early as 1940, long before the United States became involved in the war, informal conversations between British and American scientists had occurred. On July 8, 1940, the British proposed immediate and general exchange of information at the governmental and scientific levels.[56] Following a cabinet discussion of the proposal on July 11 at which the President, the Secretary of War, and the Secretary of the Navy approved the exchange, the Department of State sent a note to the British Government on July 30 informing it that the United States was in general agreement and was ready to enter conversations on the matter. A British technical mission visited the United States in September, 1940, and proposed a full exchange of information concerning research and weapons development.[57] In February, 1941, James B. Conant traveled to London to discuss more completely the interchange of information. Agreements were reached at that time under which the British were to emphasize continuing research having to do with the defense of Great Britain while long-range development was to be left to the United States. In the June 28 Executive order establishing the OSRD, Paragraph 2 gave that organization liaison responsibility in handling such interchange.[58] By the summer of 1941, then, the exchange of nuclear information on a continuing basis was an established fact.

As research progressed to the production planning stage in late 1942 and early 1943, however, the British began to doubt the willingness of the United States to exchange information on manufacturing processes. Churchill had received assurances from Roosevelt in his letter of October 11, 1941, that British and American efforts ". . . might be jointly conducted." [59] At Hyde Park on June 20, 1942, he had agreed with Roosevelt that the manufacturing stage should be conducted in the United States, far from possible attack and near to the required resources in manpower, capital, and raw materials. His agreement, however, had been contingent on Roosevelt's acceptance of the responsibility to pool all information, to work with Great Britain on equal terms and to share possible results.[60] Now in the fall of 1942, despite such accord at the top level, the British were finding it more and more difficult to obtain information at the operating level.

Consequently, in October, 1942, Akers came to the United States to try to correct the situation. At a meeting with Bush and Groves, he requested that information concerning manufacturing techniques be freely exchanged. Bush, Groves, and Conant, however, were convinced that Akers was interested more in acquiring knowledge from which to develop postwar commercial activities than in obtaining only that which was necessary to win the war.[61] In a letter to Conant on December 15, Akers pointed out the restrictions on the exchange of information which the British had noticed since the previous June and reminded Conant that the project had always been considered a cooperative effort by both Churchill and Roosevelt.[62]

On the same day the MPC succinctly stated its point of view in a report to Roosevelt:

1. The only justification for an exchange of information was to help win the war.
2. Other than the possibility that supplies of uranium and heavy water from Britain and Canada might be stopped, no undue interference with the project would result if the interchange were to cease.
3. The MPC could see no unfairness to Great Britain in cutting off the exchange of information, but it expected that it would be displeased.
4. This displeasure, however, might be outweighed by the advantages in terms of greater secrecy which restricting the transmission of such information to the British would bring.
5. Of three possible approaches — cutting off all information, complete interchange of information, or restricted interchange to the extent that Great Britain could use the information in winning the war — the Committee felt that the last was the most reasonable and thus recommended it.[63]

Apparently Roosevelt approved the recommendation.[64] As a result, the negotiations temporarily broke down; for the MED, in the absence of a formal international agreement, did not feel justified in continuing to supply information to Great Britain.[65]

Churchill, however, was not to be put off by actions of lower-level United States officials which he felt violated his Hyde Park Agreement with Roosevelt. He mentioned the matter to the President at the Casablanca Conference in January, 1943, and later claimed that he had received verbal assurances from Roosevelt that full exchange would be reinstituted.[66] While at Casablanca, Churchill also expressed his concern to Harry Hopkins who promised to look into the matter when he returned to Washington.

Finding that his Casablanca efforts brought little response, the Prime Minister kept after the Americans. On February 16, he cabled Hopkins: "I should be very grateful for some news about this, as at the present the American War Department is asking us to keep them informed of our experiments while refusing altogether any information about theirs!" [67] Through the spring of 1943, Hopkins and Churchill exchanged cables in which Hopkins asked for more specific evidence of the Casablanca agreement, the existence of which interested officials in Washington doubted; and Churchill returned with a long history of United States–British relations on exchange of information and urged quick action lest Britain ". . . be compelled to go ahead separately in this work. . . ." [68]

As a result, Hopkins discussed the problem with Roosevelt, Stimson, Bush, and Conant. But the United States' position remained unchanged when it was restated on May 25 at a White House conference attended by Hopkins, Bush, and Lord Cherwell, Churchill's scientific adviser and close friend who had accompanied the Prime Minister to Washington on May 11. Opening the discussion, Bush said that the security of the program provided the basic reason for limiting the exchange of information with the British. Cherwell replied that unless information was again supplied to the British, they would be forced to manufacture the bomb themselves despite the weakening of their war effort which such a reallocation of resources might occasion. When pressed by Bush, Cherwell admitted that, forced to go it alone, the British couldn't expect to get favorable results during the present war and that they wanted information so that they might quickly manufacture nuclear weapons in the postwar period. He disclaimed any desire for postwar commercial advantages. As a result of this meeting both Hopkins and Bush felt that exchange of information should only be reinstituted following a top-level decision involving considerations of long-range international relations. If such a decision was not forthcoming, they agreed that the existing policy should stand.[69] The United States policy then was:

. . . that information on this subject will be furnished to individuals, either in this country or Great Britain, who need it and can use it now in the furtherance of the war effort, but that, in the interests of security, information interchanged will be restricted to this definite objective.[70]

The British objection to this policy, of course, was that the United States would ultimately reap the benefits of joint research both during and after the war.

Between the end of May and the middle of July, 1943, there was no apparent change in policy. Revision, however, had come quietly at the top level. About the same time that Bush and Hopkins were stating what they considered the United States' position to be to Lord Cherwell, Roosevelt apparently was discussing the problem with Churchill at the White House. For on May 26, Churchill cabled from Washington to Sir John Anderson in London:

The President agreed that the exchange of information on tube alloys should be resumed and that the enterprise should be considered a joint one, to which both countries would contribute their best endeavors. I understand that this ruling would be based upon the fact that this weapon may well be developed in time for the present war and that it thus falls within the general agreement covering the interchange of research and invention secrets. . . .[71]

On July 20, just before he attended a conference with Churchill in London, Bush received a letter from Roosevelt which ordered the complete reversal of policy indicated in Churchill's cable. Roosevelt wrote that he and the Prime Minister had discussed the whole question of exchange of information. He understood the need for security, but he considered it necessary to a suitable understanding with Great Britain to provide for a complete exchange. He, therefore, requested Bush to reinstitute the former policy.[72] Presumably, Roosevelt felt that, at a time when the United Nations were beginning to push back the Axis in Italy, in Russia, and in the Pacific, it was not advisable to weaken British-American unity in the interest of security for the atomic project which might be protected in other ways.

To improve the situation, Stimson, Bush, and Bundy journeyed to London for discussions with the Prime Minister at No. 10 Downing Street.[73] Churchill began the conversations by recalling past cooperation between the British and the Americans and expressed his concern over recent rigid limitations imposed by the United States on the transmission of information to the British. He pointed out that such action, if continued, might seriously affect relations between the two countries. Great Britain, he remarked, was not interested in commercial exploitation of such information. Its effect on future British independence, however, was of vital importance. It would, indeed, be a serious matter if either Germany or Russia won the race to build a weapon which might be used for international blackmail. At the peace conference following the war, he could not accept any United States assertion that it alone should control the bomb. If interchange of information were not again put into effect, he concluded, Britain would have to start a parallel development although this would be a wasteful diversion of its energies from supplying other necessities of the war.

Bush, then, stated the United States' position very much as he had to Cherwell in May, emphasizing the need for security commensurate with all requirements for winning the war. Stimson next read a statement from a prepared memorandum:

1. The two governments were in possession of an unfinished, scientific project on which they were working.
2. There had been interchange of information as the project progressed.
3. The United States, at great expense, was building plants to produce the product of their combined research on the understanding that the British would share that product to win the war.
4. Now the United Kingdom wanted running reports on construction, so that after the war it could quickly produce nuclear weapons as an element of strength in case of a future war.
5. The United States was, therefore, faced with three questions. Should it grant the British request completely? Should it seek safeguards against the use of the weapon except under suitable political restrictions? Or should it refuse the British request as entirely uncalled for under the original agreements of the President and the Prime Minister?

He ended leaving his questions unanswered.

After Stimson had finished, Churchill admitted that his had been a "trenchant" analysis. He then proposed an agreement between himself and Roosevelt which would include these provisions:

1. There would be free interchange of information so that the project would be a completely shared enterprise.
2. Each government would agree not to use the bomb against the other.
3. Neither government would give information to a third party without the other's consent.
4. Each would agree not to use the bomb against third parties without the other's consent.
5. And, finally, in view of the large expenditures of the United States, the President might limit the commercial and industrial uses to which the British could apply the new force to the extent that he considered such limitations fair and equitable.

Stimson received this proposal without committing the United States to it. He promised, however, to present Churchill's views to the President. As the meeting was breaking up, Bundy informally indicated to Lord Cherwell the problems which faced the President in negotiating such agreements within the limitations of his war powers. Promises made on the periphery of such powers would inevitably raise difficulties between the President and Congress which might threaten a fair agreement with the British in the future.[74]

Stimson did not inform Roosevelt of this conversation until after his return to the United States on July 31, 1943. Soon thereafter, Sir John Anderson and Vannevar Bush, in an exchange of letters, prepared a draft agreement which embodied all of Churchill's points and in addition created a British-American Combined Policy Committee to oversee jointly the development of the bomb.[75] On August 7, Bush informed Roosevelt that he had attempted to bring about the change Roosevelt had requested in his letter of July 20. One thought, he wrote, guided his work, the ". . . conviction that all steps taken at this time should be solely for the purpose of winning the war at the earliest possible moment." [76]

Just the day before, Bundy had sent a memorandum to Stimson in which he had tried to explain the position of Bush, Conant, Marshall, Groves, and the Military Policy Committee. They had, he wrote, been trying to devise an agreement on the exchange of information in such a way ". . . that nobody, including the political opponents of the President . . . [would] be in a position to say that he had acted otherwise than under the war powers and for the sole purpose of winning the war . . . They . . . [were] trying to avoid at all costs the President being accused of dealing with hundreds of millions of taxpayers' money improvidently beyond winning the war, by turning over great power in the post-war world to Great Britain without adequate consideration of Executive and Legislative authority." [77] Thus, it would seem that United States representatives were concerned not only for the security of the program but also for the future political situation of the President as it might affect both his domestic and international policies.

What occurred between August 7 and August 19 when the Quebec Agreement was signed by Churchill and Roosevelt is difficult to determine. Roosevelt failed to consult the Military Policy Committee or Bush individually, and it is doubtful that he contacted any American on the matter at Quebec. The agreement finally negotiated was almost a replica of the British proposals. It became the official basis for the United States–British relationship during the remainder of the war.[78] The following were the important provisions of that agreement:

1. There would be complete interchange of information on atomic bomb developments.
2. Each agreed never to use "this agency" against the other.
3. Neither would use it against third parties without the other's consent.
4. Neither would communicate any information to third parties "except by mutual consent."
5. And, finally, each agreed to the establishment of the Combined Policy Committee of which Stimson was to be chairman, Bush and Conant the other American members, and Field-Marshall Sir John Dill and

the Right Honorable J. J. Llewellin, the British representatives with
the Honorable C. D. Howe representing Canada.[79]

From that time until Truman became President, British–American relations
concerned with building the atomic bomb progressed on a relatively amicable
basis. The Combined Policy Committee met seven times and developed a
working pattern for discussing technical matters involving such things as
patent rights and sources of uranium supplies. It also was instrumental in
organizing the Combined Development Trust. On June 13, 1944, Roosevelt
and Churchill signed an agreement establishing this trust, to be comprised
of British and American representatives under Groves as chairman. The
trust was given the responsibility of gaining control of supplies of uranium
and thorium in the United States, Great Britain, the Commonwealth, and in
other states. Its members were chosen by the Combined Policy Committee
and were responsible to it.[80]

The Combined Policy Committee also considered political problems from
time to time, but it took no action on such question. It did not discuss the
use of the bomb.

General Groves, working under the Military Policy Committee and Secretary Stimson, still managed the project. He, in fact, resented the agreement
with the British as a threat to his security program which carried with it no
commensurate advantage in terms of more quickly finishing the bomb. In
1954 he was to testify before the Atomic Energy Commission's Personnel
Security Board:

. . . of course, as you know and is well known, I was not responsible for our
close cooperation with the British. I did everything to hold back on it. I would
say perfectly frankly I did the things that I have . . . by implication blamed
. . . my scientists for doing. I did not carry out the wishes of our Government
with respect to cooperation with the British. . .[81]

Groves, it seems, unable to exercise complete security control over British
scientists who frequently visited his installations, did everything he could at
the administrative level to restrict their access to information so as to maintain
the secrecy of the project.

One further move to consolidate British–American efforts was made when
Churchill visited Hyde Park following the second Quebec Conference in
September, 1944, for conversations with Roosevelt. As Admiral William D.
Leahy, Roosevelt's Chief of Staff, described it, the meeting occurred between
6:00 P.M. and 8:00 P.M. on September 19. A number of military and political
matters were discussed, the most important concerning the atomic bomb.
During the discussion, ". . . an oral agreement was made that the United
States and Great Britain would continue to collaborate after the war on the
development of . . . 'tube alloys.' " [82] According to Leahy, Roosevelt refused
to agree to share the secret of the bomb with the British. "To my knowledge,"
Leahy later wrote, "no agreement was made in regard to sharing the use for

military purposes." [83] But the Admiral was mistaken. Although no one in the United States government knew of it until late June, 1945, the President and the Prime Minister had initialed an *aide-memoire* of their conversation which specifically anticipated cooperation after the war in the military as well as in the commercial development of atomic energy.[84]

TOP SECRET

TUBE ALLOYS

Aide-memoire of Conversation between the President and the Prime Minister at Hyde Park September 18, 1944.

1. The suggestion that the world should be informed regarding Tube Alloys with a view to an international agreement regarding its control and use, is not accepted. The matter should continue to be regarded as of the utmost secrecy; but when a "bomb" is finally available, it might, perhaps, after mature consideration, be used against the Japanese, who should be warned that this bombardment will be repeated until they surrender.
2. Full collaboration between the United States and the British Government in developing Tube Alloys for military and commercial purposes should continue after the defeat of Japan unless and until terminated by joint agreement.[85]

This document merits some consideration. Obviously Roosevelt and Churchill anticipated that close cooperation between their two states in the development of atomic energy for both military and commercial use would continue throughout the war and into the years beyond. The *aide-memoire* indicated the intimate, top-level collaboration that had grown between the two governments during the war. It symbolized the close United States-British relations in developing and planning for the use of the atomic bomb. Although Truman was not immediately aware of its existence in April, 1945, it ultimately proved to be one more legacy of the past which created conditions affecting his actions during his wartime months as President. The British as well as those who had worked on the project in the United States had devoted their energies over the war years to the development of an atomic bomb. When the time came for its use, they too were to be intensely interested in its disposition. Truman was to deal, therefore, with the product of an international effort. His decision for its use necessarily reflected consideration of both United States and British interests.[86]

E. *Planning for Use of the Atomic Bomb Prior to April 12, 1945*

The Hyde Park *aide-memoire* of September, 1944, denoted more than the close relationship which had grown between the United States and Great Britain in their joint development of the atomic bomb during the war. It also evidenced the willingness of Roosevelt and Churchill to employ the weapon against Japan if conditions warranted. It indicated the anticipation that the bomb would be used by those who had led in its production. Planning for such use had kept pace with the construction of the bomb. Although little had been done to incorporate considerations involving the new weapon into United States strategic plans, the air group which was to supply the bomb's carrier had been formed. Informed estimates were indicating with increasing assurance that nuclear weapons would be ready by the summer of 1945. All of those who were politically responsible for the bomb's development assumed that it would be used if the war continued. And for this purpose, they considered the war as a totality. It would not be over until both Germany and Japan surrendered unconditionally. Thus, indications during the winter of 1944–1945 that the German effort to produce such weapons had been unsuccessful failed to stop the promotion of plans for employing the bomb against Japan.

1. German Failure

Much of the motivation which had involved both scientists and the United States government in the development of nuclear weapons had resulted from the widespread fear that Nazi Germany might develop an atomic bomb and use it to conquer the world. This was considered a definite possibility among the European refugee scientists in the United States who had originally promoted governmental support for their research and who knew of the advanced state of pertinent German science. The potential force of the new weapon had been described to be of sufficient magnitude to instill in responsible officials of the government the urgency which was to characterize the entire effort after the United States became involved in the war. Although little factual information concerning German activities had been available in the United States, the driving need to forestall enemy success caused those involved in the project to exert every effort to perfect a bomb before the Germans. They were in a race to evade total defeat and, perhaps, annihilation. They had to win.[87]

This concern over the possibility of German success led General Groves to organize a military-scientific team in the fall of 1943 to investigate the state of German research and development by accompanying the armies of the United Nations as they pushed through conquered Europe. This special group was named *Alsos*, the Greek word for "groves"; and in November, 1943, Lt. Colonel Boris T. Pash of Army Intelligence was named its commanding officer.[88] Later, to provide needed scientific leadership to *Alsos*, Dr. Samuel A. Goudsmit, an experimental physicist who had been engaged in nonnuclear war work at Massachusetts Institute of Technology, was asked by Groves to share the command with Pash. The *Alsos* group landed shortly after the attack forces hit the beaches on Normandy in June, 1944. The group followed the United Nations advance across Europe, searching out German scientists, their papers, and their apparatus during 1944 and the spring of 1945 until the German surrender.[89]

The discoveries of the *Alsos* mission were at first unrewarding. It was not until after November 15, 1944, the date on which Strasbourg surrendered, that Goudsmit found encouraging evidence which indicated the failure of the German atomic program. At the University of Strasbourg he found the papers of Carl Friedrich von Weizacher, a noted physicist who had been connected with German nuclear research throughout the war. Von Weizsacher's papers demonstrated to Goudsmit that the Germans were two years behind the program underway in the United States. As of December, 1944, Goudsmit felt ". . . absolutely certain that the Germans did not have anything like an atomic bomb."[90] Since 1939, they had been attempting to separate the isotope U-235 from natural uranium by using the centrifuge process. Although they foresaw the theoretical possibility of the derivation of plutonium from the working of a heavy-water, self-sustaining pile, they had never developed the pile and never expected to utilize plutonium in a weapon. As a matter of fact, these papers indicated that the German physicists considered themselves far ahead of their adversaries in the United States; and, in any case, they never expected a nuclear bomb to be a factor in World War II.[91] They were concentrating on the production of nuclear energy rather than on the construction of an atomic bomb.[92]

After the discovery of the von Weizsacher papers, the *Alsos* group continued its work as the western front of the Germans first "bulged" and then collapsed during the winter and spring of 1945. It did so to satisfy lingering doubts of the MED that the documents might have been planted deliberately to mislead the Allies. Only after all significant German physicists had been captured and after all laboratories and possible atomic plants had been seized could there be assurance that the Germans no longer posed an atomic threat.

Goudsmit particularly desired the capture of Werner Heisenberg, a leader of recent German research and the only German physicist whom he considered sufficiently capable to construct a self-sustaining pile. On February 15, 1945, unknown to the *Alsos* mission, Heisenberg supervised construction of a pile at the small German village of Haigerloch in the Swabian Alps near Switzerland. There was, however, insufficient uranium to operate the pile and it was never activated. On April 22, 1945, the Haigerloch pile was captured by a contingent of *Alsos* men. Heisenberg was seized a few days later in Upper Bavaria where he had gone to be with his family. With his capture, the German atomic threat ended. It died at about the same time that the military power of the Third Reich collapsed completely.[93]

The Germans had never really been a nuclear threat. They had, however, been so considered by officials of the American program from the very beginning. As long as any danger existed such habits of thought, developed over a prolonged period of time, were not easily cast aside because of evidence based solely on the personal correspondence and scientific papers of the enemy. From December, 1944, the evidence of German failure was available.[94] But the MED continued its pressure to speed up production of U-235, plutonium, and an atomic bomb. At no time during the spring of 1945 was there a letup. And yet the collapse of Germany left only Japan as a target on which to cast the bomb. Japan had no nuclear weapon, and no one in the United States considered it possible for the Japanese to develop one. Given the many drains on its industry and manpower, Japan did not have the resources to handle such an immense undertaking.[95] And yet the S-1 program moved rapidly ahead. The nearer the bomb approached reality, the greater became the pressure for its realization.[96]

2.   ANTICIPATION OF SUCCESS

Production of an atomic bomb had been predicted with remarkable accuracy since the early days of the government's interest in the program. In fact, the assurance of success in developing a weapon during the war had been a major factor leading the government to take a hand. The optimistic reports of expectations by the Thomson Committee of British scientists, and the Compton Committee of scientists in the United States, led Dr. Vannevar Bush to recommend an all-out effort by the United States government in December, 1941.[97] A year later, after Fermi's success on December 2 with the West Stands pile at the University of Chicago, Bush, reporting to Roosevelt for the Military Policy Committee, refined his predictions considerably. As Compton has paraphrased his report, he forecast that:

. . . with the best of luck we could hope for atomic bombs to be ready for use in the spring of 1945. With an average share of fortune's favors they should be ready by the summer of '45 [sic]. We should surely be able to count on having the bombs ready, *if they* could be made at all, by the autumn of '45 [sic].[98]

From this time theoretical knowledge was sufficient to assume with reasonable certainty that a bomb could be built. The date of completion would depend on ". . . the time required to design and build the plants, to produce the materials, and to fabricate the materials into bombs." [99] And yet there was, throughout the program, doubt that nuclear weapons could be made at all.

One in the administration who was soon convinced of atomic potentialities was Harvey H. Bundy, an old friend of Stimson's who had worked closely with him during his term as Secretary of State in the Hoover administration.[100] Since 1941 Bundy had served with Stimson as Special Assistant to the Secretary of War and had become, through the war years, Stimson's most intimate personal assistant.[101] As the atomic program neared its successful completion, Stimson found that the project took more and more of his time; and he, in turn, allocated an increasing responsibility for administering the program to Bundy.[102] Through 1944 and the spring and summer of 1945, Bundy exercised administrative leadership over the program.[103] Although he later shared this responsibility (early in 1945 when the burden of work increased) with another Special Assistant to Stimson, George L. Harrison, Bundy continued to be the key man for the project in the Secretary's office.[104]

As early as May, 1944, Bundy was advising Stimson that some thought be given as to the place the atomic bomb should fill in the War Department's strategic planning. Thus, on May 10 he sent Stimson a memorandum in which he stated: "It will not be long before S-1 will have to be considered in our Strategic Planning [sic]." He had, he wrote, ". . . suggested to the S-1 Military Policy Committee that an up-to-date appraisal should be in the mind [sic] of the principal leaders." [105]

Apparently Bundy's suggestion was at least partially accepted. Although S-1 was not to enter military strategic planning, its future impact was to be more precisely evaluated by General Groves and the Military Policy Committee. In August, 1944, Groves predicted that a bomb would be ready by that time the following year.[106] At the second Quebec Conference in September, there was general recognition among the negotiators that they ". . . had every reason to believe [the atomic bomb] would be completed within the coming year." [107]

Finally, at Stimson's request, Bush and Conant drafted a long letter on September 30 in which they outlined their views on the future development and international post-war aspects of the atomic energy program. In their report, the two who had done so much to promote the S-1 project, estimated that ". . . there is every reason to believe that before August 1, 1945, atomic bombs will have been demonstrated and . . . in production. . . ." [108]

Bundy and Bush kept after Stimson through the winter of 1944 and 1945. On December 9, 1944, Bundy urged the Secretary of War to consider planning for handling the situation in the United States after the use of the bomb was disclosed and suggested that the time had come to let the Secretary of State, Edward R. Stettinius, Jr., in on the secret.[109] A week later he suggested that Stimson establish a "commission" to advise the President in drafting his statement following the bomb's use.[110] In two letters to Bundy, one of January 30, 1945, and another of February 1, Bush was to remind him that the ". . . time available . . . [was] none too long . . ." for the organization of this commission.[111] The need for rapid action was increasing and Bush felt it as keenly as Bundy.

Much of this attempt to institute planning of administrative action to be employed at the time the bomb was used and afterward stemmed from a report which Groves had made to General Marshall on December 30, 1944. Groves' letter began:

It is now reasonably certain that our operation plans should be based on the *gun type bomb*, which, it is estimated, will produce the equivalent of a ten thousand ton TNT explosion. The first bomb, without previous fullscale [*sic*] test which we do not believe will be necessary, should be ready about 1 August 1945. The second one should be ready by the end of the year and succeeding ones at . . . intervals thereafter.

Our previous hopes that an implosion (compression) type of bomb might be developed in the *late spring* have now been dissipated by scientific difficulties. . . .[112]

In writing this letter Groves consulted General Arnold and sent it on to Marshall who forwarded it to Stimson and Roosevelt. All read it.[113]

On January 3, Stimson followed Bundy's suggestion and informed Secretary of State Stettinius about the bomb and disclosed his expectations as to when it would be completed.[114] Stettinius recalled that he was told of the weapon "a few weeks before" January 26 in the upstairs study of the White House by Roosevelt who remarked at the time that ". . . he was not sure how long it would take to perfect . . . [the] new bomb." [115] The Secretary of State was the first in the State Department to be informed. After this conversation he saw Stimson in order to establish liaison with the military and asked Assistant Secretary of State James C. Dunn to handle the job.[116] Despite the contradictions in the two accounts, it is evident that Stettinius learned of the nuclear weapon in early January, 1945. On his way to the Crimea Conference at Yalta, Stettinius was further briefed by Major William A. Consodine of the MED. Groves had ordered Consodine to fly to Malta to provide the Secretary of State with additional information concerning the new weapon. Their discussion involved the certainty of explosion, the possible date of use on August 1, 1945, and the potential power of the bomb.[117] So by the time of the Yalta Conference the Secretary of State had been fully informed about the new weapon. Planning from then on involved consultation with the State Department. But Bundy, Stimson, and Groves were still the prime movers.

On March 3, 1945, Bundy sent another memorandum to Stimson enclosing the draft of a proposed message for the President to deliver after the bomb would be dropped sometime in 1945.[118] Following a conversation with Bundy on March 5, Stimson recorded:

We are up against some very big decisions. The time is approaching when we can no longer avoid them and when events may force us into the public on the subject.[119]

He talked later that day with Marshall to suggest that the General start thinking ". . . on this post-war set of problems." [120] On March 8, he wrote that S-1 was ". . . approaching its ripening time and matters are getting very interesting and serious." [121] To let the President know how serious he thought it was, Stimson outlined for Roosevelt, at their last White House luncheon on March 15, his anticipations in regard to the bomb and informed him ". . . when it was likely to come off and told him how important it was to get ready." [122] Although Roosevelt's remarks at this luncheon are unrecorded, it may be presumed that he was impressed with the imminence of success.

By April 12, 1945, there were strong indications that an atomic bomb would be ready sometime around August 1, 1945. Groves had informed Marshall; the Department of State had been let in on the secret; and Bundy was formulating plans for a commission to handle postwar policy and to recommend Presidential action after it was dropped.

And yet there were still doubts as to whether or not the weapon would be successful. A few who knew about the project were filled with uncertainty. Among these Admiral Leahy was, perhaps, the most skeptical. He expressed his doubts to Roosevelt as early as September 19, 1944, at the Hyde Park meeting with Churchill.[123] On September 22 following a meeting with Roosevelt, Bush, and Lord Cherwell at which Bush had outlined the progress of the S-1 program, Leahy recorded in his *Diaries* that he was "unconvinced."[124] And when Groves called on him on October 2 to inform him about the project in detail he wrote, "I have as yet received no information that leads me to have confidence in the practicality of this project." [125] Leahy was to remain unconvinced through 1944 and 1945 when he continued on as Chief of Staff to Truman.

Another who doubted the worth of the project was Assistant Secretary of State Dunn, the State Department's liaison with the Department of the Army. At their last luncheon of March 15, Roosevelt and Stimson had discussed a memorandum from Dunn in which he expressed alarm at the cost of the program. Dunn suggested that Bush and Conant should be checked by outside scientists, for he had heard rumors that they had ". . . sold the President a lemon on the subject. . . ." [126] Stimson reassured the President that such action was unnecessary although he too had qualms. "It (the atomic project) has," he wrote later, "this unique peculiarity! that, although every prophesy [sic] thus far has been fulfilled by the development and we can see that success is 99% assured, yet only by the first actual war trial of the weapon can the actual certainty be fixed." [127] This then was Stimson's attitude on the eve of Truman's accession to office. Despite the fact that Groves had formerly advised that success in the summer of 1945 was a 99 percent certainty, the Secretary of War who had been responsible for the project since May 1, 1943, was convinced that proof of success demanded a war trial.[128]

3. MILITARY PLANS

But if Secretary of War Stimson was uncertain about the success of the atomic bomb, his top military commanders were even more loathe to consider its use in their overall planning for the defeat of Japan. This can be explained by a reasonable conservatism of the military who refused to base plans involving large numbers of men, considerable time, and much money on an untested weapon. The difficult logistical problems which the United Nations would face in defeating Japan required a long-range buildup of men and supplies. Target dates, of necessity, were chosen to provide ample time to accumulate the force required for success. Bush and Groves might be predicting success for S-1 by August, 1945, but military planning could not be predicated on the validity of their predictions, particularly in the case of such a novel weapon.

Thus, military strategy devised during the last year of the war for the defeat of Japan was formulated with no consideration of the impact which the atomic bomb might have on the course of the war. For the sake of security, S-1 was never discussed in the meetings of the Joint Chiefs of Staff, although from late 1943 Marshall privately advised Arnold and King of MED developments.[129] The Joint Chiefs were told when the first bomb was ready to go. Other than that, they knew little about it except from Marshall's briefings. And, in fact, even Marshall was somewhat removed from the project; for on all international policy matters, on problems of postwar planning, and on questions handled by the Combined Policy Committee, Groves reported directly to Stimson. Only on off-continent military operations involving the bomb, did he report to Stimson through Marshall.[130] Apparently Marshall left the handling of the new weapon almost entirely to Groves while he concerned himself with the many problems of conventional warfare, which were much more pressing and with which he was much more familiar.[131]

The need for secrecy of S-1 was considered to be so critical that lower officers on Marshall's staff responsible for military plans knew little or nothing about the project until the bomb was used. The Operations Division (OPD) of the War Department General Staff, accountable to the Chief of Staff for the Army's part in strategic planning, was practically ignorant of the existence of an atomic bomb program.[132] "In the War Department the decision to use the bomb played no part in orthodox military staff work . . . OPD's planning went on virtually as if the atomic bomb did not exist." [133]

But plans for Japan's defeat had been formulated in detail by the time Truman took office. A year before, in April, 1944, the basic position had been formulated in the OPD. It envisaged that: "(a) The collapse of Japan as a result of blockade and air bombardment alone . . . [was] very doubtful; (b) The collapse of Japan can be assured only by invasion of Japan proper." [134]

With remarkable consistency the military hewed to this simple line. They, of course, collaborated to meet the needs of the vast operations necessary to implement the program. They provided roles for bombing from the air and for naval blockade. But by July, 1944, the Joint Chiefs of Staff had accepted for planning purposes the following program:

a. Concurrent advances through the Ryukyus, Bonins, and Southeast China coast for the purpose of intensifying the blockade and air bombardment of Japan and creating a situation favorable for:

b. An amphibious assault on Kyushu for the purpose of further reducing Japanese capabilities by engaging and fixing major enemy forces and establishing a tactical condition favorable to:

c. A decisive stroke against the industrial heart of Japan by means of an amphibious attack through the Tokyo plain assisted by continued pressure from Kyushu.[135]

Expanded United States operational plans were presented by the Joint Chiefs of Staff to the Combined Chiefs of Staff on January 22, 1945. The objectives remained the same:

. . . To force the unconditional surrender of Japan by:

(1) Lowering Japanese ability and will to resist by establishing sea and air blockades, conducting intensive air bombardment, and destroying Japanese air and naval strength.

(2) Invading and seizing objectives in the industrial heart of Japan. . . ."[136]

In April the field commanders in the Pacific approved the elaborate, detailed plans to accomplish the above objectives. Thus, despite later refinements in the strategy designed to meet the newly developing conditions of the war, the plans for the defeat of Japan were ready at the time of Roosevelt's death.[137] The atomic bomb had not entered the calculations of those who **had devised** the strategy.

In only one respect had the military adapted to the potentialities of the atomic program. The Army Air Forces had organized the 509th Composite Group and charged it with responsibility for dropping the new weapon. By the end of 1943, the B-29 had been chosen to carry the atomic bomb. The plane would need minor modification, but essentially the bomb had been designed to fit the airplane.[138] Earlier that summer General Arnold had assigned Colonel Roscoe C. Wilson, Commander of the 316th Bombardment Wing at Colorado Springs, as air project officer for the MED. Wilson had been authorized to utilize all necessary men and equipment to insure that any bomb produced would be dropped successfully. One of Wilson's responsibilities was to recommend pilots for the mission for Arnold's consideration. For commanding officer, Arnold chose an experienced bomber pilot, Colonel Paul W. Tibbetts, Jr. In August, 1944, Tibbets was placed in command of the 393rd Bombardment Squadron which later became the core of the 509th Composite Group, organized in December. Tibbetts chose Wendover Field, Utah, as the site of training operations. [139]

Normal training in precision bombing, using only one bomb dropped from high altitudes, had also been completed in December. In January, 1945, the squadron had participated in additional training at Batista Field, Cuba, to simulate the long, overwater flights to an island target which would characterize its attack on Japan. During February Tinian, an island north of Guam in the Marianas, had been chosen as the 509th's forward base; and work was progressing on the special installations throughout the spring. The squadron returned to Wendover from Cuba to finish its training and then to fly to Tinian in its modified B-29's in June, 1945.

The military, therefore, although not yet ready to consider the atomic weapon in their strategic planning, had provided every facility for its initial use. It was, it seems, considered by them largely as an experiment, one that had to be tested before it could be included in their evaluations of the requirements for the defeat of Japan. They, like Secretary Stimson, anticipated a war trial and were preparing for it. Truman came to office at a time when military preparations for use on Japan had long been underway. A trained squadron was almost ready to deliver the bomb. Its base was nearly finished on Tinian. Its commanders from the skipper of the 509th to the Secretary of War anticipated the fruition of their efforts later that summer.

4. VIEW FROM THE TOP

Those connected with the development of the atomic bomb expected to use it. Whether or not President Roosevelt supported such expectations and held them himself is difficult to substantiate. No official or private statement describing his position has been found. His files are nearly empty of pertinent information since he normally returned reports about atomic energy to their authors without retaining copies at the White House.[140] General Edwin M. Watson who had participated in all of the White House operations involving the atomic energy project died just before Roosevelt and left no public record.[141] Conversations were not recorded. Secrecy was too important to discuss the matter except in the most circumspect fashion and then only with a few of the highest officials. Nevertheless, indications of Roosevelt's attitudes toward use of the weapon exist. And it is important to evaluate their meaning. For Truman purposefully attempted to carry on Roosevelt's policies in conducting the war through its last months. Awed by the stature of his predecessor and humbled by his evaluation of his own capabilities, he tried to continue United States policy as if Roosevelt still lived.[142] Roosevelt's plans, so far as he could make them so, were to be his guidelines in leading the United States to peace.

What then were Roosevelt's plans for use of the atomic bomb? By implication from the history of the long and concerted effort to construct the weapon which he had fostered it seems reasonable to believe that he anticipated using the bomb if it were built before the war ended and if conditions warranted. When General Groves had assumed command of the Manhattan

Engineering District, he had been ordered to build the bomb for use. Roosevelt never modified Groves' orders.[143] And Stimson has written specifically:

. . . at no time, from 1941 to 1945, did I ever hear it suggested by the President, or by any other responsible member of the government, that atomic energy should not be used in the war. All of us, of course, understood the terrible responsibility. . . ; President Roosevelt particularly spoke to me many times of his own awareness of the catastrophic potentialities of our work. But we were at war, and the work must be done. I therefore emphasize that it was our common objective, throughout the war, to be the first to produce an atomic weapon and use it. The possible atomic weapon was considered to be a new and tremendously powerful explosive, as legitimate as any other of the deadly explosive weapons of modern war. The entire purpose was the production of a military weapon; on no other ground could the wartime expenditure of so much time and money have been justified. The exact circumstances in which that weapon might be used were unknown to any of us. . . .[144]

At least in Stimson's view, Roosevelt never doubted that the bomb should be used.

There is other evidence that this was so. The Hyde Park *aide-memoire* of September 19, 1944, indicated as much when it noted that when a bomb was available it might be used against Japan after mature consideration.[145] Roosevelt's reflections on its use were mentioned by Alexander Sachs when he recalled a discussion which he had had with Roosevelt in December, 1944. As Sachs described the conversation about a year later to Under Secretary of War Robert P. Patterson, he and Roosevelt agreed that:

. . . following a successful test, there should be arranged (a) a rehearsal demonstration before a body including internationally recognized scientists from all Allied Countries and, in addition, neutral countries, supplemented by representatives of the major (religious) faiths; . . . (c) that thereafter a warning be issued by the United States and its Allies in the Project [*sic*] to our major enemies in the war, Germany and Japan, that atomic bombing would be applied to a selected area within a designated time for the evacuation of human and animal life; and finally (d) in the wake of such realization of the efficacy of atomic bombing an ultimatum demand for immediate surrender by the enemies be issued, in the certainty that failure to comply would subject their countries and people to atomic annihilation.[146]

Whether or not Roosevelt later indicated the feelings he reportedly expressed in this discussion to Stimson or to anyone else in his administration is uncertain. No evidence has been found to indicate that anyone knew of such thoughts during the early months of Truman's regime when using the bomb was being considered. At any rate Roosevelt apparently hoped that the bomb could be used. For he is reported to have said to Miss Grace Tully, his secretary, ". . . I can't tell you what this (the atomic project) is, Grace, but if it works, and pray God it does, it will save many American lives." [147] Roosevelt, fearing the war might continue indefinitely, apparently hoped that the bomb would be used to end it *quickly*.

As success of the MED appeared more certain, detailed plans were required if facilities were to be available for the use of its product. Roosevelt's willingness to use the bomb is evidenced by his approval of those plans and the dissemination of information regarding such plans to the pertinent military commanders. Thus, General Groves' letter of December 30, 1944, to General Marshall contained these interesting suggestions:

. . . The plan of operations while based on the more certain, more powerful gun type bomb also provides for the use of the implosion type bombs when they become available . . . The time schedule must not be adversely affected by anything other than the difficulties of solving our scientific problems. *The 509th Composite Group, 20th Air Force, has been organized and it is now undergoing training* as well as assisting in essential tests.

The time has now come when we should acquaint the Assistant Chief of Staff OPD and possibly one of his assistants and the Chief of Staff of the 20th Air Force, Brigadier General Laures Norstad, with sufficient information so that the formulation of adequate plans and the necessary troop movements may be carried out without difficulty and without loss in security. It is proposed also that General Norstad . . . be authorized to give general information to the Deputy Commander [of the] 20th Air Force, Lt. Gen. M. F. Harmon, and limited information to the Commanding General of the 21st Bomber Command, Brig. Gen. [*sic*] H. S. Hansell, Jr. I also feel that it would be advisable for Admiral Nimitz to be informed of our general plans in order that we will be assured the essential Navy assistance in the area. . .[148]

The fact that the President approved these suggestions indicates that, at that time, he expected the bomb to be used and supported planning to that end.

Roosevelt's willingness to use the atomic bomb was further implied in the last conversation Stimson had with the President prior to his death. After reassuring Roosevelt that the project was progressing satisfactorily, Stimson ". . . outlined to him the future of it and when it was likely to come off and told him how important it was to get ready. . . ." The Secretary of War then went on to describe different points of view in regard to control of the weapon after the war and ". . . told him that those things must be settled *before the first projectile is used and that he must be ready with a statement to come out to the people on it just as soon as that is done.* He agreed to that. . . ."[149]

The question to Stimson and Roosevelt was not one of whether or not the bomb would be used but one which involved what their actions should be after it was used.

Other factors, however, might have caused some revision in Roosevelt's thinking, although that seems unlikely. Since the previous summer of 1944, an increasing number of scientists at the Metallurgical Laboratory had begun to doubt the advisability of using the bomb. They had organized a committee and had held seminars to discuss the political and social implications of the bomb's use. Some had come to the conclusion that it was immoral to use the weapon now that there was no possibility that Germany might use an atomic device against the United States. Others felt that it would weaken the postwar strategic position of the United States to demonstrate that it had such a weapon. One of these was Leo Szilard, who had originally helped to acquaint Roosevelt with the military possibilities of nuclear fission in 1939. He again prevailed on Dr. Albert Einstein to write to the President on March 25, 1945, urging him to grant Szilard the opportunity to present his views.[150] Szilard also obtained an appointment for an interview with Mrs. Roosevelt through whose efforts he hoped to influence the President.[151] But Roosevelt died before the appointment could be arranged. Whether or not he read Einstein's letter is doubtful. It was on his desk at the time of his death and was later referred to Byrnes.[152] Such protests from scientists at Chicago, therefore, probably failed to reach Roosevelt in time to affect his determination to use the nuclear weapon. He probably planned to use the weapon when death came.[153]

F.   The United States and the Atomic Bomb, April 12, 1945

Roosevelt's death marked only the beginning for President Truman, now responsible for the direction of the atomic program and the policies which it would affect and by which it would, in turn, be affected.

Truman had a bull by the tail. The project was now enormous and, under General Groves' direction, operating at full tilt to complete the weapon. For over four years many men had devoted their time and their energies under frequently unattractive conditions to complete the weapon. Nearly two billion dollars had been spent by an administration which had been forced to request appropriations from a Congress, generally ignorant of the purpose for which the expenditure had been made. Many men spending such money, operating in secrecy, pushed frantically on by the fear of a German atomic bomb, now free of that terror and becoming more confident of their imminent success—this was the whirlwind which Truman inherited.

By April 12, 1945, Germany no longer posed a threat. It was clear that the bomb, if used on an enemy, would be dropped on Japan. The British government, a war-long partner in the program, held agreements which established conditions Truman would have to honor if Japan was to be the victim. The squadrons of bombers had been trained to use that target.

The questions that faced Truman were serious ones. In view of Roosevelt's persistent efforts over the course of the war to involve the Soviet Union in the war against Japan, was it still in the interests of the United States to promote such a development? Was it useful to continue, unmodified,

Roosevelt's policy of unconditional surrender toward Japan? If these policies were implemented, would Japan surrender before the atomic bombs could be perfected or would it fight on to national suicide in a land torn by bombardment and invasion?

These matters required careful consideration, for in a very real sense they were important elements of Roosevelt's legacy to his successor. Truman found it necessary to formulate policy in a *milieu* which had been strongly conditioned by the long-followed policies of unconditional surrender for Japan and of Soviet participation in the Far East. But he had to do so within the military and political conditions existing in the spring of 1945. Filled with respect for his famous predecessor and accepting, in fact, requesting the advice of those who had been close to Roosevelt, he sedulously followed the ways which Roosevelt had charted.

NOTES TO CHAPTER 2

1 Smyth, *Atomic Energy for Military Purposes,* p. 82. Compton, *Atomic Quest,* pp. 104–5. Baxter, *Scientists Against Time,* pp. 435–36.

2 John D. Millett, *The Organization and Role of the Armed Service Forces* (Washington: Department of the Army, 1954), p. 47.

3 Wallace was not present at this meeting which included Stimson, General Marshall, Conant, Bush, Major General Brehon Somervell, Styer, and Groves. Smyth, *Atomic Energy for Military Purposes,* pp. 83–84. Wallace claims that this marked the end of significant activities of the Top Policy Committee. From this time, the Military Policy Committee took over any functions the Top Policy Committee had exercised. "Testimony of Henry A. Wallace," pp. 1073–74. Styer and Purnell were responsible for considering and planning military policy concerning the project to build the weapon, such planning to cover production, strategic and tactical problems, as well as research and development. Groves, as executive officer, was to carry out the policies of the MPC. See *MED Files: Harrison-Bundy Series,* "S-1 Minutes of Meeting, September 23, 1942; Folder #1" which includes Memorandum "A" of Harvey H. Bundy, Special Assistant to the Secretary of War. Memorandum "A," approved by Wallace, Stimson, Marshall, Bush, and Conant, set up the MPC.

4 U. S. Atomic Energy Commission, *In the Matter of J. Robert Oppenheimer: Transcript of Hearing Before Personnel Security Board,* "Direct Examination of General Leslie R. Groves," (Washington: 1954), p. 171.

5 Smyth, *Atomic Energy for Military Purposes,* p. 85.

6 Compton, *Atomic Quest,* p. 111. The nature of General Groves' responsibility was corroborated in a personal interview with Groves on September 8, 1960, at Stamford, Connecticut.

7 U. S. Congress, Senate, Special Committee on Atomic Energy, *Atomic Energy Act of 1946,* Hearings, 79th Cong., 2nd sess., persuant S. 1717, Part 4 (Washington: 1946), pp. 478–79. Hereafter, "Groves Statement—Number 2."

8 "Bush Statement," p. 146. Two other men who had considerable influence in an advisory capacity were Conant and Richard C. Tolman, Chairman and Vice Chairman of NDRC, who acted as Groves' scientific advisers; see Baxter, *Scientists Against Time,* p. 439. For Groves' evaluation of Conant's role, see "Groves Statement," p. 477.

[9] U. S. Atomic Energy Commission, *In the Matter of J. Robert Oppenheimer: Transcript of Hearing Before Personnel Security Board*, "Direct Examination of General Leslie R. Groves," (Washington: 1954), p. 171.

[10] There are many descriptions of this event. See: Compton, *Atomic Quest*, pp. 136–45; Fermi, *Atoms in the Family*, pp. 190–99; Laurence, *Men and Atoms*, pp. 67–72; Smyth, *Atomic Energy for Military Purposes*, pp. 91–102.

[11] Baxter, *Scientists Against Time*, p. 440.

[12] Smyth, *Atomic Energy for Military Purposes*, p. 109.

[13] *Ibid.*, p. 195.

[14] *Ibid.*, p. 204.

[15] *Ibid.*, p. 196.

[16] *Ibid.*, pp. 172–73.

[17] *Ibid.*, pp. 202–3.

[18] Compton, *Atomic Quest*, pp. 132–45. Groves, Leslie R., *Now It Can Be Told: The Story of the Manhattan Project*, (New York: Harper and Brothers, 1962), pp. 3–124. Smyth, *Atomic Energy for Nuclear Purposes*, pp. 109–11.

[19] Smyth, *Atomic Energy for Nuclear Purposes*, p. 143.

[20] Many suppliers and corporations which had contracts for specific jobs have not been mentioned.

[21] The following costs do not include those for smaller units such as the Clinton Laboratory which through June 30, 1945, absorbed about $25,000,000. See U. S. Congress, Senate, Special Committee on Atomic Energy, *Hearings on Atomic Energy,* 79th Cong., 2nd sess., persuant Senate Resolution 179, Part 1, (Washington: 1945), p. 72. Hereafter, "Groves Statement—No. 1."

[22] *Ibid.*, p. 73. These costs do not include cost of materials supplied by the Government or housing and transportation costs.

[23] *Ibid.*, pp. 44, 73.

[24] Groves, *Now It Can Be Told*, pp. 68–93.

[25] Smyth, *Atomic Energy for Military Purposes*, pp. 145–47. The necessity of letting Du Pont work on the plutonium plant without governmental interference is indicated by Stimson's forestalling antitrust action against that concern during its operations. Henry L. Stimson and McGeorge Bundy, *On Active Service in Peace and War* (New York: Harper and Brothers, 1947), p. 615. Stimson's and Bundy's book contains an expanded version of the material found in Henry L. Stimson, *"The Decision to Use the Atomic Bomb," Harper's Magazine*, CXCIV (February, 1947), pp. 97–107.

[26] Smyth, *Atomic Energy for Military Purposes*, pp. 139–41.

[27] "Groves Statement—No. 1," pp. 44, 73.

[28] In Smyth, *Atomic Energy for Military Purposes*, p. 207, and Compton, *Atomic Quest*, p. 129, this date is given. Oppenheimer, in testimony before the Personnel Security Board of the Atomic Energy Commission in 1954, recalled the choice of the site during the fall of 1943. See U. S. Atomic Energy Commission, *In the Matter of J. Robert Oppenheimer*, "Testimony of J. Robert Oppenheimer," (Washington: 1954), p. 28. Hereafter, "Oppenheimer Statement." The dates of other developments indicate that either Oppenheimer's recollection was incorrect or his account was erroneous due to a typographical error.

[29] "Groves Statement—Number 1," p. 45.

[30] "Oppenheimer Statement," pp. 30–31.

[31] U. S. Congress, Senate, Special Committee on Atomic Energy, *Hearings on Atomic Energy*, 79th Cong., 2nd Sess., persuant Senate Resolution 179, Part 3, "Statement of Commodore W. S. Parsons," (Washington: 1945), p. 384. Hereafter, "Parsons Statement." H. H. Arnold, *Global Mission* (New York: Harper and Brothers, 1949), pp.

491–92. The decision to use the B-29 may have been made as early as September, 1943. Wesley Frank Craven and James Lea Cate (eds.), *The Army Air Forces in World War II* (Chicago: University of Chicago Press, 1953), V, 705.

[32] "Parsons Statement," p. 383.

[33] "Parsons Statement," p. 384.

[34] "Groves Statement—No. 1," pp. 45, 73.

[35] In reference to his attempt to arrange with Speaker of the House of Representatives Sam Rayburn for the visit of four representatives from the House to the Clinton Works, Stimson wrote: ". . . It is rather difficult because some of the men in key places on the Appropriations Committee are not very trustworthy in regard to secrecy." *The Diary of Henry L. Stimson*, Historical Documents Department, Yale University Library, New Haven, arranged chronologically, Friday, May 4, 1945. Hereafter, Stimson, *Diary*.

[36] Stimson and Bundy, *On Active Service in Peace and War*, p. 614.

[37] Stimson, *Diary*, February 18, 1944. Stimson says this was the first meeting with members of Congress. In a later recollection Senator Styles Bridges, in a letter to Roland Young, mentioned a meeting held ". . . in late 1942 . . ." by Stimson for two Republican and two Democratic senators in Stimson's office. Roland Young, *Congressional Politics in the Second World War*, (New York: Columbia University Press, 1956), pp. 45–46. Stimson's notation has been chosen as the more accurate of the two. See Stimson and Bundy, *On Active Service in Peace and War*, p. 614.

[38] *Papers of Henry L. Stimson*, Yale University Library. This procedure is described in a Memorandum of February 24, 1944, from Bush to Bundy which appears in Stimson's papers.

[39] Joe [sic] Martin, *My First Fifty Years in Politics* (New York: McGraw-Hill Book Company, Inc., 1960), p. 101.

[40] Young, *Congressional Politics in the Second World War*, pp. 45–46. Bridges mentions that Senator Charles McNary had originally been included within the group, but his death had led to the selection of White.

[41] Alben W. Barkley, *That Reminds Me* (Garden City: Doubleday and Company, Inc., 1954), p. 266.

[42] Truman, *Memoirs: Year of Decisions*, pp. 10–11. For work of the Special Committee to Investigate the National Defense Program, see pp. 164–86.

[43] Stimson, *Diary*, February 26, March 15, May 4, and May 17, 1945.

[44] Young, *Congressional Politics in the Second World War*, p. 45.

[45] Martin, *My First Fifty Years in Politics*, p. 101.

[46] The details of the security program are here irrelevant. For good accounts see: Compton, *Atomic Quest*, pp. 115–25; Fermi, *Atoms in the Family*, pp. 200–236; Groves, *Now It Can Be Told*, pp. 138–48; Daniel Lang, *From Hiroshima to the Moon: Chronicles of Life in the Atomic Age* (New York: Simon and Schuster, Inc., 1959), pp. 1–16; Laurence, *Men and Atoms*, pp. 95–114; and William L. Laurence, *Dawn Over Zero: The Story of the Atomic Bomb* (New York: Alfred A. Knopf, Inc., 1946). U. S. Atomic Energy Commission, *In the Matter of J. Robert Oppenheimer*, "Examination of General Groves," pp. 163–80. "Compartmentalization of information" merely indicates that no man on the project was to know any more than he had to know to do his specific job.

[47] Early in the program scientists led by Leo Szilard had attempted with partial success the self-censoring of academic articles dealing with fission. "Sachs Statement," p. 557; Compton, *Atomic Quest*, pp. 115–16.

[48] James F. Byrnes, *Speaking Frankly* (New York: Harper and Brothers, 1947), pp. 268–69. James F. Byrnes, *All in One Lifetime* (New York: Harper and Brothers, 1958), pp. 247–48.

49 U. S. Atomic Energy Commission, *In the Matter of J. Robert Oppenheimer,* "Examination of General Groves," p. 173.

50 *Papers of Henry L. Stimson,* "Memo of Conference with the President," December 31, 1944.

51 Compton, *Atomic Quest,* p. 60.

52 Smyth, *Atomic Energy for Military Purposes,* Appendix 7, British Information Service Statement, "Britain and the Atomic Bomb," August 12, 1945, p. 272.

53 See p. 10.

54 "Tube Alloys" became the British Code name for the atomic bomb project. The United States used the term "S-1" to designate its program.

55 Smyth, *Atomic Energy for Military Purpose,* "Britain and the Atomic Bomb," pp. 277–78. See also Winston S. Churchill, *The Second World War: The Hinge of Fate,* (Boston: Houghton Mifflin Company, 1950), IV, 378–79.

56 *MED Files: Harrison-Bundy Series,* Folder #111, "3 [sic] Extra Copies of Diplo. [sic] History," p. 1. This folder contains three copies of a diplomatic history of the Manhattan Engineer District written by General Groves after World War II. Hereafter, "Groves History." Documents pertinent to this history are to be found in Folder #109 entitled, "Annexes-Diplomatic History-Manhattan Project." The annexes are numbered consecutively. General Groves' history will be used as the basis for the following account of British-American relations. Pagination refers to that in each copy of the history. See also Groves, *Now It Can Be Told,* pp. 125–37.

57 *MED Files: Harrison-Bundy Series,* Folder #111, "Groves History," p. 2.

58 *Ibid.,* p. 2.

59 Churchill, *The Hinge of Fate,* p. 379.

60 *Ibid.,* p. 380. See also Robert E. Sherwood, *Roosevelt and Hopkins: An Intimate History* (New York: Harper and Brothers, 1948), p. 593. Arthur Bryant, *The Turn of the Tide* (Garden City: Doubleday and Company, Inc., 1957), p. 324.

61 *MED Files: Harrison-Bundy Series,* Folder #111, "Groves' History," p. 7.

62 *MED Files: Harrison-Bundy Series,* Folder #109, Annex 7, "Akers letter to Conant."

63 At this time, and throughout the war, the second most important supplier of uranium ores to the United States was Canada where large deposits had been discovered on Lake Athabasca and other lakes in the Great Bear Lake region of the Northwest Territories. The Belgian Congo was the leading supplier. See D. M. Le Bourdais, *Canada and the Atomic Revolution* (Toronto: McClelland and Stewart Company, Ltd., 1959), pp. 43–63.

64 *MED Files: Harrison-Bundy Series,* Folder #109, Annex 6, "Military Policy Committee Report to the President."

65 *MED Files: Harrison-Bundy Series,* Folder #111, "Groves History," p. 9.

66 *MED Files: Harrison-Bundy Series,* Folder #109, Annex 11, "H. Bundy Memorandum of Meeting of July 22, 1943, at No. 10 Downing Street," p. 1.

67 Sherwood, *Roosevelt and Hopkins,* p. 703. Sherwood's account is based on a manila folder titled "Tube Alloys" which is part of *The Papers of Harry L. Hopkins* now held by the Roosevelt Library at Hyde Park, New York. The "Tube Alloys" file contains the original document and generally substantiates Sherwood's account.

68 Sherwood, *Roosevelt and Hopkins,* pp. 703–4. There is no mention of these exchanges in Churchill, *The Hinge of Fate.*

69 *MED Files: Harrison-Bundy Series,* Folder #109, Annex 9, "Memorandum of Conference by Bush."

70 Quoted from a memorandum of July 31 from Bush to Hopkins in Sherwood, *Roosevelt and Hopkins,* p. 704.

71 Churchill, *The Hinge of Fate*, p. 809.

72 *MED Files: Harrison-Bundy Series*, Folder #109, Annex 8, "Roosevelt's letter to Bush."

73 Sir John Anderson and Lord Cherwell also attended these talks. See *MED Files: Harrison-Bundy Series*, Folder #109, Annex 11.

74 *MED Files: Harrison-Bundy Series*, Folder #109, Annex 11. The foregoing account is a paraphrasing of Bundy's five-page memorandum of the meeting.

75 *Ibid.*, Annexes 13 and 14.

76 *Ibid.*, Annex 16.

77 *MED Files: Harrison-Bundy Series*, Folder #109, Annex 17.

78 *MED Files: Harrison-Bundy Series*, Folder #111, "Groves History," pp. 14–16.

79 *MED Files: Harrison-Bundy Series*, Folder #109, Annex 18, "*The Citadel Quebec Articles of Agreement.*"

80 *MED Files: Harrison-Bundy Series*, Folder #109, "Agreement and Declaration of Trust." Groves, *Now It Can Be Told*, pp. 170–84.

81 United States Atomic Energy Commission, *In the Matter of J. Robert Oppenheimer*, "*Examination of General Groves*," p. 175.

82 *Fleet Admiral William D. Leahy Diaries* (15 Vols: 1893, 1897–1952) Vol. 10, p. 85. The materials in these diaries are typed copies of the original handwritten drafts which have been destroyed. All are unofficial papers and are held by the Library of Congress, Washington, D.C. For a slightly different account see William D. Leahy, *I Was There* (New York: McGraw-Hill Book Company, 1950), p. 265.

83 Leahy, *I Was There*, pp. 265–66.

84 *MED Files: Harrison-Bundy Series*, Folder #109, Annex 28 includes a copy of the *aide-memoire* and an indication that its existence was unknown until "late spring of 1945." This copy was taken from a photostat supplied by the British on July 18, 1945. See also Stimson, *Diary*, June 25, 1945, which mentions Stimson's discovery of the *aide-memoire* and *MED Files: Harrison-Bundy Series*, Folder #37, "C.P.C. Meeting, July 4, 1945." This folder includes a letter of June 20, 1945, from Sir Maitland Wilson to Stimson which includes a copy of the *aide-memoire* as an enclosure. Apparently Wilson brought this letter and its enclosure with him when he met Stimson on June 25, for Bundy wrote a memorandum covering the conversation of that date between Stimson and Wilson which corroborates Stimson's *Diary* citation. *MED Files: Harrison-Bundy Series*, Folder #52, "S-1 British Conversations with HHB," June 25. Wilson's letter states that the *aide-memoire* is of a meeting between Roosevelt and Churchill on September 18 and refers to later conversations of which there is no record. It is possible, therefore, that Leahy's description is of that later conversation and that he was not present at the talks from which the *aide-memoire* emerged. No other evidence of a Roosevelt-Churchill conversation dealing with the atomic bomb on September 18 has, however, been found.

85 U. S. Department of State, *Foreign Relations of the United States, Diplomatic Papers: The Conference of Berlin (The Potsdam Conference), 1945* (Washington, 1960), II, 1371. Hereafter, *Potsdam Papers*. This source also includes a copy of the *aide-memoire*. Roosevelt's copy was not found among his papers at Hyde Park until after the war was over. As a result, the United States government had only the photostat of the text which Churchill sent to Stimson at his request in July, 1945. See pp. 1370–71 for Churchill's covering letter to Stimson. Although the text is dated September 18, 1944, a marginal manuscript notation indicates that it was actually written on September 19. See p. 1371, fn. 3. From other manuscript notations it appears that one copy of the original was left with Roosevelt while another was given to Leahy to hand to Lord

Cherwell who was in Churchill's party at Hyde Park. It is not known if Leahy was aware of the contents of this document. See p. 1371, fn. 2.

[86] It is not known why Roosevelt failed to inform other responsible United States officials of the existence of this agreement. One can only hypothesize as to his motivations.

(1) He might have considered the document of little immediate importance and so laid it aside until an appropriate future date. Other more pressing matters might, then, have relegated it to the background as they demanded immediate consideration. He might have simply forgotten about it, or it might have been misplaced among his papers following his death.

(2) Roosevelt might have been waiting for a politically advantageous time to distribute it. He was running for election in 1944, and he might have feared the leaking of its terms to the domestic political opposition. Then preoccupied with the events surrounding the Crimea Conference at Yalta in February, 1945, he might have been taken unexpectedly by death before he felt it wise to inform those interested few in his administration who might have opposed the agreement.

(3) He might, perhaps, have considered it merely as a formalization of the close British-American relations which had emerged in constructing the new weapon and, therefore, in itself only minimally important since others in his administration were familiar with the existence of this bilateral rapport.

(4) Finally, Roosevelt may have thought that this agreement, which he considered important to a continuation of close Anglo-American wartime relations, would have been opposed by those involved in manufacturing the bomb who had previously attempted to limit British participation. Desiring an amicable association with Churchill, he may have maintained the *aide-memoire's* secrecy so as to avoid friction between himself and those in his administration who opposed the policies which it reflected.

[87] Every account of the development of the atomic bomb which has been consulted stresses the urgency under which the program was conducted. See particularly the following: Braunbek, *The Drama of the Atom*, pp. 182–210; Compton, *Atomic Quest*, pp. 3–216, 221–51; Fermi, *Atoms in the Family*, pp. 162–249; Jungk, *Brighter Than a Thousand Suns*, pp. 71–189; Laurence, *Men and Atoms*, pp. 51–62; Stimson and Bundy, *On Active Service in Peace and War*, pp. 612–15; U. S. Atomic Energy Commission, *In the Matter of J. Robert Oppenheimer*, pp. 30–31.

[88] Jungk, *Brighter Than a Thousand Suns*, p. 157.

[89] The *Alsos* mission has been best described in Samuel A. Goudsmit, *ALSOS* (New York: Henry Schuman, 1947). Goudsmit has summarized his book in an article, "How Germany Lost the Race," *Bulletin of the Atomic Scientists*, I, (1946), pp. 4–5; and in a prepared statement left with the Senate's special committee on Atomic Energy. See U. S. Congress, Senate, Special Committee on Atomic Energy, *Hearings on Atomic Energy*, "Statement of Dr. S. A. Goudsmit," I, 261–65. Other accounts that have been consulted seem to be based on Goudsmit's works. See Compton, *Atomic Quest*, pp. 221–51; Jungk, *Brighter Than a Thousand Suns*, pp. 156–70; Lang, *From Hiroshima to the Moon*, pp. 215–46; Daniel Long, *Early Tales of the Atomic Age* (Garden City: Doubleday and Company, Inc., 1948) pp. 24–34; Laurence, *Men Against Atoms*, pp. 88–94. This account is a summary of Goudsmit's analysis of the German failure, although the other works were consulted.

[90] U. S. Senate, *Hearings on Atomic Energy*, "Statement of Dr. S. A. Goudsmit," p. 257.

[91] *Ibid.*, pp. 262–3. Goudsmit, *ALSOS*, p. 8.

[92] Goudsmit, "How Germany Lost the Race," *Bulletin of the Atomic Scientists of Chicago*, I, 4.

[93] Irving, David, *The German Atomic Bomb: The History of Nuclear Research in Nazi Germany* (New York: Simon and Schuster, Inc., 1967). This account was the first to use captured German documents extensively. Jungk, *Brighter Than a Thousand Suns*, pp. 166–70. Lang, *From Hiroshima to the Moon*, pp. 228–29.

[94] Goudsmit has described the state of German progress near the end of the war in summary form:

(1) German scientists had abandoned hope of making a bomb for this war.
(2) They concentrated their efforts on atomic energy production rather than an explosive.
(3) They had not yet succeeded in constructing a "pile" or self-supporting chain reaction.
(4) The total effort expended on the atomic energy project was small, even though it had the highest priority.
(5) German scientists had no knowledge of our work.
(6) They believed that they were ahead of our developments in atomic energy.

In the same document he has listed six reasons for German failure:

(1) German scientists lacked the vision which the allied scientists possessed.
(2) The Nazi Party and the German military placed incompetent scientists in key administrative positions.
(3) Lack of coordination caused competition rather than cooperation among the various groups.
(4) German scientists put into this field scarcely more effort than they would have into a peacetime research project, because they felt certain of their superiority.
(5) German pure science had no support from nor contact with the military.
(6) Allied bombing interfered with German progress.

U. S. Senate, *Hearings on Atomic Energy*, "Statement of Dr. S. A. Goudsmit," p. 262. For evidence that at least Stimson and Bush knew of the backwardness of the German project see *The Papers of Henry L. Stimson*, "Memorandum of talk with Bush, December 13, 1944," in which Bush indicated to Stimson that the Germans were only in the latter stages of experimentation and could not hold out long enough to produce the weapon.

[95] Compton, *Atomic Quest*, pp. 24, 225; U. S. Congress, House of Representatives, Committee on Military Affairs, *Hearings on Atomic Energy*, "Statement of Maj. Gen. Leslie R. Groves," 79th Cong., 1st sess. (Washington: 1945), p. 14.

[96] See p. 23. For indications of heightened activity in MED see Jungk, *Brighter Than a Thousand Suns*, pp. 176–77. U. S. Atomic Energy Commission, *In the Matter of J. Robert Oppenheimer*, pp. 30–33. On the other hand, General Groves refuted the case that there was a speeding up of the program. See U. S. Atomic Energy Commission, *In the Matter of J. Robert Oppenheimer*, p. 169.

[97] See, pp. 12–14.

[98] Italics are supplied. Compton, *Atomic Quest*, p. 145.

[99] *Ibid.*, p. 182.

[100] Stimson and Bundy, *On Active Service in Peace and War*, p. 193.

[101] *Ibid.*, pp. 343–44.

[102] Stimson, *Diary*, March 8 and May 28, 1945.

[103] *Notes of an Interview of General Leslie R. Groves*, by the author, September 8, 1960, Stamford, Connecticut. Hereafter, Groves Interview. Stimson *Diary*, February 9. Bundy was a Boston lawyer who took leave a few days each week without pay to handle his practice throughout the war.

104 Stimson, *Diary*, February 9. Harrison had been president of the New York Federal Reserve Bank prior to his service with Stimson during the war.

105 *MED Files: Harrison-Bundy Series*, Folder #5, "S-1 Memos. HHB to HLS," May 10, 1944.

106 U.S. Congress, Senate, *Military Situation in the Far East; Hearings Before the Committee on Armed Services and the Committee on Foreign Relations*, 82nd Cong., 1st sess. (Washington: 1951), pt. 4, p. 3120.

107 Arnold, *Global Mission* (London: Hutchinson and Company, Ltd., 1951), pp. 244–45.

108 *MED Files: Harrison-Bundy Series*, Folder #69 "S-1 Interim Committee." This letter has two enclosures attached, one a short summary of anticipations and, the second, a more complete treatment. This quotation is from the short enclosure titled, "Salient Points Concerning Future International Handling of Subject of Atomic Bombs."

109 *MED Files: Harrison-Bundy Series*, Folder #5, "S-1 Memos. HHB to HLS," Bundy Memo to Stimson in re: S-1, December 9, 1944.

110 *MED Files: Harrison-Bundy Series*, Folder #69, "S-1 Interim Committee," Bundy Memo to Stimson, December 16, 1944.

111 *Ibid.*, Bush letters to Bundy, January 30 and February 1, 1945. These letters and the Bundy memoranda immediately above include some of the earliest references to the Interim Committee which will be treated more fully below, pp. 111–150.

112 Phrases underlined by Stimson for emphasis to Roosevelt. U. S. Department of State, *Foreign Relations of the United States, Diplomatic Papers: The Conferences at Malta and Yalta, 1945* (Washington: 1955), pp. 383–84. Hereafter, *Yalta Papers*. The gun type bomb used on Hiroshima was called *Thin Man*; the implosion bomb *Fat Man* was tested at Alamagordo and dropped on Nagasaki. Groves' indication that he had anticipated a successful weapon in the "late spring" is, perhaps, substantiated by Byrnes' recollection that Patterson and Groves had informed him in December, 1944, that a bomb would be ready by April 1, 1945. See James F. Byrnes, *Speaking Frankly*, p. 258. Other evidence seems to indicate, however, that the anticipated date of success was August 1 rather than April 1.

113 *Yalta Papers*, p. 384.

114 Stimson, *Diary*, January 3, 1945.

115 Edward R. Stettinius, Jr., *Roosevelt and the Russians: The Yalta Conference* (Garden City: Doubleday and Company, Inc., 1949), p. 33.

116 *Ibid.*, p. 34.

117 U. S. Congress, Senate, *Military Situation in the Far East*, pp. 3319–20.

118 *MED Files: Harrison-Bundy Series*, Folder #74, "Interior Committee–President's Statement," March 3, 1945.

119 Stimson, *Diary*, March 5, 1945.

120 *Ibid.*, March 5, 1945. The problems involved S-1 but were not so specified in the *Diary* entry.

121 *Ibid.*, March 9, 1945.

122 *Ibid.*, March 15, 1945.

123 Leahy, *Diaries*, September 19, 1944, p. 85.

124 Leahy, *Diaries*, September 22, 1944, Vol. 10, 87.

125 *Ibid.*, October 2, 1944, Vol. 10, 90.

126 Stimson, *Diary*, March 15, 1945; Stimson and Bundy, *On Active Service in Peace and War*, p. 615.

127 Stimson, *Diary*, April 10 and 11, 1945.

128 U. S. Senate, *Military Situation in the Far East*, p. 3119. Stimson and Bundy, *On Active Service in Peace and War*, pp. 612–13, 615.

129 Ernest J. King and Walter Muir Whitehill, *Fleet Admiral King: A Naval Record* (New York: W. W. Norton and Company, Inc., 1952), pp. 620–21.

130 *MED Files: Harrison-Bundy Series*, Folder #70, "Interim Committee-Miscellaneous," notes attached to copy of project's organizational chart, May 29, 1945.

131 *Groves Interview*, September 8, 1960.

132 Ray S. Cline, *Washington Command Post: The Operations Division* (Washington: Office of the Chief of Military History, Department of the Army, 1951), Preface, p. IX. This is the second volume published in the 80 volume series, *United States Army in World War II*.

133 *Ibid.*, p. 347.

134 *Ibid.*, p. 337.

135 United States Department of Defense, *The Entry of the Soviet Union into War Against Japan: Military Plans, 1941–1945* (Washington: 1955), p. 28. This is a quotation from the files of the JCS 924 Rpt. by Joint Planning Staff, sub: "Operations Against Japan subsequent to Formosa," 30 June 44 [*sic*] and "Decision Amending JCS 924, 11 July 44 [*sic*].

136 *Ibid.*, p. 44. This quotation is from Combined Chief of Staffs file 417/11, Memo. by Joint Chiefs of Staff, sub: "Operations for the Defeat of Japan, 22 Jan. 1945."

137 See pp. 177–80 for a more comprehensive review of the military situation.

138 See p. 23.

139 Fletcher Knebel and Charles W. Bailey, II *No High Ground* (New York: Harper and Brothers, 1960), 77–81. This is an interesting popular account which has been based on Air Force documents. See also Craven and Cate, *The Army Air Forces in World War II*, V, 705–6. The 509th Composite Group consisted of a Headquarters Detachment; the 393rd Bombardment Squadron; the 390th Air Service Group (603rd Air Enginering Squadron and the 1027th Material Squadron); the 320th Troop Carrier Squadron; the 1395th Military Policy Company (Aviation); after March 6, 1945 the 1st Ordinance Squadron, Special (Aviation); and in June, the 1st Technical Detachment, War Department Miscellaneous Group, the scientists and technicians needed to service the bomb. Total personnel was 225 officers and 1,542 men.

140 Grace Tully, *F. D. R. My Boss* (New York: Charles Scribner's Sons, 1949), p. 265.

141 *Ibid.*, p. 155.

142 Truman, *Memoirs: Year of Decisions*, I, 9–10 ff; Stimson, *Diary*, April 12, 1945. Leahy, *Diaries*, April 13, 1945, II, 56.

143 *Groves Interview*, September 8, 1960.

144 Stimson and Bundy, *On Active Service in Peace and War*, p. 613.

145 See pp. 34–35.

146 This is quoted without reference to source in Jungk, *Brighter Than a Thousand Suns*, p. 175. See also "Sachs Testimony," p. 561.

147 Tully, *F. D. R. My Boss*, p. 266. Miss Tully provides no evidence to support this statement.

148 See pp. 43–44. *Yalta Papers*, p. 384. Apparently the three chief officers of OPD learned something of MED in line with their work with Marshall and Stimson. Whether their information was obtained prior to or after Groves' letter of December 30, 1944, has not been determined: Cline, *Washington Command Post: The Operations Division*, p. 347, fn. 55.

[149] Italics are supplied. Stimson, *Diary*, March 15, 1945. Stimson and Bundy, *On Active Service in Peace and War*, pp. 615–16 contains an edited account of this *Diary* entry.

[150] Jungk, *Brighter Than a Thousand Suns*, pp. 178–80. Byrnes, *All in One Lifetime*, p. 284.

[151] Alice Kimball Smith, "Behind the Decision to Use the Atomic Bomb: Chicago 1944–45," *Bulletin of the Atomic Scientists*, XIV (October, 1958), 294. An edited copy of a Memorandum which Szilard prepared for presentation to the President at his anticipated interview appears in Leo Szilard, "Atomic Bombs and the Post-War Position of the United States in the World," *Ibid.*, III (December: 1947), 351–53.

[152] Byrnes, *All in One Lifetime*, pp. 284–86.

[153] Admiral Leahy, in a conversation with Jonathan Daniels, is reported to have said later, "I know F.D.R. [sic] would have used it in a minute to prove that he had not wasted two billion dollars." Jonathan Daniels, *The Man of Independence* (Philadelphia: J. B. Lippincott Company, 1950), p. 281. Despite the doubtful quality of such evidence, it might indicate something of Roosevelt's approach to the problem of use.

CHAPTER 3

ROOSEVELT AND RUSSIA AND JAPAN — THE WAR IN THE FAR EAST

PRESIDENT Truman inherited a Far Eastern policy which, with but minor variations, Roosevelt had followed since the United States had become involved in World War II. Its major objective was to win the war by forcing Japan to unconditional surrender. This concentration on total victory as the focus of all political and military activity had been the guiding purpose of the United States Government after the Japanese attack on Pearl Harbor. It had been the lodestar followed by American statesmen throughout the conflict. The overriding objective was to win the war. Short-range military considerations, thus, took precedence over long-range political planning. First, the United States would take the lead in defeating the Axis; then, at the peace table it would negotiate a new, long-lasting peace with its Allies.

In order to defeat Japan as quickly as possible the United States sought to involve the Soviet Union. But such a task posed many difficulties. Ever since Germany had attacked and overrun much of western Russia in 1941, United States policy had been to provide sufficient support to the Soviet Union to enable it to maintain and improve its position on the eastern front against Germany. Early in 1942 Roosevelt and Churchill had agreed that the major war effort should be against Germany and that the Russians had become a most important element in that endeavor. Despite the military needs in the Far East, it had not been considered feasible to urge the Soviet government too strongly to violate the Neutrality Pact it had negotiated with the Japanese in 1941. Such an infringement might involve the Soviet Union on another and distant front against an enemy with strong forces in Manchuria. The United States government recognized the primary importance of sustaining Soviet pressure on Germany. Nevertheless, its military requirements in the Far East led it to continue to exert pressure on the Soviet Union to participate in the war against Japan.

The military need arose largely from the threat of the Japanese Kwantung Army in Manchuria. Although, as such, that army never fought more than border skirmishes with the Russians, its very existence strongly affected United States planning.[1] Despite the success of the American island-hopping strategy toward Japan as the war moved toward its climax, the Joint Chiefs of Staff frequently considered the possibility that the Japanese government might move to the mainland after its home islands had been attacked, and might continue the war with the strong military forces it still maintained in Manchuria and China. To guard against this eventuality and to win the war quickly, the United States hoped to eliminate such a threat by committing the Soviet armies to attack in Manchuria. Through coordination of United States and Russian actions thereafter, it was also hoped that the United States Army Air Force might build and use air bases in Siberia and that the United States Navy might be permitted to operate in the northern, semiclosed seas along the East Asian coast of Siberia. As a result, it had been United States policy throughout the war to involve the Soviet Union against Japan as soon as the war against Germany permitted.[2]

The earliest American efforts had been unrewarding. Stalin, deeply involved with Germany, wished to avoid a Japanese attack on eastern Siberia and the Maritime Provinces, and was most careful to observe the conditions of the Russo-Japanese Neutrality Pact. Nevertheless, it was soon after Pearl Harbor on December 8, 1941, that Roosevelt suggested indirectly in a conversation with the Soviet Ambassador, Maxim Litvinov, the possibility of Soviet–United States cooperation against Japan. On the same day, Secretary of State Cordell Hull discussed with Litvinov the question of United States use of Russian air bases and shipments of supplies to Vladivostok in Russian ships. On

December 9, Chiang Kai-shek urged the United States and the Soviet Union to support a Sino-Soviet declaration of war on Japan.[3] But Russia would not change its policy. Litvinov replied to Hull on December 11 that his government ". . . was not then in a position to cooperate . . . against Japan . . . [as it] was fighting on a huge scale against Germany and could not risk an attack by Japan." [4] The United States, despite its urgent need for Russian support in the Far East during those early days of the war, recognized the dangerous situation of the Soviet Union in Europe and discontinued its pressure for Russian action against Japan at that time.[5]

Nevertheless, over the following years the United States kept the question before the Soviet Union. As the pressure on Russia from Germany decreased, the United States stepped up its insistence on Russian cooperation against Japan. The Joint Chiefs of Staff had early been concerned with a possible Japanese attack on the Soviet Union. But despite their expression of this fear to the Soviet Government, attempts to institute military collaboration following joint staff conversations with the Russians proved fruitless throughout 1942. Although Stalin was ready to accept United States aid in his war against Germany, he was unwilling to permit United States air-group operations in Siberia or to do anything else that might provoke a Japanese attack. He put it rather bluntly to Roosevelt, in a message of January 13, 1943, in which he rejected the President's suggestion that planes attached to American units be concentrated in eastern Siberia:

> As regards sending bombing avio-units [*sic*] to the Far East, I made it clear . . . that what we want is not avio-units, but airplanes without fliers, as we have more than enough fliers of our own. . . .
>
> In the second place, we want your aid in airplanes not in the Far East, where the U.S.S.R. is not in a state of war, but at the Soviet-German front, where the need . . . is particularly acute. . . .[6]

Despite its difficulties in arranging any sort of joint military action, the United States received through 1942 and 1943 indications that Russia would ultimately enter the war against Japan. In August, 1942, W. Averell Harriman, who at that time was a special emissary representing the United States at the first meeting in Moscow between Churchill and Stalin (and who, after October, 1943, was to serve as United States Ambassador to the Soviet Union), received assurances from Stalin ". . . that it was his intention to come into the Pacific war when he was in a position to do so." [7] More positive evidence came in January, 1943. General Patrick Hurley, who had been sent by Roosevelt on a special mission to Moscow to evaluate Soviet willingness to continue fighting after the Germans had been ejected from Russian territory, reported to Admiral Leahy that Stalin had informed him that Russia would assist the United States in its war with Japan after Germany was defeated. Leahy had passed the information on to Roosevelt together with his opinion that the United States ". . . could defeat Japan without Russian assistance." [8]

Leahy's evaluation, however, was not accepted by the Army, and particularly by those who influenced General Marshall. Admiral King went along with Marshall's views. Thus, at the Washington Conference between Churchill and Roosevelt during May, 1943, a restatement of British-American strategy by the Combined Chiefs of Staff asserted the desirability of Soviet participation in the war against Japan. Later, at the first Quebec Conference in August, 1943, the Joint Chiefs of Staff presented to Churchill and Roosevelt their evaluation of the possibilities of Russian participation:

There exists between Russia and Japan a basic conflict of interest. Japan cannot enjoy complete strategic security without gaining control of the eastern region of Siberia. Russia is determined to hold that region, the strategic security of which requires the ultimate expulsion of Japan from the mainland of Asia and from southern Sakhalin. For the present, however, both Russia and Japan desire to avoid war with each other in order to be free to direct their efforts against their respective enemies. Russia is likely to intervene in the war against Japan at some stage, but not before the German threat to her has been removed. After that she will make her decision in the light of her own interests and will intervene only when she reckons that Japan can be defeated at small cost to her.[9]

The conferees, however, did not propose intensified efforts to involve the Soviet Union in the Far East. Roosevelt and Churchill recognized the difficulty of their position, particularly in view of the embarrassing delays they were experiencing in launching the Soviet's long-desired second front in Europe.

Following the Quebec Conference, Harriman assumed his post as United States Ambassador to the Soviet Union in October, 1943; and General John R. Deane joined him in Moscow as commander of the United States Military Mission. Deane's orders emphasized the Joint Chiefs' belief in the ". . . great importance . . . of Russia's full participation in the war against Japan after the defeat of Germany. . . " [10]

Further informal evidence of Russian intention to intervene against Japan arose during the Moscow Conference of Foreign Ministers which met from October 19 through October 30. During the final banquet held in the Catherine the Great Hall of the Kremlin on October 30, Stalin mentioned to Secretary of State Hull that ". . . when the Allies succeeded in defeating Germany, the Soviet Union would then join in defeating Japan. Stalin . . . brought up this subject entirely on his own, although he may have had in mind the conversations [Hull] had had on this subject with Ambassador Litvinov. He finished by saying that [Hull] could inform President Roosevelt of this in the strictest confidence. [Hull] thanked him heartily." [11] Stalin made this offer without any urging from Hull, and he attached no political strings to it. The Secretary of State considered this a promise of Russian intervention, despite the social conditions under which it was made.

During the same evening, Deane also received what he considered to be hints of Russian antagonism toward Japan. After dinner all adjourned to the Kremlin theater to view a motion picture of the Japanese occupation of Siberia in 1921. It was clear from the picture that the Russians did not like the Japanese. Since it was Deane's primary objective to induce Soviet participation in the war with Japan, it was satisfying for him to discover the Russian attitude.[12] Deane reported to the Joint Chiefs of Staff on the following day:

. . . It was significant that . . . we were shown a lengthy picture of Japanese penetration in Siberia. . . . It was distinctly anti-Japanese propaganda and we all felt it was an indirect method of telling us their attitude with regard to Japan. In private conversation with Molotov, Vashinsky [sic] and others we have heard more direct statements indicating that they will join in the Pacific war as soon as Germany is defeated.[13]

Shortly after the Moscow Conference, Molotov assured Harriman of Soviet intentions to enter the Far Eastern war. Thus, by the time of the Tehran Conference in late 1943, the Russians had clearly indicated their willingness to collaborate against Japan. No specific plans had been made. And, of course, the Russians had not committed themselves in making such general statements. It remained for Roosevelt to attempt to nail down a Russian agreement to fight Japan.

At the Tehran Conference, which met from November 27 to December 2, 1943, Roosevelt received his first direct promise of Soviet military support. Just prior to the Conference, in a memorandum estimating the situation in the Far East, the Joint Chiefs of Staff had reaffirmed to the President their position of the previous August. They still believed that, although Russia had an interest in ultimately intervening against Japan, it would only do so after its German threat had been removed.[14] They saw little chance of Russian participation before United States victories indicated that Japan was no longer a danger to the Soviet Union. Nevertheless, Roosevelt hoped to get a more precise statement of Soviet plans for the Far East than that which had been given to Hull at Moscow.

At Tehran, however, no military discussions were held with the Russians regarding the Soviet role in the war against Japan; and Stalin gave Roosevelt only indefinite reassurances as to his intentions. At the first plenary session on November 28, Stalin said that:

. . . the Soviet Government welcomed the successes of the Anglo-American forces against the Japanese; that up to the present to their regret they had not been able to join the effort of the Soviet Union to that of the United States and England against the Japanese because the Soviet armies were too deeply engaged in the West. He added that the Soviet forces in Siberia were sufficient for defensive purposes but would have to be increased threefold before they would be adequate for offensive operations. Once Germany was finally defeated, it would then be possible to send the necessary reinforcements to Siberia and then we [sic] shall be able by our common front to beat Japan.[15]

Nothing more was said about the matter at that session. But on the next day at Harriman's urging, Roosevelt gave Stalin a list of specific questions drafted for him by the Joint Chiefs of Staff.[16] The President wanted to know whether the Soviet Union would supply the United States with combat intelligence in regard to Japan; whether the Soviet Navy would desire to use United States bases in Alaska; whether the Soviets would provide assistance for a United States attack on the Kuriles; whether the Soviets would furnish data to the United States concerning Siberian ports its forces might use; and whether the Soviet Union would permit United States bombers to use air bases in the Maritime Provinces of Soviet Siberia. Stalin promised that he would study Roosevelt's questions. But it was not until December 25, after the conference had ended, that Molotov presented the Soviet response to Harriman. At that time, the Soviets agreed to exchange information but reserved consideration of the other questions to a later date.[17]

Despite their imprecision, Roosevelt placed great importance on Stalin's assurances. Thereafter, the Combined Chiefs of Staff seriously considered the possibility of Soviet involvement, and made their proposals accordingly.[18] Military pressure for definite Soviet commitments continued unabated. In their "Over-All War Plan for the Defeat of Japan" presented to Churchill and Roosevelt at Cairo following the Tehran meetings, the Combined Chiefs suggested that:

We should urge the U.S.S.R. to come in as early as possible; ask them to tell us when they propose to come in; what they propose to do when they come in; and what they want us to do to help. . . .[19]

Despite its vagueness, the Soviet declaration at Tehran was considered by Churchill and Roosevelt to be one of the two decisive events which had occurred at the conference.[20]

But the Russians had not committed themselves in detail. Following Tehran, at Roosevelt's suggestion, Ambassador Harriman and General Deane tried to pin the Soviets down to a specific date and plan of operations against Japan and to discover what political concessions they might demand as a quid pro quo. In this, Harriman and Deane were generally unsuccessful. Throughout 1944 the United States was unable to coordinate with the Russians its planning for operations against Japan. As late as January, 1945, no date for the Soviet attack had been set.

Furthermore it was not until December, 1944, that Stalin's political demands for Soviet participation were defined. Such political considerations had been discussed, at least generally, as early as the Tehran Conference. Roosevelt had apparently mentioned to Chiang Kai-Shek at Cairo the week before Tehran possible Soviet requests for concessions in the Far East. At that time he had suggested the internationalization of Dairen on the Liaotung Peninsula, and Chiang had agreed to consider the matter as long as Chinese sovereignty over the area was guaranteed.[21] At Tehran the matter came up at a luncheon on November 30 attended by Churchill, Roosevelt, and Stalin. After Churchill had raised the general question of the Soviet lack of warm water ports, Stalin asked what might be done in this regard for the Soviet Union in the Far East. Roosevelt suggested the possibility that Dairen be made a free port. Although Stalin thought that the Chinese would dislike the suggestion, the President felt that they would accept Dairen as a free port under an international guarantee.[22] In regard to the Far Eastern settlement proposed in the Communique of the Cairo Conference which planned to strip Japan ". . . of all the islands in the Pacific which she [had] seized or occupied since the beginning of the first World War in 1914 . . ." and to restore ". . . all the territories Japan [had] stolen from the Chinese, such as Manchuria, Formosa, and the Pescadores . . . to the Republic of China," Stalin expressed his thorough approval.[23]

Exploratory conversations concerning a Far Eastern political settlement had thus originated at Cairo and Tehran. No agreements had been negotiated; and Stalin, seemingly preoccupied with the war in Europe, had been obviously noncommittal. But Roosevelt already understood that in return for Russian participation in the war against Japan, some concessions would likely have to be made to the Soviet Union.[24]

One later account of the Cairo and Tehran talks remains to be considered. Roosevelt, as chairman, reported on these conversations to the Pacific War Council at its thirty-sixth meeting on January 12, 1944, at the White House.[25]

. . . [He] informed the Council that his discussions with Generalissimo Chiang Kai-Shek and with Marshal Stalin were highly satisfactory — in that both agreed that Japan should be stripped of her island possessions. . . . Marshal Stalin had specifically agreed to the idea that Manchuria, Formosa and the Pescadores should be returned to China, that the Koreans [were] not yet capable of exercising and maintaining independent government and that they should be placed under a 40-year tutelage, that Russia having no ice-free port in Siberia, [was] desirous of getting one and that Marshal Stalin [looked] with favor upon making Dairen a free port for all the world, with the idea that Siberian exports and imports could be sent through the port of Dairen and carried to Siberian territory over the Manchurian Railroad in bond. He [agreed] that the Manchurian Railway [sic] should become the property of the Chinese Government. He [wished] all of Sakhalin to be returned to Russia and to have the Kuril Islands turned over to Russia in order that they [might] exercise control of the straits leading to Siberia.

President Roosevelt stated that . . . the Generalissimo and Marshal Stalin saw "eye to eye" with him on all major problems of the Pacific and that he felt that there would be no difficulty in reaching agreements about the control of the Pacific once Japan had been completely conquered. . . .[26]

This report indicates a far more specific understanding with Stalin than the other evidence would indicate. In fact no record has been found to substantiate Stalin's agreement at the time that the Manchurian railroads should be taken over by China, or Stalin's request for Soviet absorption of Sakhalin and the Kuriles. Roosevelt was apparently expressing his anticipations based on fragmentary conversations when he indicated that, at Cairo and Tehran, there had developed a firm foundation for specific agreement on these problems involving the Far East. Nevertheless, by January, 1944, the outline, if not the blueprint, of Russian demands in the Pacific was beginning to take form.

During 1944 and early 1945, the military pressure from the Joint Chiefs of Staff for Soviet participation in the Far Eastern war continued. As early as April, 1944, the basic strategy for the defeat of Japan was being formulated in the Strategy Section of the United States Army's Operations Division. Japan's defeat as a result of blockade and aerial bombardment alone was considered very doubtful. It would only be accomplished as a result of a successful invasion of the main islands of Japan.[27] Despite objections from certain Army Air Force and Navy personnel and from Admiral Leahy, the suggestions of the Strategy Section were ultimately adopted for planning purposes by the Joint Chiefs of Staff.[28] On July 11, 1944, they accepted proposed operations including blockade and air bombardment; an amphibious assault on Kyushu on October 1, 1945; and a ". . . decisive stroke against the industrial heart of Japan by means of an amphibious attack through the Tokyo plain . . ." by the end of 1945.[29] The plan did not require Russian participation. But the Joint Chiefs pointed out that such Russian action ". . . would facilitate [the] invasion of Kyushu and [the] ultimate invasion of the heart of Japan." [30]

During the second Quebec Conference in September, 1944, the British Chiefs of Staff and, ultimately, Roosevelt and Churchill accepted plans for the invasion of Japan. Following the conference, on September 28, the Joint Chiefs of Staff through General Deane in Moscow informed the Russians of their suggestions for Soviet operations to support the United States and British attack on Japan.[31]

The question of Russian participation was seriously reconsidered in the light of military events during the winter prior to the Yalta Conference. On November 23, the Joint Staff Planners submitted a paper to the Joint Chiefs of Staff which indicated the desirability of Soviet entry although the current war planning implied the ". . . conviction that the defeat of Japan may be accomplished without Russian participation in the war." [32] The Joint Staff Planners' report emphasized the inevitability of Russia's entrance in its own interests but pointed out the importance of using United States pressure to secure the proper timing of the Russian attack. It asserted: "While the optimum advantage to us results from Russian entry prior to our invasion of Japan, the reverse is true from the Russian viewpoint. The maximum military advantage to them will obtain if they attack after our initial lodgment has been effected and Japanese forces in Manchuria have begun to move to reinforce Japan." [33] The planners concluded with two basic principles to be followed by the United States in regard to Russia's entrance into the war. First, the United States should promote ". . . Russian entry at the earliest possible date consistent with her ability to engage in offensive operations . . ."; and second, it should convince the Russians that their mission should be to conduct an offensive in Manchuria to tie down Japanese forces that might be used against the planned invasion of Kyushu and Honshu, to carry on air operations against Japan proper, and to cut lines of communications between Japan and the continent. [34]

Despite certain differences of opinion among the Joint Chiefs of Staff over the most effective way to utilize Soviet force against Japan, all were agreed that it should be solicited. In memoranda of December 4 and December 11, respectively, General Arnold and Admiral King specifically supported the general idea and suggested further study prior to the proposal of specific Russian moves. [35] On January 24, 1945, the Joint Chiefs of Staff approved a final report of the Joint Staff Planners prior to the Yalta Conference. This report, which had been transmitted to the Joint Chiefs of Staff on January 18, constituted a comprehensive statement of the United States position in the Far East. It stated as the first of two basic principles as to Russian participation in the Far Eastern war: "We desire Russian entry at the earliest possible date consistent with her ability to engage in offensive operations and are prepared to offer the maximum support possible without prejudice to our main effort against Japan." [36] The Joint Chiefs of Staff had transmitted their recommendations to Roosevelt the day before, on January 23. The opening statement of their memorandum of transmittal had included the first principle of the JPS paper of January 18. [37] By the time of Yalta, then, the President had been informed of the desire of his military leaders for Russian entry into the war against Japan. Throughout 1944 and early 1945, the Joint Chiefs of Staff had consistently assumed that Russian support in the Far East was of great importance to their planned invasion of Japan.

So much for considerations of overall planning. To be successful, such planning needed implementation; and the United States government throughout 1944 attempted to obtain military agreements with the Soviets which would permit close cooperation at the operational level after Russia had taken action against Japan. The responsibility for such negotiations lay with Ambassador Harriman and General Deane. For them the year 1944 was one of general frustration as the Russians refused to accept military commitments which would have enabled United States forces to operate on Russian territory. Stalin wanted help in the logistical buildup of supplies to support his anticipated attack on Manchuria. On the other hand, he did not desire active participation by United States troops or aircrews. Thus, United States efforts to utilize the Soviet Far Eastern territories against Japan proved practically fruitless prior to the Yalta Conference. And yet the effort had to go on. Planning for possible joint operations required some knowledge of specific Russian plans and resources. Harriman and Deane devoted considerable energy toward securing such military cooperation with the Russians during the year.

Their negotiations were made extremely difficult by the Russian reluctance to permit western troops to use their territory and the Soviet fear that Japan might attack in the Siberian Far East if it got word of any Russian or United States buildup in the areas around Manchuria. This latter consideration killed Deane's suggestion of December 26, 1943, to the Russian General Staff that the nearly empty eastern run of the Trans-Siberian railroad be utilized to haul supplies to build up a depot to the east of Lake Baikal as a means of developing a series of Far Eastern Russian-American air bases. The Russians, apparently fearing Japanese intervention, refused to consider the suggestion.[38]

Greater Russian–United States military cooperation seemed possible on February 2, 1944. During a conference with Deane and Harriman on that date, Stalin agreed to permit the operation of United States planes from Russian Far Eastern areas after the Soviet Union had gone to war with Japan. He suggested that planning for such a United States strategic air force await the arrival of top-level Soviet Air Force officers whom he had ordered to Moscow from the Far East. Apparently, the officers never arrived. Despite an inquiry by Harriman a month later in March and Stalin's promise that they would soon be available, such negotiations never took place.[39]

In the latter part of April, the Soviet Union requested delivery of five hundred heavy bombers to form the nucleus of a Soviet strategic air force. Recognizing the logistical and training problems involved as well as the time required to set up such a force, Deane recommended to the Joint Chiefs of Staff that ". . . approval of the Soviet request be conditioned on the immediate preparation of plans looking toward the establishment of both Soviet and American strategic air forces in Siberia."[40] He believed it was too late to establish such forces for use in the European war. If planning got underway with sufficient speed, these forces might be used against Japan. The possibility that the Soviet Union might acquire such aircraft was to be employed to convince the Soviets to permit the use of Siberian air bases by United States squadrons. The Joint Chiefs of Staff accepted Deane's position, and the planes were not delivered pending further negotiations.

On June 10, 1944, Harriman again reviewed the matter of joint Soviet-American military planning during a meeting with Stalin. Stalin was both more specific and encouraging in his consideration of American use of Soviet Far Eastern air bases. He indicated that there were twelve airfields in the Maritime Provinces north of Vladivostok and that the United States air forces might use six or seven of them. He felt that necessary military discussions concerning the planning of operations and the stockpiling of supplies should start promptly, but he was unwilling to specify a date for such discussions. Harriman succinctly indicated the nature of the divergent positions in his message of the following day to Roosevelt: ". . . Stalin brought up the question of the supplying by us of heavy bombers for the Red Air Force. I explained that General Arnold was ready to begin to deliver them beginning in the autumn after agreement had been reached regarding our operation from Soviet Far Eastern bases." [41] Stalin wanted United States heavy bombers and supplies. He did not welcome United States squadrons operating on Soviet soil. He therefore delayed the necessary joint planning in the hope that the United States, pressed by its need for the strategic bombing of Japan from Soviet bases, might modify its stand and entrust such missions to Soviet crews in United States planes. This the United States was unwilling to do, particularly since, as a result of its southern campaigns against Japan and the development of the long-range B-29 heavy bomber, alternative locations from which to attack the Japanese islands were available.[42]

Sporadic negotiations by Deane and Harriman through the summer proved to be fruitless in arranging joint planning of Soviet-American collaboration against Japan. Not until September 23 were their hopes again revived. On that day, Harriman and the British Ambassador to Moscow, Sir Archibald Clark-Kerr, called on Stalin to brief him on British-American negotiations which had taken place at the second Quebec Conference. From their report, Stalin noticed that the two Allies' military plans had been made without assuming a Soviet attack on Japan. As Harriman reported the matter to Roosevelt:

. . . Stalin inquired whether we wished to bring Japan to her knees without Russian assistance or whether you still wished as you suggested in Teheran [sic] Russian participation. The British Ambassador and I both assured him that Russian participation was desired but that no plans could be made for the use of Soviet resources until Marshall Stalin was ready to initiate discussions. He then stated that there was no change in his attitude as he had expressed it to you at Teheran [sic]. Russia is ready to participate in the war against Japan after Germany is defeated. . . . He was somewhat surprised that after the assurance he had given at Teheran [*sic*] we were not taking into account in our planning the participation of Russia and he appeared anxious to know specifically what role we would want Russia to play. He gave every indication of being ready and willing to cooperate but did not want to be an universal participant.[43]

As a result of this conversation, Harriman considered renewed Russian-American planning discussions a distinct possibility. Deane, who would be the United States representative in such discussions, informed the Joint Chiefs of Staff of his suggested missions for Russia in the Far East. He hoped that the Joint Chiefs of Staff would quickly approve his proposals so that he would have instructions available before the discussions might begin. Deane's suggestions were, for the most part, approved by the Joint Chiefs of Staff when, on September 28, they transmitted to him their suggested missions for the Soviet Union:

. . . The broad strategic concept of Russian participation should be aimed at the following objectives in order of priority:

    a. Securing the Trans-Siberian Railroad and the Vladivostok Peninsula.

    b. Setting up American and Soviet Strategic Air Forces for operations against Japan from the Maritime Provinces and the Kamchatka Peninsula.

    c. Interdiction of lines of communications between Japan proper and the Asiatic mainland.

    d. Destroy Japanese ground and air forces in Manchuria.

    e. Securing the Pacific supply route. . . .[44]

But again the Russians delayed as Harriman and Deane persisted. On September 29, Harriman inquired of Molotov as to when the discussions Stalin had promised might begin. He received no answer. Five days later the Ambassador asked Stalin the same question. He was put off once more.[45]

Failing in their efforts to engage in bilateral discussions, the American representatives in Moscow next planned to use Winston Churchill's approaching visit to Moscow as a means of obtaining more specific commitments from Stalin.[46] Churchill, Eden, and their military advisers arrived in Moscow on October 9, 1945.[47] Harriman held conversations with the Prime Minister during the evening of October 10. At that time Churchill agreed to a military discussion of Far Eastern matters to be held on October 14. The discussion would include Harriman and Deane as well as representatives of Britain and Russia. Harriman reported to Roosevelt that:

. . . Churchill is agreed that the primary objective of the talk should be for us to draw Stalin out on the broader subjects raised by the Chiefs of Staff in their cable to Deane, namely how soon after the collapse of Germany Stalin will be ready to take active measures against Japan and in general what Russia's capabilities will be. I believe that we can get from Stalin out of this meeting a general picture of the Soviet position which will be a useful preliminary to detailed conversations to follow between General Deane and the Red Army Staff.[48]

On October 14 Churchill, Stalin, Harriman, Deane, and the top British and Russian military advisers met at the Kremlin. During the session, Deane ". . . out-lined [*sic*] the developments of the war in the Pacific and the role Russia might play. He asked for the information desired by the Chiefs of Staff as to Russian intentions and capabilities." [49] He specifically indicated that the Joint Chiefs of Staff would like to know:

(1) How soon after the defeat of Germany may we expect Japanese-Russian hostilities to begin?

(2) How long will it take to build up Soviet forces to take the offensive?

(3) What part of the Trans-Siberian Railroad can be devoted to the building up of a Soviet-American air force?

(4) Is the Soviet Union prepared to agree to the building up of a Soviet strategic air force and to undertake a training program? [50]

Stalin showed considerable interest in Deane's remarks and pleaded the lateness of the hour in asking that the Russian reply be given on the following day.

As a result of a high fever, Churchill was unable to attend the meeting on the evening of October 15. Eden took his place among the conferees of the previous night. The meeting was largely devoted to the Russian answers to Deane's remarks of the previous evening. General Alexey I. Antonov, First Deputy Chief of the Soviet General Staff, presented Soviet intelligence estimates of Japanese strength and designated possible areas of attack by Soviet forces. He claimed that the Soviet Union would have to double its armies from thirty to sixty divisions and that this buildup would require from two and one-half to three months to complete. Then Stalin attempted to clarify the Soviet position. He emphasized his need for logistical support—for a two to three-months' supply of food for the army, fuel for the air force and ground transport, and sufficient rails to complete the railroad to Komsomolsk. He felt that the war with Japan would not last long after Russian entrance. He was not ready to provide a specific date for Soviet participation, but he thought planning should begin immediately. So far had the power of the Japanese declined, in his opinion, that he now hoped they might attack the Soviet Union first to cement the Russian people behind his actions against Manchuria. He further said he would be happy to receive four-engine bombers from the United States and instructors to train a Soviet strategic air force for use against Japan. Harriman pointed out that such requests might be fulfilled as soon as agreements were worked out regarding their use. Then Stalin indicated that the United States might use airfields in the Maritime Provinces and the naval base at Petropavlovsk on Kamchatka. But none of these assurances were definite. All needed clarification. It was decided that Harriman and Deane along with Stalin and his staff would work out the details at a following conference.[51]

On October 17, the last in the series of meetings convened. The British were voluntarily absent. Stalin first presented detailed lists of supplies which he would have to receive from the United States over the Pacific supply route before he could enter the war with Japan. He was now, he said, prepared to permit the flights of four-engine aircraft once bases were ready to receive them. He then reemphasized his fears of a Japanese attack on Vladivostok if details of his Far Eastern buildup leaked to the enemy. Anticipating a possible attack on Kamchatka he urged a United States naval thrust to the Kuriles and again offered the United States naval and air bases on Kamchatka. When Deane pointed out that, as then envisaged, Soviet ground operations were planned at about the same time as the American invasion of Japan, Stalin agreed that timing such operations should be coordinated.[52] From these discussions it seemed that the United States was finally to receive the cooperation against Japan it had so long sought. And yet Stalin refused to specify arrangements for more detailed planning. When Harriman pressed him, Stalin equivocated by indicating that he would work out an agreement with Roosevelt at their coming meeting at Yalta. He wanted the buildup of supplies to continue along with the delivery of aircraft and the training of crews. He suggested that Deane work out arrangements for consultation with suitable Soviet authorities through Antonov to prepare for his meeting with Roosevelt.[53]

During the months between the Moscow meetings and the Yalta Conference, planning for military collaboration was, if anything, more sporadic than before. Deane was unable to work out arrangements for meetings of Soviet and American staff officers despite the fact that a special group of United States planning officers was assigned to Moscow.[54] Deane saw Antonov on October 27 and was told that the problems of collaboration which he raised were still being reviewed by the Soviet General Staff. Antonov promised to appoint Soviet officers to consult with American representatives ". . . in the near future." [55] The first meeting did not take place, however, until January 26, 1945; and it was inconclusive. The United States, nevertheless, supplied the Soviets with most of the war material which they had requested.[56] It did not, however, send heavy bombers to create a strategic air force for the Russians. It neither gained access to Soviet bases or Soviet territory, nor did it operate training squadrons on Soviet fields. On December 16, 1944, Antonov informed Deane that Soviet forces would need all of the air and naval bases in the Maritime Provinces and that, therefore, United States naval and air forces would be unable to operate from them.[57] Thus, except for planning and conducting the shipment of supplies to the Russian Far East, military collaboration had practically ceased by the time of the Yalta Conference.

One further factor entered the calculations of those negotiating at Yalta. It was necessary to consider Russian political demands in the Far East in return for a definite Soviet commitment to enter the war. Aside from the hints Stalin had given Roosevelt at Tehran, there had been few indications as to what the Soviets would request in return for participation in the war with Japan.[58] Roosevelt had, nevertheless, at least on one occasion sounded out Chiang Kai-Shek in an effort to discover more definitely than he had been able to do at Cairo what Chiang might do in return for a Sino-Soviet agreement. From June 21 to June 24, 1944, Vice-President Henry A. Wallace had visited the Generalissimo in Chungking. At that time, he had raised, among other matters, the question of Chinese-Russian relations. Chiang, who desired an understanding with the Soviet Union, suggested to Wallace that Roosevelt act as the middle-man between Russia and China in arranging a settlement. This, Roosevelt was unwilling to do at that time; for he did not wish the United States to ". . . become a party or guarantor of any agreement reached between China and the U.S.S.R." [59] On the other hand, he was ready to use the good offices of the United States to bring Russia and China together.

Wallace had also emphasized the necessity of an understanding between Russia and China, if Chiang's formula for a settlement with the Chinese Communists was to be effective. Chiang had agreed and said he would seek an early opportunity for discussions with the Soviet Union. He continued to urge United States assistance.

Finally, Wallace had sounded out Chiang on the possibility of establishing Dairen as a free port in order to satisfy Russia's needs for a Far Eastern warm-water port. Chiang had replied that ". . . he had discussed the matter with President Roosevelt at Cairo and had indicated his agreement provided the U.S.S.R. cooperated with China in the Far East and provided there was no impairment of Chinese sovereignty." [60] Thus by the summer of 1944, Roosevelt had known that Chiang desired a general settlement with Russia in the Far East and that Chiang was willing to make certain concessions to obtain such an agreement, provided Russia recognized Chinese sovereignty in the areas where the concessions were to be made.

The political demands which Stalin would make were, however, not quickly defined. At Tehran, Stalin had indicated certain possible requests he might make. During 1944 he had, from time to time, indicated to Harriman that such requests for political concessions might be forthcoming.[61] In the course of the Moscow meetings of October 15 and 17 Stalin had indicated that political aspects would have to be given consideration before Russia would attack Japan.[62] But it was not until December 14 that Stalin outlined to Harriman the political price for Soviet participation in the war with Japan. At that time he suggested that the Kuriles and southern Sakhalin should be annexed by the Soviet Union so as to limit Japanese control of the approaches to Vladivostok. He further indicated a desire to lease the Chinese ports of Dairen and Port Arthur. This ran counter to Roosevelt's plan to satisfy the Russian desire for a warm-water port by making Dairen an international free port. Stalin further indicated that he wished to lease the South Manchurian Railroad linking Dairen and Harbin and the Chinese Eastern Railroad running from Manchuli through Harbin to the Manchurian border near Vladivostok. He specifically stated that he would respect Chinese sovereignty over Manchuria. His final request was that the status quo in Outer Mongolia and the maintenance of the "independent" Republic of Outer Mongolia be maintained. Harriman made no commitment concerning these political demands.[63] Their satisfaction was to await the Yalta settlement.

This then was Roosevelt's Far Eastern problem at Yalta. His military leaders had repeatedly pointed out the advantages of a Soviet attack on Manchuria in support of their planned invasion of Japan. Russian participation in the war was not necessary for success. It would, however, tie down the Kwantung army in Manchuria and thus make the invasion easier and more quickly successful in bringing about the unconditional surrender of Japan. It was true that other military advantages envisioned had not materialized as a result of Russian obstruction to military collaboration. But there was hope that the President might resolve even these difficulties in negotiations with Stalin. The price for Russian participation Roosevelt now knew might be considerable. Furthermore, from his conversations with Chiang at Cairo and from Wallace's talks with the Generalissimo at Chungking, the President had reason to believe that Chiang would accept concessions to Russia in return for a Sino-Soviet treaty of alliance which would recognize Chinese sovereignty over Manchuria and which would improve his postwar position in relation to the Chinese Communists. With such considerations in mind at the Yalta Conference, Roosevelt consummated his policy of bringing Russia into the war against Japan.

Three areas of agreement were necessary. First, the time of Russian entrance had to be fixed. Second, a political settlement had to be arranged. And, third, greater Soviet-American military collaboration had to be negotiated. Agreements in the first two areas resulted from private conversations between Roosevelt and Stalin on February 8 and 10.[64] Stalin promised that the Soviet Union would enter the war against Japan within two or three months after the surrender of Germany. He reaffirmed that China should possess full sovereignty over Manchuria, and he agreed to negotiate for the Soviet Union a treaty of friendship and alliance with the Nationalist Government of China in order to assist in its liberation from Japan. In return Roosevelt accepted the preservation of the status quo in regard to the People's Republic in Outer Mongolia and agreed to the restoration of the Russian positions in the Far East, lost as a result of the Russo-Japanese War of 1904. Such restorations included the return of southern Sakhalin and adjacent islands to the Soviet Union, joint Sino-Soviet operation of the Chinese Eastern and South Manchurian railroads, the internationalization of the commercial port of Dairen at which the preeminent interests of the Soviet Union were to be safeguarded, and the return of the Russian lease of the naval base at Port Arthur. The Kurile Islands were to be ceded by Japan to the Soviet Union. It was also agreed that the concession involving Outer Mongolia and the Manchurian ports and railroads required the concurrence of Chiang Kai-shek which Roosevelt promised to obtain.[65] Roosevelt had thus obtained from Stalin a specific agreement promising the rapid entry of the Soviet Union into the war against Japan once Germany had been defeated.

The third objective, to provide for greater cooperation in planning and preparing for operations against Japan, was also apparently achieved at Yalta. During meetings of the American and Soviet Chiefs of Staff on February 8 and 9, the United States military leveled at their Soviet counterparts a number of specific questions concerning Russian military plans in the Far East. During the second meeting General Antonov, following discussions with Stalin, answered the questions put to him by the Americans during the previous day. The questions and their answers were:

1. *Have there been any changes in Soviet plans of operations in the Far East from those described to Harriman and Deane at Moscow during October, 1944?*

   There is no change in intent and only minor changes in operations involving a slowing down of movements to the Far East of troops still engaged against the Germans in the West.

2. *Will the Soviet Union require a Pacific supply route after Soviet-Japanese hostilities erupt?*

   The Soviet Union will require such routes particularly for the shipment of food and petroleum products.

3. *Can the United States operate air forces in the Komsomolsk-Nikolaevsk area?*

   The Soviet Union agrees to the operation of United States air forces in this area and will permit advance reconnaissance and survey teams to enter the area immediately.

4. *Will United States forces be required to defend Kamchatka?*

   United States assistance in the defense of Kamchatka, far removed from the locus of Soviet military power, would be very useful.

5. *Will the Soviet Union make prewar preparations for stockpiling United States equipment in Kamchatka and eastern Siberia?*

Yes, pending the final decision as to air base requirements.

6. *Can a United States survey party depart from Alaska for Kamchatka by February 15, 1945?*

Such a departure must be delayed till the last possible minute so as not to arouse Japanese suspicions.

7. *Will the Soviets occupy southern Sakhalin and cover LaPerouse Strait and when?*

After hostilities begin the Soviet Union will occupy southern Sakhalin without United States assistance.

8. *Can the United States be assured that combined planning in Moscow will be vigorously pursued?*

Such stations may be opened after pertinent details of their estab-

9. *How will weather affect Pacific operations?*

Antonov described favorable and unfavorable periods of the year of ground and sea operations.

10. *Can the United States acquire additional weather stations in Siberia?*

Such stations may be opened after pertinent details of their establishment and operation are presented to the Soviet government.[66]

Thus, once again, the Soviet military appeared ready to increase their cooperation with the United States and to push joint planning of Soviet-American efforts against Japan. But from the time of Yalta until Truman became President, such American hopes were again frustrated. Military collaboration proceeded only in efforts to increase the shipments of supplies to Russia. Just two meetings occurred between United States and Soviet military planners in Moscow during the days following Yalta, and these resulted merely in the Russians noting American proposals and promising future action which never materialized.[67]

The survey teams for Kamchatka and for the Komsomolsk-Nikolaevsk area were never able to enter Soviet territory. By April the advantages anticipated from Siberian-based bombing of Japan appeared to be so small that the Joint Chiefs of Staff followed Deane's suggestion to cancel the bomber project.[68] Pending a specific Soviet request, the Pacific supply route was permitted to fall into disuse.

Despite the breakdown in military collaboration, most of the top military personnel believed at the time of Roosevelt's death that it would be advantageous to involve the Russians in the Far Eastern war. Since 1941 the United States government had sought such an objective. At Yalta it had apparently accomplished its goal. Invasion of Japan and a long war seemed to loom ahead. Russian intervention prior to invasion would neutralize Japanese forces in Manchuria and make the American attack easier to mount. The days between April 12 and the end of the war with Japan were to see a growing struggle within the American government over the need for Soviet participation. Yet the effect of the years of effort to that end persisted. Roosevelt's policy of promoting Russian hostilities to help in forcing the unconditional surrender of Japan added to the conditions within which Truman decided to use the atomic bombs.

NOTES TO CHAPTER 3

1 Alvin Coox, "The Myth of the Kwantung Army," *Marine Corps' Gazette*, XLII (1958), pp. 36, 38. The Japanese had tried to placate the Russians along the Manchurian-Siberian border. They had, for instance, attempted to localize military incidents, had unilaterally established a buffer zone in which their troops were restricted from operating, and had limited their reactions to Soviet air violations of Manchuria to retaliation by ground forces.

2 The most complete, though brief, account of United States efforts to involve the Soviet Union appears in U. S. Department of Defense, *The Entry of the Soviet Union into the War Against Japan: Military Plans, 1941–1945* (Washington: 1955). See also John R. Deane, *The Strange Alliance* (New York: The Viking Press, Inc., 1947). U. S. Congress, Senate, Hearings before the Committee on Armed Services and the Committee on Foreign Relations, *Military Situations in the Far East*, 82nd Cong., 1st sess., Part 5, Appendix NN, "Statement of W. Averill Harriman, Special Assistant to the President, Regarding Our Wartime Relations with the Soviet Union, Particularly as They Concern the Agreements Reached at Yalta," (Washington: 1951), pp. 3328–42. Cordell Hull, *Memoirs* (New York: The Macmillan Company, 1948), Vol. II. William D. Leahy, *I Was There* (New York: McGraw-Hill Book Company, Inc., 1950). Robert E. Sherwood, *Roosevelt and Hopkins: An Intimate History* (New York: Harper and Brothers, 1948). Stimson and Bundy, *On Active Service in Peace and War.*

3 Hull, *Memoirs*, II, p. 1112. Chiang apparently was trying to get the United States to give primary emphasis to its fight against Japan rather than to its efforts against Germany. He, thus, indicated to the United States that Russian reluctance reflected the fear that, following any such declaration, the United States would rely on the Soviet Union to shoulder the burden against Japan while it concentrated on defeating the Axis Powers in Europe.

4 *Ibid.*, p. 1111.

5 U. S. Department of Defense, *The Entry of the Soviet Union into the War Against Japan*, pp. 2–5.

6 *Ibid.*, pp. 15–16.

7 U. S. Senate, *Military Situation in the Far East*, p. 3329; see also Deane, *The Strange Alliance*, p. 226.

8 Leahy, *I Was There*, pp. 147–48, 208. See also Sumner Welles, *Seven Decisions That Shaped History* (New York: Harper and Brothers, 1950) p. 156, for indications

of this early Russian commitment to join the war against Japan after Germany's defeat.

9 U. S. Department of Defense, *The Entry of the Soviet Union into the War Against Japan*, pp. 18, 20.

10 *Ibid.*, p. 20.

11 Hull, *Memoirs*, II, pp. 1309–10. Hull's telegrams to Roosevelt transmitting this information are included in U.S. Department of State, *Foreign Relations of the United States, Diplomatic Papers: The Conferences at Cairo and Tehran*, 1943 (Washington: 1961) p. 147. Hereafter, *Tehran Papers*. Hull considered this matter so important that he sent his information in two wires, one through Army facilities and the other through those of the Navy, each transmitted in a different code.

12 Deane, *The Strange Alliance*, p. 25.

13 U. S. Department of Defense, *The Entry of the Soviet Union into the War Against Japan*, p. 22.

14 *Tehran Papers*, pp. 234, 242.

15 *Tehran Papers*, p. 489. This quotation is from the minutes of Charles E. Bohlen. Another set of minutes taken for the Combined Chiefs of Staff essentially follows the above account, *Ibid.*, pp. 499–500. For a paraphrase of the above quotation see Sherwood, *Roosevelt and Hopkins*, p. 779.

16 Harriman and Deane had felt that the Soviets were certain to enter the Far Eastern war at their convenience. Thus, on November 24, 1943, at Cairo, Harriman informed the Joint Chiefs of Staff that ". . . the Soviets had every intention of joining the U.S. [*sic*] and the British in the war against Japan as soon as Germany capitulated. They fear, however, a premature break with Japan. . . ." Deane expressed his agreement with Harriman's position. See *Tehran Papers*, p. 328, and U. S. Department of Defense, *The Entry of the Soviet Union into the War Against Japan*, p. 23.

17 Deane, *Strange Alliance*, pp. 226–27. Sherwood, *Roosevelt and Hopkins*, pp. 784–85. U. S. Department of Defense, *The Entry of the Soviet Union into the War Against Japan*, pp. 24–25.

18 *Tehran Papers*, p. 765. The Combined Chiefs of Staff included the United States Chiefs of Staff and the British Chiefs of Staff. The Soviet Chiefs of Staff were not consulted.

19 *Tehran Papers*, p. 770.

20 The other vitally important development was western approval of the cross-channel attack, *Overlord*. *Ibid.*, p. 674. See also Elliott Roosevelt, *As He Saw It*, (New York: Duell, Sloan and Pearce, Inc., 1946), p. 203, where the author records a conversation with the President at Cairo on December 5, 1943, following Tehran. The President informed Elliott that the Russians had agreed at Tehran to enter the war against Japan. In response to the question as to when they were getting in, the President replied, "Oh, not for months yet, anyway. I think he (Stalin) offered to declare war against Japan and start fighting in the Far East in order to win finally the agreement for a second front in the west. He was willing to get in as soon as he could get troops to Siberia, if we would just promise the May first invasions in the west. . . . He'll declare war against Japan. He mentioned a time period too: six months after the final defeat of Hitler!"

21 The evidence relating to the discussions between Roosevelt and Chiang on this point is inconclusive. A Chinese summary of the Roosevelt-Chiang conversation on November 23, 1943, indicates only that Chiang wanted control of Port Arthur and Dairen. See *Tehran Papers*, pp. 324–67, 562. No United States account has been dis-

covered. See p. 891 for the recollections of Dr. Hollington K. Tong who had been present at the Cairo talks and Sherwood, *Roosevelt and Hopkins*, p. 792, for Sherwood's "understanding" that Roosevelt had discussed this matter with Chiang.

22 Tehran Papers, pp. 566–67. Sherwood, *Roosevelt and Hopkins*, p. 792. U. S. Department of Defense, *The Entry of the Soviet Union into the War Against Japan*, p. 27, fn. 20. For Harriman's recollections, see U. S. Senate, *Military Situation in the Far East*, p. 3330; and *Yalta Papers*, pp. 378-79.

23 The text of the Cairo Communique appears in *Tehran Papers*, pp. 448–89; for Stalin's position, see p. 566.

24 Sherwood, *Roosevelt and Hopkins*, p. 844.

25 The Pacific War Council, made up of the representatives of states of the United Nations which were fighting in the Pacific, met from time to time in Washington; see *Tehran Papers*, p. 868, fn. 1.

26 *Tehran Papers*, pp. 868–69.

27 Cline, *Washington Command Post: The Operations Division*, p. 337.

28 *Ibid.*, pp. 338–39. See also U. S. Department of Defense, *The Entry of the Soviet Union into the War Against Japan*, pp. 28–29; Leahy, *I Was There*, p. 245; Leahy, *Diaries*, Vol. 10, p. 56.

29 U. S. Department of Defense, *The Entry of the Soviet Union into the War Against Japan*, pp. 28–29.

30 *Ibid.*, p. 29.

31 *Yalta Papers*, p. 362.

32 U. S. Department of Defense, *The Entry of the Soviet Union into the War Against Japan*, p. 39.

33 *Ibid.*, p. 41.

34 U. S. Department of Defense, *The Entry of the Soviet Union into the War Against Japan*, p. 41.

35 *Yalta Papers*, Arnold's Memorandum, pp. 375–76; King's Memorandum, pp. 377–78.

36 The complete text of this report appears in *Yalta Papers*, pp. 388–94. Excerpts are included in U. S. Department of Defense, *The Entry of the Soviet Union into the War Against Japan*, pp. 42–44. The second principle involved the Joint Staff Planners concept of Russia's mission once it had entered the war.

37 *Yalta Papers*, p. 396.

38 Deane, *The Strange Alliance*, pp. 228–29.

39 Deane, *The Strange Alliance*, p. 229. U. S. Department of Defense, *The Entry of the Soviet Union into the War Against Japan*, p. 32.

40 Deane, *The Strange Alliance*, p. 230.

41 Message from Harriman to Roosevelt, June 11, 1944, quoted in U. S. Department of Defense, *The Entry of the Soviet Union into the War Against Japan*, p. 33.

42 Deane reports that, on August 18, 1944, General H. H. Arnold had promised Lieutenant General Leonid G. Rudenko, head of the Soviet Purchasing Commission, two-hundred B-24 Liberator bombers without clearly connecting delivery with an agreement permitting United States squadrons to use Siberian bases. Deane persuaded Arnold to qualify his offer so as to maintain Deane's bargaining position with the Russians. This, apparently, was the only deviation from a consistent United States policy. See Deane, *The Strange Alliance*, p. 233.

43 U. S. Department of Defense, *The Entry of the Soviet Union into the War Against Japan*, pp. 34–35. Harriman's message to Roosevelt is quoted. See also Deane, *The Strange Alliance*, pp. 240–41.

44 U. S. Department of Defense, *The Entry of the Soviet Union into the War Against Japan*, p. 36. Deane, *The Strange Alliance*, pp. 241. *Yalta Papers*, p. 362, fn. 2.

45 Deane, *The Strange Alliance*, p. 242.

46 Roosevelt emphasized this objective in a telegram to Harriman on October 10 in which he said: ". . . As to the Far East I am a little concerned that the Prime Minister's talks with Stalin may minimize the importance of the conference that has been agreed to between General Deane and the Red Army Staff. We now have a full agreement from Stalin not only to participate in the Pacific war but to enter the war with full effort. The important thing now therefore is to ascertain what are the Russians' capabilities in the East. In this the limiting factors are of course the logistics about which we know so little. General talks are no longer needed and full discussions by General Deane are therefore the next general step. The Prime Minister's talks therefore with Stalin should emphasize the importance of the detailed staff discussions. I will try to see that the Prime Minister's conversations take this time. . . ." *Yalta Papers*, pp. 362–63.

47 There is some difference of opinion as to when Churchill arrived. The Prime Minister's statement appears in Churchill, *Triumph and Tragedy*, p. 226. Deane asserts that he arrived on October 11, 1944; see *The Strange Alliance*, p. 243.

48 *Yalta Papers*, p. 363. Churchill seems at this time to have been somewhat in the dark as to specific United States plans. In a message to Roosevelt he said: ". . . I have not yet received your account of what part of the Pacific operations we may mention to Stalin and his officers. I should like to have this, because otherwise in conversation with him I might go beyond what you wish to be said. . . . I have little doubt from our talk [Stalin] will declare war upon [Japan] as soon as Germany is beaten. But surely Averell (Harriman) and Deane should be in a position not merely to ask him to do certain things but also to tell him, in outline at any rate the kind of things you are going to do yourself, and we are going to help you to do." See Churchill, *Triumph and Tragedy*, p. 229. On October 11, Roosevelt authorized Harriman to provide Churchill information regarding American plans in the Pacific. See *Yalta Papers*, p. 364.

49 *Yalta Papers*, p. 365.

50 *Yalta Papers*, p. 367; this information was included in a wire from Deane to the Joint Chiefs of Staff. See also Deane, *The Strange Alliance*, p. 246, for a reworded account which omits the fourth query.

51 *Yalta Papers*. p. 369. The above account is taken from Harriman to Roosevelt of October 15, 1944. More general accounts appear in Churchill, *Triumph and Tragedy*, p. 237; and in Deane, *The Strange Alliance*, pp. 247–48.

52 *Yalta Papers*, pp. 370–74; these pages include both Harriman's and Deane's report of the meeting. See also Deane, *The Strange Alliance*, pp. 248–49.

53 *Yalta Papers*, p. 374.

54 U. S. Department of Defense, *The Entry of the Soviet Union into the War Against Japan*, p. 38. Deane, *The Strange Alliance*, p. 257.

55 Deane, *The Strange Alliance*, p. 250.

56 *Ibid.*, p. 249. Deane indicates that the United States delivered 80 percent of promised supplies by June 30, 1945.

57 *Ibid.*, p. 259.

58 See pp. 63–65.

59 United States Department of State, *United States Relations with China* (Washington: 1949), Annex 43, p. 550. This annex consists of summary notes of conversations

between Wallace and Chiang prepared by John Carter Vincent, Chief of the Division of Chinese Affairs, who accompanied the Vice-President.

60 United States Department of State, *United States Relations with China*, p. 558. The above account is a paraphrase of excerpts from the Wallace-Chiang conversations.

61 U. S. Senate, *Military Situation in the Far East*, p. 3330.

62 *Yalta Papers*, pp. 369-70.

63 *Ibid.*, pp. 378–79. The above is a paraphrase of Harriman's report on the conference to Roosevelt.

64 Although Churchill ultimately signed the agreement between Roosevelt and Churchill, he did not request to be consulted in its negotiation as he felt this was an American affair and not suitable for British participation; see Churchill, *Triumph and Tragedy*, pp. 388–90. Apparently Eden disagreed with the Prime Minister and urged him not to sign the document since he had not participated in its formulation; see Edward R. Stettinius, Jr., *Roosevelt and the Russians: The Yalta Conference* (Garden City: Doubleday and Company, Inc., 1949), pp. 94–95. Roosevelt negotiated the agreement without consulting Secretary of State Edward R. Stettinius, Jr. The President informed Stettinius that it was primarily a military matter and that he would consult with Harriman who had had long experience in dealing with the Russians concerning this problem; see p. 92. Harriman and Bohlen attended the meeting with Roosevelt while Molotov and Pavlov, an interpreter, accompanied Stalin; see *Yalta Papers*, p. 766.

65 Stettinius, *Roosevelt and the Russians*, pp. 93–94. *Yalta Papers*, p. 984 for text.

66 These questions and answers are paraphrased from two documents which describe the two meetings. The questions appear in the report of the first meeting on February 8; see *Yalta Papers*, pp. 757–63. The answers appear in the report of the meeting of February 9, pp. 834–36, 839–40. See also U. S. Department of Defense, *The Entry of the Soviet Union into the War Against Japan*, pp. 48–49.

67 Deane, *The Strange Alliance*, p. 261.

68 *Ibid.*, pp. 262–65.

CHAPTER 4

UNCONDITIONAL SURRENDER FOR JAPAN

THE attack on Pearl Harbor provided the emotional impetus to the development of unconditional surrender as the overall objective for victory over Japan. Enlisting Russian support had been promoted to accomplish that end more quickly. By the time of Roosevelt's death, unconditional surrender had been accepted by both the people of the United States and by their government as the *sine qua non* for ending the war with the Japanese. Truman came to office with the general objectives of United States policy toward Japan practically and politically fixed. Through years of bitter war, the American people had been conditioned to demand the unconditional surrender of Japan. The new President had lived within an atmosphere of opinion which required the fulfillment of that goal. He had personally supported it. It was to be the limiting framework within which he would develop his policies toward Japan during the last months of the war.

The policy of unconditional surrender for Japan had developed through the years of the Roosevelt administration. That policy was implicitly rooted both in the early efforts of the administration to buttress the morale of the American people in those first disastrous days following Pearl Harbor and in its parallel effort to convince the United Nations and the Axis that the United States would fight until total victory. The term, "unconditional surrender" was not used in early statements of United States policy and, as a matter of fact, was not consciously sought as an objective within the United States Department of State until the President announced it as an overall policy objective at Casablanca in January, 1943.[1] Nevertheless, the concept emerged from public statements eschewing a separate peace and promising total victory.

From December 7, 1941, throughout 1942, the pronouncements from the President and from members of his administration repeatedly proclaimed the goal of total victory. Roosevelt first set the line in his message to the Congress on the morning following Pearl Harbor when, after describing the attack, he said:

. . . No matter how long it may take us to overcome this premeditated invasion, the American people in their righteous might will win through to *absolute victory*.

I believe I interpret the will of the Congress and of the people when I assert that we will not only defend ourselves to the uttermost but will make very certain that this form of treachery should never endanger us again. . . .[2]

On January 1, 1942, the declaration announcing the wartime coalition of the United Nations against the Axis powers was published. It proclaimed that:

. . . Being convinced that *complete victory* over their enemies is essential to defend life, liberty, independence and religious freedom and to preserve human rights and justice . . . , and that they are now engaged in a common struggle against savage and brutal forces seeking to subjugate the world, . . .

Each Government pledges itself to cooperate with the Governments signatory hereto and not to make a separate armistice or peace with the enemies. . . .[3]

This declaration, of course, did not require unconditional surrender. But it did call for complete victory, and it created the obligation for each of the signatories to refuse to seek unilateral peace with the Axis.

An even stronger statement of policy appeared in the President's State of the Union Message of January 6, 1942. Again, Roosevelt repeated his call:

. . . Our own objectives are clear; the objective of smashing the militarism imposed by warlords upon their enslaved peoples — the objective of liberating the subjugated nations . . .

American armed forces must be used at any place in all the world . . . , in order to strike at the common enemy, with a view to his complete encirclement and eventual *total defeat.* . . .

Many people ask, "When will this war end?" There is only one answer to that. It will end just as soon as we make it end by . . . combined determination to fight through until the end — *the end of militarism in Germany and Italy and Japan.* Most certainly we will not settle for less. . . .

Our enemies are guided by brutal cynicism, by unholy contempt for the human race. We are inspired by a faith which goes back through all the years to the first chapter of the Book of Genesis: "God created man in His own image."

We on our side are striving to be true to that divine heritage. . . . Those on the other side are striving to destroy this deep belief and to create a world in their own image — a world of tyranny and cruelty and serfdom.

That is the conflict that day and night now pervades our lives. No compromise can end that conflict. There never has been — there never can be — successful compromise between good and evil. *Only total victory* can reward the champions of tolerance and decency and freedom and faith.[4]

Here, Roosevelt, in effect, sketched the outlines of the policy that was later to become unconditional surrender. First, the United Nations would smash competing militarism to impose total defeat on the enemy. And, second, the battle would be fought by the good to annihilate the evil. It would be a persistent drive, refusing compromise, to once and for all eliminate the enemies' "tyranny and cruelty and serfdom."

In a number of speeches during 1942 Roosevelt repeated the same theme. On June 14 before a United Flag Day rally he asked the German and Japanese peoples and those others in the areas under German and Japanese domination whether they would rather yield to dictators or be free; he went on:

We know the answer. They know the answer. We know that man born to freedom in the image of God, will not forever suffer the oppressors' sword. The people of the United Nations are taking that sword from the oppressors' hands. With it they will destroy those tyrants. The brazen tyrannies pass. Man marches toward the light. . . .[5]

And again during a radio address on September 3:

. . . our youth . . . answered the call to arms—many millions of them; and today they are determined to fight *until the forces of aggression have been utterly destroyed.* . . .[6]

Roosevelt once more demanded the destruction of Axis military power in his State of the Union Message of January 7, 1943, just before going to Casablanca:

. . . It is clear to us that if Germany and Italy and Japan—or any one of them—remain armed at the end of this war or are permitted to rearm, they will again, and inevitably, embark on an ambitious career of world conquest. They must be disarmed and kept disarmed, and they must abandon the philosophy . . . which has brought so much suffering to the world.[7]

It is true that Roosevelt here indicated certain conditions which the Axis had to accept before peace was possible. But the nature of the conditions, complete and continuing disarmament and ideological conversion, implied surrender of a sort which was likely to stem only from complete defeat.

Top officials in the Roosevelt administration expressed similar attitudes throughout 1942. On May 8, Vice-President Henry A. Wallace characterized the struggle as a fight ". . . between a slave world and a free world." He went on to say:

. . . There can be no half measures . . . the will of the American people is for complete victory.

No compromise with Satan is possible. We shall not rest until all the victims under the Nazi yoke are freed. We shall fight for a complete peace as well as a complete victory . . . , strong in the strength of the Lord, we who fight in the people's cause will never stop until that cause is won.[8]

On July 23, Secretary of State Cordell Hull proclaimed in a radio address:

. . . we shall seek our enemies and attack them at any and every point of the globe at which the destruction of the Axis forces can be accomplished most effectively, most speedily, and most certainly.

We know the magnitude of the task before us. . . . However long the road we shall press on to the final victory.

Fighting as we are in self-defense, in self-preservation, we must make certain the defeat and destruction of the world-invading forces of Hitler and the Japanese war lords. . . .

International desperadoes like individual bandits will not abandon outlawing voluntarily. They will only be stopped by force. . . .

For the immediate present the all important issue is that of winning the war—winning it as soon as possible and winning it decisively. . . .[9]

And on October 8, 1942, the Acting Secretary of State Sumner Welles also promoted the policy of absolute victory:

. . . I not only believe that we are going to win this war, but I know that however long the struggle may be, . . . the American people will never lay down their arms until the final and complete victory is won by the United Nations. . . .[10]

These remarks were typical of the general line publicly followed by the Roosevelt administration, and they indicated that the intellectual and emotional bases for the unconditional surrender formula had been consistently constructed during the year prior to the conference at Casablanca.[11] It is true that these words were spoken to develop a willingness to resist in an American public plagued with generally bad news from the fighting fronts throughout the year. And yet, even if bolstering morale was the speakers' only objective, the indirect result of their efforts was to create an atmosphere of struggle between good and evil, to develop the emotional fervor of a crusade, to form the conditions which made the enunciation of the unconditional surrender concept acceptable and meaningful in both a political and an emotional sense. Unconditional surrender had never been formalized as a policy during the first year of United States involvement in World War II. Now at Casablanca, Roosevelt would take the step which would ultimately project complete victory beyond the level of interest to the rarified realm of principle.

Accounts of the Casablanca Conference vary in explaining the specific origin of unconditional surrender. Most attribute the policy to Roosevelt. Many indicate that he announced it on the spur of the moment, with little if any forethought. And yet, despite the fragmentary evidence, it is likely that the President and others had, at least, considered the concept before Casablanca. There are even some indications that it had received serious study.

Apparently the unconditional surrender formula was first discussed at a White House meeting of the Joint Chiefs of Staff with Roosevelt on January 7, 1943. Eisenhower indicated that the matter was mentioned at that time.[12] And Wedemeyer reported that Marshall later informed him that ". . . there had been mentioned for the first time the 'unconditional surrender' formula which might be considered at Casablanca. There had been no discussion by the military staff of this fatal formula. . . "[13] At this meeting, Roosevelt ". . . announced for the first time the unconditional surrender formula as the proper aim of the allied war effort." [14] No military staff work had been done on this matter. Apparently neither the President nor the Joint Chiefs felt the question was one which required staff discussion.[15] Prior to Casablanca, then, Roosevelt had at least informed his top military commanders of his plans for unconditional surrender.

On at least one occasion at Casablanca the Joint Chiefs apparently examined Roosevelt's proposed policy of unconditional surrender. At one of their daily morning conferences, Marshall brought up the question, off the record. He had asked Wedemeyer, who had developed strong views against the policy, to present his arguments to those at the meeting. This Wedemeyer did. Possible reactions to his remarks are unrecorded. And it has been impossible to discover whether or not the Joint Chiefs again discussed the matter either among themselves, with the British, or with Roosevelt. But it seems likely that they thought the matter to be of sufficient importance to give it some consideration.[16]

The policy had probably been carefully studied, at least by Roosevelt, prior to the conference. Judge Samuel I. Rosenman, one of Roosevelt's speech writers, was ". . . sure that the gist of . . . [the unconditional surrender policy] had been carefully thought out. The President had said practically the same thing a few weeks before, in his State of Union

Message. . . ." [17] Although Sherwood is unconvinced that the policy ". . . was very deeply deliberated . . . it was a true statement of Roosevelt's considered policy. . . ." [18]

The matter probably had been discussed by Roosevelt and Churchill at the Casablanca Conference prior to Roosevelt's announcement of the policy to the press on January 24. Elliott Roosevelt records that the phrase was born at an informal luncheon attended by Roosevelt, Churchill, Hopkins, and him on January 23. The term was Roosevelt's, but Hopkins liked it immediately; and Churchill ". . . while he slowly munched a mouthful of food, thought, frowned, thought, finally grinned, and at length announced, "Perfect! And I can just see how Goebbels and the rest of 'em'll [sic] squeal!" [19] Roosevelt then remarked that he thought Stalin would be strongly in favor of the policy and asked Hopkins to work up a draft of a statement to be issued to the press the next day. The final drafts of the joint communique of the conference and of the message to Stalin were finished by 2:30 A.M., January 24. At that time Churchill raised his glass and toasted ". . . unconditional surrender." [20]

Although Churchill had no recollection of the luncheon and the toast described by Elliott Roosevelt, he certainly had had some knowledge of the policy prior to its announcement on January 24.[21] On January 20 he reported to the War Cabinet among other things:

. . . We propose to draw up a statement of the work of the conference for communication to the press at the proper time. I would be glad to know what the War Cabinet would think of our including in this statement a declaration of the firm intention of the United States and the British Empire to continue the war relentlessly until we have brought about the "unconditional surrender" of Germany and Japan. The omission of Italy would be to encourage a break-up there. The President liked this idea, and it would stimulate our friends in every country. . . .[22]

The War Cabinet reviewed the problem during the afternoon of January 20. Their message to Churchill on January 21 indicated general acceptance of unconditional surrender, but they suggested that the policy be applied to Italy as well as to Germany and Japan.[23] They did not disapprove it. Whether Churchill discussed the matter further with Roosevelt between January 21 and January 24 is questionable. Churchill does not record such consultation. He certainly did not favor the application of unconditional surrender to Italy and probably did not mention the matter to Roosevelt again during the time when the Casablanca Communique was being drafted. The draft communique was approved by Roosevelt and Churchill. It contained no reference to unconditional surrender.[24]

It may have been with some surprise, therefore, that Churchill heard the President inform the reporters of unconditional surrender on January 24. He apparently had assumed that the communique, once accepted, had superseded any previous conversations regarding unconditional surrender.[25] In any event Roosevelt expressed publicly the policy which had previously been considered only informally and in private:

. . . Another point. I think that we have all had it in our hearts and our heads before, but I don't think that it has ever been put down on paper by the Prime Minister and myself, and that is the determination that peace can come to the world only by the total elimination of German and Japanese war power.

Some of you Britishers know the old story—we had a general called U. S. Grant. His name was Ulysses Simpson Grant, but in my and the Prime Minister's early days he was called "Unconditional Surrender" Grant. The elimination of German, Japanese, and Italian war power means the unconditional surrender by Germany, Italy, and Japan. That means a responsible assurance of future world peace. It does not mean the destruction of the population of Germany, Italy, or Japan, but it does mean the destruction of the philosophies in those countries which are based on conquest and the subjugation of other people.[26]

The Prime Minister, recalling the support for the general policy which had come from the War Cabinet, recovered quickly to support the seemingly unexpected statement. After Roosevelt had finished, the Prime Minister said:

I agree with everything the President has said. . . .

I hope you gentlemen . . . will be able to build up a good and encouraging story to our people all over the world. Give them the picture of unity, thoroughness, and integrity of the political chiefs. Give them that picture and make them feel that there is some reason behind all that is being done. Even when there is some delay there is design and purpose, and as the President has said, the unconquerable will to pursue this quality, until we have procured the unconditional surrender of the criminal forces who plunged the world into storm and ruin.[27]

The policy, thus announced, became the overall wartime objective of the United Nations. Despite its cool reception by Stalin and Churchill's later efforts to redefine its implications, Roosevelt steadfastly adhered to his pronouncement until his death. Questions arise as to why he enunciated the policy in the first place and why he continued to pursue it throughout the war.

Roosevelt himself later told Sherwood that the pronouncement had been largely unplanned. "We had so much trouble getting those two French generals together," he said, "that I thought to myself that this was as difficult as arranging the meeting of Grant and Lee—and then suddenly the press conference was on, and Winston and I had no time to prepare for it, and the thought popped into my mind that they had called Grant 'Old Unconditional Surrender' and the next thing I knew, I had said it." [28]

This account has been virtually accepted by many serious and interested observers. One such is Lord Ismay, who feels that by the time of the news conference Roosevelt and Churchill might have forgotten all about unconditional surrender ". . . until Roosevelt found himself facing an army of news-hungry reporters, and . . . the phrase then recurred to his mind and was released fortuitously." [29] But the explanation is not very satisfying for a number of reasons. First, Roosevelt for some inexplicable reason liked to picture himself as a light-hearted person who frequently made ill-considered, off-hand remarks.[30] In this case, the image was far from reality. He had previously discussed this matter with his military and with Churchill. Since the beginning of the war he had been enunciating the basic tenets of unconditional surrender. And, more immediately, he had prepared a set of notes which he consulted when he faced the reporters at the January 24 press conference. Those notes included the following passage:

The President and the Prime Minister, after a complete survey of the World War situation, are more than ever determined that peace can come to the world only by a total elimination of German and Japanese warpower. This involves the simple formula of placing the objective of this war in terms of unconditional surrender by Germany, Italy, and Japan. Unconditional surrender by them means a reasonable assurance of world peace for generations. Unconditional surrender means not the destruction of the German populace, nor of the Italian or Japanese populace, but does mean the destruction of a philosophy in Germany, Italy, and Japan which is based on the conquest and subjugation of other peoples.[31]

This note should be compared with the transcript of his public remarks.[32] It contains the same explanation of unconditional surrender as his remarks before the press. The only new element is the reference to "Unconditional Surrender Grant." It seems, therefore, that the policy statement had been well prepared and that the only haphazard portion of the statement had been the reference to Grant.[33] Roosevelt had not made his policy statement accidentally as a result of confusion before the press. It seems likely that he had other more specific purposes in mind.

Some or all of the following objectives might have influenced Roosevelt's promotion of unconditional surrender at Casablanca. First, he might have been attempting to offset rumors that arose following his agreement with the pro-Vichy Admiral Jean Darlan that the United Nations might seek a negotiated peace with the Axis Powers. Such rumors weakened resistance movements in Axis-conquered areas, created doubts of an eventual United Nations victory in neutral governments causing them to hesitate before making any open break with the Axis states, and provided Axis propagandists the opportunity to weaken relations among the United Nations. Unconditional surrender might have aimed at minimizing for all of these groups the possibility that the military expediency evidenced in the Darlan deal might be repeated with other strong men in the Axis governments.

Second, Roosevelt might have been trying to evade the repetition of Nazi propaganda to the effect that Germany had never lost World War I but had merely been deceived by the Allies who had evaded the obligations of Wilson's Fourteen Points in forcing the Germans to accept the Versailles settlement. After this war there would be no Fourteen Points. This time the Germans and the Japanese and the Italians would suffer complete defeat, and there would be no later claim by succeeding governments that those states had been dealt with illegally and immorally after the peace conference.[34]

Third, Roosevelt might have been trying to reassure the Soviet Government that the British and the Americans would make no separate peace with the Germans. At Casablanca the United States military and Roosevelt had accepted the British plan for an attack on Italy which would bring another delay in fulfilling the Russian request for a second front in Western Europe. The Russians estimated that the attack on Italy would tie down relatively few German divisions and that it was but another indication that the Western Powers wished to stand in the wings while the Russians fought it out with the Germans. Casablanca would tend to confirm such opinions. Unconditional surrender would help to offset such fears and to maintain the alliance against the Axis.

And, fourth, Roosevelt might have been attempting to ensure support for a prolonged war effort at home. He recognized that as the war progressed, pressures would develop on behalf of some sort of a negotiated peace. It was true, by the time of Casablanca, that the fortunes of war had begun to turn against the Axis. And yet victory was not in sight. A long, hard war loomed ahead. Morale needed a boost. Perhaps Roosevelt tried to give the peoples of the United Nations the necessary emotional lift by promising the complete elimination of the cancerous growths of nazism, fascism, and aggressive Japanese militarism.

Thus, unconditional surrender probably satisfied a number of Roosevelt's immediate needs. Possible long-range disadvantages resulting from a prolongation of the war by desperate enemies were far in the future. He had, furthermore, sufficiently qualified his apparently inflexible statement by promising that it was not aimed at unmerciful sanctions against the Axis peoples. Once their governments, their expansionist philosophies, and their military forces had been blotted out, the peoples of Germany and Italy and Japan might expect a just and humane peace.[35]

From Casablanca until his death Roosevelt persisted against all opposition in continuing to demand unconditional surrender. Stalin, at times opposing it, at times favoring it, failed to change the President's stand. Churchill in private argument and public statement attempted to modify its impact, but Roosevelt persisted. Even some in his own government and military establishment suggested change from time to time, but the President stood firm. He might reemphasize the possibility of mercy which the defeated could expect from their righteous conquerors, but he would not change his stand on unconditional surrender.

Stalin's reaction to unconditional surrender was not overly enthusiastic. Since a statement that the policy had been adopted was not included in the message from Roosevelt and Churchill informing him of the agreements negotiated at Casablanca, he may have first learned of the policy from news reports of January 24.[36] His previous policy had been in line with the general concept of unconditional surrender, but his emphasis had been different. On November 6, 1942, he had enumerated the objectives of the Soviet Union. "It is not our aim to destroy Germany," he had said, "for it is impossible to destroy Germany. . . . But the Hitlerite state can and should be destroyed. And our first task is to destroy the Hitlerite state and its inspirers. . . . It is not our aim to destroy all organized military force in Germany, for . . . that is not only impossible . . . but inadvisable from the point of view of the victor. But Hitler's army can and should be destroyed. . . . Our third task is to destroy the hated new order in Europe. . . ." [37] Thus, he had indicated conditional surrender, but only after the annihilation of the Nazi state, its army, and its "new order," objectives which were not out of line with Roosevelt's concept of unconditional surrender. But Stalin had not emphasized unconditionality.[38]

On the other hand excerpts from his Order of the Day to the Soviet armies on May 1, 1943, indicated a shift toward acceptance of unconditional surrender, at least as applied toward Germany. In referring to rumors of German efforts to seek a negotiated peace through the promotion of a split among the Soviet Union, Great Britain, and the United States, Stalin said:

. . . But what kind of peace can one talk with the imperialist bandits from the German-Fascist camp who have flooded Europe with blood and studded it with gallows? Is it not clear that only the utter routing of the Hitlerite armies and the *unconditional surrender* of Hitlerite Germany can bring peace to Europe? [39]

Here, at least, was an apparent acceptance of unconditionality.

Later, on November 2, 1943, as a result of the Foreign Ministers Conference in Moscow preceding the Tehran Conference, the Soviet Union participated with Great Britain, the United States, and China in issuing a Declaration of General Security which began:

The Governments . . . united in their determination in accordance with the declaration by the United Nations . . . and subsequent Declarations, to continue hostilities against those Axis Powers with which they respectively are at war, until such powers have laid down their arms on the basis of *unconditional surrender* . . .[40]

Here Stalin reaffirmed his acceptance of the unconditional surrender principle applied to Germany.

But public acceptance of the concept did not indicate his approval for the application of unconditional surrender to all of the Axis Powers as a basis for negotiating peace. His doubts about the policy were forcefully stated during a dinner meeting with Churchill and Roosevelt on November 28, 1943, at Tehran. He favored the strongest possible restrictions on Germany which the victorious Allies could apply. He asserted that the ". . . Reich itself must be rendered impotent ever again to plunge the world into war." [41] Later, after Roosevelt had retired, Stalin more strongly than ever proposed to Churchill ". . . the strongest possible measures against Germany." [42] And yet as ". . . a war-time measure . . . [he] questioned the advisability of the unconditional surrender principle with no definition of the exact terms which would be imposed upon Germany. He felt that to leave the principle of unconditional surrender unclarified merely served to unite the German people, whereas to draw up specific terms, no matter how harsh, and tell the German people that this was what they would have to accept, would, in his opinion, hasten the day of German capitulation." [43] This was, perhaps, the clearest statement of Stalin's position on unconditional surrender. He was not adverse to imposing severe terms on the Germans after achieving their complete defeat. He too wished to avoid any separate peace which might split the alliance against the Axis. But he could see no sense in feeding the German propaganda mill and leading the German people and armies to fight to the bitter, desperate end by raising an undefined unconditional surrender to the level of immutable principle.[44]

Furthermore, the Soviet Union would have limited the concept to Germany, the major threat, and would have used the lure of a negotiated peace to wean away from the Reich its allies. The Soviet Government favored a negotiated peace with Italy in September, 1943, and began negotiating armistice with Finland early in 1944. Throughout the early months of 1944, it favored modification of unconditional surrender toward such states as Finland, Hungary, Bulgaria, and Rumania.[45] Such Soviet insistence, supported by that of the British and the State Department, resulted in a modification of the general applicability of the principle on May 12, 1944, when the three Allies issued a joint statement which promised the Axis satellites more lenient terms than unconditional surrender in return for withdrawal from the war.[46]

Stalin's efforts to obtain some specific definition of unconditional surrender continued through 1944 and early 1945. At the Yalta Conference during the second plenary session on February 5, 1945, Stalin raised the question as to how the policy should be applied to Germany. Did it mean, for instance, that if Hitler's government accepted unconditional surrender, the Allies would deal with his government? And shouldn't the Germans be told exactly what the Allies expected after surrender in regard, say, to dismemberment and reparations?[47] He was answered by Churchill. Roosevelt evaded the question. The Prime Minister, desiring to put off specific plans for the dismemberment of Germany, replied to Stalin that if some other German group than the Hitler government sued for peace, the Allies:

. . . would present terms of surrender, but if Hitler or Himmler should offer to surrender unconditionally the answer was clear—. . . . [they] would not negotiate under any circumstances with any war criminals and then the war would go on. He added it was more probable they would be killed or in hiding, but another group of Germans might indicate their willingness to accept unconditional surrender. In such case the three Allies would immediately consult together as to whether they could deal with this group, and if so terms of unconditional surrender would immediately be submitted, if not, war would continue and . . . [they] would occupy the entire country under a military command.[48]

Roosevelt offered no direct comment in regard to Churchill's position. Publicly-undefined unconditional surrender continued to be the policy of the United Nations.

Despite his unwillingness at Yalta to define unconditional surrender by outlining plans for the specific dismemberment of Germany, Churchill had since its introduction been attempting to modify its possible impact on German resistance by describing the policy publicly in moderate terms as applied to the German people. Thus, on February 11, 1943, reporting on the Casablanca Conference to the House of Commons, he had said:

. . . our inflexible insistence upon unconditional surrender does not mean that we shall stain our victorious arms by wrong and cruel treatment of whole populations. But justice must be done upon the wicked and the guilty, and, within her proper bounds, justice must be stern and implacable. No vestige of Nazi or Fascist power, no vestige of the Japanese war-plotting machine will be left to us when the work is done. . . .[49]

Later, on August 14, 1943, he had noted to Eden that there was no need to discourage the disintegration of the Nazi regime ". . . by continually uttering the slogan 'Unconditional Surrender.' As long as we do not have to commit ourselves to dealing with any particular new figure or new Government, our advantage is clear. We certainly do not want . . . to get them all fused together in a solid desperate block for whom there is no hope. . . ."[50]

Following the Tehran Conference, through the early spring of 1944, Churchill had supported Stalin's efforts for some modification of unconditional surrender, at least toward the East European satellites of Germany.[51] On February 22, 1944, he described the policy in moderate terms:

. . . Here I may point out that the term "unconditional surrender" does not mean that the German people will be enslaved or destroyed. It means . . . that the Allies will not be bound to them at the moment of surrender by any pact or obligation. There will be, for instance, no question of the Atlantic Charter applying to Germany as a matter of right . . . Unconditional surrender means that the victors have a free hand. It does not mean that they are entitled to behave in a barbarous manner nor that they wish to blot out Germany from among the nations in Europe. If we are bound, we are bound by our own consciences to civilization. We are not to be bound . . . as the result of a bargain struck. That is the meaning of "unconditional surrender. . . ." [52]

Churchill continued to support the President's policy while seeking its moderation. He too wished to eliminate the Nazi government and to wipe out Germany as a threatening power. He did not, however, desire to prolong the war by stubbornly following a slogan in such a way as to promote unity among the Germans and Japanese.

Despite the efforts of Stalin and Churchill, Roosevelt publicly persisted in following unconditional surrender as the general objective of Allied policy. He continued to do this over the objections of Secretary of State Hull and despite pleas for its modification from his military leaders, particularly from Eisenhower, who saw it as reinforcing the German and Japanese will to resist.[53] Roosevelt emphasized that the formula applied to Japan as well as to Germany, and as late as March 1, 1945, in his report to the Congress on the Yalta Conference he reiterated:

. . . There will be no respite for . . . [the Nazis]. We will not desist for one moment until unconditional surrender . . .

But the unconditional surrender of Japan is as essential as the defeat of Germany. I say that advisedly, with the thought in mind that that is especially true if our plans for world peace are to succeed. For Japanese militarism must be wiped out as thoroughly as German militarism.[54]

Though he was from time to time during the war to redefine unconditional surrender, he never wavered from support for the general principle.[55]

Despite the public impact of his statements, Roosevelt's approach to unconditional surrender was not far different from Churchill's and Stalin's. He considered the principle to be useful.[56] And yet he also frequently defined the policy in humanitarian terms. In an address to the White House Correspondents Association on February 12, 1943, he asserted:

. . . the only terms on which we shall deal with any Axis factions are . . . "unconditional surrender." We know, and the plain people of our enemies will eventually know, that in our uncompromising policy we mean no harm to the Axis Nations. But we do mean to impose punishment and retribution in full upon their guilty, barbaric leaders.[57]

Perhaps, however, the best indication of what unconditional surrender meant to Roosevelt appears in two messages he sent to Hull when the Secretary of State was trying, in line with British and Russian pressures, to obtain some modification of the formula in regard to the Axis satellites. The first, sent on March 25, 1944, read, in part:

. . . It would be a mistake, in my judgment, to abandon or make an exception in the case of the words "unconditional surrender." As a matter of fact, whom do we mean these words to apply to? Evidently our enemies.

In August, 1941, at the time of the Atlantic Charter, and in January, 1943, at the time of Casablanca, Hungary, Bulgaria, Rumania, and Finland were the Axis satellites. But they were not our enemies in the same sense that Germany and Italy were. These . . . states were enemies under the duress of Germany and Italy.

I think it a mistake to make exceptions. Italy surrendered unconditionally but was at the same time given many privileges. This should be so in the event of the surrender of Bulgaria or Rumania or Hungary or Finland . . . That is the spirit I want to see abroad—but it does not apply to Germany. Germany understands only one kind of language.[58]

The second message was sent to Hull on April 5:

. . . I want at all costs to prevent it from being said that the unconditional surrender principle has been abandoned. There is real danger if we start making exceptions to the general principle before a specific case arises.

We all know that this would happen if we were to make any exceptions to the principle which would thereafter apply in all cases.

I understand perfectly well that from time to time there will have to be exceptions not to the surrender principle but to the application of it in specific cases. That is a very different thing from changing the principle. . . .[59]

Roosevelt, it seems, did not greatly differ with his wartime colleagues. He was willing to be flexible in interpreting unconditional surrender when the occasion demanded it. But he continued to think of the policy as a principle, to be generally maintained at all costs.

Throughout the war he continued to promote unconditional surrender. He would impose it for the benefit of the common people of the Axis states by freeing them from the restrictions of their tyrannical governments. Thus, during his speech explaining Yalta to the Congress, he said:

. . . The German people, as well as the German soldiers, must realize that the sooner they give up and surrender . . . the sooner their present agony will be over. They must realize that only with complete surrender can they begin to reestablish themselves as people whom the world might accept as decent neighbors. . . . Unconditional surrender does not mean the destruction or enslavement of the German people.

And yet despite Roosevelt's willingness to interpret the policy flexibly when necessary, despite his efforts to make it applicable to governments and philosophies and militarism, his frequent use of the term—his brave reassertion of its grave import for the Axis—developed, it seems, in the minds of the American people the impression that unconditional surrender was the immutable objective of United States policy. Suggested deviations from its requirements were frequently met by cries of appeasement from the press and from both Democrats and Republicans in the Congress. A general atmosphere demanding complete military victory over Germany and Japan was created for the incoming Truman administration. Roosevelt's death brought with it the possibility of policy revision. In effect, however, the policies he had followed limited the choice of alternatives for Truman. The limitations were both direct and indirect. Direct restrictions were imposed by public opinion and by official opposition to change from holdovers of Roosevelt's administration. Indirect restraints resulted from the interaction of Roosevelt's policies and the character and thinking of his successor.

NOTES TO CHAPTER 4

[1] Hull, *Memoirs*, II, p. 1570. For details concerning the Casablanca announcement see pp. 85–89.

[2] Leland M. Goodrich (ed.), *Documents on American Foreign Relations*, (Boston: World Peace Foundation, 1942), IV, pp. 116–18. The complete text of Roosevelt's message is included. Italics are supplied.

[3] *Ibid.*, p. 208. Italics are supplied.

[4] Goodrich (ed.), *Documents on American Foreign Relations*, IV, pp. 45–53, includes complete text. Italics are supplied.

[5] *Ibid.*, p. 78. The text of this address appears on pp. 77–79.

[6] *Ibid.*, V, p. 13. Complete text appears, pp. 12–16. Italics are supplied.

[7] *Ibid.*, pp. 38–42.

[8] *Ibid.*, IV, p. 69. Complete text appears, pp. 62–69.

[9] *Ibid.*, V, July 1942—June, 1943, pp. 1–12.

[10] *Ibid.*, p. 17. Complete text appears, pp. 16–22.

[11] See also Samuel I. Rosenman (comp.), *The Public Papers and Addresses of Franklin D. Roosevelt* (New York: Harper and Brothers, 1950), X, XI, XII, XIII; for a chronological and annotated compilation of Roosevelt's statements during World War II.

[12] Dwight D. Eisenhower, *Crusade in Europe* (Garden City: Doubleday and Company, Inc. 1948), p. 489. This is a reference to footnote 7 of Chapter 8 which cites ". . . OPD (Operation Division) Exec. 10, Stern 45, Department of the Army." See below, note 14.

[13] Albert C. Wedemeyer, *Wedemeyer Reports!* (New York: Henry Holt and Company, 1958), pp. 185–86. General Wedemeyer was, at that time, the Army Planner in OPD.

[14] Cline, *Washington Command Post*, p. 217. Cline cites the same file containing the minutes of this meeting that Eisenhower does. See above, note 12.

[15] *Ibid.*, p. 217.

[16] The only account of this meeting appears in Wedemeyer, *Wedemeyer Reports*, pp. 186–87. Wedemeyer indicates that the Joint Chiefs ". . . expressed no views for the record and . . . [he could] find nothing now. The only reference that . . . [he] had was the notes . . . [he] made and kept for . . . [himself]." He gives no date for the meeting. See also Leahy, *I Was There*, p. 145. Leahy states that as far as he could determine, unconditional surrender had never been discussed by the Combined Chiefs of Staff prior to January 24. He says nothing of possible consideration by the Joint Chiefs. The failure of Sir John Slessor or Lord Alanbrooke to mention discussion of

the question in their accounts might indicate that the British Chiefs of Staff were not consulted. See Sir John Slessor, *The Central Blue* (New York: Frederick A. Praeger, Inc., 1957). Arthur Bryant, *The Turn of the Tide* (Garden City: Doubleday and Company, Inc., 1957).

[17] Samuel I. Rosenman, *Working with Roosevelt* (New York: Harper and Brothers, 1952), p. 371. Rosenman was one of Roosevelt's trusted advisers.

[18] Sherwood, *Roosevelt and Hopkins*, p. 696.

[19] Roosevelt, *As He Saw It* (New York: Duell, Sloan and Pearce, Inc., 1946), p. 117. It should be noted, however, with regard to this source, that Churchill later made a caustic comment on such reports of alleged table conversation; see Churchill, *The Hinge of Fate*, pp. 680–85.

[20] Roosevelt, *As He Saw It*, pp. 117–19.

[21] Much later, on July 21, 1949, in answer to a question in the House of Commons, Churchill stated that the first he had heard the term "unconditional surrender" had been from Roosevelt at the press conference on January 24 and that Roosevelt had spoken without consulting him. In later checking his files, he found that he had been in error. See Churchill, *The Hinge of Fate*, pp. 687–88. Lord Hankey, *Politics Trials and Errors* (Chicago: Henry Regnery Company, 1950), p. 31.

[22] Churchill, *The Hinge of Fate*, p. 684.

[23] *Ibid.*, p. 686.

[24] Churchill, *The Hinge of Fate*, p. 286. See also Goodrich (ed.), *Documents on American Foreign Relations*, V, 251–53, for text of the communique.

[25] Churchill, *The Hinge of Fate*, pp. 686–87. See also General Lord Ismay, *Memoirs* (New York: The Viking Press, Inc., 1960), p. 290.

[26] Text appears in Rosenman (comp.), *The Public Papers and Addresses of Franklin D. Roosevelt*, XII, 37–40. See also Goodrich (ed.), *Documents on American Foreign Relations*, V, 254–55.

[27] Rosenman, pp. 40–42.

[28] Sherwood, *Roosevelt and Hopkins*, p. 696. The two generals mentioned were Henri H. Giraud and Charles de Gaulle who had been reconciled, at least outwardly, at Casablanca.

[29] Lord Ismay, *Memoirs*, p. 290. This attitude may also indicate something of Churchill's thoughts; for he has written that Ismay ". . . knew exactly how . . . [his] mind was working from day to day . . ." during the conference. See Churchill, *The Hinge of Fate*, p. 687.

[30] Sherwood, *Roosevelt and Hopkins*, p. 696.

[31] *Ibid.*, pp. 696–97.

[32] See p. 87.

[33] Much has been written concerning the President's misuse of history in making the reference to Grant at the Casablanca Conference. It is pointed out that Grant demanded unconditional surrender not from Lee but from the Confederate commander of Fort Donelson, Simon Bolivar Buckner, in 1862; and, further, that Grant at Fort Donelson was merely demanding the unconditional surrender of a single enemy commander rather than establishing an overall object for the Civil War. See Anne Armstrong, *Unconditional Surrender: The Impact of the Casablanca Policy Upon World War II* (New Brunswick: Rutgers University Press, 1961), pp. 13–14; and B. H. Liddell Hart, *The Defense of the West* (New York: William Morrow and Company, Inc., 1950), pp. 52–61, on which Armstrong relies. Careful review of the documents reveals no Roosevelt mistake in historic allusion at Casablanca. In his explanation to Sherwood he merely mentioned the difficulty of getting Grant and Lee together and then the transfer

of his thoughts to the relationship of Grant and the term "unconditional surrender." The press conference transcript of January 24 refers only to "Unconditional Surrender" Grant and makes no reference to Lee. Another account cites one of Roosevelt's advisers at Casablanca as indicating that Roosevelt wanted to use the Grant-Lee exchange at Appomattox to indicate that, despite unconditional surrender, the populations of the defeated Germany, Japan, and Italy might expect mercy at the hands of the victors. See Wallace Carroll, *Persuade or Perish* (Boston: Houghton Mifflin Company, 1948), pp. 309–11. If Roosevelt had this in mind at the time, there is little other specific evidence to indicate it. It might be implied from the wording of the transcript of the press conference which promised mercy to the conquered peoples. Perhaps much of this confusion has resulted from the remarks made off-the-cuff by Roosevelt at another press conference held over a year later on July 29, 1944, in Honolulu. At that time the President, in referring to the Casablanca policy, not only made the incorrect allusion to Grant's demand for unconditional surrender from Lee at Appomattox but also indicated Grant's mercy as an indication of how unconditional surrender might be applied to the vanquished in World War II. See Rosenman (comp.), *The Public Papers and Addresses of Franklin D. Roosevelt*, XIII, 209–10.

[34] Sherwood, *Roosevelt and Hopkins*, p. 697.

[35] This analysis relies heavily on that proposed in Carroll, *Persuade or Perish*, pp. 306–12. See also Armstrong, *Unconditional Surrender*, pp. 39–40; Paul Kecskemeti, *Strategic Surrender: The Politics of Victory and Defeat* (Stanford University Press, 1958), pp. 217–18.

[36] *Stalin's Correspondence with Churchill, Attlee, Roosevelt and Truman, 1941-45* (New York: E. P. Dutton & Company, Inc., 1958), pp. 86–87.

[37] Goodrich (ed.), *Documents on American Foreign Relations*, V, 203–4. There are excerpts from a speech by Stalin to the Moscow Soviet.

[38] Stalin's remarks were assumed to have been made on November 6, 1943, in Armstrong, *Unconditional Surrender*, pp. 56–57. Armstrong substantiates her position by citing William Henry Chamberlin, *America's Second Crusade* (Chicago: Henry Regnery Company, 1950), p. 289.

[39] Goodrich (ed.), *Documents on American Foreign Relations*, V, 210. Italics are included.

[40] *Soviet Foreign Policy During the Patriotic War: Documents and Materials*, I (London: Hutchinson and Company, no date), 241–42. This volume and two others include translations of Soviet documents. Italics are the author's. See also Goodrich (ed.), *Documents on American Foreign Relations*, VI, 229.

[41] *Tehran Papers*, p. 510.

[42] *Ibid.*, p. 511.

[43] *Tehran Papers*, p. 513. This latter quotation is from a Supplementary Memorandum to the Minutes of the dinner meeting prepared by Bohlen. It is doubtful that Roosevelt saw or, at least, remembered the memorandum; for he later assured Hull that the matter had never been brought up in his presence at Tehran. See Hull, *Memoirs*, II, 1572.

[44] Hull, *Memoirs*, II, 1573.

[45] *Ibid.*, pp. 1576–80.

[46] Hull, *Memoirs*, II, 1580.

[47] *Yalta Papers*, pp. 612, 624. These are references to two sets of minutes—those of Bohlen and those of Matthews.

[48] *Yalta Papers*, p. 613.

[49] House of Commons, *Parliamentary Debates* (London: His Majesty's Stationery Office, 1943), Fifth Series, CCCLXXXVI, 1473.

[50] Churchill, *Closing the Ring*, p. 663.

[51] Hull, *Memoirs*, II, 1579.

[52] *Parliamentary Debates*, House of Commons, Fifth Series, Vol. CCCXCVII, 698–99.

[53] Hull, *Memoirs*, II, 1570–82. Harry C. Butcher, *My Three Years with Eisenhower* (New York: Simon and Schuster, Inc., 1946), 386, 518. Carroll, *Persuade or Perish*, 306, 314, 319.

[54] Rosenman (comp.), *The Public Papers and Addresses of Franklin D. Roosevelt*, XIII, 574, 584.

[55] Rosenman, *Working with Roosevelt*, p. 371.

[56] William S. White, *Majesty and Mischief: A Mixed Tribute to F.D.R.* (New York: McGraw-Hill Book Company, 1961), pp. 48–49. White asserts that Roosevelt ". . . approached the war's problems in the notion . . . that slogans, high-minded and quite sincere ones, could themselves become the partial solvents of great issues and mighty contests of arms." Hence, among others, unconditional surrender was a slogan which became a principle.

[57] Rosenman (comp.), *The Public Papers and Addresses of Franklin D. Roosevelt*, XII, 80.

[58] Hull, *Memoirs,* II, p. 1576.

[59] *Ibid.,* p. 1577.

[60] Rosenman, (Comp.), *The Public Papers and Addresses of Franklin D. Roosevelt*, VIII, 575

CHAPTER 5

PRESIDENT HARRY S. TRUMAN

FRANKLIN D. Roosevelt died during the early afternoon of April 12, 1945. By 7:09 that evening Harry S. Truman had been sworn in as President and had fallen heir to Roosevelt's political legacy.[1] He was now head of a government which had long been involved in developing an atomic weapon. This tremendous project was moving rapidly, to the successful conclusion then being predicted by its directors. In Europe, German power had nearly been eliminated. Plans were already being made to divert United States strength from Europe to the Far East in order to hasten Japan's unconditional surrender. To insure such complete defeat, the United States government was continuing its persistent effort to involve the Soviet Union in the war against Japan. At this time when Roosevelt's policies were apparently leading to the successful conclusion of a prolonged and bitter war, it would have been difficult and, perhaps, unwise for any successor to have departed significantly from his long-accepted formulas. In view of Truman's inexperience and background, it was highly improbable that he would move along other paths from those already mapped by his predecessor.

Truman's roots lay deep in the soil of the rural, middle-class, Middle West of the late nineteenth century. Both of his grandfathers had been moderately successful neighboring farmers in Jackson County, Missouri.[2] His parents, John Anderson Truman and Martha Ellen Young, had moved to Lamar, Missouri, before Harry's birth in May, 1884. After a brief few years back on Grandfather Young's farm at Grandview, the family moved to Independence, Missouri, in 1890. Truman was to spend most of the period prior to his election to the Senate in 1934 in or near Independence. It is still his home.

In Independence, Harry grew through high school. It was there that he found he needed eyeglasses, discovered in Sunday School a childhood sweetheart who was later to become his wife, obtained his first job at eleven working in a drugstore, and recognized the joys to be derived from music and history. Perhaps because his fear of breaking his glasses made the rough play of the school yard a threat, Harry turned to reading and to piano playing. He was a sensitive boy and a favorite with his mother. In fact, he was to develop a sentimental, almost overemotional regard for women, particularly for women of his household. His mother, his wife, and his daughter were the paragons of feminine virtues throughout his life.

Harry's father, John, was, at times, a livestock broker, a real estate dealer, and a part-time farmer. He was generally successful until he lost heavily, speculating in grain market futures in 1903, shortly after Harry had graduated from high school in 1901.[3] John had been raised a Democrat, had attended the Democratic Convention in 1900 in Kansas City, and had instilled in his son a belief in the traditional rightness of the Democratic Party. Harry was to be an ardent partisan throughout his life.

In 1903, the Trumans moved to Kansas City; and Harry, who had had his hopes for a military career dashed when his eyes proved to be too poor to meet the requirements for entrance to West Point, went to work. During the summer he had been a timekeeper for a railroad contractor and had worked for two weeks in the mailing room of *The Kansas City Star*. By 1904 when his parents moved back to the Young farm at Grandview, Harry stayed on in Kansas City as a bank clerk and cashier at the National Bank of Commerce and later as a bookkeeper at the Union National Bank. By 1906 he was needed back on the farm. During the following years he farmed the land with his father.[4] John Truman died in 1914, and Harry went to war in 1917. He came back to the farm after his military duty in France. He was a farmer when he took his first public office in 1922.

From this experience Truman derived certain habits and beliefs which were still to characterize him in the spring of 1945. Among these was a devoted Protestantism. His family had been Baptists but not "hard-shell" Baptists. They had gone to a Presbyterian church when they had moved to Independence and, later, Truman was to attend Episcopalian services. Thus, his Protestantism was secure but not narrow. Despite his experiences with the rough railroad gang in 1902, despite his years until 1906 working within the "sinful" atmosphere of Kansas City, despite his reaction to the demoralizing impact of fighting in the field in France, and despite his later relationships with the Pendergast machine of Kansas City, he was to maintain a certain rigorous line of Protestant morality. He apparently developed a tendency to see matters, particularly matters about which he had a superficial knowledge, such as foreign affairs, in relatively simple terms of right or wrong, black or white.[5]

It was also during this period that he became a Mason in Belton, Missouri, in 1909. He continued to work within the organization, rising steadily, if slowly, until in 1940 he was elected Grand Master of Masons in Missouri.

Thus, his early life had established for him the role of the average, diligent young man of the middle border of Missouri: Mason, Protestant, Democrat; member of a smalltown, middle-class family, uncertain in its finances but backstopped by a family farm; farmer, both diligent and enterprising; lover, both sensitive and constant; student, above average and devoted to history. This was Harry Truman, uncertain of his future but moving ahead.

Perhaps because of accommodations which he found it necessary to make during his youth, Truman was to become over the years between 1922 and 1945 a practicing, practical politician. His decision to go into politics was made in 1922 after somewhat unfortunate experiences in zinc mining, oil speculation, and the haberdashery business.[6] As a reserve major of artillery, he participated in local veterans' organizations. He gained strength from his lodge connections, from his "old" Missouri family, from his connections with both rural and small-town interests, and, above all, from his relationship with Michael J. (Mike) Pendergast through his son James M. (Jim) Pendergast who had served with Truman in France.[7] The circumstances under which Mike Pendergast, brother of Thomas J. (Tom) Pendergast who controlled the Kansas City Democratic machine, first urged Truman to run for Judge of the County Court for the Eastern District of Jackson County are unclear.[8] It remains certain, however, that he supported Truman in the election of 1922.[9]

Despite his election in 1922, Truman at first had rough going in politics. He was defeated in his effort for reelection in 1924. But he ran successfully in 1926 and was never again defeated in a political campaign. Although he closely allied himself with the Pendergast organization, at that time a practical necessity in Jackson County, Truman was able to establish a reputation for scrupulous honesty in developing an excellent county road system and in building a new county courthouse at Independence. He was useful to the Pendergast organization and the organization helped him. He refused to be ruled by it, but he was always loyal to it. Loyalty and partisan consistency were always basic tenets of Truman's political creed.

Truman was not Tom Pendergast's first choice for the Democratic nomination for United States Senator in 1934. He had already been turned down for Governor and United States Representative and twice for the lucrative job as Collector of Internal Revenue. But Pendergast could obtain the services of no one else. Despite the poor chances of winning the nomination, Truman, the loyal party member, agreed to run. He was aided by his good record as county judge, by his many contacts developed in trips around the state as Federal Reemployment Director of Missouri, a nonpaying job he had taken on in 1933, and by his ability to attract many who opposed Pendergast despite his close support from the machine. He won the nomination handily and was elected easily on a ticket pledging support to Franklin D. Roosevelt's New Deal. Somewhat to his surprise Truman found himself in Washington as the junior Senator from Missouri.

In the Senate, Truman was known originally as the "Gentleman from Pendergast." [10] He was under such a cloud that Roosevelt refused to see him during the first six months he was in Washington. But Truman shrewdly, if slowly, began to rid himself of the stigma. Following a lifelong practice, he quietly observed the Senate's activities and traditions. Later, explaining this technique, he was to write: ". . . I used to watch my father and my mother closely to learn what I could do to please them, just as I did my school-teachers and my playmates. Because of my efforts to get along with my associates I usually was able to get what I wanted. It was successful on the farm, in school, in the Army, *and particularly in the Senate*." [11] He spoke seldom, and then in modest terms. Although he tried to follow the wishes of the Kansas City Democrats, he was not bound by them and occasionally asserted his independence. He supported Roosevelt's legislative proposals with little reservation. Not particularly glib in telling a joke, he was, nevertheless, a popular conversationalist with his fellow Senators; for he was one of those rarities, an excellent listener who really enjoyed the humor of others. He handled his committee assignments well, did his homework so that he was sufficiently well informed, and demonstrated a sincere and beguiling modesty in his relations with other Senators and Members of the House. Although not widely known outside the Senate, by the time he was up for reelection in 1940, he had apparently weathered Tom Pendergast's disgrace in 1939, had developed a reputation as a liberal Senator supporting the New Deal, and had decided to run again.

The odds appeared to be against Truman as he sought a second term. Despite his support for Roosevelt's program, the President had sent him a note late in 1939 indicating that he could not win in Missouri and offering to appoint him to the Interstate Commerce Commission.[12] Earlier that year Tom Pendergast had pleaded guilty to income tax invasion, and Truman's connection with Pendergast's Kansas City machine seemed to create an insurmountable obstacle to his reelection. Truman had, unlike some others, continued his friendship with the discredited Boss. But despite the fact that Roosevelt supported Governor Lloyd C. Stark, his competitor for the nomination, Truman decided to run. He won by a narrow margin against great odds. This time he had won on his own. He had proved himself to be the Senator from Missouri rather than the Senator from Pendergast.

Truman's second term in the Senate marked his rise to considerable national fame as Chairman of the Senate's Special Committee to Investigate the National Defense Program, which was popularly known as the Truman Committee. The Committee had been Truman's idea. He believed that tremendous waste and inefficiency characterized the defense program already beginning to mushroom during 1941. A Senate committee, he reasoned, might check such losses before they began by thoroughly, if quietly, investigating defense practices and publishing recommendations for improvements. At no time did he desire it to become another Joint Committee on the Conduct of the War with which the Congress had so plagued Lincoln during the Civil War. That Committee had concerned itself with operations during the war as well as with other purely military matters clearly within the province of the President as Commander-in-Chief. Truman's Committee would only investigate inefficiencies, bottlenecks, and waste in war production in order to aid the President in directing military operations.

The Truman Committee was one of the best-publicized activities of the Senate during the war. Almost always it had a good press. Favorable references to Truman's name appeared frequently in newspapers throughout the country, and by 1944 his Committee was reported to have saved the taxpayers an estimated fifteen billion dollars.[13] In a poll conducted by *Look Magazine*, Truman was considered by Washington correspondents to be one of the ten most valuable men in Washington in the conduct of the war. He was the only member of Congress listed.[14]

Undoubtedly his reputation as chairman of the Truman Committee was the major positive factor in his selection as the Democratic Vice Presidential candidate in 1944. But other considerations also played a part. Truman was a Protestant; he had developed no major enemies either inside or outside of the Congress; he came from a Middle West border state; his record on civil rights was such that it would not alienate northern Negroes; but his position had not been stated vigorously in public, and some of his best friends in the Congress were from the South; he was well liked by labor and by Roosevelt for his support of the President's policies. Despite these advantages, he was not too well known outside of Washington. Other, more powerful men in the Democratic Party hoped for the nomination in view of the opposition within the party to Vice President Henry A. Wallace and their varying evaluations of the President's health.

Truman neither expected nor sought the nomination prior to the Democratic Convention of 1944.[15] In fact he frequently denied that he would accept it and even agreed to place the name of James F. Byrnes, one of the more likely candidates, in nomination. Truman saw too many others in the field. He also liked his work in the Senate. He had no apparent desire to fill the office which had been a political dead end for many of those who had held it.

All who campaigned for the nomination, however, developed serious political opposition. Vice-President Wallace was opposed by the conservative South and the leaders of the Party's organization in the large cities. He was too liberal. On the other hand, James F. Byrnes, who had resigned from the Supreme Court in 1942 to become Director of the Office of Economic Stabilization and later head of the Office of War Mobilization and who was popularly known as the "Assistant President," was too conservative. He was unacceptable to Edward J. Flynn, the leader of the Democratic organization in the Bronx; to labor, particularly to Sidney Hillman of the Garment Workers; and to the liberal wing of the Party. He was a Catholic who had left the church at the time of his marriage and who might, therefore, alienate the Catholic vote. His association with the South might lose the black vote in the large northern cities. Byrnes, like Wallace, thought he had Roosevelt's support.

Alben W. Barkley, Majority Leader of the Senate, was another hopeful. He was ruled out on the grounds that he was too old, although he was to run successfully for the office four years later. Justice William O. Douglas of the Supreme Court was one of those acceptable to Roosevelt, but he had little backing beyond that. Since no other was "available," the choice fell on Truman who accepted only after a personal plea from Roosevelt. He was nominated on the second ballot. Throughout the fall of 1944 he campaigned vigorously and was elected with Roosevelt in November. In this way, the quiet man from Missouri, relatively unknown, became first in line to the most powerful position on earth.

During the few months between his inauguration and Roosevelt's death, the new Vice-President fit comfortably back into his beloved Senate. Unlike Wallace he enjoyed his role as President of the Senate. He developed a close relationship with Majority Leader Barkley and Speaker Rayburn of the House of Representatives, and managed the give-and-take of debate with an experienced touch. Perhaps he missed the lost prestige of chairing his committee; undoubtedly he recognized the decline in his influence as he moved from active Senator to the Chair. But as a faithful Democrat, as a man who gave his loyalty to those who had supported him, he filled the role with his usual energy. Somewhat paradoxically, on April 11, just one day away from that awesome power of the Presidency, he was able to exercise one of his powers as Vice-President. When the opposition proposed to limit the President's power on the renewal of the Lend-Lease Act by forbidding him to use the program for postwar relief, reconstruction, or rehabilitation in foreign states, Truman used his vote to break a 39-39 tie by voting "no." [16]

To those characteristics reflecting Truman's early life and political career, add another which may be significant in analyzing his decision to use the atomic bomb. Truman was both personally and publicly honest when it came to handling the money of others. To a certain degree this resulted from a family training which taught him that honest people always paid their debts. Thus, when his haberdashery store folded in 1922 he refused to take the easy way out by declaring bankruptcy; and, although it took fifteen years, he eventually met all of his obligations.[17]

During his tenure as Judge of Jackson County Court, Truman was openly proud of his efficiency, frugality, and honesty. Despite frequent charges aimed at the Pendergast machine, Harry Truman was never implicated. Associated with the Kansas City machine, he found it necessary to be purer than pure. Not even his most bitter enemies were able to charge him with dishonesty. When money was appropriated for roads, he saw to it that the public got good roads. When he constructed a new courthouse, he made sure that it was well built.

It was, thus, consistent with his principles and experience when he suggested the creation of his Senate Committee to insure efficiency and honesty in defense expenditures during World War II. By thorough investigation and responsible publicity before waste occurred, he would "save" the people billions of dollars. And in all of their investigations, he and his committee were apparently above persuasion in the conclusions they drew.

In a personal sense, Truman had the poor man's approach to money. Roosevelt, the patrician, never short of funds, seldom carried cash. Truman, the common man, always had plenty in his wallet.[18] It was as if his frequent experience with insufficient assets had impressed on him the importance of ready cash. Money brought with it respectability. And he wanted to be respectable. He had a sense of the importance of small transactions. At the time he became President, his grocer is reported to have said, "Mr. Truman [was] a man who everlastingly [knew] the price of a can of peas." [19]

Thus, it was a man who had been careful of unwarranted expenditures who made the decision to use the atomic bomb. He was a man who would reasonably have been sympathetic to arguments that the two billion dollars spent on the project should not prove to be a waste, and, more important, that it should not appear as a waste to Congress and to the people of the United States. Much money had been spent in developing the product. Under the conditions which existed, it most likely seemed reasonable to Truman to justify the expenditure by demonstrating the usefulness of the weapon in ending the war.

Along with his respect for money, Truman brought to the White House a profound respect for history which he had developed since his early school days. To Truman, history was always men, not concepts or trends. His earliest reading included *Abbott's Lives*, and *Great Men and Famous Women* edited by Charles F. Horne. These books were written to impress upon the young the virtues of the great and the good.[20] During his boyhood he also read and reread the family copy of *Plutarch's Lives* and later was frequently struck with the similarities between ancient and present political problems. Stories about soldiers were his favorites, and tales of the heroes of the Civil War provided the basis for his desire to attend West Point and for his later military activity in the Missouri National Guard.

From his study of the history of the United States, particularly of its wars and its Presidents, he developed an emotional patriotism which was the result of the educational system of his times. He was convinced that the United States had a mission to perform and that its cause was intrinsically right. From his investigation into the lives of successive Presidents, he developed a certain understandable awe of the office and its responsibilities. He has said about it, "The Presidency of the United States is a terrible responsibility for one man . . ."; and "The President has an executive job that is almost fantastic. There has never been one like it. I think no absolute monarch has ever had such decisions to make or the responsibility that the President . . . has. It is really fantastic. . ." And again, "No man really can fill the Presidency. The Presidency has too many and too great responsibilities. All a man can do is try to meet them. He must be able to judge men, delegate responsibility and back up those he trusts." [21]

To Truman there was ". . . nothing new in the world except the history you do not know." [22] He saw history as a series of exciting examples of human greatness. The great included among others Darius of Persia, Alexander of Greece, Marcus Aurelius Antonius and Julius Caesar of Rome, Hannibal of Carthage, Henry the Fourth and Napoleon Bonaparte of France, and Jefferson and Jackson of the United States.[23] The legions of the great more immediately included the leaders of the United Nations in World War II—Roosevelt and Churchill, Stimson and Marshall, Forrestal and Leahy. Roosevelt was now dead, but the others remained to fight the good fight with Harry S. Truman. He now filled that awesome position; he now operated among the great.

The impact of history upon Truman's thinking at the time he became President should, however, be considered in the light of his very real humility. Harry Truman was seldom pretentious. When he first arrived in Washington, he distinguished himself by his studiousness, by his quietness, and by his unwillingness to act any differently toward others as Senator than he had toward his neighbors back in Missouri. Joe Martin, who was at the time an established leader of the Republican Party, recalls that, at his first meeting with Truman prior to World War II, Truman ". . . was very modest and unassuming, and as we chatted, I could as easily have imagined him setting [sic] on the moon as occupying the White House." [24]

Truman was a Senator who would call on a Washington correspondent from an opposition Missouri paper to request advice about Washington and his new job. He was a Senator who seldom presumed to speak on the floor and then only for a limited time. He was the Senator who did his job with little publicity and with few efforts to project his image on the national political scene.

The differences between him and Roosevelt became obvious during the campaign of 1944 and his short period as Vice-President in 1945.

Roosevelt always was confident. For a time Truman seemed to lack self-assurance. Roosevelt enjoyed flattery, though he did not demand it. Truman was a little embarrassed by it. Roosevelt felt good about his patrician ancestry. Truman was satisfied with his own Missouri farm origin. Roosevelt loved to talk and tell stories. Truman was a better listener. Roosevelt laughed engagingly at his own stories. . . . Truman laughed best when a friend told him a good one.[25]

Truman, a small, quiet, attentive man, was to replace the more flamboyant, forceful extrovert who had been President for over twelve long years.

Truman's reactions when he became President demonstrated his characteristic humility. Some saw in them weakness; but others recognized them for what they were—evidence of the almost overwhelming awe of the position which so quickly had been thrust upon him and the native self-effacement of a modest man.

On his way to the White House for his first morning on the job he stopped his car to give Ernest B. Vaccaro, a reporter for the Associated Press, a lift. During the ride Truman remarked in "quiet, almost prayerful tones" that ". . . few men in history equalled the one into whose shoes [he] was stepping and that [he] silently prayed to God that [he] could measure up to the task." [26]

At noon that same day he again did the unusual. He arranged for luncheon with the leaders of Congress in the office of Les Biffle, Secretary of the Senate. On leaving the luncheon he was surrounded by reporters with whom he shook hands and said: "Boys . . . if you ever pray, pray for me now. I don't know whether you fellows ever had a load of hay fall on you, but when they told me yesterday what had happened, I felt like the moon, the stars, and all the planets had fallen on me. I've got the most terribly responsible job a man ever had." [27]

On April 16, the Monday following Roosevelt's burial at Hyde Park, Truman delivered his first message to Congress. Some of its excerpts again demonstrate his plea for support, his self-effacement, and his humility. It was, on the whole, a strong speech assuring the continuation of Roosevelt's policies. But it was couched in terms which expressed his plea for help, from the people, from Congress, and from God: "With great humility I call upon all Americans to help me keep our nation united in defense of those ideals which have been so eloquently proclaimed by Franklin Roosevelt." And, later: "You, the Members of Congress, surely know how I feel. Only with your help can I hope to complete one of the greatest tasks ever assigned to a public servant. With Divine guidance, and your help, we will find a new passage to a far better world, a kindly and friendly world, with just and lasting peace." And, finally: "At this moment, I have in my heart a prayer. As I have assumed my heavy duty, I humbly pray Almighty God, in the words of King Solomon:

" 'Give therefore thy servant an understanding heart to judge thy people, that I may discern between good and bad; for who is able to judge this thy so great people?'

"I ask only to be a good and faithful servant of my Lord and my people." [28]

Some of his associates like Senator Barkley thought he was carrying his self-depreciation too far, both for his own interests and for the prestige of the Presidency. Barkley went to him, as did some of the others, and urged him to stop minimizing his ability to carry on with his tasks. Barkley recalls that he said to Truman:

'. . . God raised up leaders. We do not know the process, but, in the wisdom of Almighty God, you have been made President. You will have all of the help any of us can give you. Have confidence in yourself. If you do not, the people will lose confidence in you. However humble and contrite you feel, you have got to go forward and lead this nation out of war. Have trust in the God Who brought this about and He will enable you do do what you have to do.' [29]

Truman thanked the Majority Leader, who later concluded that his warning had been effective. "Gradually," Barkley wrote, "he grew more sure of himself and, commencing to act with vigor and assurance, he became a forceful and confident Chief Executive." [30]

It would appear, therefore, that Truman in these early days after his succession, self-trained in the history and responsibilities of the Office and recognizing his own limitations, was quite understandably very uncertain of himself and of his capabilities. When he recalled his first meeting with Roosevelt in 1935, he described how courteous Roosevelt was to him and then commented, "It was quite an event for a country boy to go calling on the President of the United States." [31] Now that Roosevelt was dead it was a much greater event for the country boy to enter the White House.

Truman's knowledge of the responsibilities of the Presidency and his feeling of inadequacy predisposed him to delegate authority to those who had been responsible for the war effort under Roosevelt. He had already demonstrated in his assignments to members of the Truman Committee that he believed in assigning responsibility to others.[32] Now as a new President, surrounded by men he believed to be both great and competent, it would have seemed presumptuous to have asked them to resign. One of his first acts on April 12, therefore, was to assure the Roosevelt cabinet that he had no desire to remove them and that he would continue ". . . both the foreign and the domestic policies of the Roosevelt administration." [33]

The next morning he met for the first time with the Joint Chiefs of Staff, Stimson, and Forrestal and said much the same thing. He directed them ". . . to adhere to the same lines of procedure [they] had followed with his predecessor."[34] After the meeting he successfully urged Leahy to stay on as his Chief of Staff in the same role the Admiral had filled under Roosevelt. Leahy later recalled that one of his first tasks was to draft a reply to Churchill's letter of condolence on Roosevelt's death. Truman wrote to Churchill in part: ". . . I wish to send you this personal assurance that, with God's help, I will do everything in my power to move forward the great work to which President Roosevelt gave his life . . ." [35]

In his address to Congress on April 16, he assured his listeners that he would carry on in seeking the ends of the Roosevelt administration. He strongly proclaimed that the United States would ". . . never become a party to any plan for partial victory . . .!" Its demand had been and remained ". . . Unconditional Surrender"! [36]

Despite his willingness to carry on Roosevelt's policies and despite his inclination to delegate authority to those who worked with the former President, Truman had a strong sense of his own responsibility for decision-making. From his first assumption of office, he never shirked the burden of final action. In fact, his tendency seems to have been to rely heavily on the advice of those who worked with Roosevelt and then to make quick and definite decisions. Perhaps this attitude stemmed from his knowledge of the functions of the Presidency, perhaps from certain insecurities which he camouflaged by openly positive action; but, whatever the cause, a reading of Truman's record leaves one with the feeling that he seemed to be pre-occupied with the necessity for making decisions. He emphasized to that first cabinet meeting that he would assume full responsibility for the decisions he might have to make.[37] Later, commenting on the Presidency, he emphasized that ". . . every final important decision has to be made right here on the President's desk, and only the President can make it. . . ." [38] Throughout those early days as President, his letters home to "Mama and Mary" held allusions to "making all sorts of decisions, everyone of which would touch millions of people . . . ," and the necessity for him ". . . to begin making decisions an hour and a half before [he] was sworn in . . . ," and that he had ". . . been making them ever since." [39] He knew all too well that he must formally make important decisions. His most important ones at this time were to follow Roosevelt's policies and to delegate their implementation to the men who had carried out such responsibilities under his predecessor.

And yet this was quite probably a necessity for the new President, for he was quite unavoidably ignorant of many of the factors relating to the international position of the United States. He had never really been involved in the operations of the Roosevelt administration. Roosevelt, it is true, relegated to his Vice-President responsibility for smoothing relations between the White House and the Senate, for engineering Senatorial confirmation for former Vice-President Henry A. Wallace's nomination as Secretary of Commerce, and for helping to steer certain pieces of legislation through the upper house of Congress. But he seldom, if ever, discussed foreign or military policy with his Vice-President.

In fact, Roosevelt had seldom talked personally with Truman between the time of his nomination in July, 1944, and April, 1945. On August 18 he had lunched with Truman to discuss campaign plans.[40] On September 9 he had again lunched with Truman. He had talked with Truman for about half an hour on October 3. On November 10, after their election victory, Roosevelt had ridden with Truman in the victory parade from Union Station to the White House.[41] Another luncheon with Truman had occurred on December 21. On January 2 and January 9, 1945, the President had met with his Congressional leaders, Wallace, Rayburn, Barkley, McCormack, and Truman at the White House. He had attended inauguration ceremonies with his Vice-President and soon afterward had left for the Crimea Conference. On his return he again had consulted Truman, Rayburn, Barkley, and McCormack at the White House on March 8 and March 19. But that was all. Aside from a few cabinet meetings where Roosevelt seldom discussed anything important, Truman had talked extensively with the President only twice since his inauguration and then in the company of Congressional leaders. In fact, during the campaign, after the election, and following the inauguration, Truman had only been with Roosevelt ten times during which conversation was possible, and the meetings apparently did not involve foreign or defense policy.[42] Obviously Roosevelt had not groomed his Vice-President for the responsibility of assuming the Presidency.

The result was that Truman knew little specific about foreign or defense policy when he came to office on April 12. He had supported Roosevelt's domestic policies and was familiar with them.[43] But he found it necessary to rely on Roosevelt's men to inform him about the history of the war and about United States relations abroad. He called on James F. Byrnes for information on the Crimea Conference. He relied on Admiral Leahy, Harry Hopkins, and Averell Harriman for accounts of the relations with the Soviet Union and Great Britain. He was not to be informed of the existence of the atomic program until soon after he had become President.[44] Here, then, was a man facing overwhelming responsibilities, operating with considerable ignorance, and dealing with a number of strong-willed, knowledgeable men who had long been intimately involved with defense and foreign policy, who now had to make the decisions which would involve the future of the United States. His reasonable course was to act in line with how he was instructed Roosevelt might have acted.

Accounts left by his associates indicate their uncertainty of Truman's capacity for the Presidency, their efforts to lead him along the way already planned, and their support for his efforts to carry on after Roosevelt. Leader of the Republican opposition, Senator Arthur H. Vandenberg, somewhat tersely wrote in his diary on April 12:

President Roosevelt died today. . . . The gravest questionmark in every American heart is about Truman. Can he swing the job? Despite his limited capacities, I believe he can.[45]

Churchill, in later considering his decision not to attend Roosevelt's funeral, commented with characteristic clarity on Truman's position:

. . . It seemed to me extraordinary, especially during the last few months, that Roosevelt had not made his deputy and potential successor thoroughly acquainted with the whole story and brought him into the decisions that were being taken. This proved of great disadvantage to our affairs. There is no comparison between reading about events afterwards and living through them from hour to hour. . . . The Vice-President of the United States steps at a bound from a position where he has little information and less power into supreme authority. How could Mr. Truman know and weigh the issues at stake at this climax of the war? Everything that we have learnt [sic] about him since shows him to be a resolute and fearless man, capable of making the greatest decisions. In these early months his position was one of extreme difficulty, and did not enable him to bring his outstanding qualities fully into action.[46]

Churchill rightly described the temporary lapse in Presidential leadership. The void was to be filled by the joint efforts of the holdovers from the Roosevelt regime.

One of these was James F. Byrnes. Only recently resigned from the Roosevelt administration, Byrnes was quickly called back to Washington and just as quickly closeted with the new President to inform him not only of domestic political difficulties but also of what had transpired at the Crimea Conference. Byrnes, who had come so close to the Vice-Presidential nomination, clearly recognized Truman's difficulties. He wrote later:

The task of the President at that time was unusually heavy. President Roosevelt had found it unbearably hard to conduct our foreign affairs in time of war and at the same time kept pace with events on the domestic front. He had had years of experience in the office and had learned to live with his problems as they accumulated; in contrast, President Truman was facing without warning unfamiliar hazards both at home and abroad, with his Secretary of State necessarily absent from the capital. While I remained in Washington I saw him daily, giving him what help I could.[47]

Although Byrnes did not remain long in Washington that April, he was able to inform Truman of many of the programs bequeathed to him by Roosevelt, including that of the atomic bomb.[48]

The reactions of Admiral Leahy, Roosevelt's Chief of Staff, were somewhat more graphic as he wrote in his *Diary* on April 12:

One cannot yet see how the complicated critical business of the war and the peace can be carried forward by a new President who is completely inexperienced in international affairs. The Captain of the Team is gone, and we are all at loose ends and confused as to who may be capable of giving sage advice and council to the new leader in his handling of the staggering burdens of war and peace that he must carry.[49]

The next day Leahy was impressed with the ". . . President's expressed desire and intention to follow accurately the procedure established by Mr. Roosevelt." [50] Truman at that time asked him to stay on as Chief of Staff, and during the weeks that followed he became one of the new President's most influential advisers. He and Harry Hopkins spent long hours schooling Truman in the affairs of the nation.[51]

It was, however, Stimson, who had been responsible for the development of the atomic weapon, who was, perhaps, most interested in the views of the new President and in guiding them to fit the requirements of the war situation as he had seen it develop. He believed correctly that the President had heard nothing of the atomic bomb, and he wished to enlighten Truman in such a way that he would support the continuation of the project. The Secretary of War described his thoughts during the evening of April 12 when Truman had been sworn in:

No one knows what the new President's views are—at least I don't. But we all feel that there is nothing to do but to close in and take a solid phalanx along the pattern which had been followed hitherto. Stettinius, Forrestal and I said something to that effect in our answers to Truman's statement to the group. . . .

The new President on the whole made a pleasant impression but it was very clear that he knew very little of the task into which he was stepping and he showed some vacillations on minor matters that came up for decision a little bit as if he might be lacking in force. I hope not.[52]

In his next *Diary* entry on April 13 he noted:

He (Truman) made the impression on me of a man who is willing and anxious to learn and to do his best but who was necessarily laboring with the terrific handicap of coming into such an office where the threads of information were so multitudinous that only long previous familiarity could allow him to control them.[53]

And so the "solid phalanx" of the experience formed around Truman, the new President.

Truman, it seems, was ignorant about the major problems of war and peace. His humility and his penchant for delegating authority to the experienced led him to rely on those who had been intimately involved with handling such problems under Roosevelt. He would work hard, and he would learn. But there was insufficient time before the war's end to become more than superficially competent in understanding the problems facing him. As he soon began to discover the facts concerning the development of the atomic bomb, it became clear to him not only that he would have to rely on the advice of those who had participated in its construction but also that, if it failed, he would have to explain to the United States and the Congress the ". . . greatest and most costly fizzle in the history of the world." [54] He was now dealing with great men, with the men who made history. And to him two of the greatest were Marshall and Stimson.[55] It was largely on their advice that he would rely as he began to make the intermediate decisions which would lead ultimately to his authorization to drop the bombs on Hiroshima and Nagasaki. Truman had just left the top of the slide. Within the restrictions imposed by his circumstances, his character, and his associates, there was little chance either to stop or to get off.

NOTES TO CHAPTER 5

[1] The timing of the ceremony is uncertain. Truman reports that he had finished taking the oath by 7:09 P.M. Harry S. Truman, *Memoirs: Year of Decisions* (Garden City: Doubleday and Company, Inc., 1955), I, 8. In his diary, Forrestal records the time as 6:45 P.M. Walter Millis (ed.), *The Forrestal Diaries* (New York: The Viking Press, Inc., 1951), p. 43. And Leahy indicates that the ceremony took place at 7:10 P.M. Leahy, *Diaries*, XI, 56.

[2] Jackson County includes Kansas City. The best accounts of Truman's life appear in his *Memoirs*; in William Hillman, *Mr. President* (New York: Farrar, Straus and Young, 1952); and in Jonathan Daniels, *The Man of Independence* (Philadelphia: J. B. Lippincott Company, 1950).

[3] Daniels, *The Man of Independence*, pp. 59–60.

[4] *Ibid.*, pp. 67–74.

[5] In recalling his leave in Paris just after the armistice in 1918, Truman has written about the "disgusting performance" he saw at the *Folies Bergere*, the "gambling hell" of the Casino at Monte Carlo, and the "let down" he and his buddies felt when they saw the Princess of Monaco drinking beer in the Casino de Paris. See Hillman, *Mr. President*, pp. 172–73.

[6] See p. 105.

[7] Daniels, *The Man of Independence*, p. 109.

[8] Truman's accounts in his *Memoirs*, I, 136–37, and in Hillman, *Mr. President*, p. 173–74, contain slightly differing versions. Judges of county courts in Missouri are

administrative rather than legal officers. They levy taxes; make expenditures for roads, homes for the aged, schools for delinquent children; and support the insane in state institutions.

[9] Truman had held certain other political positions in the county prior to this time. He had been overseer of roads in Washington Township of Jackson County, Democratic clerk at every election since 1906, and a postmaster at Grandview for a period before World War I. Truman, *Memoirs*, I, 137.

[10] Daniels, *The Man of Independence*, p. 175 ff.

[11] Italics are supplied. See Truman, *Memoirs*, I, 125.

[12] Daniels, *The Man of Independence*, p. 197.

[13] Truman, *Memoirs*, I, 186.

[14] Daniels, *The Man of Independence*, pp. 227–28.

[15] Much remains to be clarified concerning the race for Vice-President during 1944. Certain discrepancies appear in the accounts which exist, and many are personal points of view reflecting either satisfaction or dissatisfaction with Roosevelt's actions. The following account relies in part on: Alben W. Barkley, *That Reminds Me* (Garden City: Doubleday and Company, Inc., 1954) pp. 188–91; James F. Byrnes, *All in One Lifetime* (New York: Harper and Brothers, 1958), pp. 216–32; Daniels, *The Man of Independence*, pp. 230–54; James A. Farley, *Jim Farley's Story: The Roosevelt Years* (New York: McGraw-Hill Book Company, Inc., 1948), pp. 363–68; Edward J. Flynn, *You're The Boss* (New York: The Viking Press, Inc., 1947), pp. 178–83; William D. Leahy, *I Was There* (New York: McGraw-Hill Book Company, Inc., 1950), pp. 147–48; Russell Lord, *The Wallaces of Iowa*, (Boston: Houghton Mifflin Company, 1947), pp. 526—41; Samuel I. Rosenman, *Working with Roosevelt,* (New York: Harper and Brothers, 1952), pp. 438–54; Truman, *Memoirs*, I, 187–93; Grace Tully, *F. D. R. My Boss* (New York: Charles Scribner's Sons, 1949), pp. 275–77.

[16] *The New York Times*, April 12, 1945, p. 1.

[17] Hillman, *Mr. President*, p. 173; Daniels, *The Man of Independence*, pp. 105–9.

[18] William M. Rigdon with James Derieux, *White House Sailor* (Garden City: Doubleday and Company, Inc. 1962), pp. 182–83.

[19] John Chamberlain, "Washington in June," *Life*, XVIII (June 11, 1945), 102.

[20] Daniels, *The Man of Independence*, pp. 50–51.

[21] Truman quoted in Hillman, *Mr. President*, p. 10.

[22] *Ibid.*, p. 81.

[23] *Ibid.*, pp. 81–87.

[24] Joe Martin, *My First Fifty Years in Politics*, p. 177.

[25] Rigdon, *White House Sailor*, p. 182.

[26] Truman, *Memoirs*, I, 13; Bernard Asbell, *When F. D. R. Died* (New York: Holt, Rinehart and Winston, Inc., 1961), p. 137.

[27] Truman, *Memoirs*, I, 19.

[28] *Public Papers of the Presidents of the United States*: *Harry S. Truman, 1945* (Washington: United States Government Printing Office, 1961), pp. 1–6. This work contains the complete text.

[29] Barkley, *That Reminds Me*, p. 197.

[30] *Ibid.*, p. 197.

[31] Hillman, *Mr. President*, p. 24.

[32] *The New York Times*, April 15, 1945.

[33] Truman, *Memoirs*, I, 9.

[34] Leahy, *I Was There*, p. 347.

[35] *Ibid.*, p. 348.

[36] *Public Papers of the Presidents of the United States: Harry S. Truman, 1945*, p. 2.

37 Truman, *Memoirs*, I, 9.

38 Hillman, *Mr. President*, p. 10.

39 Truman, *Memoirs*, I, 63, 74, 293–94. "Mary" was the President's sister, Miss Mary Jane Truman.

40 The dates of these meetings appear in the copy of the Presidential Appointment Diary kept by Roosevelt's secretary, Miss Grace Tully. They were corroborated by entries in a similar diary kept for Mrs. Roosevelt. The diaries do not indicate the nature of the discussions. They are now in the Roosevelt files at the Franklin D. Roosevelt Library at Hyde Park, New York: F. D. R. Group 13, P. P. F. 1–0 (2), *Presidential Appointment Diaries*, 1943-45, Box 192. See William D. Hassett, *Off the Record with F. D. R.* (New Brunswick: Rutgers University Press, 1958), 1942-1945, p. 265.

41 Hassett, *Off the Record with F.D.R.*, 1942-1945, pp. 395–96.

42 Daniels, *The Man of Independence*, p. 259. Daniels cites the Roosevelt files to indicate eight meetings. He has apparently omitted the November 10 parade and the inauguration on January 20 .

43 See William S. White, *Majesty and Mischief: A Mixed Tribute to F.D.R.* (New York: McGraw-Hill Book Company, Inc., 1961) for an analysis which indicates that for some time prior to his death Roosevelt had been moving to the right away from his former New Deal positions and that Truman's continued support for the former liberalism constituted what to Roosevelt would have seemed an anachronism.

44 See p. 112.

45 Arthur H. Vandenberg, Jr. (ed.), *The Private Papers of Senator Vandenberg* (Boston: Houghton Mifflin Company, 1952), p. 165.

46 Winston S. Churchill, *The Second World War: Triumph and Tragedy* (Boston:, Houghton Mifflin Company, 1953), VI, 479–80.

47 James F. Byrnes, *All in One Lifetime*, p. 280. During most of Truman's first three months in office, Secretary of State Stettinius was at the United Nations conference in San Francisco.

48 See p. 116–17.

49 Leahy, *Diaries*, XI, 1945, 55.

50 *Ibid.*, p. 56.

51 Rigdon, *White House Sailor*, p. 184. See also Leahy, *I Was There*, pp. 248–49, and Sherwood, *Roosevelt and Hopkins*, p. 883.

52 Stimson, *Diary*, April 12, 1945 .

53 *Ibid.*, April 13, 1945.

54 Daniels, *The Man of Independence*, p. 266.

55 See Churchill, *Triumph and Tragedy*, p. 481, for Lord Halifax's evaluation of Truman's veneration of Marshall.

CHAPTER **6**

THE INTERIM COMMITTEE

HARRY S. Truman came to the Presidency unprepared to solve the difficult problems which faced him. He recognized his insufficiencies, however, and sought the counsel of those who had been close to Roosevelt and involved in the tremendous undertakings occasioned by the war. This was particularly so in the case of the atomic bomb project, for in that area Truman was most uninformed. After his first Cabinet session as President on April 12, 1945, he had been told by Stimson of an immense project which had been developing a new explosive of tremendous power. The Secretary of War, however, had not felt it necessary at that time to provide the new President with details of the project. On April 13, James F. Byrnes had given Truman additional information on the new project. Since Byrnes had had only a brief relationship with the atomic bomb program, it is doubtful that this conversation could be considered a briefing. Later, perhaps that same day, Vannevar Bush called at the White House to present a scientist's view of the bomb.[1]

It was not, however, until nearly two weeks later that Truman was adequately briefed. Preoccupied with other more pressing matters, he gave little attention to the atomic bomb; and in line with his general approach he permitted those who had been responsible for its development to continue in authority.

Secretary of War Stimson, who carried overall responsibility for the project, took the initiative in briefing Truman on the anticipated nature of the weapon and on the domestic and international problems associated with its use. On April 24 Stimson prepared a memorandum on the prospects of atomic energy development and on the problems which the atomic program might pose for the United States. He then wrote to Truman to ask him for an appointment to discuss the matter. Stimson had prepared his memorandum on the basis of a summary of the S-1 program which had been presented to him the previous day by General Groves and George L. Harrison, his Special Consultant.[2] During the morning of April 25, Stimson carefully reviewed his memorandum with Harrison and Bundy and later showed it to Groves and General Marshall. All approved the document.[3]

At the same time Stimson decided that General Marshall should not accompany him when he went to the White House. The close watch which reporters maintained on Marshall might endanger the secrecy of the project. In place of Marshall, General Groves was asked to be present at the White House meeting. He was directed to go to the White House separately and to enter by the back door. Stimson preceded him to the conference. Groves was admitted a short time after Stimson had begun to brief Truman.[4]

During the short period prior to Groves' appearance, Stimson had impressed Truman with the revolutionary nature of the new weapon and the effects it might have on civilization, as well as the decisive influence it would have on United States foreign relations.[5] He then presented his S-1 memorandum to Truman:

1. Within four months we shall in all probability have completed the most horrible weapon ever known in human history, one bomb of which could destroy a whole city.
2. Although we have shared its development with the U.K., physically the U.S. is at present in the position of controlling the resources with which to construct and use it and no other nation could reach this position for some years.

3. Nevertheless it is practically certain that we could not remain in this position indefinitely.

   (a) Various segments of its discovery and production are widely known among many scientists in many countries, although few scientists are now acquainted with the whole process which we have developed.

   (b) Although its construction under present methods requires great scientific and industrial effort and raw materials, which are temporarily mainly within the possession and knowledge of U.S. and U.K., it is extremely probable that much easier and cheaper methods of production will be discovered by scientists in the future, together with the use of materials of much wider distribution. As a result, it is extremely probable that the future will make it possible to be constructed by smaller nations, or at least by a large nation in a much shorter time.

4. As a result, it is indicated that the future may see a time when such a weapon may be constructed in secret and used suddenly and effectively with devastating power by a willful nation or group against an unsuspecting nation or group of much greater size and material power. With its aid even a very powerful unsuspecting nation might be conquered within a very few days by a very much smaller one. . . .

5. The world in its present state of moral advancement compared with its technical development would be eventually at the mercy of such a weapon. In other words, modern civilization might be completely destroyed.

6. To approach any world peace organization of any pattern now likely to be considered, without an appreciation by the leaders of our country of the power of this new weapon, would seem to be unrealistic. No system of control heretofore considered would be adequate to control this menace. Both inside any particular country and between nations of the world, the control of this weapon will undoubtedly be a matter of the greatest difficulty and would involve such thoroughgoing rights of inspection and internal controls as we have never heretofore contemplated.

7. Furthermore, in the light of our present position with reference to this weapon, the question of sharing it with other nations and, if so shared, upon what terms, becomes a primary question of our foreign relations. Also our leadership in the war and in the development of this weapon has placed a certain moral responsibility upon us which we cannot shirk without serious responsibility for any disaster to civilization which it would further.

8. On the other hand, if the problem of the proper use of this weapon can be solved, we would have the opportunity to bring the world into a pattern in which the peace of the world and our civilization can be saved.

9. As stated in General Groves' report, steps are underway looking towards the establishment of a select committee of particular qualifications for recommending action to the Executive [sic] and legislative branches of our government when secrecy is no longer in full effect. The committee would also recommend the actions to be taken by the War Department prior to that time in anticipation of the postwar problems. All recommendations would of course be first submitted to the President.[6]

The President was deeply impressed with Stimson's concern over the impact the bomb would have in shaping the future history of the world and with his hopes of imminent success.

After Groves had joined the conference, Truman read the memorandum Groves had prepared on April 23. The President asked many questions which Stimson answered. Groves answered queries involving the manufacturing process. Much of the conversation involved international affairs, particularly relations with the Soviet Union. As the conference ended Truman agreed that the project should be continued and expressed confidence in the capabilities of Stimson and Groves to carry it through to a successful conclusion.[7] He authorized the establishment of a committee to function as Stimson had suggested in paragraph 9 of his memorandum.[8]

By April 25, then, Truman had been extensively briefed on the state of the S-1 program as well as on possible future repercussions which possession of the weapon might have on United States foreign relations and on the very existence of civilization. Problems of establishing domestic and international control of the weapon, of relating it to the emerging United Nations, of sharing United States knowledge with other states, and of planning for its proper use loomed before him. A committee of experts chosen from interested government agencies would be invaluable in giving him the advice he needed to resolve such issues. His lack of scientific knowledge of S-1 and the magnitude of the weapon obliged him, in the name of prudence, to rely on such advice. Thus, the way was cleared for a continuity of policy and for the continuing control of the weapon by those who had worked so hard in its development.

But Truman's assertion that he chose the committee can only be accepted in the sense that he authorized Stimson to go ahead with its formation. For the committee had been in the administrative works long before Truman assumed control of the government. It, too, was part of the legacy which he had inherited from his predecessor.

Perhaps the earliest roots of the committee lay in the concern of those involved in the development of S-1 that plans for its control and use be available when it became a reality. Stimson had foreseen such a need in the late summer of 1944 when he had asked Vannevar Bush and James B. Conant for their views on the postwar international effects of the atomic weapon. Bush and Conant had replied in a memorandum to Stimson on September 30, 1944, in which they had made six points:

1. "There is every reason to believe that before August 1, 1945, atomic bombs will have been demonstrated. . . ."
2. "The art will expand rapidly after the war, and the military aspects may become overwhelming."
3. "Unless it develops that Germany is much further along than is now believed it is probable that the . . . United States . . . [is] . . . in a temporary

position of great ascendency. It would be possible, however, for any nation with good technical and scientific resources to reach our present position in three or four years."

4. Basic knowledge was widely known and it would be impossible to maintain complete secrecy after the war. They, therefore, advocated complete disclosure of the history of the development of S-1 except for manufacturing and military details as soon as the first bomb had been detonated. "This demonstration might be over enemy territory, or in our own country, with subsequent notice to Japan that the materials would be used against the Japanese mainland unless surrender was forthcoming."

5. Partial secrecy would lead to a secret international armaments race with Russia and other countries including the defeated enemies.

6. "There is hope that an arms race on this basis can be prevented, and even that the future peace of the world may be furthered, by complete international scientific and technical interchange on this subject, backed up by an international commission acting under the association of nations and having the authority to inspect." [9]

Here, with amazing prescience, they had given an outline of future developments and accompanying problems. At the same time they had indicated the pressing importance of adequate planning for its use and later handling.

Throughout that winter Bush and Bundy were to urge Stimson to name a planning committee. During a conversation with Stimson on December 13, 1944, Bush suggested the formation of a committee to explore and report on the prospects of S-1 and on its postwar control in the United States.[10] On December 16, 1944, Bundy sent a memorandum to Stimson suggesting that ". . . a Commission composed of six might be appointed by the President now to make studies and preliminary recommendations . . ." concerning a public statement the President might make following the use of S-1. He further suggested that the commission include representatives of the Secretary of War, the Secretary of State, and the Secretary of the Navy as well as ". . . three leading scientists familiar with the project." [11] Bush was again after Bundy on January 30, 1945, when he wrote urging that the proposed committee under Mr. Harrison be set up soon. He ended with the admonition that ". . . there is none too much time for them to do their work." [12]

A month later Bush wrote to Bundy describing more specifically the nature of the suggested committee and stating that he had discussed the matter with Conant and Assistant Secretary of State James Dunn at a conference which Bundy had arranged. He felt that General Groves should be advised of the proposal in order to obtain his suggestions before the committee was named. The committee, Bush thought, should deal entirely with postwar matters. He then proposed possible members and tried to exclude as scientific members, Conant and himself, as well as Ernest O. Lawrence and Arthur H. Compton, on grounds of their overburdening administrative responsibilities. Once more he ended on a note of urgency: for ". . . the new committee will have a great deal to do, and the time available is none too long." [13]

There is little evidence of additional efforts to set up the committee during February and March of 1945. Citations in Stimson's *Diary* indicate his growing preoccupation with S-1 and his conviction that its future development required careful planning. He wrote on March 5:

We are up against some very big decisions. The time is approaching when we can no longer avoid them and when events may force us into the public on the matter.

Later that day he called in General Marshall and urged him to begin thinking ". . . on this post-war set of problems." [14] Three days later he again mused that ". . . this matter now is taking up a good deal of my time and even then I am not doing it justice. It is approaching its ripening time and matters are getting very very interesting and serious." [15]

Stimson's growing concern was also evidenced by the increased frequency of his consultations with Bundy on S-1. During this period, Bundy and Harrison were apparently involved in suggesting members for the committee. Although there is little evidence to substantiate this conclusion, a memorandum of March 14 from Bundy to Harrison suggested such continuing activity. The memorandum began as follows: "Other names for the possible top level committee are . . ." and went on to mention Bernard Baruch, Owen Young, Conant, Robert P. Patterson, Dr. Frank Graham; ". . . possible representation from the Hill, Truman, Lister Hill, Sen. George, Sen. Tydings, and possibly one Sen. from the Republican side, also possibly one Dem. and one Rep. from the House." [16] At the same time, Bundy indicated that such congressional representation would not be consistent with a small working committee.[17]

It seems apparent, therefore, that the idea for a planning committee for S-1 had been considered within the War Department for some time before Truman came to office. Some attention had been given to its purpose and to its membership. Stimson was merely describing its evolution when he indicated in paragraph 9 of his memorandum to Truman of April 25 that ". . . steps are underway looking towards the establishment of a select committee of particular qualifications."[18] Truman, it is true, might have stopped its formation. But he had no reason to do so, for the committee met the needs of his intention to rely on Roosevelt's policies and Roosevelt's men to carry him through this period of his unavoidable inadequacy. He, therefore, authorized Stimson to go ahead and appoint a committee. Only indirectly can it be said that he appointed the committee himself.

Developments that occurred between the Stimson-Truman conference of April 25 and May 9 when the Interim Committee held its first informal meeting indicate the key role which Stimson and the War Department played in naming the committee's members and fixing its responsibilities. On May 1 at 10:00 A.M., Harrison and Bundy went to Stimson's office with a memorandum written by Harrison which outlined the need for a committee, indicated its functions, and suggested its membership.[19] The Harrison memorandum is interesting for a number of reasons. It first reviewed Stimson's objectives in suggesting the committee to Truman on April 25. "You had in mind," the memorandum began, "the advisability of setting up a committee of particular qualifications for recommending action to the executive and legislative branches of the government when secrecy is no longer required. The committee would also be expected to recommend actions to be taken by the War Department in anticipation of the post war [sic] problems." [20] There was no indication that the committee was to consider the question of use of the weapon.

The memorandum then went on to indicate the urgency of instituting the committee:

In view of the possibly short time available *before actual military use* and the relaxation of secrecy, it seems to me—and as you know both Dr. Conant and Dr. Bush agree—that it is becoming more and more important to organize such a committee as promptly as possible. This committee should, I think, be a relatively small committee which should be prepared to serve . . . until Congress might appoint a permanent Post War Commission [sic] to supervise, regulate and control the use of the product.

Certain things, however, must be done now *before use* if we are to avoid the risk of grave repercussions on the public in general and on Congress in particular.[21]

Such "grave repercussions" as Harrison had in mind were not defined, and it can only be surmised that they might have involved such matters as the necessity for continuing appropriations and the possibility of a critical evaluation of the morality involved in the use of the bomb. Certainly Harrison was presuming that it would be used. This assumption is clearly implied by his following suggestions that the committee should concern itself with preparing the statements to be issued by the President and Secretary of War *after its use* and with steps to provide essential *controls after use*. "It seems clear," the memorandum continued, "that some machinery is essential now to provide for continuous and effective controls and to insure or provide for the necessary and persistent research and development of the possibilities of atomic energy in which the United States now leads the way. If properly controlled by the peace-loving nations of the world this energy should insure the peace of the world for generations. If uninsured it may lead to the complete destruction of civilization." [22] Harrison's memorandum indicated that he felt it most important to plan for postwar regulation and for the control of this new energy by the "peace-loving nations," presumably including the United States. There is no indication that the committee was to decide on whether or not the bomb should be used. The memorandum went on:

In the circumstances I suggest that a committee of six or seven be set up at once to study and report on the whole problem of temporary war controls and publicity, and to survey and make recommendations on post-war research, development and controls, and the legislation necessary to effectuate them.[23]

It concluded with the suggestions that the committee be appointed by the Secretary of War with the President's approval and that it operate through appropriate military, scientific, and legislative panels of advisers. Appended was a list of names suggested for membership: Stimson; Harrison as Stimson's alternate; Conant; Bush; Karl T. Compton; William L. Clayton, Assistant Secretary of State; Ralph A. Bard, Under Secretary of the Navy; and an unnamed special representative of the President.[24]

A number of considerations need to be mentioned concerning these latter suggestions. First, Harrison's suggestion that a committee be set up indicated that, as of May 1, it was not in existence. This refutes Stimson's account that it was named during April.[25] Second, there was no indication that Harrison expected the committee to consider use of the weapon. And, third, the choice of those who were to serve on the committee rested initially on Harrison and probably on Bundy. Stimson accepted Harrison's suggestions for which he later obtained General Marshall's approval. By the time Stimson took his recommendations to Truman, the Interim Committee, with one exception, had in effect been chosen.[26]

On May 2, Stimson again brought the matter to Truman's attention. Truman accepted the list of proposed names but was cool to the addition of any personal representative, a step which he felt was unnecessary. Stimson, who wanted greater political power on the committee, persisted. He said that he would ". . . prefer to have such a representative and suggested that he should be such a man (a) with whom the President had close personal relations, and (b) who was able to keep his mouth shut." Truman then agreed to ". . . try to think up such a man. . . ." [27] The next day Stimson consulted Harrison, Bundy, and Groves, who favored the appointment of James F. Byrnes. They selected Byrnes, whom they expected to be the next Secretary of State, because they thought he had the complete confidence of the President and because he was strong politically.[28] Stimson telephoned Truman to suggest Byrnes; and later in the day Truman called back to say that Byrnes was a fine choice, that he had called him at his home in South Carolina, and that Byrnes had accepted the appointment. Stimson was overjoyed. "So *my* committee is complete," he wrote in his *Diary*. "Bundy and Harrison are tickled to death with this Byrnes suggestion and now we can start to work on preparing for the many things that must be planned for S-1." [29]

Stimson was eager to get started. Following a Cabinet meeting on May 4, he asked Truman when Byrnes would arrive in Washington. He mentioned that the committee's agenda was already in preparation and that he wanted to start committee action as soon as Byrnes arrived. Truman answered that Byrnes was to be available from Saturday, May 5, until the following Wednesday. Stimson expected to be ready to begin meetings on Monday, May 7, or certainly on Tuesday.[30] During the same day he wrote identical letters to the prospective members asking them to serve on the committee. The introductory paragraphs of his letters read:

With the approval of the President, I am appointing an Interim Committee on S-1 to study and report on the whole problem of temporary war controls and later publicity, and to survey and make recommendations on post war [sic] research, development and controls, as well as legislation necessary to effectuate them.[31]

None of the members of the committee, therefore, were informed that they were to make a decision on whether or not to use the bomb. It seems doubtful that this was to be their function.

Harrison stayed in Washington over the weekend in order to describe the S-1 program to Byrnes if he should show up; but it was not until Tuesday, May 8, that the briefing was held. At 3:30 that afternoon, Stimson, Bundy, Harrison, and Groves told Byrnes the story of S-1 and discussed with him the functions of the Interim Committee. Byrnes was apparently well received, for Stimson recorded that ". . . during the meeting it became very evident what a tremendous help Byrnes would be as a member of the Committee." [32]

The first informal meeting of the Interim Committee was held on May 9, 1945, from 9:30 A.M. until 12:30 P.M. All but Conant were present, and Bundy attended by invitation.[33] The opening statement by Stimson indicated that the committee was to ". . . study and report on the entire problem of temporary wartime controls and later publicity, and to survey and make recommendations on postwar research, development, and control, and on legislation necessary for these purposes." [34] He made no reference to the necessity for a decision as to whether or not to use the bomb. Stimson went on to explain the reason for the committee's name and to point out that its recommendations would go first to him and then to the President. After the Secretary had explained the basic facts concerning S-1, the committee went to Harrison's office to hear and discuss Groves' report of April 23. Before it adjourned, the committee also discussed the Quebec Agreement with the United Kingdom.[35] The minutes of this meeting and of those which followed barely indicate the course of events. Seldom was there an indication of the nature of the discussion. Yet certain conclusions can be reached. The committee was learning about a program completely foreign to some of its members. It was interested in the relationship which had developed with the British. It did not discuss the use of the atomic bomb.

A second informal meeting convened May 14, with Harrison in the chair, Conant still absent, and Groves present by invitation. The committee named Arthur H. Compton, Ernest O. Lawrence, J. Robert Oppenheimer, and Enrico Fermi as its advisory scientific panel. Each of these men had been intimately connected with the development of the atomic bomb. At the suggestions of Bush and Conant they were to be permitted to present their views on political as well as scientific aspects of the problem. The choice of a military panel was put off pending further discussion among Stimson, General Marshall, and Admiral King. The committee decided against appointing an industrial panel. They then considered what the President should say if the anticipated bomb test in the United States should occasion wide publicity and designated William L. Laurence of the *New York Times,* under contract to the Manhattan Project, to prepare drafts of public statements to be issued after the bomb was used. They again considered the Quebec Agreement. Copies of a memorandum from certain scientists at Chicago to Arthur H. Compton were distributed to Byrnes and Bard for further study.[36] The question of the future status of the Metallurgical Laboratory at Chicago was put off until ". . . after the weapon was put to offensive use." [37]

Once more, certain conclusions seem important. The use of the bomb was not discussed. But Laurence was to prepare statements to be issued *after its use* and the Metallurgical Laboratory was to continue until *after it might be employed offensively.* The reasonable implication is that use was presumed.

A third informal session met on May 18. Harrison again acted as chairman, Bush was absent, and Groves and Arthur W. Page, a friend and assistant to Stimson, were present by invitation. First, the committee agreed to meetings with the scientific panel and certain interested industrialists on May 31 and June 1. Second, they considered the Quebec Agreement and the British proposal of setting up a committee similar to the Interim Committee in the United Kingdom. And, third, they discussed the nature of publicity to be issued after the first test but before the bomb was dropped on Japan. They agreed that the ". . . nature of the statements would depend in large measure on the results of the test and of the actual use, and that changes might be necessary in terms of the international situation existing at the time of the release." [38] The presumption of use is as always quite obvious. The committee needed only to confirm this at its formal meeting of May 31.

While the Interim Committee was preparing for its full dress meeting on May 31, Stimson was operating outside the committee to prepare the way for the use of the atomic bomb. On May 8, he informed the Secretary of the Navy, James Forrestal, and the Acting Secretary of State, Joseph C. Grew, about the Interim Committee and received their approval of Bard's and Clayton's appointments.[39] The military situation in the Far East came up for review in a short talk with Marshall on May 10. Stimson particularly ". . . wanted to find out whether or not we couldn't hold matters off from very heavy involvement in casualties until after we had tried out S-1. [He] found that probably we could get the trial before the locking of arms came and much bloodshed." [40] He was torn two ways. On the one hand, he wanted a field test of S-1; on the other, he wanted to avoid casualties.

At the same time, Stimson was keeping the British informed of plans for S-1 in line with United States obligations under the Quebec Agreement. On May 14, during a conference at the Pentagon with British Foreign Minister Anthony Eden, he ". . . outlined . . . the progress which . . . [had been] made and the time table as it stood now, and told . . . [Eden his] own feeling as to its bearing upon our present problems of an international character." [41] He asked Eden to transmit this information to Churchill.

The British, however, had already been informed of United States strategic plans for use of the bomb. A British scientist, Dr. W. G. Penney, had been a member of a special group in Washington which, since November, 1944, had been studying possible targets in Japan. He and Groves, who headed the group, had regularly informed Field Marshal Sir Henry Maitland Wilson, head of the British Joint Staff Mission in Washington, of their plans; and Wilson had then been reporting such information to the Lord President of the Council, Sir John Anderson, in London. Through the spring of 1945, the British had been increasingly concerned over the form which their consent to the use of the bomb should take. On April 30 Wilson had informed Anderson that the United States intended to use the bomb in August, 1945. Wilson had also asked for Anderson's views on whether the British should agree to employment of the weapon on Japan, whether any warning should be given, and how British consent should be given. On May 2, Anderson informed Churchill of Wilson's report and suggested that he should consider the British role under the Quebec Agreement and direct Wilson to inform General Marshall that he was consulting with the Prime Minister. But it was not until May 21 that Churchill asked Anderson to draft a reply to Wilson, and the Prime Minister failed to consider Anderson's draft until June 18 when it was finally sent to Washington.[42] Churchill, it seems, was not extremely concerned with the British participation in planning the use of the bomb. He had tacitly left to the United States that responsibility when he had accepted its lead in producing the weapon, and his immediate problem was merely to devise a suitable method for recording British compliance.

As British-American diplomacy moved toward formal joint acceptance of the weapon's use, preparations for employment of the bomb progressed rapidly within the War Department. The strategy had already been devised by General Groves in consultation with Marshall and Stimson.[43] On May 6 the first ground echelons of the 509th Composite Group sailed for Tinian. They arrived on May 29, shortly after the advance air elements which had flown in on May 18.[44]

Meanwhile, despite the German surrender which removed the urgency from the atomic race, the effort to deliver the first weapon to the 509th went on. At Los Alamos, the need for additional speed in finishing the weapon became pressing. As Oppenheimer later recalled:

. . . After the collapse of Germany, we understood that it was important to get this ready for the war in Japan. We were told that it would be very important— I was told I guess by Mr. Stimson—that it would be very important to know the state of affairs before the meeting at Potsdam at which the future conduct of the war in the Far East would be discussed. . . . I believe we were under incredible pressure to get it done before the Potsdam meeting. . . .

Mr. Garrison has asked me . . . whether there was any change in tempo after the war against Germany ended. There was, but it was upward. It was upward simply because we were still more frantic to have the job done and wanted to have it done so that if needed, it would be available.

In any case, we wanted to have it done before the war was over, and nothing much could be done. I don't think there was any time where we worked harder at the speedup than in the period after the German surrender and the actual combat use of the bomb.

. . . I did suggest to General Groves some changes in the bomb which would make more efficient use of the material . . . He turned them down as jeopardizing the promptness of the availability of bombs . . . the very fact that any delay was involved was unacceptable.[45]

Although General Groves has stated that there was no increase in the urgency to produce the bomb in time to use it against Japan since no one in the government expected the war to end within a reasonably short time, the need to speed the completion of the weapon seems to have been very pressing to those at Los Alamos.[46]

As the completion of the bomb rapidly approached, work continued in the War Department on the draft statement which the President would make after the bomb was dropped. As early as February 13, Bundy had drafted a possible statement which began: "On ——— 1945, the United States Armed Forces used against the enemy an entirely new weapon. . . ." [47] By May 28, the original draft of the statement had been completed and sent to Harrison. It began: "Two hours ago an American airplane dropped a bomb on the Nagasaki Naval Base, and the Naval Base ceased to exist." [48] Of necessity in both cases the presumption of those writing the draft statement was that the bomb would be employed.

To insure funds for its completion while protecting its security against possible leaks from Congressmen, Stimson continued his policy of informing a few selected Congressional leaders of the bomb's development. However, one Congressman, Clair Engle, threatened that unless he saw the S-1 plant he would make a critical and open speech on the floor of the House of Representatives. To blunt this threat, Stimson first mollified Engle and then arranged a visit to the Clinton works by four key members of the House Appropriations Committee on May 17.[49] The trip fulfilled its aims, for Groves was able to inform Stimson on May 30 that the Congressmen were back from Tennessee and that they were now friendly to the project.[50]

By May 31, then, preparations for use of the bomb were well on the way to completion. Stimson had been able to ensure continuing congressional appropriations; the first draft of Truman's declaration was finished; the bomb was being rushed to completion; military preparation for its use were progressing rapidly; and steps had been taken to obtain British concurrence. Stimson, facing an uncertain future relationship with the Soviet Union and recognizing the power that S-1 would provide for the United States in resolving such relations in a favorable manner, decided to devote himself to its development and use.[51] On May 28 he wrote in his *Diary*, "I have made up my mind to make that subject (S-1) my primary occupation for these next few months, relieving myself as far as possible from all *routine matters in the Department*." [52] Thus, by the time the Interim Committee was to meet again on May 31, the Secretary of War and those interested in S-1 within the War Department had generally planned the anticipated use of the atomic bomb.

One other factor must be considered before describing the May 31 meeting of the Interim Committee. Prior to that time, despite delays occasioned by Roosevelt's death, efforts of nuclear scientists to stop the bomb's use had at least become known to those who sat on the committee.

Certainly Stimson knew that certain scientists who had worked on S-1 objected to its use. Prior to the appointment of the Interim Committee, General Groves had informed him of the concern of scientists at the Metallurgical Laboratory over use of the bomb and over the necessity of planning for future development and control of atomic energy.[53] He may also have received indications that some scientists questioned the desirability of using the weapon from Vice-President Wallace who had discussed the matter over breakfast with Arthur H. Compton and James Franck near the end of April.[54] Undoubtedly Stimson had been in close touch with Bush, Conant, and Groves, all of whom were familiar with the growing doubts which some scientists entertained about using the bomb. Such doubts were transmitted to Stimson in a letter from Conant on May 5 in which Conant stated his reservations about serving on the Interim Committee.

There is a growing restlessness among this group, some of which concerns the international implications of the work on which they are engaged. Many of the scientists have a feeling of reluctance about the whole endeavor and wish, as I certainly do, that there had been some physical reason why the undertaking proved to be impossible. I know you share this feeling.

I know that many of the active scientists are now deeply concerned about the international problems arising from the use of this weapon. In particular, they are concerned about our relations with Russia in this respect. They suppose that there has been no transmission of any information on this subject to our Russian allies, and they fear lest this fact endanger the future of our relations with that country and that we may soon be involved in a secret armaments race with that nation—particularly if use should occur before the Russians were notified of the existence of the weapon. . . .[55]

Interestingly enough, Conant's letter indicated a preoccupation with relations with the Soviet Union after the bomb's use. It merely implied a moral concern about the use on Japan.

It seems certain, therefore, that Stimson knew of scientific unrest when the Interim Committee met on May 31. He had, however, only heard of it indirectly through those who were administering the program. He apparently had no direct contact with those nonadministrative scientists who were fearful of the international consequences which might result from the fruition of their work. His interest in reducing such fears was sufficient enough for him to approve the appointment of the scientific panel to give the scientific group at least the semblance of representation in the work of the Interim Committee.

Byrnes was another member of the committee who knew of scientific objections to use prior to May 31. On May 28, at Spartanburg, South Carolina, he had been visited by Leo Szilard; Walter Bartky, Associate Dean of the Physical Sciences at the University of Chicago; and Harold Urey. There they reviewed with Byrnes, Szilard's memorandum of the previous March to President Roosevelt. The Spartanburg meeting had come about in a somewhat indirect manner. After Roosevelt's death, Szilard had enlisted Bartky's help in trying to obtain an appointment with Truman. Matt Connelly, the President's appointments secretary, had informed them that Truman had suggested that they discuss the matter with his personal adviser, Byrnes. Bartky and Szilard had decided to call in Urey, and the three scientists had gone to Spartanburg.[56]

Byrnes and Szilard got on poorly. To Byrnes, the professional politician, Szilard's obvious desire to ". . . participate in policy making . . ." was unthinkable.[57] He considered Szilard's suggestion that scientists should discuss the use of the bomb with the cabinet most rash. To Bartky and Urey who were ". . . neither as aggressive nor apparently as dissatisfied . . ." he could listen. But Szilard was just too much.[58] Byrnes, however, was a master of persuasion. After soliciting the information that Szilard (despite his criticism of Bush, Conant, and Compton) greatly admired Oppenheimer, Byrnes appeased him with the information that the latter would sit with the Interim Committee.

The three scientists, on the other hand, were considerably disturbed by their understanding of Byrnes' attitude toward the bomb. They considered him to be ignorant of its significance and much more concerned about justifying the large expenditure involved in its production and in using the weapon as a power factor in negotiating with the Russians than in devising a long-term plan for eliminating a future nuclear armaments race. Most of their time was spent in familiarizing Byrnes with the application of atomic energy to the production of power. They had little opportunity to discuss Szilard's March memorandum or to explore Szilard's most recent idea ". . . that the interest of peace might best be served and an arms race avoided by not using the bomb against Japan, keeping it a secret, and letting the Russians think that . . . work on it had not succeeded." [59] They were, however, able to arouse Byrnes' ". . . fears of the terrible weapon they had assisted in creating." [60]

Besides Stimson and Byrnes, others who sat with the Interim Committee on May 31 knew of the scientists' misgivings concerning use of the bomb. Bush and Conant, working very closely with Groves on the Military Policy Committee (MPC), of course, were familiar with the problem. Groves himself was well informed and had, as a matter of routine, ordered that the three scientists who had gone to see Byrnes be followed to Spartanburg by one of his intelligence officers.[61] He was so disturbed by the visit that he later asked Bartky to come to Washington to discuss the problem with him. At that time Bartky assured him that scientific misgivings went far beyond those of Szilard alone and that opposition to use of the weapon resulted from efforts other than his.[62]

Arthur Compton, in charge of the Metallurgical Laboratory, had long known of the doubts of some of his scientists. He had apparently considered the matter so important that he had asked for the creation of the Franck Committee in order to place the opinions of such men on record for use by the Interim Committee.[63]

It is likely that others on the Interim Committee knew of the opposition developing at Chicago, but they had little information concerning such opposition. Karl Compton, Lawrence, Fermi, and Oppenheimer were familiar with the divergent viewpoints. They were, however, somewhat removed from the center of opposition and with the exception of Compton were deeply involved in the pressing day-to-day problems of bomb development. As Oppenheimer was later to recall ". . . the hotbed of discussion [on the desirability of using the bomb in Japan] was in Chicago, rather than in Los Alamos. At Los Alamos I heard very little talk about it. We always assumed, if they were needed, they would be used. But there were places where people said for the future of the world it would be better not to use them." [64]

Harrison, Bard, and Clayton had been present at the second informal meeting of the Interim Committee on May 14 when copies of a memorandum to Arthur Compton from certain scientists at Chicago had been distributed.[65] The memorandum presumably dealt with scientific misgivings about use of the weapon. It was, however, passed over without recorded comment.[66]

In varying degrees, then, by May 31 the members of the Interim Committee were familiar with scientific criticism concerning use of the bomb. The effect of such knowledge seems to have been minimal in their considerations. It resulted in the Interim Committee's meeting on May 31 with the scientific panel. But apparently this was not an attempt to provide representation for such dissident opinions. It was, it seems, an effort to provide scientific participation in making the decision by involving administrative scientists who were either out of sympathy with such views or were so preoccupied with other problems that they had little time for doubtful matters.

Stimson had prepared carefully for the meeting of May 31. He had devoted all of the previous day to planning the agenda with Bundy, Harrison, Groves, and Marshall. As was the case with previous sessions, preparation for the meeting had been concentrated largely within the War Department. The final agenda of the May 31 meeting reflected suggestions which the Secretary had received in a memorandum of May 30 from his subordinates. The memorandum first suggested that the general purpose of the committee was ". . . to study and report on the whole problem of temporary controls and publicity during the war and to survey and make recommendations on post war [sic] research, development and controls, both national and international." A second purpose was ". . . to give the Committee chance to get acquainted with the scientists and vice versa." No suggestion was made of the possible purpose of discussing the use of the bomb. The memorandum went on to list the questions that were expected to come up. They were those involving future military prospects, international competition, future research, future controls, and the possibility that they might be used to extend democratic rights and the dignity of man, and future nonmilitary uses. The memorandum included no indication of the possibility that use of the bomb might be discussed.[67]

During the May 30 discussions, Stimson and his assistants also ". . . talked over the subject very thoroughly of how [they] should use this implement in respect to Japan." [86] It seems that they were presuming use on the very eve of the committee's meeting where such an action might be considered. At 8:40 the next morning Stimson again reviewed his previously formulated plans in conversation with Harrison and Marshall.[69] The Secretary of War was taking no chances on being unprepared. The agenda had been fixed, and he was well briefed to expedite its consideration.

All of the members of the Interim Committee along with Marshall, Groves, Bundy, and Page, who were present by invitation, met with the scientific panel at 10:00 A.M. on May 31 in Stimson's office.[70] Stimson opened the discussion reading from a carefully prepared statement. He first emphasized the revolutionary nature of the new weapon. Second, he pointed out that he and General Marshall shared responsibility for making recommendations to the President in regard to military applications of the weapon and indicated the advisory function of the committee. In an attempt to ensure their participation in the discussion, he then urged the scientists present to express themselves freely on any phase of the subject.[71]

Intent on demonstrating to them the reasonableness and understanding of the members of the committee, Stimson went on to say that ". . . we did not regard it as a new weapon merely but as a revolutionary change in the relations of man to the universe and that we wanted to take advantage of this; that the project might even mean the doom of civilization; that it might be a Frankenstein [sic] which would eat us up or it might be a project by which the peace of the world would be helped in becoming secure." [72] He concluded by suggesting the following topics for discussion: future military weapons; future international competition; future research; future controls; and future developments, particularly those of a nonmilitary nature.[73]

The discussion which followed that morning covered a wide range of topics dealing with nuclear energy. It is significant that it did not include consideration of the use of the bomb. Of those present who have since described the meeting, Compton recalled that ". . . throughout the morning's discussions it seemed to be a foregone conclusion that the bomb would be used." [74] Bard later remembered no intensive discussion of the question of use throughout the meeting, and Oppenheimer has testified that no consideration of the use of the bomb took place while he was present.[75] The question of use was apparently peripheral; Stimson had not even included it on his agenda.

Following Stimson's opening remarks, the committee heard descriptions from Oppenheimer, Bush, Conant, and Compton of the anticipated destructive potential of the new weapon. They tried to get across to the others the ". . . novelty, the variety, and the dynamic quality of this field . . . that this was not a finished job and that there was a heck of lot [they] didn't know." [76] They were, however, able to predict the course of future developments in bomb destructiveness. The bomb they were developing would have the impact of between 2,000 and 20,000 tons of TNT. During a second stage in the year and a half following January, 1946, bombs with the force of between 50,000 and 100,000 tons of TNT might be developed. And in a third stage to follow three years after the second, a bomb with the equivalent of between 10,000,000 and 100,000,000 tons of TNT was a possibility.

Such predictions had a sobering effect on those who listened. They turned their thoughts toward devising ways of ensuring the United States' lead in the production of nuclear energy. Lawrence, the Comptons, and Oppenheimer stressed the vital necessity of continuing United States predominance. Lawrence recommended the expansion of existing production facilities and suggested that new plants be located around the country to make a crippling attack more difficult. He also urged that ". . . at the same time a sizable stock pile [sic] of bombs and material should be built up." [77] Karl T. Compton supported Lawrence's suggestion that production should be expanded to produce bombs for an atomic stockpile. Stimson then summarized his understanding of how the program should develop. First, the present industrial plant should be maintained; second, a sizable stockpile of material for military use and for industrial and technical use should be accumulated; and, third, industrial development should be pursued.

The talk progressed logically to a consideration of postwar research. The scientists involved in the project had long chafed at the restrictions on research which they felt had been imposed by the program of compartmentalization. They recognized the necessity of such measures for wartime security. They thought, however, that United States progress in nuclear development after the war would be hamstrung if similar security restrictions imposed obstructions to the free flow of scientific information on which such progress depended. Evidencing this line of thinking, Oppenheimer, Bush, Arthur H. Compton, and Fermi each emphasized the importance of postwar, nonrestricted, fundamental research. They seized this opportunity to impress on the political and military people present that future development depended on elimination of the sterility of research imposed by concentration on specific goals and needs of the war.

But if research was to be freed of security restrictions, the problem of postwar, international control under effective inspections would have to be solved. And this involved the future relationship with Russia. These were the matters which occupied the committee during the remainder of the morning. The major question considered was whether or not to give information on S-1 to the Russians. Some, like Oppenheimer and Karl T. Compton, favored free exchange of information of a general nature without giving them the details of productive processes. Bush, on the other hand, pointed out that despite the fact that during the war our advantage over totalitarian states had been tremendous, he was doubtful ". . . of our ability to remain ahead permanently if we were to turn over completely to the Russians the results of our research under free competition with no reciprocal exchange." [78]

General Marshall then stated the military position. He felt that the apparent uncooperative attitude of Russia in military matters arose from their necessity of maintaining security. He accepted this evaluation of Russia's motives and acted accordingly. Although he was in no position to comment on the post-war situation involving other than military matters, ". . . he was inclined to favor the building up of a combination among like-minded powers, thereby forcing Russia to fall in line by the very force of the coalition." [79] But he had no fear that the Russians, given information concerning the bomb, would disclose it to the Japanese. And he went so far as to raise the question as to whether it was desirable to invite two prominent Russians to the first test.[80]

Arthur H. Compton supported Marshall's view. He too wanted to ". . . secure agreements for cooperation with other like-minded nations and at the same time work toward solidifying our relations with the Russians." [81] He recommended freedom of research consistent with national security, a combination of democratic powers for cooperation in the field of nuclear energy, and the formulation of an understanding with Russia.[82]

It was left for Byrnes, the politician and practitioner of compromise, to suggest an approach sufficiently general to satisfy everyone. If information were given to the Russians, even in general terms, Stalin would ask to be brought into the British-American partnership. Byrnes then ". . . expressed the view, *which was generally agreed to by all present*, that the most desirable program would be to push ahead as fast as possible in production and research to make certain that we stay ahead and at the same time make every effort to better our political relations with Russia." [83]

After discussion of Byrnes' proposal the meeting adjourned for lunch at 1:15 P.M. Compton's account is the best existing report of the luncheon, which lasted for an hour. During his conversation with Stimson who was seated next to him, he ". . . asked the Secretary whether it might not be possible to arrange a nonmilitary demonstration of the bomb in such a manner that the Japanese would be so impressed that they would see the uselessness of continuing the war." [84] Stimson presented this question for general discussion. As alternative suggestions for a test were suggested, each was struck down as being unwise or inexpedient.

It was evident that everyone would suspect trickery. If a bomb were exploded in Japan with previous notice, the Japanese air power was still adequate to give serious interference. An atomic bomb was an intricate device, still in the development stage. The operation would be far from routine. If during the final adjustments of the bomb the Japanese defenders should attack, a faulty move might easily result in some kind of failure. Such an end to an advertised demonstration of power would be much worse than if the attempt had not been made. It was now evident that when the time came for the bombs to be used we should have only one of them available, followed afterwards by others at all-too long intervals. We could not afford the chance that one of them might be a dud. If the test were made on some neutral territory, it was hard to believe that Japan's determined and fanatical military men would be impressed. If such an open test were made first and failed to bring surrender, the chance would be gone to give the shock of surprise that proved so effective. On the contrary it would make the Japanese ready to interfere with the atomic attack if they could. Though the possibility of a demonstration that would not destroy human lives was attractive, no one could suggest a way in which it could be made so convincing that it would be likely to stop the war.[85]

Thus, Compton described the luncheon conversation. From the facts that the luncheon lasted only an hour and that it was attended by all but Bard, it seems improbable that these matters received any but cursory consideration. And yet the account is interesting for two reasons. It points out the attitude of those present toward Japan, and it also indicates that tactical rather than strategic considerations influenced their thoughts. The question was not one of whether or not the weapon should be used, but one of how it could be used most effectively.

It is difficult to determine what caused Stimson to raise the question of use of the weapon during the afternoon session which began at 2:15 P.M. He has not recorded his purpose in his *Diary*. He may have been influenced by the luncheon conversation. At any rate, although it was not on the agenda for the meeting, the first topic considered that afternoon was the effect of the bombing on the Japanese and on their will to continue fighting.[86] Again, however, the matter was phrased in such a way as to presume use.

First, the force of the attack was portrayed as being similar in effect to that of any conventional air attack of similar dimensions. Oppenheimer remarked that the visual effect would be tremendous and that life would be endangered within a radius of two-thirds of a mile from the point of impact. He recommended several simultaneous strikes. Groves objected to Oppenheimer's recommendation for three reasons: because the additional knowledge which might be gained from each successive bombing would be lost; because simultaneous attacks would require a rush job by those assembling the bombs which might render them ineffective; and because the effect would not be sufficiently distinct from regular bombing.

After much discussion concerning various types of targets and the effects to be produced, the Secretary expressed the conclusion, on which there was general agreement, that we could not give the Japanese any warning; that we could not concentrate on a civilian area; but that we should seek to make a profound psychological impression on as many of the inhabitants as possible . . . The Secretary agreed that the most desirable target would be a vital war plant employing a large number of employees and closely surrounded by . . . houses.[87]

This ended the discussion of use of the bomb during the afternoon session. Other matters, however, came up. Groves complained that some of the scientists working on S-1 were of doubtful discretion and uncertain loyalty. It was agreed that nothing could be done about them until after the bomb had been used or at least until after it had been tested. The meeting ended with the suggestion that the scientific panel inform their fellow scientists about the

Interim Committee and of their connection with it but that they should not divulge its membership. The committee wanted the scientists to know that the government was taking an active interest in the project and was giving its problems careful consideration.

To demonstrate further governmental consideration for any doubts which scientists had concerning the bomb's use, the scientific panel was asked to report on whether they might devise a demonstration that might end the war without using the weapon on Japan. As Oppenheimer later recalled:

We were asked to comment on whether the bomb should be used. I think the reason we were asked for that comment was because a petition had been sent in from a very distinguished and thoughtful group of scientists: "No, it should not be used." It would be better for everything that they [sic] should not. We didn't know beans about the military situation in Japan. We didn't know whether they could be caused to surrender by other means or whether the invasion was really inevitable. But in back of our minds was the notion that the invasion was inevitable because we had been told that. . . .[88]

The scientific panel was to meet later in June to draw up its recommendations.

The May 31 meeting ended, therefore, on a similar note to that on which it had begun. It had been held to symbolize scientific participation in considering important decisions to be taken in relation to S-1. It had not been held to discuss specifically and in depth the question of whether or not the bomb should be used. That this question rose at all seems to have been incidental. The presumption of use appears obvious. One possible explanation is that the War Department tried to muster arguments against peaceful demonstration of the bomb when scientific protest began to reach the Pentagon. Thus, at the May 31 meeting, the impact of scientific advice on matters involving the development of S-1 and its planned use was minimal.

To round out the picture of civilian, scientific, and military cooperation in deciding to use the weapon, Stimson had called another Interim Committee meeting for the next day, June 1, with representatives from industries which had participated in building S-1. All members of the committee were present with Marshall, Groves, Bundy, and Page again invited to sit in. Representing industry were George H. Bucher, president of Westinghouse; Walter S. Carpenter, president of Dupont; James Rafferty, vice-president of Union Carbide; and James White, president of Tennessee Eastman.[89] Stimson first welcomed the industrialists and praised the contribution of their companies to the S-1 program. He then urged them to offer suggestions that might help in solving the international problems resulting from the development of nuclear energy. After pointing out that ". . . a most important factor in making decisions concerning the problem of international cooperation was the question of how long it would take other nations to catch up with the United States . . . ," he asked for their estimates of this time factor.[90]

The industrialists spent most of their time with the committee answering Stimson's question. Carpenter estimated that it would take Russia four or five years to construct a plant similar to that at Hanford, even assuming that it had access to the basic plans. With the help of captured German scientists, it might proceed more rapidly. White felt that Russia's greatest problem would be in finding skilled personnel, but Clayton thought they were likely to solve that difficulty by utilizing the services of the captured Germans. Bucher estimated that, even with German scientific help, it would take Russia three years to put an electromagnetic pilot plant into operation. He guessed that Germany would require fifteen to eighteen months, Italy the same, and Britain about a year before they reached the production stage. To build the gaseous-diffusion plant, Rafferty anticipated, would require ten years for the Russians if they were not given basic knowledge of production techniques. Even with information obtained through espionage, Russia would require three years to get such a plant into operation. This, apparently, was all that the industrialists contributed. They made no suggestions on use of the bomb. They gave no consideration to other international problems. Before they left the meeting at 2:15 P.M., they made recommendations on the postwar domestic organization of the development of nuclear energy. They said nothing on the problem of use.

After the representatives from industry had left the meeting, however, the members of the committee considered more pressing problems. They discussed the preparation of legislation to authorize the postwar organization of the project and decided to utilize the recommendations of the scientific panel as a basis for such an enactment. They talked about the necessity of devising ways to obtain appropriations after June, 1946, when existing authorizations would expire. And they advised Stimson to use the bomb.

The notation in the minutes which refers to the recommendation that the bomb be used indicates no discussion of the matter. It seems that Byrnes who made the suggestion was merely reiterating the feeling of the group which had been expressed the previous day. The minutes read:

Mr. Byrnes *recommended,* and the Committee *agreed,* that the Secretary of War should be advised that, while recognizing that the final selection of the target was essentially a military decision, the present view of the Committee was that the bomb should be used against Japan as soon as possible; that it be used on a war plant surrounded by . . . homes; and that it be used without prior warning. It was the understanding of the Committee that the small bomb would be used in the test and that the large bomb (gun mechanism) would be used in the first strike over Japan.[91]

In connection with their recommendation, the committee briefly discussed both publicity to be given to the bomb's use and possible targets. In connection with the latter, Harrison restated the agreement that the choice of targets was a responsibility of the military. He informed the committee that ". . . in the past few days the Secretary has held discussions with General Marshall and Arnold concerning targets and would probably discuss the question further with Admiral King and General Marshall. This committee was not considered competent to make a final decision on the matter of targets, this being a military decision." [92] The meeting ended after the committee had agreed to reconvene on June 21. Significantly, they decided that the agenda for that meeting would include postwar organizational proposals for the peacetime United States atomic energy program, legislation to effectuate a proposed organization, and the situation at the time in relation to the issuance of publicity following the bomb's use. There was no mention of further consideration of the question of use and no suggestion of possibly reconsidering their recommendations as a result of the anticipated report of the scientific panel.[93]

The May 31 and June 1 meetings of the Interim Committee were pivotal in understanding its approach to use of the atomic bomb. At no time was the question of use widely discussed. The important questions, if there were such, were *where* it was to be used, *how* it was to be used, and *when* it was to be used rather than *whether* it should be used. After accepting the suggestion that the bomb be used against Japan on a war plant surrounded by civilian homes and without prior warning, the committee left the questions of when and how to employ the weapon to the War Department. After recommending that use occur as soon as possible, it left the timing of delivery to the military. It was far more concerned with domestic control, *after use*; with international regulation, *after use*; with keeping the information from the Russians and employing the new weapon to better the United States position vis-à-vis the Soviet Union, *after use*; with ensuring appropriate publicity through statements by the President and the Secretary of War, *after use*; and with providing the public a suitable picture of careful civilian consideration of the question of use, *after use*.

Stimson has written that the ". . . first and greatest problem [for the committee] was the decision on the use of the bomb—should it be used against the Japanese, and if so, in what manner?" [94] While this may be true, it is possibly significant that the committee, chosen largely by the War Department, was predisposed to use of the bomb and served primarily to support a decision which Stimson had already reached independently.[95] A perceptive biographer of Stimson hit close to the mark when he wrote:

They [those on the Interim Committee who had lived with the knowledge of atomic energy for a long time] did not go into the meetings of the Interim Committee on May 31 cold. They had attitudes already developed—independently and by informal collaboration on a common task. The Interim Committee was appointed to give their opinions ordered form, some corporate structure, as the need for a defined decision was presented. The effort to give the decision this kind of support, to invest it with the sanction of a formal judgment reached by orderly procedures, a canvass and resolution of all considerations at some given moment in time, was the expression of the natural desire to make all human acts and decisions appear not only wise but the product of system and right reason. The Interim Committee, insofar as the special matter of using the bomb was concerned, was, in a sense, a symbolic act to demonstrate with what care this enormous conclusion had been considered. . . .[96]

The committee was formed with the intention of giving the decision to use the bomb the appearance of resulting from "right reason." Indications of careful committee perusal and a thorough canvass of all points of view are apparently unwarranted.

The work of the committee was as yet unfinished. It was to meet again on June 21 and a number of times thereafter before the war with Japan was ended; but for all practical purposes the committee's connection with the use of the bomb had ended. This situation was not recognized, however, by certain scientists attempting to stop such use and by the members of the scientific panel. Between June 1 and June 21, interested scientists increased their efforts to change the plans of the War Department. During that time the scientific panel attempted to devise an alternative to use.

Between the first of June and the committee's June 21 meeting the efforts of scientists to propose suitable alternatives to use centered in the Franck Committee of the Metallurgical Laboratory at the University of Chicago.[97] The Social and Political Implications Committee, as it was formally named, has been popularly labeled with the name of its chairman, James Franck, a noted physicist and an exile from Nazi Germany.[98]

The earliest records of the Franck Committee are dated June 5 and describe the meeting of the previous day. Recollections of its members indicate, however, that the committee had met previously, at least informally, and that the June 4 meeting was held merely to collate previous decisions.[99] The discussion at the June 4 meeting reflected primarily a concern for postwar international control. Although the members were undoubtedly moved by moral considerations, no mention was made of the moral and humanitarian positions against use of the bomb. Rather, the arguments against its employment rested on the impact which it would have on United States efforts to develop international regulation and on the postwar strategic position in which the United States might find itself. The United States, they felt, would be more vulnerable to future atomic attack than other states because of the relatively intensive geographic concentration of its industry. Convinced that future benefits to the United States would result from international control, the committee discussed a number of what were to them more acceptable alternatives than use. Among them were the following: ". . . refraining from use but building a stockpile for the future, announcing that we had the bomb but would not use it, and a demonstration on an uninhabited island before our Allies and the Japanese, with the United Nations deciding about its use if Japan did not immediately surrender." [100] Although a later account by Arthur H. Compton indicates a division within the committee, the recollections of committee members and the minutes of the meeting on July 4 indicate unanimous acceptance of the report. By June 11 the report of the committee was ready. It remains a remarkably prophetic document. In summary it stated:

The development of nuclear power not only constitutes an important addition to the technological and military power of the United States, but also creates grave political and economic problems for the future of this country.

Nuclear bombs cannot possibly remain a "secret weapon" at the exclusive disposal of this country for more than a few years. The scientific facts on which their construction is based are well known to scientists of other countries. Unless an effective international control of nuclear explosives is instituted, a race for nuclear armaments is certain to ensue following the first revelation of our possession of nuclear weapons to the world. Within ten years other countries may have nuclear bombs, each of which, weighing less than a ton, could destroy an urban area of more than ten square miles. In the war to which such an armaments race is likely to lead, the United States, with its agglomeration of population and industry in comparatively few metropolitan districts, will be at a disadvantage compared to nations whose population and industry are scattered over large areas.

We believe that these considerations make the use of nuclear bombs for an early unannounced attack against Japan inadvisable. If the United States were to be the first to release this new means of indiscriminate destruction upon mankind, she would sacrifice public support throughout the world, precipitate the race for armaments, and prejudice the possibility of reaching an international agreement on the future control of such weapons.

Much more favorable conditions for the eventual achievement of such an agreement could be created if nuclear bombs were first revealed to the world by a demonstration in an appropriately selected uninhabited area.

In case chances for the establishment of an effective international control of nuclear weapons should have to be considered slight at the present time, then not only the use of these weapons against Japan, but even their early demonstration, may be contrary to the interests of this country. A postponement of such a demonstration will have in this case the advantage of delaying the beginning of the nuclear armaments race as long as possible.

If the government should decide in favor of an early demonstration of nuclear weapons, it will then have the possibility of taking into account the public opinion of this country and of the other nations before deciding whether these weapons should be used against Japan. In this way, other nations may assume a share of responsibility for such a fateful decision.[101]

The Franck Report appears to have had little impact on the decision to use the atomic bomb. It was formulated only after the Interim Committee had made its decision, and it presented no argument which the committee's members had not previously, if informally, evaluated. Furthermore, it never reached most of the members of the committee.

As soon as the report was completed on June 11, Franck personally carried it to Washington to ensure that the proper authorities would receive it. There, he enlisted the help of Arthur H. Compton and his assistant, Norman Hilberry. The next day Compton attempted, through Harrison's office, to arrange a meeting between Franck and Stimson; but the Secretary of War was not in town. According to Compton, Harrison then assured him that the report would be given to Stimson. Compton, therefore, left the report with Harrison along with a covering letter which Franck had asked him to write.[102] The Interim Committee's log, however, indicates that Compton may not have seen Harrison. His letter with the Franck Report was left with R. Gordon Arneson, the Secretary of the Committee on June 12. Three days later Arneson reported to Harrison on the meeting with Compton. Whether Harrison saw Compton or his letter or the Franck Report before June 15 is, therefore, uncertain.[103]

At any rate, by June 15 the documents were before him. Any impact that the Franck Report might have made was probably blunted by the doubtful note struck by Compton's covering letter.[104] After describing the genesis of the report, Compton finished his letter with these words:

The proposal is to make a technical but not military demonstration preparing the way for a recommendation by the United States that the military use of atomic explosives be outlawed by firm international agreement. It is contended that its military use by us now will prejudice the world against accepting any further recommendation by us that its use be not permitted.

I note that two important considerations have not been mentioned:
1. that failure to make a military demonstration of the new bombs may make the war longer and more expensive in human lives, and,
2. that without a military demonstration it may be impossible to impress the world with the need for national sacrifices in order to gain lasting security.[105]

Harrison, seeing nothing pressing in the Franck Report, decided that the scientific panel rather than the Interim Committee should deal with it.[106] He later reported this decision to the Interim Committee on June 21. So except indirectly through the ultimate report of the scientific panel and through Harrison's report of his handling of the matter, the Interim Committee apparently never saw the Franck Report. Any impact the report might have made was filtered out by the scientific panel's refusal to accept its recommendations.[107] It seems doubtful that Stimson ever saw the Franck Report during this period, and certainly the matter was not considered by the President.[108]

Just as the Franck Report had little effect on the decision to use the bomb, so the work of the scientific panel had a minimal impact. The panel had been asked by the Interim Committee on May 31 to consider an alternative to military use. About ten days later, it met over a long weekend at Los Alamos.[109] Oppenheimer recalled that the panel had been assigned two tasks. It had been asked to produce a plan for a peacetime atomic energy organization and ". . . to comment on whether the bomb should be used." He considered the second task to be ". . . quite slight." [110] The panel, it seems, was to give further corroboration to the decision which had been taken previously. It was formed to demonstrate that every effort had been made to devise an alternative to military use.

Although the scientific panel took into account the general opposition to use among some of the scientists involved in developing S-1, it did not have a copy of the Franck Report on hand for its discussions. That report was only completed on June 11, presumably after the panel's meeting. Furthermore, Harrison did not decide to submit it to the panel before June 15. And he only presented the Report to the scientific panel for study and recommendation at the time of the June 21 meeting of the Interim committee.[111] It is, therefore, doubtful that the panel perused the Franck Report in formulating its report which was sent to the Interim Committee on June 16. Of course, by June 12 at least Arthur H. Compton knew of the Franck Report. But between then and the time of the submission of the scientific panel's report, he probably attended no further meeting of the panel. The panel, of course, might have delayed drafting its report while waiting for the Franck Report. But it seems more likely that since the Franck Report was in Washington in Harrison's office, and since the scientific panel's report was being written in Los Alamos, the delay between the meeting of the panel and transmission of its recommendations on June 16 was occasioned merely by the technicalities of drafting its report.[112]

The recommendations of the scientific panel were transmitted as three reports, which were attached to a letter from Oppenheimer to the Secretary of War for Harrison's attention. The first report which included recommendations on future policies and the third report which suggested interim recommendations for policies of domestic control were irrelevant to the question of use. The second report, "Recommendations on the Immediate Use of Nuclear Weapons," indicated that the panel had overruled objections from their scientific colleagues and reaffirmed the confirmation of the decision to use the bomb which had resulted from the Interim Committee's meetings of May 31 and June 1. It read:

You have asked us to comment on the initial use of the new weapon. This use, in our opinion, should be such as to promote a satisfactory adjustment of our international relations. At the same time, we recognize our obligation to our nation to use the weapons to help save American lives in the Japanese war.

1. To accomplish these ends we recommend that before the weapons are used not only Britain, but also Russia, France, and China be advised that we have made considerable progress in our work on atomic weapons,

that these may be ready to use during the present war, and that we would welcome suggestions as to how we can cooperate in making this development contribute to improved international relations.

2. The opinions of our scientific colleagues on the initial use of these weapons are not unanimous: they range from the proposal of a purely technical demonstration to that of the military application best designed to induce surrender. Those who advocate a purely technical demonstration would wish to outlaw the use of atomic weapons, and have feared that if we use the weapons now our position in future negotiations will be prejudiced. Others emphasize the opportunity of saving American lives by immediate military use, and believe that such will improve the international prospects, in that they are more concerned with the prevention of war than with the elimination of this specific weapon. We find ourselves closer to these latter views; we can propose no technical demonstration likely to bring an end to the war; we see no acceptable alternative to direct military use.

3. With regard to these general aspects of the use of atomic energy, it is clear that we, as scientific men, have no proprietary rights. It is true that we are among the few citizens who have had occasion to give thoughtful consideration to these problems during the past few years. We have, however, no claim to special competence in solving the political, social, and military problems which are presented by the advent of atomic power.[113]

This report suggests that the panel was primarily influenced by considerations of saving American lives and by international relations following its use. It had reviewed the position taken by scientists in opposition to use and had rejected it. Although recognizing the gravity of its choice, it could propose no alternative. It was, in effect, substantiating a position which the Interim Committee had already taken.

While the scientific panel fruitlessly considered alternatives to use and the Franck Committee transmitted futile objections to Washington, the War Department's preparations to use the bomb went on during the first three weeks of June. The President was told of the Interim Committee's recommendations in regard to use. At the same time the statements which he and the Secretary of War were to make following use were being drafted. And planning for negotiation of more formal and specific British concurrence went forward. Overriding all was the rush within the Manhattan Engineer District to complete the weapon and test it by Groves' target date in July.

There is some doubt about how Truman first heard of the Interim Committee's recommendations. He recalls that Stimson brought him its report on June 1.[114] The committee recommended ". . . that the bomb be used against the enemy as soon as it could be done . . ." and ". . . further that it should be used without specific warning and against a target that would clearly show its devastating strength. . . . The final decision of where and when to use the weapon . . ." was Truman's to make.[115] Despite the President's recollection, it seems more likely that Byrnes gave him the news of the committee's actions on June 1. Thus, Byrnes has written, "As the President's representative on the committee it was my duty to report to him the reasons for our various recommendations . . . I reported these conclusions to the President. . . . He expressed the opinion that, regrettable as it might be, so far as he could see, the only reasonable conclusion was to use the bomb." [116] And again, ". . . the day the committee reached agreement, I communicated its decision to President Truman. He said he had been giving thought to the problem and, while reluctant to use this weapon, saw no way of avoiding it. Thereafter, Secretary Stimson formally presented him a written statement, setting forth our recommendations. . . " [117] Stimson's *Diary* seems to corroborate Byrnes' statements. The Secretary of War wrote on June 6 of a conference with the President on that date. During the meeting he told Truman of the work of the Interim Committee the previous week. The President, in turn, informed him that Byrnes had already described the committee's work and that Byrnes was pleased by what had been done.[118] Hence, it seems apparent that Byrnes informed Truman of the committee's suggestions soon after its June 1 meeting and that Truman decided at that time that the United States should use the bomb. From then on, he was concerned primarily with the timing and location of use. Unlike Byrnes, Stimson waited until June 6 to make a complete report of the committee's work. The delay can be explained by his possible expectation that Byrnes would give the President preliminary explanations.

The conference between Truman and Stimson on June 6 involved no discussion of the question of use of the weapon. Three major topics were considered:

1. The effect of the bomb on United States–Soviet relations and the position of the United States on international control after use.
2. Stimson's concern about holding the Air Force to precision bombing in Japan.
3. The choice of Senators to be sent to the Clinton Works in Tennessee.

The latter two matters took little time. Truman approved the idea of sending the Senators and left to Stimson the later choice of who would go.[119] In regard to Air Force bombing, Stimson explained to Truman that he was demanding the utmost in precision ". . . first, because [he] did not want to have the United States get the reputation of out-doing Hitler in atrocities; and second, [because he] was a little fearful that before we could get ready [with S-1] the Air Force might have Japan so thoroughly bombed out that the new weapon would not have a fair background to show its strength." Truman said he understood.[120] It seems that the Secretary was seriously interested in setting a suitable stage for the use of the bomb. He wanted its terrible nature to be fully understood by the Japanese.

Stimson's primary concern at the meeting was over Russian reaction to the knowledge that the United States had the new weapon. Both he and the

President agreed that no revelation relating to the bomb should be made ". . . to Russia or anyone else . . ." until the first bomb had been successfully ". . . laid on Japan." [121] Stimson felt that the Russians might ask to participate in the development of the atomic bomb at the forthcoming meeting at Potsdam. If the request were made, he suggested that Truman should reply directly in a ". . . simple statement that as yet we were not quite ready to do it." If the question of future controls came up, the United States should favor, first, each country's promising to make its work public and, second, the creation of an international committee of control with full powers to inspect such work. In any case, he suggested the request for a *quid pro quo* in return for Russian partnership. Truman ". . . said he had been thinking of that and mentioned the same things that [Stimson] was thinking of, namely the settlement of the Polish, Rumanian, Yugoslavian, and Manchurian problems." [122] He also told his Secretary of War that ". . . he had postponed [the Potsdam Conference] until the 15th of July on purpose to give [him] more time . . ." to employ the weapon against Japan before the Russians might ask to join in the program.[123]

From Stimson's account of this conference it seems that neither he nor Truman gave much consideration to the problem of use. That decision had been made. They were not again to give the question much time at the top level. Their major concern involved the question of the impact of the weapon's use on United States–Soviet relations. They saw its success as a political tool which, if properly used, might increase their ability to obtain Russian concessions in areas where, as yet, they had not had the strength to force a Russian retreat.[124]

President Truman had approved the decision to use the bomb. The completion of drafts of statements which he and Stimson were to issue after its use was still necessary. This work went on within the War Department. As early as March 3, 1945, Bundy had sent Stimson a draft of a possible statement by the President. Laurence's original draft had been ready for comment by May 28.[125] Now, in the early weeks of June, further revisions were made. By June 7, the draft of the President's statement which was to be considered by the June 21 meeting of the Interim Committee was ready. It began: ". . . two hours ago an American airplane dropped one bomb on the Nagasaki Naval Base [*sic*] and destroyed its usefulness to the enemy. . . ." [126] On June 15, Harrison received from Arneson the first draft of the Secretary of War's statement.[127] Both drafts were sent to Groves for comment and later revised slightly. They were ready for consideration on June 21.[128] Both necessarily presumed the use of the atomic bomb.

Before the June 21 meeting considerable thought had been given to acquiring British consent to use of the weapon. Under the Quebec Agreement of August, 1943, such consent was required before use against third parties and before publication of any information concerning S-1. This objective had been discussed at the Interim Committee meetings of May 9, May 14, and May 18. During this same period the British had been devising a method to formalize their consent. But apparently this was unknown to many in the United States Government, for the matter received considerable attention through early June.

The evidence of such attention is spotty. On June 13 Arneson delivered to and discussed with Byrnes a copy of the Quebec Agreement and documents leading to the agreement. Byrnes was mostly interested in discovering whether there was a requirement to provide the British information about United States' plants and their construction. The documents revealed no such obligation or previous exchange.[129] Two days later Groves sent a memorandum to Stimson urging him to transmit the following message to the proper British authorities:

> Under the terms of the Quebec Agreement signed by President Roosevelt and Prime Minister Churchill, each government agreed to secure the consent of the other before using any Tube Alloy weapon against third parties and before communicating any information about the weapon to third parties.
>
> As you are aware we are now preparing to use such a weapon against Japan at an early date. We feel that it will be necessary or advantageous to both of our nations following such use or possibly following unforeseen effects during contemplated tests to make certain limited public disclosures as to what has been accomplished and possibly future effects. The consent of the Government of the United Kingdom . . . to such use and release of information is requested.[130]

This memorandum was interesting for a number of reasons. It demonstrated Groves' rapid preparation for the use of the bomb and the fact that the British had already been informed of United States plans. It indicated that Groves, who knew that the British had been discussing the nature of their consent since the previous April, wanted to light a fire under them in order to obtain their concurrence before conditions were right for dropping the bomb.

But British action was already underway. On June 18, Churchill finally sent to Field Marshal Wilson in Washington instructions to consider the Quebec Agreement loosely so as not to insist on its legalistic interpretation.[131] Since Stimson and Marshall were not in Washington, Wilson decided to mention the matter to Bundy, the United States Secretary to the Combined Policy Committee, through Roger Makins, his British counterpart. On June 19, Makins mentioned to Bundy ". . . the necessity of recording the consent of the British Government to the use of S-1 against Japan and it was then suggested that this could be accomplished by a memorandum of the Combined Chiefs of Staff." [132] Makins and Bundy agreed to see if this arrangement would be satisfactory to their superiors.

By June 21, therefore, efforts to record British consent to use of the bomb were well underway. The British had, in effect, done everything but formalize their concurrence with United States policy. Truman had been informed of the May 31 and June 1 recommendations of the Interim Committee and had accepted them. The scientific panel had found no acceptable alternative to such recommendations. The Franck Committee's efforts to bring about a reconsideration had been unsuccessful. The Manhattan Project rushed rapidly toward the completion of its product. The stage was set for the sixth meeting of the Interim Committee.

The committee met in Harrison's office at 9:30 A.M. on Thursday, June 21. All members were present except Stimson. Groves, Bundy, and Page sat in by invitation.[133] The committee first reviewed the drafts of statements to be made by the President and the Secretary of War after the weapon had been used. They suggested that both statements be released to the press at the same time and gave Groves the responsibility for issuing future publicity after that concerning initial use. Second, they discussed clause two of the Quebec Agreement which provided that the weapon should not be used against a third state without the mutual consent of the parties to the pact. "After serious consideration *Mr. Bard* made *the motion that the Secretary of War be advised that the Interim Committee favored revocation of Clause Two by appropriate action. The motion was unanimously carried.*" [134] So far as can be ascertained this recommendation was never acted upon by Stimson or Truman. The fact that the motion was made might indicate that the committee had no knowledge of negotiations between the War Department and the British to obtain the latter's consent to use of the bomb against Japan. Since Bundy was present, however, and since he very likely would have indicated the nature of such negotiations, it seems probable that the committee was trying to free the United States from the obligation of seeking British concurrence for possible future use of such weapons. At any rate, the recommendation was not implemented.

After recessing for luncheon at 1:15 P.M. the committee reconvened at 2:00 P.M. and heard the report of the scientific panel.[135] The committee accepted the first and third sections of the report and agreed that a permanent commission should be set up and that the committee should defer judgment to it once it had been established. After he presented the second section, Harrison informed the committee that he had received the Franck Report from Compton and would present it to the scientific panel. He pointed out that it suggested, among other things, ". . . that the weapon not be used in this war but that a purely technical test be conducted which would be made known to other countries." [136] After hearing the second section in which the scientific panel admitted that it saw no acceptable alternative to direct military use, the committee *reaffirmed* the position taken at the May 31 and June 1 meetings that the weapon be used against Japan at the earliest opportunity, that it be used without warning, and that it be used on a dual target, namely, a military installation or war plant surrounded by or adjacent to homes or other buildings most susceptible to damage.[137]

This brief account merits some comment. The scientific panel was not present to discuss its report or the Franck Report with the committee. Although Harrison informed the committee of the existence of the Franck Report, he did not transmit it to them and merely let them know how he had handled it. There is no indication in the minutes that any of the members saw the Franck Report at that time. There is no evidence that the matter received extensive discussion. Apparently the Interim Committee received Harrison's remarks and the scientific panel's report as a matter of form and, with little further consideration, reaffirmed their previous acceptance of the War Department's plans to use the atomic bomb. This was to be the last time that the question of use came before the Interim Committee. From then until August 6, when Hiroshima was bombed, any revision of the policy of use would come from the top—from Stimson or from Truman.

After reaffirming its approval of the use of the bomb, the committee gave more extensive consideration to the problem of what the President might say about the project to the Russians at the forthcoming Potsdam Conference. They saw the importance of maintaining operational secrecy, and yet they felt that future control of nuclear weapons might rest on Russia's willingness to cooperate after the war. The minutes record their recommendation:

In the hope of securing effective future control and in view of the fact that general information concerning the project would be made public shortly after the conference, the Committee unanimously *agreed* that there would be considerable advantage, if suitable opportunity arose, in having the President advise the Russians that we were working on this weapon with every prospect of success and that we expected to use it against Japan.

The President might say further that he hoped this matter might be discussed some time in the future in terms of insuring that the weapon would become an aid to peace.[138]

If the Russians asked for additional details, the President should say that the information could not presently be furnished. In view of the commitments of the Quebec Agreement, the committee suggested that the President should go over the whole matter with Churchill prior to the Potsdam Conference.

The Interim Committee met twice again, on July 6 and on July 19. Stimson, who was either traveling to the Potsdam Conference or at Potsdam, attended neither meeting. The committee reviewed such matters as ways to obtain political control of newly found uranium deposits in Sweden; British objections to publicity for scientific information after use; postwar legislation to regulate atomic energy development; the type of commission to be established to administer the program; and the possibility of a United Nations' mechanism for international control.[139] At no time, apparently, did the Interim Committee again review its decision to use the atomic bomb. As far as its members were concerned, the question was closed. The die was cast.

Efforts of Franck and Szilard and other like-minded scientists of the Metallurgical Laboratory at Chicago to stop the use of the weapon continued. They were, however, no longer to be the concern of the Interim Committee, for they never got beyond the War Department through which they were channeled.[140]

Another objection to use came from an unexpected source. The Interim Committee had been unanimous in its acceptance of the use of the bomb on Japan. But by June 27, Ralph Bard, Under Secretary of the Navy, had changed his mind. Bard had come to the conclusion that ". . . the Japanese were practically ready to capitulate . . . and . . . that for our position in history it would be much more desirable if . . . a warning was given." [141] He felt that it would be better for the United States if it did not disclose the fact that it had the bombs in reserve. He, therefore, transmitted his objections to Harrison on June 27 in the following memorandum:

MEMORANDUM ON THE USE OF S-1 BOMB

Ever since I have been in touch with this program I have had a feeling that before the bomb is actually used against Japan that Japan should have some preliminary warning for say two or three days in advance of use. The position of the United States as a great humanitarian nation and the fair play attitude of our people generally is responsible in the main for this feeling.

During recent weeks I have also had the feeling very definitely that the Japanese government may be searching for some opportunity which they could use as a medium of surrender. Following the three-power conference emissaries from this country could contact representatives from Japan somewhere on the China Coast and make representations with regard to Russia's position and at the same time give them some information regarding the proposed use of atomic power, together with whatever assurances the President might care to make with regard to the Emperor of Japan and the treatment of the Japanese nation following unconditional surrender. It seems quite possible to me that this presents the opportunity which the Japanese are looking for.

I don't see that we have anything in particular to lose in following such a program. The stakes are so tremendous that it is my opinion very real consideration should be given to some plan of this kind. I do not believe under present circumstances existing that there is anyone in this country whose evaluation of the chances of the success of such a program is worth a great deal. The only way to find out is to try it out.[142]

What caused Bard to change his mind is difficult to determine. He has stated his motivations in his memorandum. Others have indicated that he was influenced by personnel in the Navy Department such as Rear Admiral Lewis L. Strauss who desired a demonstration of the weapon for the Japanese before using it on Japan.[143] Certainly some in the Navy anticipated that naval and air blockade would be sufficient to defeat Japan. They thought that Japan was, in effect, already defeated. Admiral Leahy, Truman's Chief of Staff, and one of the few naval officers to know of the atomic bomb expressed the Navy point of view forcefully in his *Diaries*. On May 20 and on June 4, he wrote of separate meetings with Byrnes at which he expressed his doubts of the effectiveness of the new weapon. On June 18, he wrote: "It is my opinion at the present time that a surrender of Japan can be arranged with terms that can be accepted by Japan and that will make fully satisfactory provision for America's defense against future trans-Pacific aggression." [144] Bard may have been influenced by such considerations. But his memorandum also indicated a growing concern within the Navy over Russia's position in the Far East after the termination of hostilities. Although its language is obscure, it would seem to suggest that Japan be approached so as to secure some sort of rapproachment to offset any improved political position Russia might occupy on the Asian continent.[145] General Groves, when asked later as to Bard's motivations, was at a loss to explain the reversal of opinion. He pointed out, however, that Bard never expressed his revised view at the meetings of the Interim Committee. He changed his position only after the Interim Committee had met on June 21.[146]

Whatever caused Bard's change of mind, it had little if any effect on the plans to use the atomic bomb. Harrison transmitted Bard's memorandum to Stimson sometime before July 2 when it was delivered along with a copy of Harrison's letter of transmittal to Byrnes.[147] So far as is known, neither Stimson nor Byrnes passed it on to Truman. Neither changed his approach to the use of the bomb on Japan.[148] The Bard memorandum, like the views of scientists opposed to use of the weapon on Japan, failed to influence the decision which had been made. The bomb would be used. The War Department had decided. The Interim Committee had voiced its approval. The President had sanctioned the decision. The weapons would be used when completed and when weather conditions were suitable over Japan.

NOTES TO CHAPTER 6

[1] James F. Byrnes, *All in One Lifetime* (New York: Harper and Brothers, Publishers, 1958), p. 282. William Hillman, *Mr. President* (New York: Farrar, Straus and Young, 1952), pp. 247–48. Elting E. Morison, *Turmoil and Tradition: A Study of the Life and Times of Henry L. Stimson* (Boston: Houghton Mifflin Company, 1960), p. 616. Harry S. Truman, *Memoirs* (Garden City: Doubleday and Company, Inc., 1955), I, 10–11. Other than Truman's account of Bush's visit, which fails to mention the time it took place, no evidence has been found that Bush saw the President. Also, there is the chance that Bush's visit occurred after Truman's briefing by Stimson on April 25.

[2] Stimson, *Diary*, April 24, 1945. Citations of February 9, 1945, indicate that Harvey H. Bundy, Special Assistant to the Secretary, was given general responsibility for handling S-1. After March 15, Harrison, reporting back from an illness, took over much of the work in order to relieve Bundy of some of his many responsibilities. Bundy, how-

ever, was closely associated with the War Department's administration of S-1 throughout. General Groves recalls that Bundy, rather than Harrison, was in administrative leadership all the way. *Groves Interview, September 8, 1960.*

³ Stimson, *Diary*, April 25, 1945.

⁴ *MED Files*: Folder #24, Tab D. This information comes from an account of the Stimson-Truman conference included in a memorandum which General Groves wrote for his files.

⁵ Truman, *Memoirs*, I, 87.

⁶ Stimson, *Diary*, April 25, 1945. The text of this memorandum also appears in Henry L. Stimson, "The Decision to use the Atomic Bomb," *Harper's Magazine*, CXCIV (February, 1947) 199; Henry L. Stimson and McGeorge Bundy, *On Active Service in Peace and War* (New York: Harper and Brothers, Publishers, 1947), pp. 635–36. The latter work does not include paragraph 9 of the memorandum.

⁷ *MED Files*: Folder #24, Tab D, "Groves Memorandum."

⁸ Truman, *Memoirs*, pp. 87, 419. Truman states that he set up the committee indicating that it resulted from his choice of members.

⁹ *MED Files*: *Harrison-Bundy Series*, Folder #69, "S-1 Interim Committee." The above resume is a paraphrase of parts of the Bush-Conant letter and its two attached appendices.

¹⁰ *Papers of Henry L. Stimson*, "Memorandum of Talk with Bush, December 13, 1944." This may have been the genesis of the Interim Committee.

¹¹ *MED Files*: *Harrison-Bundy Series*, Folder #69, "S-1 Interim Committee."

¹² *MED Files*: *Harrison-Bundy Series*, Folder #69, "S-1 Interim Committee." The wording of this letter indicates that there had been some consultation on establishing a committee during the last two weeks of 1944. No other evidence of such development has been discovered.

¹³ *Ibid.*

¹⁴ Stimson, *Diary*, March 5, 1945.

¹⁵ *Ibid.*, March 8, 1945.

¹⁶ *MED Files*: *Harrison-Bundy Series*, Folder #69, "S-1 Interim Committee."

¹⁷ *Ibid.*

¹⁸ Byrnes has indicated that the original suggestion that such a committee might be desirable had come from General Groves; Byrnes, *All in One Lifetime*, p. 283. No other confirmation of this has been found except that Groves recalls that he worked with Bundy and Harrison in planning the committee; *Groves Interview*, September 8, 1960.

¹⁹ Stimson, *Diary*, May 1, 1945.

²⁰ *MED Files*: *Harrison-Bundy Series*, Folder #69, "S-1 Interim Committee."

²¹ *Ibid.* Italics are supplied.

²² *MED Files*: *Harrison-Bundy Series*, Folder #69, "S-1 Interim Committee."

²³ *Ibid.*

²⁴ *Ibid.*

²⁵ Stimson and Bundy, *On Active Service in Peace and War*, p. 616.

²⁶ Stimson, *Diary*, May 1, 1945. General Groves was also consulted on the choice of members. He recalls that the choice of members lay with Stimson, Bundy, and himself. Stimson suggested, and Groves agreed, that he not be on the committee. The suggestion of Clayton came from Groves. *Groves Interview*, September 8, 1960.

²⁷ *Ibid.*, May 2, 1945.

²⁸ Stimson, *Diary*, May 3, 1945, *Groves Interview*, September 8, 1960.

²⁹ Stimson, *Diary*, May 3, 1945.

³⁰ *Ibid.*, May 4, 1945.

31 *MED Files: Harrison-Bundy Series,* Folder #69, "S-1 Interim Committee." This is the first time the name Interim Committee was used. An explanation of the choice of the name appears in a memorandum of May 30, 1945, to the Secretary of War. This memorandum is unsigned, but it is probably from Bundy or Harrison. It states that Stimson used the name *Interim Committee* ". . . merely because . . . [he] anticipated that when there [was] no longer need for secrecy it [was] likely that the Congress [would] want to consider the establishment of a permanent post war [sic] commission to supervise, regulate and control the manufacture and use of the product." *MED Files: Harrison-Bundy Series,* Folder #100, "Interim Committee–Minutes of Meetings."

32 Stimson, *Diary,* May 8, 1945.

33 The membership of the Interim Committee included: Henry L. Stimson, Secretary of War, Chairman; George L. Harrison, Special Consultant to the Secretary of War, Alternate Chairman; Ralph A. Bard, Undersecretary of the Navy; Vannevar Bush, Director, Office of Scientific Research and Development; James F. Byrnes, Special Representative of the President; William L. Clayton, Assistant Secretary of State; Karl T. Compton, Chief, Office of Field Service, Office of Scientific Research and Development; and James B. Conant, Chairman, National Defense Research Committee. See *MED Files:Harrison-Bundy Series,* Folder #100, "Interim Committee Minutes." Stimson and Bundy, *On Active Service in Peace and War,* p. 616. Stimson, *Diary,* May 9, 1945. Some accounts indicate that the first meeting of the committee occurred on May 31, 1945. They are accurate in the sense that this was the first session with the scientific panel. See Gar Alperovitz, *Atomic Diplomacy: Hiroshima and Potsdam* (New York: Simon and Schuster, Inc., 1965), which mentions no meeting prior to May 31. Knebel and Bailey, *No High Ground,* p. 102. Louis Morton, "The Decision to Use the Atomic Bomb," *Foreign Affairs,* XXXV (January, 1957), p. 337. Morton's article also appears in Kent Roberts Greenfield, *Command Decisions* (Washington: Office of the Chief of Military History, Department of the Army, 1960, pp. 493–518. Michael Amrine, *The Great Decision: The Secret History of the Atomic Bomb* (New York: G. P. Putnam's Sons, 1959), p. 81.

34 *MED Files: Harrison-Bundy Series,* Folder #100, "Interim Committee Minutes." An account of this and following meetings appears in outline form in Folder #98, "Interim Committee Log," of the same *MED Files.* The minutes of this meeting are dated May 17, 1945. The delay is occasioned by the fact that the secretary who wrote these and succeeding minutes, R. Gordon Arneson, a second lieutenant attached to Bundy's and Harrison's offices, was not appointed until the second meeting on May 14. Whether or not Arneson was present at the first meeting is uncertain.

35 *MED Files: Harrison-Bundy Series,* Folder #100, "Interim Committee Minutes". Stimson, *Diary,* May 10, 1945. Stimson indicates that this meeting began at 9:50 A.M.

36 The implication here is that the others had seen this memorandum. See pp. 128–31.

37 *MED Files: Harrison-Bundy Series,* Folder #100, "Interim Committee Minutes." At Harrison's suggestion, Arneson was chosen secretary of the committee.

38 *Ibid.*

39 Stimson, *Diary,* May 8, 1945; Walter Millis (ed.), *The Forrestal Diaries* (New York: The Viking Press, Inc., 1951), p. 54. Forrestal's impression was that Stimson had indicated the committee was ". . . to be headed by Jimmy Byrnes. . . ."

40 Stimson, *Diary,* May 10, 1945.

41 *Ibid.*

42 John Ehrman, *Grand Strategy,* VI (London: Her Majesty's Stationery Office, 1956), 295–97. This account follows Ehrman closely. Little other evidence of this group has been discovered.

43 Compton, *Atomic Quest,* p. 221. *Groves Interview,* September 8, 1960.

[44] Wesley Frank Craven and James Lea Cate (eds.), *The Army Air Forces in World War II: The Pacific—Matterhorn to Nagasaki, June 1944 to August 1945,* V (Chicago: University of Chicago Press, 1953), 707.

[45] U. S. Atomic Energy Commission, *In the Matter of J. Robert Oppenheimer,* pp. 31–33. These are excerpts from Oppenheimer's testimony. Lloyd K. Garrison was Oppenheimer's counsel before the board conducting the hearings.

[46] U. S. Atomic Energy Commission, *In the Matter of J. Robert Oppenheimer,* p. 167.

[47] *MED Files: Harrison-Bundy Series,* Folder #74, "Interim Committee—President's Statement." This folder includes a memorandum from Bundy transmitting his proposal to Stimson on March 3, 1945.

[48] *Ibid.* The original draft appears in this folder. Attached to it is an unsigned document titled *Objectives.* A notation in pencil on the attached document indicates Arneson transmitted it to Harrison on May 28, 1945. The document includes some interesting suggestions as to points to be made by the President in his speech. Among others, those pertinent are as follows:

Notify world we have atomic bomb 1,000 to 1. It seems wise not to mention that bigger ones will follow for we want to have our acts more dreadful than our words to the Japs.

Call on the Japs to surrender. Making it clear that if they do not all subsequent slaughter is their guilt; making it clear also we do not count on the bomb but intend to follow it with the foot soldiers and fleet. . . .

Notify the Russians that they do not get the secret for nothing but might if a proper international organization were effected. . . .

Get the fact that the British are partners but we have the credit and the plants and have spent the money—before it is brought out by a critic. . . .

Choose a military target like a naval base if possible so that wholesale killing of civilians will be on the heads of the Japanese who refused to surrender to our ultimatum.

[49] Stimson, *Diary,* February 26, March 15 and 31, May 17, 1945. Those on the visit were J. Buell Snyder of Pennsylvania, George H. Mahon of Texas, John Taber of New York, and Clair Engle of California.

[50] *Ibid.,* May 30, 1945.

[51] *Ibid.,* May 14 and 15, 1945.

[52] *Ibid.,* May 28, 1945.

[53] Arthur H. Compton, *Atomic Quest,* p. 233. Compton suggests a causal relationship between these conversations and the appointment of the Interim Committee, pp. 233–34.

[45] Alice Kimball Smith, "Behind the Decision to Use the Atomic Bomb, Chicago, 1944–45," *Bulletin of the Atomic Scientists,* XIV (1958), 294. Mrs. Smith indicates that Franck used a memorandum he had written on April 21 as a basis for this discussion. That memorandum contained many of the suggestions which were later to be incorporated in Stimson's report to Truman on April 25 and in the *Franck Report* of June 11. She feels that this might indicate a relationship between the Franck memorandum and Stimson's report. Stimson's accounts in *Harper's Magazine,* in *On Active Service in Peace and War,* and in his *Diary* do not mention any consultations with Wallace during this period. For a consideration of the impact of the *Franck Report,* see pp. 139–41.

[55] *MED Files: Harrison-Bundy Series,* Folder #69, "S-1 Interim Committee." Conant also suggested that a few leading scientists be called in to present their views

on the international situation. This request was satisfied by the appointment of the scientific panel.

56 Smith, *Bulletin of the Atomic Scientists*, XIV, 293, 296. The two accounts of this Spartanburg meeting are fragmentary at best. Mrs. Smith's account is based on discussions with Bartky, Szilard, and Urey. See also Byrnes, *All in One Lifetime*, pp. 284–85.

57 Byrnes, *All in One Lifetime*, p. 284.

58 *Ibid.*, p. 284.

59 Smith, *Bulletin of the Atomic Scientists*, XIV, 296.

60 Byrnes, *All in One Lifetime*, p. 285.

61 *Ibid.*, p. 285.

62 Smith, *Bulletin of the Atomic Scientists*, XIV, 296.

63 The origins of the Franck Committee are still in doubt. Mrs. Smith cites recollections of its members to substantiate its existence through late April and May, 1945. She points out, however, that such recollections differ and that the first record of the committee's meeting was on June 5. *Ibid.*, p. 300.

64 U. S. Atomic Energy Commission, *In the Matter of J. Robert Oppenheimer*, p. 33.

65 See p. 125.

66 It has been impossible to find this document or any other reference to it. It probably was the Franck memorandum of April 21. See p. 128. Mrs. Smith has written that in 1957 Bard informed her that he knew nothing about the Manhattan Project until the May 31 meeting. This seems to be unlikely, since Bard had attended the previous meetings of May 9, May 14, and May 18. See Smith, *Bulletin of the Atomic Scientists*, XIV, 297.

67 *MED Files: Harrison-Bundy Series*, Folder #100, "Interim Committee Minutes." The unsigned memorandum appears in this folder. It presumably was written by Harrison but, perhaps, by Bundy. Its suggestions were followed very closely by Stimson in his opening statement before the May 31 meeting of the Interim Committee. See pp. 132.

68 Stimson, *Diary*, May 30, 1945.

69 *Ibid.*, May 31, 1945.

70 *MED Files: Harrison-Bundy Series*, Folder #100, "Interim Committee Minutes." The following account of the May 31 meeting of the Interim Committee is based on undated notes signed by the secretary, Arneson.

71 Apparently getting the scientists to talk was a major preoccupation for Stimson. He has recorded in his *Diary* that he opened the meeting with remarks about the weapon and afterward ". . . telling what we expected of these scientists in getting them started and talking." Stimson, *Diary*, May 31, 1945.

72 *Ibid.*, May 31, 1945. Slightly different versions of Stimson's remarks appear in the minutes of the committee. Arneson has recorded that Stimson said: "While the advances in the field to date had been fostered by the needs of war, it was important to realize that the implications of the project went far beyond the needs of the present war. It must be controlled if possible to make it an assurance of future peace rather than a menace to civilization." *MED Files: Harrison-Bundy Series*, Folder #100, "Interim Committee Minutes." It is interesting that Stimson neither in his *Diary* nor in the minutes of the committee indicates any request for discussion of use of the weapon. On the other hand, Compton, in recalling Stimson's remarks, implies that the Secretary desired committee consideration of possible use of the bomb. He writes that Stimson said: "Gentlemen, it is our responsibility to recommend action that may turn the course of civilization. In our hands we expect soon to have a weapon of wholly unprecedented destructive power. Today's prime fact is war. Our great task is to bring this war to a prompt and successful conclusion. We may assume that our new

weapon puts in our hands overwhelming power. It is our obligation to use this power 'with the best wisdom we can command. To us now the matter of first importance is how our use of this new weapon will appear in the long view of history." Compton, *Atomic Quest*, p. 219.

73 *Med Files: Harrison-Bundy Series*, Folder #100, "Interim Committee Minutes."

74 Compton, *Atomic Quest*, p. 238. This statement is taken somewhat out of context, for it is part of an account that indicates that the morning discussion included consideration of the bomb's use. The minutes of the committee indicates no such consideration.

75 Smith, *Bulletin of the Atomic Scientists*, XIV, 297. Bard's failure to remember *any* exploration of use is explained by the fact that he left following the morning meeting and was absent when the matter was brought up at the afternoon session. See Elting E. Morison, *Turmoil and Tradition: A Study of the Life and Times of Henry L. Stimson* (Boston: Houghton Mifflin Company, 1960), p. 627.

76 U. S. Atomic Energy Commission, *In the Matter of J. Robert Oppenheimer*, p. 34. Byrnes, *Speaking Frankly*, p. 260. Byrnes, *All in One Lifetime*, p. 282. Compton, *Atomic Quest*, p. 236.

77 *MED Files: Harrison-Bundy Series*, Folder #100, "Interim Committee Minutes."

78 *Ibid.*

79 *Ibid.*

80 *Ibid.*

81 Compton's account indicates that this morning session involved a refusal by Stimson to consider Kyoto as a target and a statement by Marshall on the use of the bomb: "General Marshall stated that from the point of view of the post war [*sic*] safety of the nation he would have to argue against the use of the bomb in World War II, at least if its existence could be kept secret. Such use, he said, would show our hand. We would be in a stronger position with regard to future military action if we did not show the power we held." Later in his work Compton states that from subsequent conversation, he concluded that Marshall was merely voicing a valid military objection and that the General was nevertheless convinced that the bomb should be used. See Compton, *Atomic Quest*, pp. 237–38. There is no record of such statements by Stimson or Marshall in the committee's minutes.

By this time in the discussion it is likely that Stimson had left the meeting to attend a White House conference. He has written in his *Diary* that he left after an hour and a half and that Marshall took over for him as chairman. Stimson, *Diary*, May 1, 1945. The minutes do not mention his departure.

82 These comments are interesting inasmuch as they were made at a time when the United States was involved at San Francisco in promoting the United Nations as an international organization with universal membership as an ideal.

83 *MED Files: Harrison-Bundy Series*, Folder #100, "Interim Committee Minutes." General Groves has expressed the opinion that Byrnes was the key person on the Interim Committee in formulating decisions. Bush, Conant, and Groves as expert advisers were important in presenting the facts concerning S-1 upon which the decisions were based. *Groves Interview*, September 8, 1960.

84 Compton, *Atomic Quest*, p. 238.

85 *Ibid.*, pp. 238–39.

86 Although Compton claims that the committee went into executive session after lunch and only later recalled the members of the scientific panel, there is no such suggestion in the minutes. In fact Arneson's record states that all were present but Marshall, thus indicating that Bard had returned. The fact that Oppenheimer, at least,

participated in the afternoon's discussions indicates that the scientific panel might have been present. See Compton, *Atomic Quest*, p. 239. *MED Files*: *Harrison-Bundy Series*, Folder #100, "Interim Committee Minutes."

87 *MED Files*: *Harrison-Bundy Series*, Folder #100, "Interim Committee Minutes."

88 U. S. Atomic Energy Commission, *In the Matter of J. Robert Oppenheimer*, p. 34. Compton, *Atomic Quest*, p. 239.

89 The Interim Committee Log indicates that copies of the A. H. Compton report were given to the committee. The writer has been unable to determine the nature of the report. A reasonable guess might indicate that it further emphasized scientific misgivings. See *MED Files*: *Harrison-Bundy Series*, Folder #98, "Interim Committee Log," 1 June, 1945. See also Folder #100, "Interim Committee Minutes of Meetings" for Harrison's memorandum of June 1 to the Secretary of War which suggested the agenda for the meeting that day. An interesting statement appears in paragraph 4 of that memorandum. Harrison wrote, ". . . we cannot be quite as frank with them as we were yesterday. They all know the tremendous power of the weapon. They all know its approaching success. They, of course, do not know and should not know anything about targets or precise schedules." Apparently they were not to be consulted about the use of the bomb.

90 *MED Files*: *Harrison-Bundy Series*, Folder #100, "Interim Committee Minutes," undated, "Notes of the Interim Committee Meeting Friday, 1 June, 1945, 11:00 A.M.-12:30 P.M., and 1:45 P.M.-3:30 P.M." signed by Arneson. Byrnes indicates that he introduced the question of how long it would take other governments to produce atomic bombs. See Byrnes, *All in One Lifetime*, pp. 283–84, and Byrnes, *Speaking Frankly*, p. 261.

91 *MED Files*: *Harrison-Bundy Series*, Folder #100, "Interim Committee Minutes," 1 June, 1945. The phrase, "the present view of the Committee," might suggest that they foresaw the possibility of later changing their opinion. Subsequent developments both within the committee and among other interested individuals indicate, however, that no reversal occurred except on the part of Bard. See pp. 149–50.

92 *Ibid.* Presumably the committee did not consider itself endowed with such competence.

93 See pp. 141–43.

94 Stimson and Bundy, *On Active Service in Peace and War*, p. 617.

95 *Ibid.*, p. 617. The implication of prior decision is the author's.

96 Morison, *Turmoil and Tradition*, p. 629–30.

97 See p. 128.

98 Smith, *Bulletin of the Atomic Scientists*, XIV, 299. Mrs. Smith's account of the Franck Committee's work is the most authoritative that has been found. The following account, with noted exceptions, is based on her article. The other members of the committee were Donald Hughes, J. J. Nickson, Eugene Rabinowitch, Glenn Seaborg, Joyce Stearns, and Leo Szilard. According to General Groves, the moving force behind the committee's actions was Szilard who had a strong influence on Franck. *Groves Interview*, September 8, 1960.

99 See Compton, *Atomic Quest*, pp. 234–35, for an indication that the Franck Committee had rushed to present its conclusions prior to the May 31 meeting of the Interim Committee.

100 Smith, *Bulletin of the Atomic Scientists*, XIV, 301.

101 Hereafter, *Franck Report*. Text Appears in *Bulletin of the Atomic Scientists*, I (May 1946), p. 1.

102 Compton, *Atomic Quest*, p. 236. Smith, *Bulletin of the Atomic Scientists*, XIV, 302. Compton's account implies incorrectly that the attempt to get the report to Stimson occurred prior to the May 31 meeting of the Interim Committee.

103 *MED Files: Harrison-Bundy Series*, Folder #98, "Interim Committee Log," June 12, 1945, and June 15, 1945.

104 This letter was addressed to Stimson, for the attention of Harrison, causing some doubt that it was ever meant for Stimson. The original and an attached copy of the *Franck Report* appears in *MED Files: Harrison-Bundy Series*, Folder #76, "S-1 Interim Committee—Scientific Panel." This copy of the Franck Report closely approximates the text of report included in this paper.

105 *Ibid.* See also Compton, *Atomic Quest*, p. 236.

106 *MED Files: Harrison-Bundy Series*, Folder #98, "Interim Committee Log," June 15, 1945.

107 See pp. 142–43.

108 Stimson specifically mentions seeing only the report of the scientific panel which was written on July 16. He indicates, however, that the committee was a channel for suggestions from scientists and that one such suggestion questioned any use of the bomb against the enemy. Henry L. Stimson, "The Decision to Use the Atomic Bomb," *Harper's Magazine*, CXCIV, 101.

109 The timing of this meeting is uncertain. Compton mentions that ten days after the May 31 meeting of the Interim Committee he spent a long weekend at Los Alamos. See Compton, *Atomic Quest*, p. 239. If the meeting occurred over a weekend it would have begun on June 9, a Saturday. It is likely that the panel met over the weekend of June 9 and 10.

110 U. S. Atomic Energy Commission, *In the Matter of J. Robert Oppenheimer*, p. 34.

111 *Med Files: Harrison-Bundy Series*, Folder #100, "Interim Committee Minutes." See also, Smith, *Bulletin of the Atomic Scientists*, XV, 306. Mrs. Smith very effectively indicates that the scientific panel did not consider the *Franck Report* as such in preparing its report. She states that Oppenheimer is certain that he never saw it until after the war.

112 See Herbert Feis, *Japan Subdued: The Atomic Bomb and the End of the War in the Pacific* (Princeton: Princeton University Press, 1961), p. 42, fn. 81. Feis felt that the delay probably resulted from the panel's desire to see the *Franck Report* before submitting its recommendations. This is, of course, possible. But the timing would indicate that, even if the panel had seen it, the *Franck Report* had little if any impact on its recommendations. The citation in the "Interim Committee Minutes" suggests that they had not seen it. In the revised edition of his work (Herbert Feis, *The Atomic Bomb and the End of World War II* [Princeton: Princeton University Press, 1966], p. 53), he states that "It . . . remains undetermined whether the panel had in hand a complete copy of the Franck memo when they met, or merely knew of its reasoning and proposals."

113 *MED Files: Harrison-Bundy Series*, Folder #76, "S-1 Interim Committee— Scientific Panel." See also Stimson, "The Decision to Use the Atomic Bomb," *Harper's Magazine*, CXCIV, 101.

114 Truman, *Memoirs*, I, 419. Truman implies that he received the conclusions of the scientific panel at the same time. Since the report was not written until June 16, it seems that his recollections are faulty.

115 *Ibid.*, p. 419.

116 Byrnes, *Speaking Frankly*, pp. 261–62.

117 Byrnes, *All in One Lifetime*, p. 286.

118 Stimson, *Diary*, June 6, 1945. See also Feis, *Japan Subdued*, p. 39, fn. 23.

119 Stimson made his choice after consultation with Senator Kenneth McKellar, President pro tempore of the Senate. McKellar suggested Carl Hayden of Arizona and Wallace H. White of Maine. Stimson asked for Alben W. Barkley, the Majority Leader. Although McKellar thought that appropriations were assured, Stimson was doubtful. He wanted McKellar to assume responsibility for the selection so that the Senate later wouldn't think that the choice had been his. See Stimson, *Diary*, June 6, 1945.

120 Stimson, *Diary*, June 6, 1945.

121 *Ibid.*, June 6, 1945.

122 *Ibid.*, June 6, 1945.

123 *Ibid.*, June 6, 1945.

124 Feis indicates that the Interim Committee's recommendations ". . . were revised or at least reworded in another recorded statement of them on June 7th. The differences were not significant. Presumably Stimson used the first version when talking with the President on June 6th." See Feis, *Japan Subdued*, p. 39, fn. 24. Feis, *The Atomic Bomb and the End of World War II*, p. 49, fn. 35. It has been impossible to discover a formal rewording or revision of the committee's recommendations. A notation in the "Interim Committee Log," on June 7, 1945, refers to a discussion between Harrison and Stimson concerning the recommendations of May 31 and June 1. This conference seems to have been called to clarify and reaffirm for Stimson what the committee had done. It could be a misdated briefing, preparing Stimson for his conference with Truman. The note mentions the following recommendation:

"(1) the present program, including Chicago, be continued at present levels for the duration of the war; (2) the bomb be used without prior warning against Japan at earliest opportunity, the targets to be a military target [*sic*] surrounded by houses; (3) a Military Panel be established; and (4) work to be started promptly on legislation." Stimson agreed with (1) and (2). He didn't favor (3). In reference to (4) he wanted to give first priority to legislation for a domestic control, with problems of international relations and controls to be handled by a permanent postwar commission established by law. See *MED Files: Harrison-Bundy Series*, Folder #98, "Interim Committee Log," June 7, 1945. The above citation is hardly a reworking of the earlier decision.

125 Arthur W. Page was also assigned to work on the President's message. See *MED Files: Harrison-Bundy Series*, Folder #98, "Interim Committee Log," May 19, 1945.

126 *MED Files: Harrison-Bundy Series*, Folder #74, "Interim Committee—President's Statement," June 7, 1945.

127 *MED Files: Harrison-Bundy Series*, Folder #98, "Interim Committee Log," May 19, 1945. Arneson had been assigned to work on Stimson's draft.

128 *Ibid.*, June 15, 18, 20, 1945.

129 *MED Files: Harrison-Bundy Series*, Folder #98, "Interim Committee Log," June 13, 1945.

130 *MED Files: Harrison-Bundy Series*, Folder #37, "S-1 C.P.C. Meeting, July 4, 1945," June 15, 1945. It has been impossible to determine whether Stimson requested this information or Groves initiated its transmission.

131 Ehrman, *Grand Strategy*, VI, 297.

132 *MED Files: Harrison-Bundy Series*, Folder #52, "S-1 British—Conversations with HHB," June 19, 1945.

133 The account of this meeting is based on Arneson's undated minutes. See *MED Files: Harrison-Bundy Series*, Folder #100, "Interim Committee Minutes." It is interesting that Stimson failed to attend and that he was not present at any of the succeeding

meetings. Apparently he could rely on Harrison to handle the lesser matters which the committee had under consideration.

[134] Italics are Arneson's. *MED Files*: *Harrison-Bundy Series*, Folder #100, "Interim Committee Minutes."

[135] See pp. 142–43. The scientific panel was not present at this meeting.

[136] *MED Files*: *Harrison-Bundy Series*, Folder #100, "Interim Committee Minutes."

[137] *Ibid.*, Italics are Arneson's.

[138] *MED Files*: *Harrison-Bundy Series*, Folder #100, "Interim Committee Minutes."

[139] *Ibid.*, July 6 and July 19, 1945. At the conclusion of the meeting of July 19, Conant suggested that the next meeting be held on August 2. The committee, however, set no time for a following meeting and the files do not contain minutes of any subsequent meeting. Presumably, that of July 19 was the last.

[140] See pp. 220–24.

[141] From a letter of August 15, 1958, from Ralph A. Bard.

[142] This is from a copy sent by Bard in his letter of August 15, 1958. A copy is also included in Knebel and Bailey, *No High Ground*, pp. 109–10.

[143] Knebel and Bailey, *No High Ground*, p. 109.

[144] Leahy, *Diaries*, II, 86, 92, 99.

[145] Millis (ed.), *The Forrestal Diaries*, p. 53.

[146] *Groves Interview*, September 8, 1960.

[147] *MED Files*: *Harrison-Bundy Series*, Folder #98, "Interim Committee Log," July 2, 1945.

[148] Stimson had conferences with Truman on July 2 and 3, 1945. He mentions nothing about Bard's memorandum. In fact, at no place in his *Diary* does he indicate that he saw it. Stimson, *Diary*, June 27 to August 6, 1945.

CHAPTER **7**

A FALLING SUN

BEFORE the Potsdam Conference convened on July 16, 1945, the Interim Committee had given its support for the use of the atomic bomb on Japan. It had recommended to Secretary of War Stimson and to President Truman that the bomb be used, it had suggested the nature of the target, and it had recommended that no warning be given either to the Japanese people or to the Japanese Government. By July 16 at Alamogordo, New Mexico, an atomic bomb was detonated successfully. The components of two additional but different weapons were on their way to Tinian. The 509th Bombing Group was already practicing bomb runs from North Field on Tinian. Unless Truman withdrew his sanction, the bombs would be used. The decision to change the policy rested, at least in part, on the United States Government's evaluation of the Japanese position and on its ability to force the Japanese Government to unconditional surrender through the use of conventional weapons.

The general image of the Japanese held by those in policymaking positions in the United States Government was strongly influenced by the bitter fighting of Japanese troops during the war. Many had fought long after defeat had been inevitable. Many had fought to the death. The determined resistance of Japanese troops on Iwo Jimo and on Okinawa, when projected to the defense of the Japanese home islands, provided the prospect of a nation in arms, defending its homeland with harsh retaliation against the invaders despite the probability of national death.

Most of the top officials in Washington, although they recognized the disparity between the growing power which the United States could now concentrate against Japan since the defeat of Germany and the diminishing power of Japan, were strongly conditioned by the belief that the Japanese would never surrender.[1] Prevailing opinion held that Japan, despite the severe reduction of its naval and air forces, could still muster a large army backed by a zealous population to make its eventual defeat most costly. Secretary of War Stimson, reviewing the situation in July, 1945, later wrote:

As we understood it in July. there was a very strong possibility that the Japanese government might determine upon resistance to the end, in all of the areas under its control. In such an event the Allies would be faced with the enormous task of destroying an armed force of five million men and five thousand suicide aircraft, belonging to a race which had already amply demonstrated its ability to fight to the death.[3]

This attitude deeply influenced Truman's thoughts during the days before Potsdam. His feelings during June and July were evidenced in his *Memoirs*:

The war in the Pacific had been hard and costly in the years since December 7, 1941. We had come a long way back from Pearl Harbor and Bataan. From Australia and New Caledonia in the south and island bases on Hawaii in the eastern Pacific, our forces had fought their way back to the Philippines and to the last island chain before the Japanese home islands. Okinawa and Iwo Jima 'had been defended fiercely by the enemy, and our loss of lives had been very heavy. But we now had bases from which direct attacks could be launched on Japan. We also knew that the closer we came to the home islands the more determined and fanatical would be the resistance. There were still more than four million men in the Japanese armed forces to defend the main Japanese islands, Korea, Manchuria and North China. The Japanese were also building up a "National Volunteer Army" at home for a last ditch stand.

The Chiefs of Staff were grim in their estimates of the cost we would have to pay to invade the Japanese mainland.[3]

There were few in the United States Government who accepted a different position, and those who did were in the lower echelons of intelligence from which they had difficulty in influencing the top policymakers. One such official was Captain Ellis M. Zacharias, a naval intelligence officer who had spent some time in Japan prior to the war. In proposing Operation Plan I-45 for a series of radio broadcasts to Japan which would emphasize the futility of resistance he indicated the weakening Japanese situation by reviewing the positions of the Japanese military leadership:

. . . c.   Certain members of the Japanese High Command realize that the war is irretrievably lost; the others of the High Command recognize the seriousness of the present situation is bound to deteriorate in the future.

d.   The plans for victory of the Japanese High Command are contingent upon continued unity of thought between the Army and the Navy and upon an all-sacrificing prosecution of the war.

e.   Great conflict of opinion exists within the High Command as to the past, present, and future conduct of the war.

f.   Field commanders in highest echelon are blaming the High Command for inept leadership in the war.

. . . h.   For the first time since the Russo-Japanese war, the Premier has been instructed to participate in the deliberations of the High Command. . . .

i.   For the first time in twenty-four years criticism of the government and the High Command is openly voiced. . . .

. . . r.   There are a great many highly placed individuals in Japan who realized that war with the United States meant "the finish of the Japanese empire and a great loss to the United States. . . ." [4]

He then went on to assume:

. . . c.   It is known that groups already exist whose position in favor of a cessation of hostilities would receive the required stimulus and support for concerted action in the direction desired by this plan.

d.   That cessation of organized resistance in Germany . . . would give the Japanese High Command the pretext for withdrawal from the war, particularly if such a "face-saving" course is encouraged. . . ."[5]

But Zacharias found it difficult to promote this position.

Another attempt to dispel the myth of Japanese willingness to fight to national death was made by the Foreign Morale Analysis Division in the Office of War Information. Commander Alexander H. Leighton, Chief of the Division, has written that on June 1, 1945, his organization published a report which indicated a serious deterioration of morale among the civilian Japanese and the great possibility that the Japanese Government would surrender on almost any terms the United States suggested.[6] The report had been ready by May, but the ". . . Office of War Information Japan Section in the office of the Deputy Director for the Far East held up the report's publication and required that it be toned down." [7] Just who saw the report is unclear. Leighton says nothing about its distribution. It apparently had little, if any, effect on the men at the top.

The opinion at the higher levels continued to be that Japanese military and civilian morale was practically unbreakable.

There were many men in top command and policy-making positions who felt that Japanese morale was a solid wall of uniform strength which nothing could destroy except the actual killing of the men who displayed it. Every Japanese soldier was regarded as an ideal fighting machine—fearless, fanatic, obeying instantly, something not quite human that looked only for an opportunity to die for the Emperor.[8]

For whatever reason, whether in reaction to the original underestimate of Japanese capability, to the willingness of some Japanese soldiers to fight on after all hope was gone, or to the misunderstanding of the Japanese suicide rite of *hara-kiri* and its more recent manifestation, the *Kamikaze,* those responsible for United States policy steadfastly adhered to the stereotype of the Japanese who would accept death rather than surrender.

This attitude within the United States Government was only partially reflective of fact. It was, perhaps, true that most Japanese would accept death rather than dishonor that symbol of Japanese nationalism, the Emperor. On the other hand, as Zacharias and Leighton were trying to point out, there was in the Japanese Government a growing movement for peace. The course that Japanese policy was to follow, at least after April, 1945, was to reflect the growing influence of the peace group in the highest governmental agency, the Supreme Council for the Direction of the War ((SCDW).[9]

The details of political interaction within the government of Japan which ultimately led to covert action seeking avenues of possible surrender have been frequently reviewed and need not be repeated here.[10] Certain events, however, must be considered. On April 5, the government of General Koiso Kuniaki fell, and on April 7 Admiral Suzuki Kantaro became Premier.[11] Suzuki had been chosen by the *Jushin*, a council of former premiers or Elder statesmen, who were called together by the Lord Keeper of the Privy Seal, the Marquis Kido Koichi. Kido was the Emperor's political adviser and the link between the throne and the government. One of his functions was to advise the Emperor on the choice of a new Premier after a government had fallen.[12] In this case Kido, who favored peace and who knew that the Emperor supported him, overrode the objections of former Premier, General Tojo Hideki, and with the support of the other *Jushin,* most of whom also supported a policy of peace, prevailed on the aged Admiral to become Premier.[13] Suzuki was looked upon as a moderate who could implement the desire for peace.

The peace movement, however, had developed even before the Suzuki government came to power in 1945. The former Foreign Minister, Shigemitsu Mamoru, had believed that his ". . . most important duty was the quest for peace . . ." when he had come to office in 1943.[14] He had also learned from Kido at that time that ". . . the Emperor's will was crystal clear; he desired peace at the earliest moment. So long as Japan's good name were maintained, the question of her overseas possessions was immaterial." [15] As the military position of Japan worsened during 1943 and 1944, Kido and Shigemitsu continued to promote peace within the palace and the government respectively. And yet they had had to move slowly and secretly, for the army and its effective internal police system might very well liquidate them. In fact, the pattern of their efforts would be repeated under the Suzuki regime. The peace group found it expedient to follow a fine and narrow line promoting their ends without incurring the premature and open opposition of army leaders who wished to carry on the war and who were not above using the tool of political assassination to eliminate their more flexible opposition.

Shigemitsu's last speech to the Privy Council on March 30, 1945, illustrated the problem of the peace group. For some time he had felt that Japan should go directly to the United States and Great Britain to open negotiations for peace. Russia, he thought, was likely to attack Japan at any moment and could not be relied on for mediation. He had stated these views privately to a gathering of senior statesmen. Now he decided to indicate his feelings openly to the Privy Council. And yet his remarks represented a masterpiece of indirection. After stating that the German war had nearly reached its last phase he remarked that ". . . when a continental country becomes enfeebled on land and in the air, the war is nearing its end; the same argument applies to an island country when it loses its mastery at sea and in the air. In these days of mechanized mass warfare, the defeat of the weaker country comes very suddenly." [16] He next mentioned that Hitler meant to fight it out to the end, and then as an apparent afterthought he pointed out that the ". . . position of Nazi-Germany differs from that of Japan with her Imperial Throne." [17] Shigemitsu finally warned that Russian protestations of neutrality meant nothing and that Japan should be ". . . prepared for her to descend on Manchuria in overwhelming strength. The time has come when Japan must give grave consideration to her future course of action." [18] He made no direct recommendation. But the course he implied was negotiated peace.

On April 9, Suzuki appointed Togo Shigenori as the new Foreign Minister to replace Shigemitsu. Togo had formerly been Ambassador to Russia and had served as Foreign Minister at the time of Pearl Harbor. Despite the fact that he was widely thought of in the United States as one of those responsible for the war, he was on his accession to office in 1945 strongly devoted to the negotiation of peace.[19] His major purpose in reluctantly assuming the post of Foreign Minister was to end the war as soon as possible. He seized the occasion of German defeat to "try to get agreement to making peace while [Japanese] military strength was not yet wholly exhausted. . . ." [20]

Togo, perhaps, influenced by the knowledge he had acquired of the Soviet Union during his term as Ambassador in Moscow, decided that Japan's only course was to attempt to improve relations with the Soviet Union. It was true that the Soviet Government had announced to the Japanese on April 5, 1945, that it could not renew the Russo-Japanese Neutrality Pact which had been the basis of the relations between the two states during the war. Under its terms, however, the pact was to be in force for a year after the announcement to terminate. Togo acted quickly, therefore, to obtain Soviet assurance that the neutrality obligations would be observed by urging the Japanese Ambassador in Moscow, Sato Naotake, to determine the Russian position. On April 27 Vyacheslav M. Molotov, the Soviet Foreign Minister, told Sato that the Soviet attitude toward neutrality had not changed.[21] Togo then set his course to improve relations with the Soviet Union, despite the buildup of Russian arms in the Soviet Far East, and to secure Russian mediation between Japan, on the one hand, and the United States and Great Britain, on the other.

On May 10, he began to implement this policy. His first step was to convince the members of the SCDW that they should meet without the subordinate staff who customarily attended their meetings. Quite realistically, he recognized that the younger staff officers were far more fanatic in their support for continued hostilities than the more senior members of the SCDW. He feared not only their actions in the SCDW but also the possibility that they might promote rebellion of the military against their superiors on the council. Most of the important decisions concerning the course of the war and the effort to negotiate a peace were handled by secret "members meetings" of the SCDW. As Togo wrote:

The guarding of secrecy was vital, because it was certain that should the discussions at the meetings become known at the lower levels, fanatical opposition would be raised by some of the military officers, and the effort to make peace would be seriously hampered or even frustrated.[22]

In the subsequent meetings of the SCDW, a general division developed between the group who favored peace, ultimately at almost any price, and those who favored continuing the war in order to obtain a stronger bargaining position for negotiating a settlement following anticipated victories in the home islands. The peace group argued that the possibility of such victories was illusory and that Japan's position showed every evidence of continued deterioration. But the three on the SCDW who favored continuing hostilities were strongly affected by their belief in the willingness of the Japanese people to fight for their homeland. Togo, Admiral Yonai Mitsumasa, and frequently General Suzuki Korechika favored an active effort to negotiate peace. Anami, General Umezu Yoshijiro, and Admiral Toyoda Soemu, backed by most of the military, favored resistance. The peace group had the continuing, if tacit, support of the Emperor and the open backing of Kido and most of the *Jushin*, particularly former Premier Konoye Fumimaro.

Following the German collapse, the SCDW held a number of meetings from May 11 to May 14 to discuss the course of Japanese policy. A general agreement was made to seek a rapprochement with the Soviet Union. Anami, the representative from the army, wanted only a renewal of Soviet-Japanese neutrality which would keep the Russians out of the war. The navy, on the other hand, suggested closer commercial relations with the Soviet Union which might provide its ships with additional petroleum and other supplies. Foreign Minister Togo warned both groups that any rapprochement with the Soviet Union was impossible. It was too late. He emphasized that the Soviet Government was realistic in its respect for power and had quite likely recognized Japan's worsening position. He suggested that the best Japan might get from the Soviet Government was an agreement to mediate and that Japan would have to provide considerable concessions in order to obtain that. The result of these discussions was a decision to make an approach to the Soviet Union in the following order of preference: "(1) the prevention of Russian entry into the war; (2) inducing the U.S.S.R. so far as might be possible to adopt an attitude favorable to . . . [Japan]; and (3) opening a way to peace." [23]

To secure possible mediation, the use of China, Switzerland, Sweden, and the Vatican was considered; but each was considered a less hopeful channel for mediation than the Soviet Union. Only the latter was sufficiently influential to negotiate a modification of the United States policy of unconditional surrender. A major difference of opinion arose between Togo and Anami when it came to suggesting terms of peace acceptable to Japan in the solicitation of Russian mediation. Anami, backed by Umezu, favored terms which would emphasize that extensive areas were still held by the Japanese army and that it was in no sense defeated. Togo, on the other hand, felt that Japan should seek peace on realistic terms reflecting the superior position of the enemy considering the general trend of the war. The resultant impasse led to the tabling of the effort to negotiate Russian mediation. The possibility of realizing a rapprochement with the Soviet Union was to be explored first.

To sound out the Russian Government as to the possibilities of closer relations with Japan, Togo chose the career diplomat. Hirota Koki, who, as a former Foreign Minister and Premier, was recognized as an expert on Russo-Japanese relations. Hirota met with the Soviet Ambassador to Japan, Jacob A. Malik, on June 3 and 4 at the Gora resort hotel in the Hakone Mountains near Tokyo. Following his conversations with Malik, Hirota reported to Togo that Malik and he had exchanged opinions on fundamental problems, that the discussion had been friendly, but that Malik had been noncommittal and had requested a delay prior to additional negotiations so that he might contact his government.[24] The delay was to last until June 14.

In the meanwhile, on June 6 the army struck to offset the movement in the SCDW toward a mediated peace. As a result of a meeting of the SCDW and its staff called unexpectedly on June 6; of Premier Suzuki's apparent acceptance of the army's position at that meeting; of the sanction of the Imperial Conference on June 8; and of its announcement to an Extraordinary Session of the Diet which met from June 9 until June 13, the Japanese Government apparently made a complete reversal of the policy suggested in the SCDW in May and accepted a "Fundamental Policy to be Followed Henceforth in the Conduct of the War." [25]

This policy, accepted in silence by the Emperor and enunciated in the name of the highest authority, was essentially the ". . . army's final, comprehensive demand that the nation engage the enemy on Japan's own shores, for only thus . . . could the imperial land be preserved and the national policy maintained." [26] The change was openly accepted by Suzuki and Yonai because they hoped the harder line would improve the morale of the Japanese people when the policy was openly proclaimed before the Diet and because they were unwilling to accept a direct confrontation with the army at a time when they were so uncertain as to the meaning of unconditional surrender. Togo objected to the changed "Fundamental Policy" but with little success. Both he and Kido, however, attached little importance to the development; for they expected the deteriorating military situation to cut away the basis for such a last-ditch defense. They became even more determined to search for an acceptable peace.[27]

The reinstitution of the government's effort to seek Russian mediation, however, came quite quickly. At a meeting of the top six of the SCDW on June 18, it was determined to seek ways of promoting Soviet mediation. However, all agreed that fighting would have to continue as long as the United States and Great Britain demanded unconditional surrender. The next day Togo urged Hirota to do everything possible to renew his conversations with Malik. On June 22, the day that the United States announced that Okinawa had been secured, the SCDW convened in an Imperial Conference to receive the Emperor's suggestion that they ". . . exert every effort to make an end to the war with the greatest expedition." [28]

On June 24 Hirota again met with Malik who now requested a concrete statement of Japan's intentions although he had formerly seemed to have only a cursory interest in Hirota's advances. On June 29 Hirota met with Malik for the final time. At this session he presented Japan's offer in specific terms. In return for Soviet acceptance of a nonaggression pact with Japan, the Japanese Government would grant independence to Manchuria, would trade Japanese fishing concessions in Soviet waters for Soviet oil shipments, and would consider any other matters the Soviet Union might wish to discuss.[29] After a short conversation Malik promised he would transmit the Japanese proposals to Moscow and indicated he would resume negotiations after he had received an answer. Despite Togo's efforts to expedite Soviet consideration of the Japanese offer through Sato, Malik was never again to discuss the matter with Hirota.

By early July the military situation had become critical for Japan. Heavy bomber attacks and carrier-based bomber and fighter forays swept Japan practically unimpeded by defensive air cover. Togo gave up hope for success from a continuation of the Hirota-Malik talks and decided to seek Soviet mediation directly. On July 10 the SCDW accepted Togo's plan to dispatch a Special Imperial Envoy to Moscow to negotiate Russian participation in peace negotiations. Thus began the last, futile Japanese effort to attract the support of the Soviet Union, already committed to entering the war against Japan. But this the Japanese did not know, and this the Russians did not disclose.

The Russians sought to avoid Japan's requests for mediation in order to delay its capitulation to the United States. At the same time the Soviet Union hastened its military buildup in the Far East to establish at least a token participation in the war as a basis for exercising political influence after the Japanese had been defeated. Sato, therefore, experienced nothing but frustration in trying to obtain rapid Soviet acceptance of the mission of the Imperial Envoy.

On July 11, Togo wired Sato that while continuing to foster the completion of the Hirota-Malik talks, he would now explore directly the possibility of Soviet mediation since the ". . . foreign and domestic situation for the Empire is very serious, and even the termination of the war is now being considered privately." [30] He urged Sato to meet Molotov immediately in order to ascertain Russian intentions. On July 12, he indicated Japan's desire to send Konoye as an Imperial Envoy to Moscow. He asked Sato to obtain Russian acceptance of Konoye's mission and to arrange for a meeting between Konoye and the Russian authorities as soon as they returned to Moscow from the pending Three Power Conference at Potsdam. In general terms he described the purpose of the Konoye visit:

His Majesty the Emperor is greatly concerned over the daily increasing calamities and sacrifices faced by the citizens of the various belligerent countries in this present war, and it is His Majesty's heart's desire to see the swift termination of the war. In The Greater East Asia War, however, as long as America and England insist on unconditional surrender, our country has no alternative but to see it through in an all-out effort for the sake of survival and the honor of the homeland. The resulting enormous bloodshed would indeed be contrary to His Majesty's earnest hope that peace may be restored as speedily as possible for the welfare of mankind.[31]

In a following wire, Togo, somewhat naively, prompted Sato to impress on the Soviet Government the need for absolute secrecy.

Sato responded with a somewhat blunt message to Togo on July 12. The Ambassador stated that obtaining Soviet aid in terminating the war as Japan desired was nearly hopeless. Japan, he argued, was in no position to be responsible for the maintenance of peace in East Asia since the United States and Britain were assuming Japanese prerogatives there. "If indeed our country is pressed by the necessity of terminating the war," he wired, "we ourselves must first of all firmly resolve to terminate the war." [32]

The next day Sato informed Togo that, because of Molotov's pending departure for Potsdam he had been unable to see the Soviet Foreign Minister. He had, however, presented the matter of the requested Konoye mission to Deputy Foreign Minister Alexander Lozovsky who had promised a reply to the Japanese request as soon as possible.[33] In a following message Sato strongly recommended that the purpose of the Konoye mission ". . . should be nothing other than a proposal for peace and termination of hostilities."[34] And, finally, before the Potsdam Conference convened, the Japanese Ambassador wired his Foreign Minister that ". . . a peace treaty by negotiation is something which cannot win the support of the Soviet Union. In the final analysis, if our country truly desires to terminate the war, we have no alternative but to accept unconditional surrender or something very close to it." [35]

By July 16, the date on which the Potsdam Conference convened, some in the Japanese Government at the highest level were seeking a peace short of unconditional surrender, which was generally considered an intolerable threat to the position of the Emperor. Despite the mistaken belief among those at the top of the United States Government that Japan was likely to fight on until completely defeated, active steps had been taken within the Japanese Government toward a resolution of the war. The war party in the SCDW and among the lower ranks in the military still constituted a threat to the hopes of the group which sought peace. And yet the latter persisted and developed strength as the military repeatedly demonstrated its incapacity to meet the growing United States and British pressure. Furthermore, the United States Government had some reason to recognize Japanese peace moves.

From September, 1944, until July 16, 1945, semiofficial and unofficial attempts had been made by a number of Japanese to negotiate peace through channels in Spain, Sweden, Switzerland, the Vatican, and the Soviet Union. Because of the threat of military opposition in Tokyo, most such efforts were conducted privately and by intermediaries rather than by government officials. Apparently few intimations of these developments ever reached the United States Government and, then, generally at its lower levels.

During Shigemitsu's term as Foreign Minister the most important peace effort had originated in mid-September, 1944, in conversations between Suzuki Bunshiro, a spokesman for a peace group headed by Konoye, and the Swedish Minister to Japan, Widar Bagge.[36] Suzuki proposed that Bagge request that the Swedish Government initiate through London peace feelers based on Japan's willingness to surrender all conquered territories, possibly including Manchuria. Bagge reported these conversations to Stockholm and continued his talks with Suzuki during the fall and winter.

In March, 1945, just before a planned visit to Sweden, Bagge informed another friend, Sakaya Tadashi, former Japanese Minister to Finland, that he believed that the United States and Great Britain would modify unconditional surrender to permit the retention of the Emperor if only Japan would take the initiative in seeking peace.[37] Sakaya reported this to Shigemitsu who scheduled a meeting with Bagge later that month. As a result of the conversations with Shigemitsu, Bagge was impressed with the sincerity of the Foreign Minister's request that he do whatever he could to explore Japan's chances of arranging a negotiated peace.[38]

Bagge's return to Sweden was delayed until after the fall of the Koiso government. On April 11, Sakaya informed Togo, the incoming Foreign Minister, of the negotiations with the Swedish Minister. This was welcome news to Togo, for he was already much interested in exploring the possibility of a Swedish approach to the United States.[39] Since Bagge left for Sweden the next day, however, Togo was unable to arrange a meeting with him.

Bagge arrived in Sweden early in May and on May 10 contacted the Japanese Minister to Sweden, Okamoto Suemasa. He was surprised to discover that the latter had received no instructions concerning Swedish mediation. Okamoto informed Togo of his conversation with Bagge. As Togo interpreted Okamoto's message, Bagge expected to act to determine the intention of the United States following a Japanese request for Swedish action. Togo was not ready to go so far, since he was at the same time attempting to promote mediation by the Soviet Union. He was willing to continue the effort only if Sweden, rather than Japan, took the initiative. This it was unwilling to do, and the negotiations were terminated.

Whether or not such efforts might have been successful is problematical. But the United States Government had been informed of these negotiations in May, 1945. At that time, Bagge had had a long conversation with United States Ambassador, Herschel V. Johnson, in which he comprehensively described his contacts with the Japanese.[40] It may be assumed that Johnson reported his conversation to Washington. Little evidence has been discovered to indicate whether the information ever reached the top-level policymaking group in the United States Government.

However, Johnson did inform Washington later of an unofficial and independent attempt to secure Swedish mediation by the Japanese military attache, Major General Onodero Makoto.[41] The Swedish Government had complained to the Japanese about Onodero's unauthorized efforts, and Togo had disavowed them. But Johnson reported that Onodero had said that he and not the Japanese Minister had been authorized to enter negotiations and that, while Onodero stated the Emperor must be maintained as a condition of surrender, he specified no other terms.[42] No further action was taken. Much later at Potsdam, Truman apparently had these incidents in mind when he mentioned to Stalin on July 18 that he had indications of a Japanese peace feeler through Sweden.[43]

Other overtures for peace had been originated unsuccessfully by Foreign Minister Shigemitsu. He ". . . played with the idea of Madrid, where many influential British of Cabinet rank resided, but the project came to nothing." [44] He also apparently initiated peace efforts through the Papal Nuncio in Tokyo.[45] There is little evidence that such attempts were known in the United States. Admiral Zacharias reports, however, that in April and May, 1945, ". . . peace feelers were coming in to Washington in amazingly large numbers. The most persistent of these came via the Vatican. . . ." [46] The Vatican was informed that the Archbishop of Tokyo was acting for the Emperor who was urgently requesting that the Pope serve as an intermediary in arranging peace. The Vatican, however, would only act as a channel of communication. Among Zacharias' group in Washington, these efforts were considered to be propaganda on the part of Japan insofar as the Japanese concerned were inconsistent in their requests for intervention.[47] Whether this information ever went higher than intelligence levels has not been determined.

Unofficial attempts to arrange a peace settlement were also made through Japanese officials in Switzerland. Togo, feeling that Switzerland had insufficient influence with the Allies to mediate peace effectively and basing his hopes on Soviet action, refused to sanction official efforts through the Swiss Government. But other Japanese in Switzerland went ahead anyway.[48]

On May 8, 1945, the Japanese naval attache to Switzerland, Commander Fujimura Yoshiro, urged his superiors to utilize the United States Office of Strategic Services (OSS) in Switzerland as a channel for peace negotiations. Fujimura had first contacted the OSS group through Dr. Friedrich Hack, a German national employed by the Japanese Navy. Hack had met representatives of the Dulles organization on April 23, 1945 in Berne.[49] After receiving Fujimura's assurance that he wished to promote direct negotiations between the Japanese and United States Governments, the Dulles group informed Washington and asked for instructions. On May 3, the Department of State authorized the OSS agents to continue conversations with Fujimura in order to verify his intentions and credentials but warned them not to commit the United States to any arrangement.[50] On May 4, the Dulles group informed Fujimura of its authorization to hear his proposals provided he had the support of his government. Since he had acted only on his own initiative, he could not satisfy this requirement. Despite repeated efforts through May and June, Fujimura was unable to obtain the Japanese Government's sanction for his negotiations. By June 21, the talks between the Dulles group and Fujimura had been terminated.

It appears that the Department of State knew of the OSS-Fujimura conversations in Berne.[51] However, some doubt exists as to whether Allen Dulles had been informed of the talks. On June 14 when Admiral Leahy asked Dulles to visit him in his office, the director of the OSS group denied any knowledge of the talks. Leahy recorded in his *Diaries*:

> I told him [Dulles] that reports had been received to the effect that some of his agents are endeavoring to arrange for conversations with Japanese officials regarding peace terms with Japan.
>
> He replied that he has no knowledge of any such activity and that he does not believe any of his group are involved. He is returning to Switzerland tomorrow where he will, upon arrival in Berne, make a personal investigation of the matter.[52]

No further entry concerning this matter appears in the *Diaries*, and no evidence has been discovered to indicate a follow-up by Dulles. Given the close relationship existing between Truman and Leahy, it seems likely that the President heard at least in general terms about Fujimura's unsuccessful efforts to negotiate a settlement to end the war.

Another attempt similar to Fujimura's was made by Lieutenant General Okamoto Seigo in Zurich and in Basel. Together with Kitamura Kojiro and Yoshimura Tsuyoshi, two officials of the Bank for International Settlements in Basel, he obtained the good offices of Per Jacobsson, a Swedish economic advisor to the bank who was on friendly terms with officials at the United States consulate at Berne, and with Allen Dulles whose headquarters were then at Frankfurt am Main in Germany. Jacobsson arranged to see Dulles at Frankfurt. During their conversations on July 14 Dulles informed Jacobsson that the United States was not opposed to retention of the Emperor following surrender, but that it could presently make no firm commitment. "All it could do was state its *understanding* that the imperial institution would be maintained if Japan surrendered." [53] In addition, the constitution of Japan would have to be changed; and no commitment could be made concerning the disposition of Korea and Formosa which the Japanese desired to retain. Jacobsson returned to Basel with Dulles' suggestions. The Okamoto group decided, with the help of the Japanese Minister, Kase Shunichi, to enlist the support of Tokyo. As in the case of Fujimura, however, it was unable to obtain the backing of the Japanese Government; and negotiations came to an end prior to the meeting at Potsdam.

There is no evidence to indicate top-level United States knowledge of the Okamoto-Dulles negotiations prior to the Potsdam Conference, and it is uncertain that Dulles had authorization for his statements concerning the Emperor. He did, however, fly to Berlin on July 20 to inform Stimson of the Japanese negotiations.[54] Although Stimson made no comment, it may be assumed that he passed the information on to Truman.[55]

Indications of such clandestine moves by individual Japanese might have reinforced the opinions of various officials within the United States Government who concluded from events in Japan that under certain conditions, particularly if the Emperor might be retained, the Japanese might surrender. There is considerable doubt that such opinions ever reached Truman or others in the top-level group in Washington.

Eugene H. Dooman, of the Department of State, who became chairman of the Far East Subcommittee of the State, War, and Navy Coordinating Committee in February, 1945, recalled in 1951 another incident which indicated the Japanese desire for peace.[56] In March or April, 1945, Colonel Dana Johnson, Chief of Psychological Warfare in Hawaii, had visited Dooman and Acting Secretary of State Joseph G. Grew in Washington. From interrogation of high-ranking Japanese prisoners of war, Johnson believed that Japan was ready to surrender as long as the Emperor was not tried as a war criminal and punished.[57] Johnson also believed that the change in governments which brought in Suzuki as Premier was an indication that the Japanese desired to surrender.

Suzuki's rise to power was also considered as a move toward peace by Zacharias' secret branch of Navy Intelligence, devoted to psychological warfare and bearing the designator OP–16–W.[58] The new Premier's moderate statement of condolence to the American people on April 14, just after Roosevelt's death, was felt to indicate a conciliatory line on the part of the Japanese Government. While affirming his determination to continue fighting for the prosperity and coexistence of all nations, Suzuki admitted that ". . . Roosevelt's leadership has been very effective and has been responsible for the Americans' advantageous position today." He went on, "For that reason I can easily understand the great loss his passing means to the American people and my profound sympathy goes to them." [59] This expression was a far cry from the angry joy which Roosevelt's death occasioned in the German Government.

More important to the Zacharias group were intelligence reports indicating a Japanese willingness to accept surrender, or at least a cessation of hostilities prior to the invasion of the home islands. Among these was a most significant report submitted from a neutral capital as early as December, 1944:

It outlined in great detail the course Japan intended to take and stated that General Koiso would soon resign and permit the appointment as prime minister of Admiral Suzuki, an old confidant of the Emperor and leader of what . . . had come to [be called] the "peace party." Moreover, the document indicated that the Emperor himself was leading a group of influential personalities desirous of obtaining peace terms under the most favorable circumstances. And finally, the document informed us that when such a formula could be worked out and our unconditional surrender terms modified to permit the continuation of the Emperor on the throne, Admiral Suzuki would resign in favor of an imperial prince who would effect Japanese surrender. . . .[60]

It is doubtful that any agency outside of OP–16–W gave this report serious consideration or that it was ever brought to the attention of the White House or the Joint Chiefs of Staff.[61]

The White House did, however, have information concerning "rumors" which the Russians had heard concerning Japanese peace efforts. During the conversations between Truman's emissary, Harry Hopkins, and Marshal Stalin in Moscow in late May, 1945, Stalin indicated that he had heard of talks between the British and Japanese regarding unconditional surrender. He went on to say that:

Japan was doomed and they knew it and already so-called Republican movements were beginning to arise behind the scenes which were attempting to play up to the Soviet Union that they could split the Allies.[62]

Hopkins then inquired as to what form Stalin thought Japanese peace overtures might take. Stalin denied having precise information and claimed that his statements were based on what had been heard at the Japanese embassy in Moscow and from sources in Japan. Hopkins then mentioned ". . . that we had heard rumors from Switzerland of the desire of the Japanese industrial families to preserve their position and save Japan from destruction. . . . He thought that these matters in regard to the surrender of Japan should be discussed between the three Allies *and the sooner the better since time was short*." [63] Apparently Hopkins, despite the Joint Chiefs' expectations of months of vigorous fighting, anticipated the possibility of a rapid end to Japanese resistance. On May 30 he cabled Truman that ". . . certain elements in Japan are putting out peace feelers. Therefore, we should consider together our joint attitude and act in concert about the surrender of Japan." [64]

It is unlikely that Truman heard about the Hirota-Malik talks or the Sato-Togo communications prior to the Potsdam Conference. And yet persistent rumors circulating in the United States in regard to Japanese peace offers gave considerable concern to the State Department. As early as February 7, 1945, Under Secretary of State Joseph C. Grew had received an International News Service report which mentioned peace feelers launched by business groups in Japan. These peace feelers had come to the attention of high United States military figures. Grew had been against publishing the article, for he had felt that the Japanese Government might consider it as evidence that the people of the United States were pressing their government to explore the possibility of ending the war. Grew had also believed that businessmen in Japan were in no position to control the Japanese military.[65]

On July 5, Grew had talked on the telephone with Walter Fitzmaurice of *Newsweek* who had heard of Japanese peace offers which had been made by individuals who were not in a responsible position and who did not speak for the Japanese Government. Grew stated positively that ". . . the 'offers' were very unimportant and we had paid no attention whatever to them.

He [Fitzmaurice] could . . . go all out in supporting [Grew's] categorial denial that this Government had received any peace offers from the Japanese Government." [66]

A further incident occurred on July 10 when another International News Service release on the peace movement in Japan was brought to Grew's attention for possible censoring. Despite the fact that he expected that the press release he was about to make on Japanese peace offers could counteract public reaction to the article, it was forbidden publication the next day.[67]

Apparently Grew considered that the publication of such unofficial Japanese efforts to open negotiations for peace might indicate to Japan an unwillingness on the part of the American people to support the war. To dispel any such illusions, Grew issued a press release on July 10 which asserted that the United States had received ". . . no peace offer from the Japanese Government, either through official or unofficial channels. Conversations relating to peace have been reported to the Department from various parts of the world, but in no case has an approach been made to this Government, directly or indirectly, by a person who could establish his authority to speak for the Japanese Government, and in no case has an offer to surrender been made." [68] Grew felt that this would counteract the impact of what he and others considered to be Japanese propaganda for peace. At the same time, the press release indicated that the Department of State had heard of certain informal Japanese attempts to open discussions. Presumably this information, as sketchy as it was, had been relayed to Truman. At Potsdam he was to receive concrete evidence of Japanese efforts to enlist Russian mediation.[69]

The Togo-Sato messages which reflected the decision of the Japanese Government to seek Russian mediation were almost immediately available to the United States Government due to its ability to intercept and decipher communications between Tokyo and Moscow.[70] The first of these messages was read by Lewis L. Strauss, Special Assistant to the Secretary of the Navy, and Secretary Forrestal on July 13.[71] From that time on, Forrestal saw all of the Japanese cables. He was greatly impressed by Sato's realism, and the exchange convinced him more than ever that Japan would capitulate if unconditional surrender were modified so as to preserve the imperial institution.[72] So that their impact might be felt at Potsdam, Forrestal transmitted the intercepts to Admiral Leahy as soon as they were received.[73] Later, on July 28, he flew to Potsdam, although uninvited, and presented the complete files to Byrnes who saw them in detail for the first time.[74] In addition to Byrnes, Stimson also had been informed. He reported that he had heard of Japanese maneuvers for peace on July 16.[75] And Dooman testified later that the State Department had been informed of the messages.[76] News of the Togo-Sato telegrams reached the top when they were mentioned to President Truman at Potsdam, probably by Admiral Leahy.[77] Thus, before and during the

Potsdam negotiations, all of those in the highest decision-making positions knew at least generally of the course of the last, desperate efforts of the Japanese to negotiate peace through Russian good offices.

Despite the suspected maneuvering of the peace group in the Japanese SCDW; despite information which the United States had obtained of formal and informal Japanese attempts to open peace negotiations indirectly; and despite the obviously crippling losses sustained by both the Japanese military and Japan's population, the United States Government, hewing to the line of unconditional surrender, and strongly conditioned by the overriding assumption that Japan would fight until complete military defeat, followed a remarkably consistent policy in the development of its military plans for the defeat of Japan. These plans had originated in the Operations Division (OPD) of the Army's General Staff in April, 1944. At that time, the basic overall strategy that was finally to be utilized against Japan had first been formulated. In its original phraseology, the Strategy Section of OPD had suggested: "a. The collapse of Japan as a result of blockade and air bombardment alone is very doubtful. b. The collapse of Japan can be insured only by invasion of Japan proper." [78] Basing its action on the Strategy Section's recommendations and their elaboration by the Joint War Plans Committee and the Joint Staff Planners, the Joint Chiefs of Staff (JCS) had proposed on July 11, 1944, that the Combined Chiefs of Staff (CCS) accept the following overall strategy for the defeat of Japan:

Our successes to date, our present superiority in air and sea forces, and the prospective availability of forces following the defeat of Germany, lead us to believe that our concept of operations against Japan following Formosa should envision an invasion of the industrial heart of Japan. While it may be possible to defeat Japan by sustained aerial bombardment and the destruction of her sea and air forces, this would probably involve an unacceptable delay.[79]

The schedule of operations envisioned an amphibious attack on Kyushu on October 1, 1945, and a ". . . decisive stroke against the industrial heart of Japan by means of an amphibious attack through the Tokyo plain . . ." by December 1, 1945.[80] On July 29, 1944, the British Chiefs of Staff had accepted the United States plan, and at the second Quebec Conference (Octagon) in September the general strategy had been approved by both the CCS and by Roosevelt and Churchill.

More vigorous resistance by the German military which had culminated in the serious reversal of the Battle of the Bulge, caused the JCS to revise their plans for the defeat of Japan. The changed timing had been outlined in a report from the CCS to Roosevelt and Churchill at the Yalta Conference on February 9, 1945. The general objective had remained ". . . to bring about at the earliest possible date the unconditional surrender of Japan." [81] This was to be accomplished by lowering the Japanese will to resist by means of air bombardment, air and sea blockade, and destruction of the Japanese Navy and Air Force. This softening-up was to be followed by an invasion of the industrial heart of Japan. At this time, however, the planning dates for the end of the war were to be projected farther into the future: Germany's defeat was expected to occur by July 1, 1945, at the earliest; and the planning date for the end of the war with Japan was fixed at eighteen months after German surrender.[82] Despite the fact that allowances must be made for the usual conservatism which marks most military planning, the CCS with the approval of the President and the Prime Minister, had anticipated a long and difficult war before Japan would capitulate.

Now, in April, 1945, Truman was President. One of his first conferences was with the JCS, Forrestal, and Stimson on April 13, the day after he had been sworn in. At that time the JCS revised the time schedule accepted at Yalta by predicting German defeat in six months and the fall of Japan eighteen months thereafter.[83] Truman directed his military advisers to proceed along the lines followed by Roosevelt.[84] He "knew and respected" all of these men and was comforted to know that he would be advised by such capable leaders.[85]

A complete review of the military strategy toward Japan, presented by the Joint Staff Planners (JPS) to the JCS on April 24, generally confirmed the existing policy. Since it was to become the basis for United States planning toward Japan, which, with but few modifications, would remain unchanged until Japan surrendered, the report merits some study. The general objective was still to ". . . bring about at the earliest possible date the unconditional surrender of Japan." [86] Although questioning the necessity of continuing the unconditional surrender policy, the report reaffirmed that if that objective were continued ". . . there is no alternative to annihilation and no prospect that the threat of absolute defeat will bring about capitulation. The accomplishment of . . . unconditional surrender . . . must be entirely brought about by force of arms." [87] The report went on to support the planned invasion of Japan to bring about unconditional surrender as rapidly as possible. After intense air and naval bombardment and a continuing blockade of Japan, the plan envisaged an attack on Kyushu by November 1, 1945, as a prelude to the main attack over the Tokyo plain on Honshu on March 1, 1946. Together with continuing air and naval action, the operations would require 2,700,000 men and would be completed about the fall of 1946.[88] Although the Japanese were still thought to possess the large, well-equipped Kwantung Army in Manchuria, the increasing ability of the United States to interdict movement of such forces from the mainland to Japan made Russian entrance into the war no longer necessary to make invasion feasible.[89]

On May 10, 1945, this report was officially accepted by the JCS and became the basis for all future planning. The first directive ordering Mac-

Arthur, Nimitz, and Arnold to prepare for an invasion of Kyushu on the target date, November 1, 1945, was issued on May 25.[90] Thenceforward, from a planning point of view, the strategy was settled.

Despite the fact that the unanimity of the JCS had been outwardly maintained by their action of May 10, there had been a considerable difference of opinion among them as to the necessity for an invasion of Japan. Generally speaking, the naval and air leaders believed that air and naval bombardment and blockade would bring a Japanese surrender. However, all admitted that, as long as the general objective was the most rapid possible unconditional surrender of Japan, the bitter resistance anticipated from the Japanese would require an invasion before surrender was likely.

Prior to the April 23 meeting, General Marshall had solicited opinions on the basic issue, to invade or not to invade, from his field commanders.[91] MacArthur had replied on April 20, that, of those alternatives available, the most preferable plan was one which supported an invasion of Kyushu in order to obtain bases from which air forces could provide cover for the final assault on Honshu.[92]

Admiral Nimitz's comments had only arrived in Washington on April 28 after the meeting on April 24. He had pointed out the importance of continuing the naval and air actions to encircle and isolate Japan, but he had agreed that the invasion of Kyushu should occur at the earliest possible date. Symptomatic of the general military attitude, he had ended his message with these serious forebodings:

We must be prepared to accept heavy casualties whenever we invade Japan. Wherever our best troops have met the Japanese army . . . in prepared defensive positions it has been a competent fighting force. Our previous successes against ill-fed [sic] and poorly supplied units cut down by our overpowering naval and air action should not be used as the sole basis of estimating . . . the resistance we will meet in the Japanese homeland where the enemy lines of communication will be short and enemy supplies more adequate. . . ."[93]

General Arnold, who consistently emphasized the impact which his strategic bombers were making on the Japanese population and its industrial and commercial capabilities, felt that Japan was on the verge of collapse. He found it difficult to see how it could continue to fight very long after the defeat of Germany. He, nevertheless, accepted the plans for invasion since the attack on Kyushu was to be preceded by intensified bombing.[94]

Other navy doubts of the usefulness of the invasion of Japan were expressed fully by Admiral King and Admiral Leahy. King later reported, ". . . as he had pointed out many times, that the dilemma (the invasion of Japan) was an unnecessary one, for had we been willing to wait, the effective naval blockade would, in the course of time, have starved the Japanese into submission through lack of oil, rice, medicines, and other essential materials." [95] Both he and Leahy have written that at the time they believed the invasion unnecessary, but they acquiesced in order that the decisions of the JCS might appear unanimous.[96]

The army's view which favored an invasion, promoted by Marshall and supported by MacArthur, prevailed. It did so largely because of generally exaggerated anticipations of Japanese resistance and because of the recognition by both naval and air force leaders that prior to the invasion on November 1, they would have a considerable time in which to demonstrate the effectiveness of naval and air techniques in securing the surrender of Japan.

The basic strategy was reaffirmed finally before the Potsdam Conference in mid-June. On June 14, Admiral Leahy informed the JCS that Truman would like to be briefed by them on the following matters on June 18, in preparation for the coming conference:

. . . He will want information as to the number of men of the Army and Ships [*sic*] of the Navy that will be necessary to defeat Japan.

He wants an estimate of the time required and an estimate of the losses in killed and wounded that will result from an invasion of Japan proper.

He wants an estimate of the time and the losses that will result from an effort to defeat Japan by isolation, blockade and bombardment by sea and air force.

He desires to be informed as to exactly what we want the Russians to do.

He desires information as to what useful contribution, if any, can be made by other Allied nations.

It is his intention to make his decision on the campaign with the purpose of economizing to the maximum extent possible in the loss of American lives.

Economy in the use of time and in money cost is comparatively unimportant. . . .[97]

It appears from Leahy's memorandum that Truman, prior to this date, had not been fully informed about the JCS plans for operations against Japan.

Truman received answers to his queries at a conference on June 18 with the JCS; Secretary of War Stimson; his Assistant Secretary, John J. McCloy; and Secretary of the Navy Forrestal.[98] On Truman's invitation Marshall first described the general war plans against Japan. Korea had been practically cut off as a source of Japanese reinforcements. The JCS had selected November 1, 1945 as the target date for an attack of Kyushu. By that time Japan's industry, its navy, its air force, and many of its urban areas would have been destroyed. The invasion of Kyushu was necessary both in order to tighten the blockade and to prepare for the invasion of Honsu on the Tokyo plain. Marshall then repeated the basic concept underlying the planning for Japanese defeat:

We are bringing to bear against the Japanese every weapon and all the force we can employ and there is no reduction in our maximum . . . bombardment and blockade while at the same time we are pressing invasion preparations. It seems in the field they will do it when faced by the completely hopeless prospect occasioned by (1) destruction already wrought by air bombardment and sea blockade, that if the Japanese are ever willing to capitulate short of complete military defeat coupled with (2) a landing on Japan indicating the firmness of our resolution, and also perhaps coupled with (3) the entry or threat of entry of Russia into the war.[99]

Although he hesitated to make any estimate of losses in numbers, he expected that they would be heavy for the United States and considerably heavier for Japan. Asserting that he had the support of MacArthur, Marshall again recommended an invasion, since air power and sea power alone would not be sufficient to knock Japan out of the war.[100]

Admiral King, who previously had been cool toward the invasion of Kyushu, supported Marshall's plea for an invasion.[101] He in turn was followed by General Ira C. Eaker, Arnold's deputy, who stated his own support for Marshall's proposal and indicated he had just received a cable from General Arnold giving the plan his wholehearted endorsement. Although Admiral Leahy was to introduce a slight element of doubt into this apparently complete accord by indicating his opinion that, perhaps, the casualties anticipated from an invasion would be too great a price to pay, the other military leaders felt that they would be reasonable in relation to the advantages derived from the attack.

Truman then said ". . . that as he understood it the Joint Chiefs of Staff, after weighing all possibilities of the situation and considering all possible alternative plans, were still of the unanimous opinion that the Kyushu operation was the best solution under the circumstances." [102] The JCS replied that this was their position. With Stimson's and Forrestal's agreement, the President finally accepted the plan for the Kyushu invasion ". . . from a military standpoint and, so far as he was concerned, the Joint Chiefs of Staff could go ahead with it; . . . we can do this operation and then decide as to the final action later." [103]

Thus, the military plans for invasion of Japan received Presidential approval. Despite obvious United States military superiority and Japanese peace maneuvers, some of which were known to the United States Government, the overriding pessimism concerning an early Japanese surrender, which was engendered by an almost inflexible belief in the willingness of the Japanese to fight to national death, led the JCS and President Truman to prepare for the invasion of Japan. Truman went to Potsdam with the knowledge that ". . . it would require until the late fall of 1946 to bring Japan to her knees." To him this ". . . was a formidable conception . . . ," and he ". . . realized fully that the fighting would be fierce and the losses heavy." [104]

On June 29, the JCS informed the CCS of their plans for Japan. No significant changes were made by the CCS. Kyushu and Honsu were to be the areas of invasion. November 1, 1945, and March 1, 1946, respectively, were to be the dates set for the attacks. On July 16, the very day that the first test of the atomic bomb proved successful at Alamogordo, the CCS noted the American proposal for the defeat of Japan. It is, perhaps, as significant of the revolutionary character of the atomic bomb as much as of the conservatism of the military approach to Japan that the planning for Japanese defeat never included consideration of the possible use of the novel weapon.[105]

Even as the JCS were planning the ultimate invasion of Japan, the military and technical preparations for the testing and final use of the bomb rolled on. It is doubtful that any of the JCS except Marshall and Arnold and, perhaps, not even they, were abreast of the rapid developments taking place within the Manhattan Engineer District (MED) at the time. It is very unlikely that Truman, burdened with many immediate and unfamiliar problems, had either the time or the inclination to concern himself with MED developments aside from the recommendations of the Interim Committee. Below the level of top military policy, however, General Groves rammed his project through to completion.

As the late spring witnessed the German surrender and as the early summer months of 1945 led into the Potsdam negotiations, Groves seemed to sense an even greater need for urgency in the completion of the atomic bomb. This was evidenced in a number of ways. The design of the Fat Man (implosion) model for the bomb had been recognized as being faulty, and those working on it in March, 1945, had become concerned with the need for redesigning it in line with their present knowledge.[106]

They realized, however, that this program could not be allowed to interfere with their main task, which was to get the existing model ready as soon as possible. . . . Today a great deal of attention would doubtless be given to this problem and possibly many would argue that the improvements should be completed before the bomb was actually used in combat. . . . [Groves] overruled any such idea and insisted that there be no delay in the use of existing models, which were satisfactory, though they did not have the explosive power that the redesigned Fat Man would have had.[107]

During these last days before Potsdam, Groves's efforts to hasten delivery of the weapon persisted. Even before the Alamogordo test, components of the Thin Man were dispatched to Tinian. The major portion of the bomb was shipped from Los Alamos on July 14. After a somewhat hectic trip by truck, airplane, and finally from San Francisco to Tinian by the cruiser U.S.S. *Indianapolis*, these components arrived at Tinian on July 26.[108] On July 12 Captain Charles B. McVay, III, skipper of the *Indianapolis*, had been ordered to make his ship ready within four days, much earlier than had been planned. On July 15 he received additional instructions to pick up a small but vital and top secret cargo at Hunter's Point Navy Yard at San Francisco. He was ordered to sail at high speed for Tinian. Although he was not informed as to the nature of his cargo, he was told to preserve it at all costs, even in a life-boat if his ship was sunk. McVay steamed for Tinian at full speed and made the run in a record time of ten days.[109] Other components of Thin Man were shipped to Tinian by airplane. The necessity for speed underlay the entire operation.

Rapid delivery of the weapon related to the nature of the Potsdam Declaration.[110] Groves knew that the declaration would be issued late in July. Consequently he could not wait to test Thin Man.

. . . the indications for success were strong enough so that no one urged us to change our plans of dropping the first gun-type bomb in combat without prior tests. In any case, we simply had to take the chance, because the production of U-235 was so slow . . . that we could not afford to use it on a test. We could now establish firmly that the first atomic bomb drop on Japan would be sometime around the first of August.[111]

In discussing the Alamogordo test of Fat Man, Groves himself has explained the relationship between use of the weapons and the Potsdam Declaration:

I was extremely anxious to have the test carried off on schedule. One reason for this was that I knew the effect that a successful test would have on the issuance and wording of the Potsdam ultimatum. I knew also that every day's delay in the test might well mean the delay of a day in ending the war; not because we would not be ready with the bombs, for the production of fissionable material would continue at full tilt anyway, but because a delay in issuing the Potsdam ultimatum could result in a delay in the Japanese reaction, with a further delay to the atomic attack on Japan. Obviously, a reasonable time had to be allowed for the Japanese to consider the ultimatum.[112]

After the test at Alamogordo, Groves again mentioned the relationship of the test and the Potsdam Declaration.

. . . the reassurance that we would be ready for the first bombing of Japan on July 31, weather permitting, froze the previously tentative decision that it was now time to issue the Potsdam ultimatum. . . . Just how differently the ultimatum would have been worded without this knowledge, no one knows, but with the news of our success in hand President Truman and Mr. Churchill were able to see it dispatched with a great deal more confidence than otherwise might have been the case.[113]

Given the military situation at the time, it is difficult to understand why Truman and Churchill needed additional strength as a basis for issuing the Potsdam Declaration. Groves' sense of urgency certainly seemed tied to the ultimatum. He saw in its possible delay a further obstacle to the use of his weapon.[114]

So Groves rushed the testing of Fat Man at Alamogordo and the shipment of Thin Man components to Tinian. He also took steps, during the spring and early summer, to assure that the other operational problems involved in the use of the bombs were solved.

Among these, an important consideration involved the choice of targets in Japan. Authorized to choose the targets by General Marshall, Groves and General Arnold organized a committee of MED and Air Force personnel to make target recommendations. They also established the criteria which were to guide the committee in making its choices. These were: (1) ". . . that the targets should be places the bombing of which would most adversely affect the will of the Japanese people to continue the war"; (2) they should be generally of a military character, ". . . either important headquarters or troop concentrations, or centers of production of military equipment and supplies"; (3) they should not have been previously bombed so as to provide untouched measuring facilities for the explosive force of the weapons; and (4) at least, the first target should be sufficiently large enough to contain the complete blast of the weapon so that its power could be measured.[115]

The committee met for the first time on May 2. In choosing the targets it was to consider the maximum range of the loaded B-29's of the 509th; the need for visual bombing; the anticipated weather conditions; the nature of expected blast and damage; and the advantages derived from having three targets available for each bombing.[116] On May 28, the Target Committee chose three targets: Kyoto, the ancient capital of Japan, and an urban, industrial city large enough to include within its limits the anticipated damage from the bomb; Hiroshima, a port of embarkation for the Japanese army and convoy assembly point for the navy as well as an industrial city; and Niigata, a growing port on the Sea of Japan and also a center of industry. Later, in June, after Stimson had rejected Kyoto because of its historical and religious significance to the Japanese, the Kokura Arsenal, one of the largest munition plants in Japan, was substituted for it.[117] Nagasaki was chosen much later, probably early in July, by the staff of Major General Curtis E. LeMay who had operational control of the 509th. It was a large shipbuilding and repair center and a major military port. It was, however, added to the list as the least desirable of the targets.[118]

While seeing to it that suitable targets were selected, Groves and Arnold also were concluding that final control over the use of the bombs should rest in Washington. This was necessary because some in the air force assumed that, like other new weapons, the bombs would be used when ready at the discretion of the officer in command in the field. Groves and Arnold, however, believed that Stimson and Marshall would not relinquish control of this important weapon. Groves ". . . had always assumed that operations in the field would be closely controlled from Washington, probably by General Marshall himself, with Mr. Stimson fully aware of and approving the plans." [119] He expected that Truman would ". . . share in the control, not so much by making original decisions as by approving or disapproving the plans made by the War Department." [120] The JCS and CCS were not to be involved in the operation both for security reasons and to avoid the opposition of Admiral Leahy who doubted the practicality of the weapon and felt that, even if it were a success, it need not be used to induce the surrender of Japan.[121] There was, apparently, never any doubt that control of the weapon would be in Washington and in the hands of Marshall and, ultimately, Stimson.

Another important chore faced Groves during the period prior to Potsdam. It was necessary to select a group to stage the final experiments and tests and to assemble the bombs on Tinian. The group was chosen early in May, 1945, and was placed under the direction of Commander William S. Parsons. Although it included some civilians, it was named the First Technical Service Detachment of the Army. Its functions did not include advising on the use of the weapon it was preparing.[122]

By July 16, General Groves' work was nearing completion. A Fat Man bomb had been successfully detonated, and another was expected to be ready early in August. The Thin Man, not to be tested until Hiroshima, was expected to be ready by the beginning of August. Targets had been chosen, and a group of experts was already on Tinian ready to assemble the materials when they arrived. The line of control had been established from Stimson, through Marshall to Groves, and then to the operational forces.

By July 16 the 509th was nearly ready to carry the weapon. Its long training at Wendover and come to an end, and early in May had begun to stage out to Tinian. On May 6 the first ground echelons left Seattle by ship. The advanced air echelon flew in to North Field on Tinian on May 18, eleven days prior to the arrival of the ground contingents from Seattle. The combat air crews began to arrive on June 11. After training missions against bypassed, Japanese-held Pacific islands through June and early July, the 509th's crews, simulating conditions expected during the atomic attacks, began combat strikes on Japanese cities on July 20. Following strikes on July 24, 26, and 29, they were ready for Hiroshima.[123]

The military decisions for the defeat of Japan had thus been solidified soon after the United States delegation arrived at Potsdam. The 509th was preparing itself for its atomic mission, its targets had been chosen and its bombs would be ready. Lines of command had been defined. Completely aside from the rapid effort to test the Thin Man and the Fat Man under combat conditions, the Joint Chiefs of Staff had developed their plans for blockade, bombardment, and invasion of Japan. Serious consideration of inconclusive information concerning Japanese peace moves had been practically precluded by a profound respect for Japanese willingness to fight to the death. Japan was unlikely to accept the unconditional surrender which the United States demanded. The anticipated result was a prolonged war with large casualties. Military anticipations at Potsdam proved to be the basis for apparently sound arguments supporting the use of the atomic weapons. Only from a change in circumstances which might result from intervening political decisions leading to a redefinition of unconditional surrender; from a revised evaluation of the emerging relationship with Russia; or from top-level reaction to requests for reconsideration of use made by certain scientists within the MED, might the atomic holocaust planned for Japan be avoided.

NOTES TO CHAPTER 7

1 Ellis M. Zacharias, *Secret Missions: The Story of an Intelligence Officer* (New York: G. P. Putnam's Sons, 1946), pp. 324, 332–34.

2 Henry L. Stimson, "The Decision to Use the Atomic Bomb," *Harper's Magazine*, CXCIV (February, 1947), 102. This excerpt from Stimson's article also appears in Henry L. Stimson and McGeorge Bundy, *On Active Service in Peace and War* (New York: Harper and Brothers, Publishers, 1947), p. 618.

3 Harry S. Truman, *Memoirs* (Garden City: Doubleday and Company, Inc., 1955), I, 315.

4 Zacharias, *Secret Missions*, pp. 342–43. Text of Operation Plan I-45 appears on pp. 342–45.

5 *Ibid.*, p. 343.

6 Alexander H. Leighton, *Human Relations in A Changing World* (New York: E. P. Dutton and Company, Inc., 1949), p. 60. The text of the report appears in Appendix B, pp. 227–91. The information on which the report was based was supplied by interrogations of prisoners of war, captured military documents, military intelligence documents, Japanese publications, Japanese radio broadcasts, and reports from neutrals who had been in Japan.

7 Leighton, *Human Relations in A Changing World*, p. 60.

8 *Ibid.*, p. 46.

9 This council of six members had been formed on August 8, 1944, to ". . . shape and determine fundamental policies on the conduct of the war and to adjust and harmonize the requirements of the Supreme Command and the government." See Kase Toshikazu, *Eclipse of the Rising Sun* (London: Jonathan Cape, 1951), p. 88. It included during the period of the last wartime government under the Premier, Admiral Suzuki Kantaro, the following: the Premier; Foreign Minister Togo Shigenori; Minister of War, General Anami Korechika; Chief of the Army General Staff, General Umezu Yoshijiro; Minister of the Navy, Admiral Yonai Mitsumasa; and Chief of the Navy General Staff (after May 19, 1945), Admiral Toyoda Soemu. The Supreme Council followed the role of unanimity in making decisions, was required to submit its decision to the Cabinet for ratification, could request the Emperor's attendance at its meetings, and could be called into special sessions by the Emperor. See Robert J. C. Butow, *Japan's Decision to Surrender* (Stanford: Stanford University Press, 1954), pp. 37–38.

10 Of the many works which have considered Japanese peace moves the most reliable are those upon which the following general account is based: Butow, *Japan's Decision to Surrender*. William Craig, *The Fall of Japan* (New York: The Dial Press, Inc., 1967). David H. James, *The Rise and Fall of the Japanese Empire* (London: George Allen and Unwin, Ltd., 1951), pp. 297–349. F. C. Jones, *Japan's New Order in East Asia* (London: Oxford University Press, 1954), pp. 401–68. Kase, *Eclipse of the Rising Sun*. Kate Masuo, *The Lost War: A Japanese Reporter's Inside Story* (New York: Alfred A. Knopf, Inc., 1946), pp. 196–264. Yale Candee Maxon, *Control of Japanese Foreign Policy: A Study of Civil-Military Rivalry, 1930–1945* (Berkeley: University of California Press, 1957), pp. 189–219. Shigemitsu Mamoru, *Japan and Her Destiny: My Struggle for Peace* (New York: E. P. Dutton and Company, Inc., 1958). The Pacific War Research Society (comp.), *Japan's Longest Day* (Tokyo: Kodansha International, Ltd., 1965). Togo Shigenori, *The Cause of Japan* (New York: Simon and Schuster, Inc., 1956), pp. 268–339. United States Strategic Bombing Survey (Pacific), Naval Analysis Division, *Interrogations of Japanese Officials* (Washington: United States Government Printing Office, 1946), II, 313–26. United States Strategic Bombing Survey, *Japan's Decision to End the War* (Washington: United States Government Printing Office, 1946). Yoshida Shigeru, *The Yoshida Memoirs* (London: William Heinemann, Ltd., 1961), pp. 1–30.

11 The best account of the selection of Suzuki as Premier appears in Kase, *Eclipse of the Rising Sun*, pp. 110–15.

12 *Ibid.*, p. 53.

13 Suzuki was seventy-eight years old, had retired from active naval service in 1929, and had served the Emperor after his retirement as Grand Chamberlain and Privy Councillor. He had been attacked and seriously wounded for his moderate sentiments in the army uprising of 1936. See Togo, *The Cause of Japan*, p. 268 (fn. 1).

14 Shigemitsu Mamoru, *Japan and Her Destiny*, p. 299.

15 *Ibid.*, p. 300.

16 *Ibid.*, pp. 336–37.

17 *Ibid.*, p. 337.

18 *Ibid.*, p. 338.

19 He was *not*, as Kase reports, war minister in 1941. See Kase, *Eclipse of the Rising Sun*, p. 121, fn. 8. Togo was convicted by the International Military Tribunal for the Far East of conspiracy to wage aggressive war and sentenced to twenty years imprisonment. He died in an American military hospital in Tokyo in 1950. See Togo, *The Cause of Japan*, Translators' Introduction, pp. 1–2.

20 Togo, *The Cause of Japan*, pp. 275–76.

21 *Ibid.*, p. 279.

22 *Ibid.*, p. 284.

23 *Ibid.*, p. 286. The account of the May 11–14 meetings presented here relies on Togo's work, pp. 284–86; Butow, *Japan's Decision to Surrender*, pp. 81–85; and Kase, *Eclipse of the Rising Sun*, pp. 169–70. Kase states the objectives somewhat differently:

1. Try to negotiate for the extension of the neutrality pact.
2. If this were gained, broaden the negotiations, aiming at a nonaggression treaty.
3. If the worst became unavoidable, request the Soviet Government to use its good offices with the United States and Great Britain for the restoration of peace.

He further states that No. 3 above was only to be sought if Nos. 1 and 2 proved unattainable.

24 Togo, *The Cause of Japan*, p. 289.

25 Butow, *Japan's Decision to Surrender*, pp. 92–93.

26 *Ibid.*, p. 93.

27 Togo, *The Cause of Japan*, p. 293.

28 *Ibid.*, p. 297.

29 Butow, *Japan's Decision to Surrender.* p. 122. Togo, *The Cause of Japan*, p. 298.

30 The complete texts of the telegrams exchanged by Togo and Sato are included in U.S. Department of State, Bureau of Public Affairs, Historical Office, *Foreign Relations of the United States, Diplomatic Papers: The Conference of Berlin* (Washington: United States Government Printing Office, 1960), I, 874–83. Hereafter, *Potsdam Papers.*

31 *Potsdam Papers*, I, 876.

32 *Ibid.*, pp. 878–79.

33 *Ibid.*, pp. 879–80. An interesting error appears in Kase, *Eclipse of the Rising Sun*, where Lozovsky is referred to consistently as Rozovsky.

34 *Ibid.*, p. 881.

35 *Ibid.*, p. 883.

36 Suzuki was publisher of the newspaper *Asahi*. He should not be confused with Admiral Suzuki Kantaro who became Premier in April, 1945. Butow, *Japan's Decision to Surrender*, p. 40.

37 *Ibid.*, p. 54. No evidence has been discovered to indicate that this opinion resulted from conversations with either of the two Allied governments. In fact it is doubtful that the British received information of Bagge's talks with Suzuki or that information concerning them reached the United States Government. See also Shigemitsu, *Japan and Her Destiny*, p. 339.

38 Butow, *Japan's Decision to Surrender*, p. 55.

39 Togo, *The Cause of Japan*, p. 277.

40 Butow, *Japan's Decision to Surrender*, p. 56, fn. 80.

41 *Potsdam Papers*, II, 1589. In reporting this effort Butow indicates that the attache's name was Ono; see *Japan's Decision to Surrender*, p. 56, fn. 82. The name included in Johnson's cable to the Secretary of State on July 6, 1945, has been chosen.

42 *Ibid.*

43 *Potsdam Papers*, II, 1589, fn. 1.

44 Shigemitsu, *Japan and Her Destiny*, p. 339.

45 *Ibid.*, p. 339.

46 Zacharias, *Secret Missions*, p. 364.

47 *Ibid.*, p. 364.

48 Butow, *Japan's Decision to Surrender*, p. 88.

49 *Ibid.*, 104. The OSS organization was named for its director, Allen Dulles, who did not participate in the negotiations himself. However, his American secretary and his advisor on Japanese problems did meet with Hack, and it seems likely that Dulles was cognizant of the course of the talks. Tsuyama Shigeyoshi, an executive of the *Osaka Shosen Kabushki Kaisha*, and Ryu Shintaro, correspondent for the *Tokyo Asahi Shimbun*, both residents of Switzerland, collaborated with Fujimura. None had official standing with the Japanese Government.

50 Butow, *Japan's Decision to Surrender*, p. 105.

51 This assumption rests on Butow's unsubstantiated assertion; and the author's assumption of its reliability reflects his evaluation of Butow's scholarship.

52 William D. Leahy, *Diaries*, XI, June 14, p. 96. See also William D. Leahy, *I Was There*, p. 384.

53 Butow, *Japan's Decision to Surrender*, p. 110. This account is based on Butow, pp. 109–111, and on Fletcher Knebel and Charles W. Bailey, II, *No High Ground*, pp. 18–24. There are certain minor discrepancies in the two accounts.

[54] Knebel and Bailey, *No High Ground*, pp. 108–9.

[55] Stimson, *Diary*, July 20. See Zacharias, *Secret Missions*, p. 363, for an account of another effort to seek peace through Switzerland. This one involved a Japanese newspaperman, Toguchi Jiro. who early in June, 1945, had sent Togo a message urging him to seek peace. A copy of the message, secured by the OSS in Switzerland, had been forwarded to Zacharias for his use. Toguchi, acting on his own initiative, had contacted the United States Minister, Leland Harrison, who did not take his efforts seriously because he had no official backing. No other evidence has been found to corroborate this account, and there is no indication that the information ever reached top-level officials.

[56] The State, War, Navy Coordinating Committee was a policymaking committee which included the Secretaries of the three Departments and which formulated policy at the level just below the President. Its recommendations in regard to Japan were generally based on the reports of its Far East Subcommittee, made up of the interested Assistant Secretaries in the three Departments. See U. S. Congress, Senate, Subcommittee to Investigate the Administration of the Internal Security Act and Other Internal Security Laws of the Committee on the Judiciary, *Hearings on the Institute of Pacific Relations*, 82nd Cong., 2nd sess. (15 Parts, Washington: 1953), Part 3, p. 704. Hereafter, *IPR Hearings*.

[57] *Ibid.*, pp. 727–28.

[58] Zacharias, *Secret Missions*, pp. 302–60.

[59] *The New York Times*, April 15, 1942, quoting an English wireless dispatch to North America recorded by the Federal Communications Commission.

[60] Zacharias, *Secret Missions*, p. 335. No specific information is provided concerning the source of the report.

[61] *Ibid.*, p. 335.

[62] *Potsdam Papers*, I, 43–44. These citations are from a memorandum of the May 28, 1945, conversations between Hopkins and Stalin prepared by Charles E. Bohlen. Harriman also was present. See also Sherwood, *Roosevelt and Hopkins*, pp. 902–3. Hopkins reported his conversations in detail to Truman and the State Department.

[63] *Potsdam Papers*, I, 45. Italics are added. This last opinion was omitted from Hopkins' report to Truman. Sherwood, *Roosevelt and Hopkins*, p. 903.

[64] *Ibid.*, p. 160.

[65] *Grew Conversations*, 1945, 3 vols., February 9, 1945. This folder is among the *Grew Papers* at Harvard University. It contains carbons of Memoranda of Conversations listed by date with no pagination or index.

[66] *Ibid.*, July 5, 1945.

[67] *Ibid.*, July 10 and 11, 1945.

[68] *Ibid.*, July 10, 1945. See also Butow, *Japan's Decision to Surrender*, p. 111, and fn. 24.

[69] See *Potsdam Papers*, pp. 902–93, for Grew's explanation of the press release to Byrnes.

[70] See pp. 168–69.

[71] Lewis L. Strauss, *Men and Decisions* (Garden City: Doubleday and Company, Inc., 1962), p. 188. Walter Millis (ed.), *The Forrestal Diaries* (New York: The Viking Press, Inc., 1951), p. 74.

[72] Millis (ed.), *The Forrestal Diaries*, p. 76.

[73] Strauss, *Men and Decisions*, p. 188.

[74] *Ibid.*, p. 189. See also Byrnes, *All in One Lifetime*, p. 297.

[75] Stimson, *Diary*, July 16; Henry L. Stimson, "The Decision to Use the Atomic Bomb," *Harper's*, CXCIV, 101.

[76] *IPR Hearings*, p. 728.

[77] *Potsdam Papers*, p. 873. This conjecture is the author's although, since Leahy has not recorded his actions in this respect, the only evidence is derived from Strauss' statement that Forrestal informed Leahy, from Leahy's desire to end the war quickly without invasion, and from the Admiral's close relationship to Truman as his personal Chief of Staff.

[78] Ray S. Cline, *Washington Command Post: The Operations Division* (Washington: Office of the Chief of Military History, Department of the Army, 1951), p. 337. Cline's work is based on OPD files. See pp. 41–44.

[79] *Ibid.*, p. 339.

[80] *Ibid.*, p. 338. U. S. Department of Defense, *The Entry of the Soviet Union into the War Against Japan: Military Plans, 1941–1945*, p. 28.

[81] *Yalta Papers*, p. 827. The complete text of the "Report of the Combined Chiefs of Staff to President Roosevelt and Prime Minister Churchill" appears on pp. 827–33.

[82] *Ibid.*, pp. 829–30.

[83] Harry S. Truman, *Memoirs*, I, 17.

[84] Leahy, *Diaries*, XI, 56, April 13, 1945.

[85] Harry S. Truman, *Memoirs*, I, 17.

[86] U. S. Department of Defense, *The Entry of the Soviet Union into the War Against Japan*, p. 62. Complete text of this reports answers on pp. 62–68.

[87] *Ibid.*, p. 63.

[88] *Ibid.*, pp. 66–67.

[89] U. S. Department of Defense, *The Entry of the Soviet Union into the War Against Japan*, p. 67. See also Alvin Coox, "The Myth of the Kwantung Army," *Marine Corps' Gazette*, XLII (July, 1958), 36–43, for a detailed statement of the decline of the Kwantung Army by early summer, 1945. Its combined strength was over 700,000 troops which were organized in twenty-four under-strength infantry divisions as a bluff to delay an anticipated Russian attack. In 1941 terms, the Kwantung Army contained the equivalent of only 8.5 elite divisions. It had poor or nonexistent equipment; insufficient air cover; and troops, many of whom were either overaged men or young boys.

[90] U. S. Department of Defense, *The Entry of the Soviet Union into the War Against Japan*, p. 68. On April 3 the JCS had decided on command arrangements in the field for the final actions in the Pacific War. General MacArthur was to be Commander in Chief, U. S. Army Forces in the Pacific, and Admiral Nimitz was to command all naval forces in the Pacific, while strategic control was to remain with the JCS. General Arnold was to command the strategic bombing forces of the Army, under direct control of the JCS. *Ibid.*, pp. 53–54.

[91] U. S. Department of Defense, *The Entry of the Soviet Union into the War Against Japan*, pp. 54–55.

[92] U. S. Department of Defense, *The Entry of the Soviet Union into the War Against Japan*, pp. 55–56. For a contradictory statement of MacArthur's position, see Courtney Whitney, *MacArthur: His Rendezvous with History* (New York: Alfred A. Knopf, Inc., 1956), pp. 198–99. Whitney states that MacArthur was opposed to landings on Japan and that he predicted the end of the war before January 1, 1946, which differed with the current Navy view of eighteen months after the defeat of Germany. MacArthur thought Japanese collapse would be "sudden and unheralded," possibly within

six months. This statement is apparently refuted by MacArthur's message to Marshall on April 20, 1945. In it he does mention that the pressure of combined Allied forces might force Japanese surrender earlier than expected, but he goes on to anticipate a decisive assault in early 1946.

93 U. S. Department of Defense, *The Entry of the Soviet Union into the War Against Japan*, pp. 59–60.

94 Henry H. Arnold, *Global Mission* (Harper and Brothers, Publishers, 1951) pp. 564, 576.

95 Ernest J. King and Walter Muir Whitehill, *Fleet Admiral King: A Naval Record* (New York: W. W. Norton and Company, Inc., 1952) p. 621.

96 *Ibid.*, p. 598. See also Leahy, *I Was There*, pp. 384–85.

97 U. S. Department of Defense, *The Entry of the Soviet Union into the War Against Japan*, p. 76.

98 *Potsdam Papers*, I, pp. 903–10, contains the minutes of the June 18 meeting. These minutes also appear in U. S. Department of Defense, *The Entry of the Soviet Union into the War Against Japan*, pp. 77–85 .Lieutenant General Ira C. Eaker attended for General Arnold.

99 *Potsdam Papers*, I, 904–95.

100 *Ibid.*, p. 906. See Stimson, "The Decision to Use the Atomic Bomb," *Harper's*, CXCIV, 102, where the Secretary of War states that he had been told that ". . . such operations might be expected to cost over a million casualties to American forces alone. Additional losses might be expected among our Allies, and . . . if we could judge by previous experience, enemy casualties would be much larger than our own."

101 *Potsdam Papers*, I, 906–12. Leahy, *I Was There*, p. 384.

102 *Potsdam Papers*, p. 908.

103 *Ibid.*, p. 909.

104 Truman, *Memoirs*, I, 416.

105 Cline, *Washington Command Post*, p. 347.

106 The Fat Man model was that used at Alamogordo and Nagasaki. The Thin Man, also called Little Boy, a guntype bomb, was used for the first time on Hiroshima.

107 Leslie R. Groves, *Now It Can Be Told; The Story of the Manhattan Project* (New York: Harper and Brothers, Publishers, 1962), p. 262.

108 *Ibid.*, pp. 305–6.

109 Richard F. Newcomb, *Abandon Ship! Death of the U. S. S. Indianapolis* (New York: Henry Holt and Company, 1958), pp. 23–28. The *Indianapolis* was sunk four days after delivering its components of Thin Man on July 30 by the Japanese submarine I-58 under Lieutenant Commander Hashimoto Mochitsura. For his account of the sinking, see Hashimoto Mochitsura, *Sunk: The Story of the Japanese Submarine Fleet, 1942–1945* (London: Cassell and Company, Ltd., 1954), pp. 157–69.

110 See, p. 242.

111 Groves, *Now It Can Be Told*, p. 305.

112 *Ibid.*, pp. 292–93.

113 *Ibid.*, p. 304.

114 The first Thin Man was ready by August 1. On the other hand, the first Fat Man after Alamogordo was not ready until August 6. The second was expected to be available August 24 and others at an accelerating rate, possibly three in September to as many as seven in December. See *MED Files*, Folder 5a, Tab C, "Groves Memorandum to Marshall, July 24, 1945." See also Groves, *Now It Can Be Told*, p. 309, which indicates that the Thin Man was to be ready by July 31.

115 Groves, *Now It Can Be Told*, p. 267. See also, Arnold, *Global Mission*, p. 492.

[116] Groves, *Now It Can Be Told*, p. 268. See also Richard G. Hewlett and Oscar E. Anderson, Jr., *A History of the United States Atomic Energy Commission: The New World, 1939/1946* (University Park: The Pennsylvania State University Press, 1962), p. 365, and fn. 2 on p. 692. Hewlett and Anderson cite Notes on the Initial Meeting of the Target Committee to indicate it first met on April 27. Groves mentions an April meeting with Air Force personnel, but indicates that this was preparatory to the establishment of the Target Committee.

[117] Hewlett and Anderson, *The New World, 1939/46*, p. 365. See Groves, *Now It Can Be Told*, pp. 272–73. Groves indicated that all four cities were chosen originally by the committee. He, however, fails to mention, except in general terms, the date of the choice. It is possible that his account combines the two operations. See also Stimson and Bundy, *On Active Service in Peace and War*, p. 625.

[118] Groves, *Now It Can Be Told*, pp. 309–19, 343. It is unclear as to how Nagasaki was added to the list of target cities. The probability of LeMay's staff being responsible is advanced in Wesley Grank Craven and James Lea Cate (eds.), *The Army Air Forces in World War II* (Chicago: The University of Chicago Press, 1953), V. 710.

[119] Groves, *Now It Can Be Told*, p. 271.

[120] *Ibid.*, p. 271.

[121] *Ibid..* p. 117. See also Leahy, *I Was There*, pp. 440–41 and Leahy, *Diaries*, X, 85, 87, 90; XI, 86, 92. See Craven and Cate (eds.), *The Army Air Forces in World War II*, V, 707, which indicates that the line of command in the last missions was from the President to Stimson, with whom Arnold consulted alone or sometimes with Marshall, to Groves.

[122] Groves, *Now It Can Be Told*, p. 282.

[123] Craven and Cate (eds.) *The Army Air Forces in World War II*, V, 707–9, Groves, *Now It Can Be Told*, pp. 283–84.

CHAPTER 8

PRELUDE TO POTSDAM

A NUMBER of officials in the United States Government during the spring and early summer of 1945 thought that the war might be ended rapidly without invasion of Japan provided the policy of unconditional surrender were more clearly defined. At the same time, others were convinced that the military situation, even without a modification of unconditional surrender, no longer warranted United States efforts to involve the Soviet Union in the war against Japan. Thus, two generally overlapping lines of pressure developed within the government, each seeking to affect the existing and postwar political situation in the Far East. One sought to reduce official pressure for Russian intervention and to limit Russian influence in the Far East following the anticipated defeat of Japan. The other attempted a redefinition of unconditional surrender, at least to the extent of indicating to the Japanese that their defeat would not result in the elimination of their Emperor.

This effort to assure the retention of the Emperor despite unconditional surrender proved to be impossible to achieve. Throughout the war the Emperor had been blamed by many in the United States for the original attack on Pearl Harbor and for later Japanese indignities.[1] The struggle against Japan was peculiarly the war of the United States. The pride of its people had been wounded by initial Japanese successes; and hurt pride stimulated by wartime journalism sought an outlet in revenge on the symbol of the enemy, the Emperor. Unconditional surrender promised just retribution. Such revenge would be unacceptably diluted if the very object of its application, the Emperor, continued as head of the Japanese political system. The voices of public opinion, the words of lesser politicians, and the repeated statements of the President himself continued to demand unconditional surrender and the humiliation of Hirohito. Japan was the Emperor, and both the Emperor and Japan must suffer punishment for their crimes.

This atmosphere was all the more pervasive because of the widespread ignorance in the United States concerning, first, the role of the Emperor in the Japanese polity and, second, his resultant lack of power to influence the policies of the Japanese Government. The Emperor was looked upon as a warmonger and was closely identified with Japanese militarism and expansion. Emperor-worship was widely believed to be a cult of violence, a basis for the perpetuation of authoritarian class privilege. The Emperor was thought to be the willing partner of political and military leaders who used this cult to further their imperialist goals. Some thought the Imperial Palace should be bombed to dramatize to the Japanese people the end of their antiquated Emperor-worship.[2]

But the Emperor was far more to the Japanese than a popular, militant leader. He was, in his being, the human incarnation of an eternal god. He was the most recent of a genealogical line descended directly from the Sun Goddess who ruled the heavens and who had charged her descendants with the rule of Japan. The Emperor symbolized, in his being, Japan itself. He was of Japan, and Japan was of him. Theoretically, it was he who ruled Japan. He was the symbol which unified the nation and promised its continuity. To permit the Emperor to be humiliated as a defendant in a war crimes trial, to accept his deposition or his death as part of unconditional surrender was to permit the liquidation of the Japanese nation. Death itself was preferable. Losing their Emperor probably seemed a far greater personal blow to the Japanese than the loss of a secular leader would have been to the people of another nation. Unlike a Churchill, a Stalin, a Hitler, or a Roosevelt, the Emperor was divine.[3]

Furthermore, the Emperor was apparently all things to all people. As a national symbol, his significance received from individual Japanese a wide variety of interpretations reflecting their personal predilections. Thus, ". . . to the expansionists and militarists he was a strong war leader bent on liberating the East from Western domination; to those who were . . . opposed to war, the Emperor was . . . a man of peace deceived by the warmongers in Japan; to the partisans of democracy, he was a democrat at heart; to the simple and uneducated he held supernatural powers; to the sophisticated he represented the highest ideals of Japanese culture." [4]

Despite his supreme position as the divine bridge between the gods and Japan and as the theoretical monarch of the nation, the Emperor had practically no power in determining the policy of the Japanese Government. Decisions were formally made by his government in audience before him in an Imperial Conference; but the Emperor seldom intervened, and then only when asked to do so. Arguments took place within the government before the Emperor was consulted. By the time policy was presented to the Emperor, it had already been formulated. His only function was to signify consent. His silence was interpreted to imply concurrence. Consultation with him was generally a formality, a ritual to demonstrate respect to the myth of the God-Emperor. Illustrative of this was the shock which occurred among those in the Supreme Council for the Direction of the War (SCDW) as it met before the Emperor on August 9, 1945, shortly after the second atomic bomb was dropped on Nagasaki. Premier Suzuki decided to seek the Emperor's opinion as to whether to accept the Potsdam Declaration and to substitute the imperial opinion for the decision of the SCDW.

This announcement . . . electrified the whole gathering and all participants gasped, not having anticipated such a step. It was most unusual to convene an imperial conference without arranging beforehand both the agenda and the final decision. . . . The imperial conference was held merely to maintain the fiction that the Emperor sanctioned such a decision in person. As a matter of fact the Emperor was always a dummy who sat through the sessions silently without ever taking an active part. Thus, to solicit the advice of the Emperor was an extraordinary deviation from time-honored practice.[5]

And yet, despite the inconsistencies between the Emperor's political impotence and the absolute power attributed by myth to the human-divine, many in Japan were seemingly willing to fight on to national suicide rather than to surrender that myth. They could only live as Japanese if the Emperor remained.

Many Japanese had been whipped into a fatalistic and frenzied desire to die heroic deaths—"One hundred million people die in honor," ran the slogan. "Better to die than seek ignominious safety." To the average Oriental mind there was nothing insincere about this theme. The Orientals' conception of death is far different from that of the West. Death is a simple matter of fact which may be adorned with a pleasant sort of glamour if it can be made to serve a remotely useful purpose.[6]

Loss of the Emperor was, to the Japanese, the greatest ignominy. Death might serve the useful purpose of escaping this last indignity.

A few in the United States Government recognized the importance of the imperial institution to the people of Japan. They believed that the Japanese might fight beyond any hope of success if they interpreted unconditional surrender to mean the elimination of that institution. On the other hand, they anticipated that the Japanese might very well surrender quickly if it could be demonstrated that continued resistance held no hope for victory and if the unconditional surrender policy were publicly amended to preserve the position of the Emperor. Thus, they devoted their energies, despite possible public disapproval, to redefine the unconditional surrender formula so as to permit the retention of the Emperor. Such efforts were made by a number of individuals in different agencies at both lower and higher administrative levels. The more important were pursued in the War Department, the Department of State, the Navy Department, and the Office of War Information (OWI).

One of the most perceptive attacks on unconditional surrender was made in the Foreign Morale Analysis Division of the OWI. From its interrogations of Japanese prisoners and its other sources, the Division came to the conclusion that attacks on the Emperor were at best wasteful and at worst likely to reinforce Japanese loyalty to him. "There could then be renewed determination and the feeling that death would be preferable to submission before an enemy who vilified the values that were the foundation of existence. It would seem better to lose one's life than to lose hope." [7] The Division, basing its conclusions on such assumptions, issued a report titled "Current Psychological and Social Tensions in Japan" on June 1, 1945.[8] Despite the fact that the report was said to be based on pertinent discussions with top policymakers in the spring of 1945, there is no indication as to who was consulted. The Japan Section in the OWI read it earlier in the spring and decided that it should be toned down and held up until June 1.[9] Whether anyone outside of the OWI read it is problematical. No other reference to it has been found. Apparently its recommendations ran counter to the opinions of those in higher OWI positions, and the report did not receive wide distribution among those responsible for top-level United States decisions.

Certain statements and conclusions made in the report merit consideration. The Foreign Morale Analysis Division indicated that although there appeared to be an increase in criticism of all other leaders in Japan, there had ". . . been no weakening of attitudes toward the Emperor and the Imperial Institution." [10] It anticipated a struggle in Japan between those who favored making a last-ditch fight and others who would save Japan from devastation by seeking peace. This latter group would ". . . not for the most part be liberal, but would likely be less-extreme militarists, bureaucrats, and business-men who would try to protect their positions by avoiding the disintegration of the system upon which they depended for their prominence. It was likely that they would assume control to promote peace through the Emperor." [11] It was, therefore, suggested that the Emperor not be attacked and that every attempt be made to define unconditional surrender, stressing its positive aspects.[12]

Such suggestions apparently ran counter to the desires of Elmer Davis, the director of the OWI. His attitude had been expressed clearly in a radio broadcast on August 15, 1944, when he had stated that the United States objective of world security demanded ". . . that all the conquests of Japan for half a century past be disgorged, and that the power of Japan to commit aggression be broken utterly." [13] Nearly a year later on May 28, 1945, just prior to the completion of the Division's report, Davis was to confirm his inflexible attitude to modifying unconditional surrender by reacting violently to a State Department suggestion that the Emperor be retained and by stat-ing that he would have none of it.[14] Thus, it is unlikely that the OWI went on record at the time as favoring the Division's position.

Intelligence officers within the Navy Department found similar difficulties in promoting the modification of unconditional surrender. Captain Ellis M. Zacharias and his intelligence group, OP–16–W, had come to the conclusion during the spring of 1945 that the Emperor should be retained. They had obtained reliable information which ". . . indicated that all Japan hoped to salvage from the war was her sovereignty." [15] The men of OP–16–W under-stood that the term *sovereignty* had a unique meaning to the Japanese:

It [had] a theocratic undertone in addition to its legalistic meaning. Sovereignty [was] closely linked to the sovereign in a combination of sacred-secular interpre-tation reminiscent of the feudal interpretation of the term, when the sovereign was God, the last representative of an unbroken line of divine rulers descended from the Sun Goddess, an irrational dogma elevated to the rank of anachronistic politi-cal philosophy.[16]

They understood that to Admiral Suzuki, the new Premier of Japan, a guar-antee of clemency for the Imperial House was the primary objective of Japa-nese policy. Suzuki was willing to pay with Japan's Empire if necessary for the assurance that his Emperor would reign. Zacharias, therefore, came to the conclusion that the term *unconditional surrender*, which was even imper-fectly understood in the United States, should be further clarified.[17]

From May 8 to August 4, Zacharias, with the concurrence of Secretary of the Navy Forrestal, was to make a series of fourteen broadcasts to Japan seeking to convince the Japanese Government that Japan's cause was hopeless and that unconditional surrender did not imply the elimination of the Japanese polity.[18] These broadcasts, supplemented by an important anonymous letter which he wrote to the *Washington Post* to which he knew the Japanese had access through neutral governments, were used by Zacharias to try to convince Suzuki that unconditional surrender did not intend the destruction of the national structure of Japan.

In his letter to the *Post*, the Japanese Government was urged to open diplomatic negotiations to determine what unconditional surrender meant beyond public statements issued by the United States Government. The secrecy guaranteed by such channels would enable those in Japan who requested clarification to evade any public admission of weakness.

If, as Admiral Suzuki revealed in the Diet, the chief concern is over Japan's future national structure (*Kokutai*), including the Emperor's status after surrender, the way to find out is to ask. Contrary to widespread belief, such a question can be answered quickly and satisfactorily to all those who are concerned over the future peace of the Orient and the world.[19]

In his broadcasts, particularly that of July 21, Zacharias tried to demonstrate that unconditional surrender applied only to the cessation of hostilities and not to the condition of postwar Japan. Unconditional surrender might include the continuation of the Japanese polity and peace and prosperity for Japan.[20] To the Japanese, however, Zacharias' efforts probably seemed to be the work of a clever propagandist. Despite the fact that he was introduced over the air as "an official spokesman for the United States Government" prior to his July 7 broadcast, to the Japanese his efforts might have appeared to be the bait to lure them into the trap of surrender.[21] At no time was he able to state specifically that, despite unconditional surrender, the institution of the Emperor would be maintained. At no time did any higher political figure in the United States Government announce such a clarification. His efforts, therefore, fell short of their mark. His message, given top-level support in public statements and couched in more specific language concerning the position of the Emperor, might have led to an earlier peace. As it was, the intransigence of the United States Government concerning public acceptance of the retention of the imperial institution nullified Zacharias' actions.

Zacharias' broadcasts could only have taken place with Forrestal's permission.[22] By May, 1945, the Secretary of the Navy had begun to anticipate the power relationships that might exist in the Far East after the war. He questioned whether it was to the interests of the United States to eliminate Japan as a counterweight to the power of the Soviet Union. He strongly supported, therefore, Acting Secretary of State Grew's efforts to reinterpret unconditional surrender so as to provide for the retention of the Emperor as a way to possible peace in the Far East before the elimination of Japanese power.[23] In line with this thinking, Zacharias' broadcasts were used as a means to persuade the Japanese that unconditional surrender would not threaten the Emperor's position. Consistently, until the war's end, Forrestal and the Navy would support the modification of the terms of unconditional surrender.[24]

While steps were being taken within the Navy Department to modify United States surrender terms, similar conclusions were being drawn by some in the Department of War. On April 18, 1945, in a paper entitled "Defeat of Japan by Blockade and Bomb," the Joint Intelligence Committee of the Joint Chiefs of Staff (JCS) suggested that ". . . clarification of Allied intentions with regard to the Japanese nation might bring nearer the possibility of unconditional surrender [and that] . . . there is a possibility that some constitutional Japanese central government, backed by the Emperor, may seek and accept a rationalized version of unconditional surrender before the end of 1945." [25] This paper was generally concerned with the possible duration of the war and only incidentally with unconditional surrender. And yet it indicated the Joint Intelligence Committee's hope for a changed policy toward Japan.

In their review of the overall strategy in the Pacific for the Joint Chiefs of Staff on April 24, the Joint Staff Planners presented their estimates as to the course of future operations in the Far East.[26] As part of their presentation, they considered the possibility of modifying unconditional surrender:

It is by no means certain that . . . "unconditional surrender" can be brought about by any means. What can be accomplished is decisive military defeat and the results equivalent to unconditional surrender, similar to the present situation in Germany. In no case to date in this war have organized Japanese units surrendered. The concept of "unconditional surrender" is foreign to Japanese nature. Therefore, "unconditional surrender" should be defined in terms understandable to the Japanese, who must be convinced that destruction or national suicide is not implied. This could be done by the announcement on the governmental level of a "declaration of intentions" which would tell the Japanese what their future holds. Once convinced of the inevitability of defeat, it is possible that a government could be formed in Japan that would sign and could enforce a surrender instrument.

. . . Unless a definition of unconditional surrender can be given which is acceptable to the Japanese, there is no alternative to annihilation. . . .[27]

The Joint Chiefs of Staff considered the overall report and approved it. There is no indication that serious consideration was given to changing unconditional surrender.

Two studies made by the Strategy and Policy Group of OPD at the request of Secretary Stimson pointed out OPD opinion on unconditional surrender. The first concluded that the point when the Japanese would surrender was unpredictable since it depended on their hopes for a conditional surrender.[28] The second considered more carefully the problem of unconditional surrender.

It suggested that the ". . . proposal of a public declaration of war aims, in effect giving definition to 'unconditional surrender' has definite merit." [29] Continued military pressure should be brought to bear against Japan; but, in addition, political and psychological techniques should be used to persuade the Japanese to yield.

These studies, sent to the Secretary of War on June 4 and June 15 respectively, reinforced Stimson who, at the time, was exploring possible ways of inducing Japanese surrender. Although he consistently supported Acting Secretary of State Grew's efforts to modify the unconditional surrender formula through June and July, Stimson did not look on the change in policy as a means to bring Japanese capitulation prior to use of the atomic bombs. His plans, in fact, involved an effort to get Japan to surrender by giving a warning ". . . after she had been sufficiently pounded possibly by S-1." [30] To Stimson the bombs might be used to force surrender before the United States became involved in an invasion of Japan.

The greatest pressure for a change in the unconditional surrender policy came, however, from within the Department of State from Acting Secretary of State Grew.[31] Grew believed that Truman's statements on unconditional surrender did not go far enough to reassure the Japanese in regard to the fate of their Emperor. In his first major address to the Congress, the President firmly called for unconditional surrender. At that time he defined the term by saying:

We will not traffic with the breakers of peace on the terms of peace.

The responsibility for the making of the peace . . . must rest with the defenders of the peace. We are not unconscious of the dictates of humanity. We do not wish to see unnecessary or unjustified suffering. But the laws of God and of man have been violated and the guilty must not go unpunished. Nothing shall shake our determination to punish the war criminals even though we must pursue them to the ends of the earth.[32]

Here, indeed, he implied leniency, but not for war criminals: and he did not exclude the Emperor from this group.

On May 8, following his announcement of Germany's defeat, Truman released a "Statement . . . Calling for Unconditional Surrender of Japan."

Nazi Germany has been defeated.

The Japanese people have felt the weight of our land, air and naval attacks. So long as their leaders and their armed forces continue the war the striking power and intensity of our blows will steadily increase and will bring utter destruction to Japan's industrial war production, to its shipping, and to everything that supports its military activity.

The longer the war lasts, the greater will be the suffering and hardships which the people of Japan will undergo—all in vain. Our blows will not cease until the Japanese military and naval forces lay down their arms in *unconditional surrender*.

Just what does unconditional surrender of the armed forces mean for the Japanese people?

It means the end of the war.

It means the termination of the influence of the military leaders who have brought Japan to the present brink of disaster.

It means provision for the return of soldiers and sailors to their families, their farms, their jobs.

It means not prolonging the present agony and suffering of the Japanese in the vain hope of victory.

Unconditional surrender does not mean the extermination or the enslavement of the Japanese people.[33]

This declaration by Truman contained everything Grew wanted except a statement to the effect that ". . . unconditional surrender would not mean the elimination of the present dynasty if the Japanese people desired its retention." [34] Apparently it also indicated a willingness on Truman's part to moderate unconditional surrender. He has since written about his attitude:

. . . National pride outlives military defeat. It is a delusion to think otherwise. I also think that it is a mistake to insist on unconditional surrender for moral or educational purposes. Any surrender is at the will of the victor, whether the surrender terms be conditional or unconditional. If there is any reason for unconditional surrender, it is only the practical matter of taking over a defeated country and making its control easier. . . .

Warfare, no matter what weapons it employs, is a means to an end, and if that end can be achieved by negotiated settlements of conditional surrender, there is no need for war. I believe this to be true even in the case of ruthless and terroristic powers ambitious for world conquest.[35]

It may reasonably be assumed that Truman's thought at the time was in line with this later statement. It may also be assumed that Grew saw in the May 8 declaration evidence of this attitude. Grew decided to try to convince the President that he should amplify his statement of May 8 to reduce Japanese fears about their Emperor.

The Acting Secretary of State had believed for some time that the Emperor might be useful to the United States in a number of ways after the defeat of Japan. The Emperor might, for instance, be persuaded to issue an imperial rescript, sacred to the Japanese, urging his soldiers to surrender thus making the United States task an easier one.[36] From the time he had assumed direction of the Division of Far Eastern Affairs in the Department of State on May 1, 1944, Grew had believed that, despite public sentiment against the Emperor, the United States Government should not rule out use of the Emperor to maintain order in defeated Japan. He had written to Secretary of State Hull about that time, that "Any cult which has been artificially created, as has the Shinto cult, can always be molded to suit new conditions, and if the institution of the Japanese Throne can in future be turned toward peaceful international cooperation, as it was in the days of the Shidehara diplomacy, Shintoism, since its essence is support of the throne, can and may prove to be an asset rather than a liability in a healthy postwar reconstruction. The Japanese are past masters at executing the maneuver of right-about-face." [37] The Department of State had followed a noncommittal approach toward the retention of the Emperor. To have rejected the continuation of the imperial institution might have added to the strength of the Japanese military who would then gain the opportunity to stimulate increased hatred of the United States among the Japanese people. To have supported his retention might have discouraged any popular movement in Japan to eliminate the imperial institution.[38] During May, 1945, Grew, however, continued to promote the idea of using the Emperor if appropriate; and, to this end, he suggested that the United States publicly define unconditional surrender to permit the Emperor's retention if the Japanese so desired.

Others in the State Department supported this position during the spring of 1945. Most influential among these were Eugene H. Dooman, chairman of the Far East Subcommittee of the State, War, Navy Coordinating Committee; Joseph W. Ballantine, director of the Office of Far Eastern Affairs; and George Hubbard Blakeslee, chairman of the Far Eastern Area Committee of the Department.[39] All were men who knew Japan well. To Dooman it was clear from intercepts of messages between the Japanese Government and its ambassador in Moscow and from other indications that the Japanese were ready to surrender if it were made clear to them that it was not United States policy to try the Emperor as a war criminal and to disestablish the monarchial system.[40] On this assumption, about the middle of May, he and Grew began to prepare a draft of a Presidential proclamation indicating the possible retention of the Emperor. Dooman's final draft of the paper was presented to Grew on May 24. Grew approved the draft and called a meeting of the State Department's Policy Committee which included the Assistant Secretaries of State and the legal adviser. Grew read Dooman's paper to the Policy Committee. There was no dissent until the item regarding the Emperor came up. Then Assistant Secretaries Dean Acheson and Archibald MacLeish protested strongly that the retention of the Emperor was distasteful to them.[41]

Despite apparent dissent within the Policy Committee, the Acting Secretary presented the draft proclamation to Truman on May 28. He pointed out to Truman that ". . . once the military extremists [of Japan] have been discredited through defeat, the Emperor, purely a symbol, . . . [could] and possibly . . . [would] be used by new leaders who will be expected to emerge. . . ." [42] He then suggested that the President define unconditional surrender so as to include retention of the Emperor. Truman told Grew that he ". . . had already given some thought to this matter . . . and that it seemed . . . a sound idea." [43] He asked Grew to consult with the Joint

Chiefs and the State-War-Navy Coordinating Committee in order to obtain the opinions of all concerned before he made his decision.[44]

During the next day, May 29, Grew presented his case for retention of the Emperor to the Joint Chiefs of Staff, Forrestal, and Stimson in the latter's office. Marshall, Forrestal, and Stimson indicated that they supported Grew's position in principle, but that it was inadvisable for the President to make the statement at that time since the fighting on Okinawa was still in progress and modification of the unconditional surrender formula might be construed by the Japanese as a sign of weakness.[45] This point of view prevailed. Although Grew failed to obtain immediate support for his proposal, the meeting still proved useful to him; for it originated the growing collaboration among Grew, Forrestal, and Stimson to promote change in the unconditional surrender formula.[46] Later that day, Grew reported the decision of the group to Truman, and the matter was temporarily dropped.[47]

On June 1, Truman issued a dramatic call for unconditional surrender in a special message to the Congress. After reviewing the course of the war and the successes of Allied forces against Japan, Truman concluded on a militant note:

> We are faced with a powerful Japanese military machine. These are the same Japanese who perpetrated the infamous attack on Pearl Harbor . . . ; they are the same Japanese who ordered the death march from Bataan; they are the same Japanese who carried out the barbarous massacres in Manila.
>
> They now know that their dreams of conquest are shattered. They no longer boast of dictating peace terms in Washington.
>
> This does not mean that the Japanese have given up hope. . . . They hope that our desire to see our soldiers and sailors home again and the temptation to return to the comforts of peace will force us to settle for some compromise short of unconditional surrender.
>
> They should know better. . . .[48]

Here was no indication of a modification of unconditional surrender. Despite Truman's personal tendency to accept a change, his public pronouncements indicated no salvation for the Emperor. Before Grew and Forrestal and Stimson lay the difficult job of convincing the President to make the change.

At a State-War-Navy Coordinating Committee meeting on June 12, the matter of unconditional surrender was again discussed. All agreed that this was a most serious question; and Stimson said that while the ". . . national objective was to secure the de-militarization of Japan it was equally true that no one desired the permanent subjugation of Japan, the enslavement of her people or any attempt to dictate what kind of government the country should have." [49] Grew indicated, as the meeting broke up, that the State Department was giving continuing study to the problem of defining war aims more precisely.

Grew appealed to Truman again on June 15. Once more he presented the President with a draft of a proclamation which he suggested be issued after the fall of Okinawa. The proclamation would include a reference indicating that the Japanese might maintain their political structure.[50] Truman delayed his decision until the matter could be discussed from a military point of view by the Joint Chiefs of Staff on June 18. He asked Grew and, on the latter's suggestion, Dooman to attend the meeting with the Joint Chiefs.[51]

Truman met with Grew again on June 16. At that time the President suggested that the proclamation might be issued as a joint announcement of the heads of government from Potsdam, for he felt that his May 8 release and his speech of June 1 defined unconditional surrender sufficiently for the present. Possibly the President was taking a more rigid attitude against Grew's suggestions as the latter pushed more rigorously for a modified surrender formula. He informed Grew, however, that he would accept Grew's further considerations for review before the July 18 meeting with the Joint Chiefs.[52] That same day Grew left a letter with Rosenman for Truman's perusal. In it he stated that the surrender policy should be defined so as to permit the Japanese to choose their own government. He also stated strongly that he didn't see any reason to delay announcement of such a change until the Potsdam meetings. It would be worthwhile to start the Japanese thinking about surrender as soon as possible in order to reduce the loss of life in the coming military campaigns.[53]

For some unexplained reason Grew and Dooman did not meet with the Joint Chiefs of Staff, Forrestal, Stimson, and McCloy, on July 18. During that morning Grew had again urged Truman to make an immediate statement more specifically defining unconditional surrender. Truman then had informed Grew that he had decided to hold up the statement until the Potsdam meeting. Grew argued strongly against delay, but Truman remained adamant and asked Grew to place the matter on the agenda for the meeting at Potsdam.[54]

That afternoon, during the Joint Chiefs of Staff meeting with Truman, military plans for the defeat of Japan ultimately received the President's endorsement. Neither Stimson nor Forrestal raised the political question involving the change in unconditional surrender except indirectly. Stimson merely asserted that he felt there might be a submerged class in Japan which would fight tenaciously if attacked on their homeland. He still hoped for some fruitful accomplishment through other means than invasion and asked to be permitted to speak on the matter of an alternative later.[55] Forrestal accepted the necessity for the attack on Kyushu.

During the meeting Assistant Secretary of War McCloy and Admiral Leahy presented the strongest arguments for changing unconditional surrender. After the conference had agreed to military plans against Japan, McCloy stated that he thought the time was propitious to study means of using the submerged class mentioned by Stimson. No one picked this up. But Leahy, also seeking a political settlement, said:

. . . he could not agree with those who said to him that unless we obtain the unconditional surrender of the Japanese that we will have lost the war. He feared no menace from Japan in the foreseeable future, even if we were unsuccessful in forcing unconditional surrender. What he did fear was that our insistence on unconditional surrender would result only in making the Japanese desperate and thereby increase our casualty lists. He did not think this was at all necessary.[56]

Truman's response was illuminating, if unusual. He said that ". . . it was with that thought in mind that he had left the door open for Congress to take appropriate action with reference to unconditional surrender. However, he did not feel that he could take any action at this time to change public opinion on that matter." [57] Between May 28 and June 18, Truman had come to the position of refusing to further redefine unconditional surrender. Furthermore, on June 18 he made the seemingly irrelevant reference to Congressional participation. What he meant by leaving the door open for Congress to take action is difficult to determine. It seems likely that the President was equivocating, for it was within his authority to define unconditional surrender. Apparently public opinion, which appeared to be strongly antagonistic to the Emperor, led him to refuse any suggestion that he publicly change the policy of unconditional surrender.

As the conference was breaking up, McCloy suggested a political attempt to end the war before invasion was attempted. He thought that a warning should be issued to Japan before the atomic bombs were used, and that the Japanese should be permitted to retain the Emperor and a form of government of their own choosing.[58] This suggestion apparently threw the gathering into a furor; but, McCloy recalls, it appealed to the President and to Leahy.[59] Nothing, however, resulted from McCloy's efforts. The meeting adjourned without further considering modification of unconditional surrender.

At the weekly State-War-Navy meeting the next day, Stimson, Grew, and Forrestal agreed that some way should be found to induce the Japanese to discontinue fighting before an invasion became necessary. Each supported an indication to the Japanese ". . . that they would be allowed to retain their own form of government and religious institutions. . . ." [60] Grew then stated that he believed Truman was now against such a move. Stimson, however, disagreed with Grew's evaluation of the President's position. Truman, he felt, did not want to make the change at once for fear it would weaken the American war effort, a position with which Stimson agreed.[61] Stimson's ". . . only fixed date [was that] the last chance warning . . . must be given before an actual landing of the ground forces on Japan, and fortunately the plans [provided] for enough time to bring in the sanctions to our warning in the shape of heavy ordinary attack and an attack by S-1." [62] Stimson was not planning, it seemed, to employ the warning to Japan to eliminate the necessity of using the atomic bomb. The warning and the bomb would be complementary devices to force Japan to surrender before an invasion needed to be launched.

After this meeting with Grew and Forrestal, Stimson drafted a warning for the President to issue to the Japanese.[63] He presented his draft to Grew and Forrestal at the next State-War-Navy meeting on June 26. After some discussion, a subcommittee of McCloy, Dooman, Ballantine, and Correa was directed to rewrite the draft as the proposed text of the warning by Truman. All agreed that the provision referring to the retention of the Emperor be included. On July 29 McCloy sent Stimson a short form of the proposed declaration. In it he included an item suggesting the maintenance of the dynasty. "This may cause repercussions at home," he wrote, "but without it those who seem to know most about Japan feel there would be very little likelihood of acceptance." [64] By June 30, the revised draft was ready. McCloy and Stimson again went over it and made a number of changes.[65] On July 2, the War Department copy was sent for approval to the State Department. The latter suggested modifications as to form, but the substance relating to the possibility that the Japanese might continue a "constitutional monarchy under the present dynasty" remained.[66]

On July 2, Stimson presented to the President a long memorandum detailing his evaluation of the military and political situation. He then stated that he thought there was an alternative to a costly invasion and that was to give ". . . them a warning of what is to come and a definite opportunity to capitulate." [67] He did not think that the Japanese were mad fanatics, and he believed that there were many in its population who might be relied on to reconstruct Japan after it had surrendered. He, therefore, urged the President to issue a warning to the Japanese which, in effect, would redefine unconditional surrender as a criterion for capitulation. The warning would indicate:

1. The magnitude of United States military force;
2. The inevitability and completeness of the destruction in Japan if this force were employed;
3. The determination of the Allies to destroy the authority which misled the country to attempt world conquest;
4. The determination of the Allies to limit Japan to its home islands and to eliminate its ability to start another war;
5. The disavowal of any desire to eliminate the Japanese as a race or as a nation;
6. A reassurance that Japan would be permitted to develop economically and commercially;
7. A willingness to withdraw from Japan when the above ends had been achieved;

8. And, finally, a reassurance to Japan that it might choose to maintain ". . . a constitutional monarchy under her present dynasty, [which] would substantially add to the chances of acceptance." [68]

The warning was purposefully constructed so as to hold out hope if Japan surrendered and destruction if it fought on.

Truman seemed to be impressed by the memorandum. He mentioned that the draft warning ". . . necessarily could not be completed until they knew what was to be done with S-1." [69] It is noteworthy that Stimson did not mention that Truman accepted his suggestions in regard to retention of the imperial dynasty in Japan. That he had some hope that the President concurred may be indicated by the comment in his *Diary* referring to his attempt to shorten the war with Japan by modifying United States surrender terms:

. . . I have to meet and overcome the zeal of the soldier . . . and . . . I have to meet the feeling of war passion and hysteria which seizes hold of a nation like ours in the prosecution of a bitter war. The President so far has struck me as a man who is trying hard to keep his balance.[70]

While Stimson tried to influence Truman directly, Grew was busy on another tack. In each of two briefing book papers prepared for the President to study on his way to the Potsdam Conference, references were made to the retention of the Emperor. The first, drafted on June 29, asserted that the Japanese should be informed that when they were no longer a threat to peaceful international relations, their political institutions might be retained. In the second paper of July 3 concerning the treatment of the Emperor by the anticipated United States military government in postwar Japan, the State Department emphasized that the occupation authorities should not prejudice the ". . . continuance of the institution of the Emperor against the will of the Japanese people. . . ."[71]

Although its importance was not clearly recognized at the time, an event occurred on July 3 which was ultimately to negate the efforts to modify unconditional surrender so as to provide for the possible continuance of the imperial institution. James F. Byrnes was sworn in as Secretary of State. No longer would Grew have direct access to the President. Truman now consulted Byrnes rather than Grew. Truman now gave Byrnes the responsibility for handling Stimson's draft declaration.[72] By July 7, Truman and Byrnes were on their way to Potsdam.[73]

Byrnes, who ultimately was to decide on the definition of unconditional surrender, left in Washington most of those who advocated retention of the Emperor. And yet even as he prepared to leave for Potsdam, Byrnes was subjected to conflicting influences. Just before embarkation, Byrnes telephoned former Secretary of State Hull at his apartment to request Hull's opinion on the substance of Stimson's draft declaration. Hull, despite the fact that he had (when Secretary of State) suggested the possibility of modifying unconditional surrender so as not to eliminate the institution of the Emperor, now advised Byrnes to delete the item relating to the Emperor from Stimson's draft. He told Byrnes that

> . . . since he was leaving in a few minutes, there was no time to write anything for him, but that the statement seemed too much like appeasement of Japan, especially after the resolute stand we had maintained on unconditional surrender. [He] pointed out that, as it was worded, it seemed to guarantee continuance not only of the Emperor, but also of the feudal privileges of a ruling caste under the Emperor. [He] said that the Emperor and the ruling class must be stripped of all extraordinary privileges and placed on a level before the law with everybody else.[74]

Grew, on the other hand, tried to influence Byrnes differently. As Byrnes was leaving his office to depart for Potsdam, Grew handed him the State Department draft of the proposed declaration. Grew had been trying to interest Byrnes in his position on the Emperor since Byrnes had become Secretary, but Byrnes had been too preoccupied with preparation for his departure to discuss the matter. His last action, on leaving the office, was to place Grew's document in his pocket.[75] That evening Grew expressed to Forrestal his satisfaction with the draft that had finally been written making unconditional surrender more specific. He was afraid that it would be ditched on the way to Potsdam by those with the President, like Bohlen, who felt that any change in unconditional surrender would be construed by the Russians as an attempt to end the war before they had an opportunity to enter.[76] This was a new argument against modification of the surrender formula. No other evidence has been discovered to support Grew's remarks.

On July 6, another effort was made to influence Byrnes. Assistant Secretary of State MacLeish sent a memorandum to Byrnes to inform him that the Staff Committee of the State Department had split on the question of changing the surrender policy. Both he and Acheson felt that if unconditional surrender were changed to surrender on the irreducible Japanese terms of nonmolestation of the Emperor, then ". . . the American people have a right to know it." [77] Furthermore, he believed that the change in the policy toward Japan was inconsistent with the policy already followed toward Germany. If the Emperor were retained he might be used in the future as he had been at the start of this war. He urged that no statement be issued until the differences within the Staff Committee were reconciled, and that if one was issued that it should be made clear that the policy of unconditional surrender was being replaced by one of conditional surrender.[78]

The next day the Secretary's Staff Committee in the State Department met to iron out their differences on unconditional surrender. MacLeish mentioned his memorandum to Byrnes and restated his point of view. Grew fought back. He indicated that the draft which had been completed the day before and given to Byrnes, had been approved by Stimson, Forrestal, King, and probably

Marshall, as well as by himself.[79] The discussion continued with Grew opposing Acheson and MacLeish. Assistant Secretary Dunn and Legal Adviser Green H. Hackworth suggested compromises. Dunn wondered why it was necessary to go beyond a statement that the Japanese might be allowed to form a government that was peaceful. Hackworth suggested that the statement merely say that the Japanese might develop a government of their own choice. Grew ended the discussion, emphasizing that the Staff Committee was not responsible for the draft he had given Byrnes and urging Dunn, who was going to Potsdam, to keep the committee's discussion in mind.[80]

Concerned as he was about the forces lining up against change, Grew urged McCloy, who also was on his way to Potsdam, to let Stimson know how strongly he favored changing the surrender formula.[81] But he went even further. On July 13 he wrote directly to Byrnes urging him to support modification of unconditional surrender. He ended this plea by stating that he hoped ". . . that an early action may be taken on the proposed statement by the President which I gave you before your departure spelling out a little more definitely what unconditional surrender will mean." [82]

It is ironic that Grew, the man who had fought most vigorously for a change in the surrender formula, might have been an instrument for the omission of the reference to the Emperor in the Potsdam Declaration. And yet, such seems to have been the case. Grew had offered the communications services of the State Department to Hull to contact Byrnes at Potsdam. On July 16 Hull sent, through Grew, his views on unconditional surrender. He felt that the general public would construe the statement in the draft proclamation regarding the Emperor as an indication that the Allies would preserve the Emperor and his monarchy in case of victory. He went on:

The theory is that somehow the influences and persons who listen to the Emperor and his religion would fight and resist less hard and so save allied lives and shorten the war. . . . Undoubtedly, if this undertaking should prove successful it would be still more appealing. The other side is that no person knows how the proposal would work out. The militarists would try hard to interfere. Also should it fail the Japs would be encouraged while *terrible political repercussions would follow in the U. S.* Would it be well to await the climax of allied bombing and Russia's entry into the war?[83]

The next day Byrnes replied, and Grew dutifully phoned his message to Hull:

I agree that the issuance of the statement should be delayed and, when made, should not contain commitment to which you refer.[84]

Hull wasn't sure as to what commitment Byrnes had in mind, but Grew reassured him that it was the change concerning the Emperor. The Acting Secretary must have been somewhat embittered by this evidence of the failure of his efforts; yet, strangely enough, he informed Hull that he too felt the declaration should be delayed. Grew was, it seems, a good loser.

By the time the Potsdam Conference met the effort to eliminate the military solution of blockade, bombing, and invasion as a means of achieving Japanese surrender and to replace it with a political solution by modifying the unconditional surrender formula had apparently failed. Grew probably hoped that Dunn, McCloy, and Stimson might still prevail upon Byrnes. And yet Byrnes' message to Hull on July 17 seemed to preclude that development. His approach, reflecting that of Hull and in line with Truman's, apparently was based on the conclusion that there was too much to lose politically in appearing to preserve the Emperor. He was willing to issue the declaration with its implication of moderation in the treatment of a defeated Japan. He was not willing to say anything specific in assuring the Japanese that they might retain their Emperor.

As in the case of attempts to modify the surrender formula, efforts to revise the policy of involving the Soviet Union in the war in the Far East also were ineffective. Such actions must be considered within the general deterioration of relations between the Soviet Union, on the one hand, and Great Britain and the United States, on the other, which took place during the spring and early summer of 1945. As the power of Germany and Japan declined, the similarity of interests which bound the allies during the greater part of the war dissipated. Widespread distrust of Soviet intentions developed quietly within the British and American Governments as they witnessed Soviet expansion into Eastern Europe, Soviet domination of Poland, and Soviet pressures on the Eastern Mediterranean and the Middle East. Such actions seemed to violate the terms of agreements negotiated at the Yalta Conference. Although hope remained that the Soviets might withdraw once hostilities had ended, some high in the United States Government saw such Soviet moves as forerunners to later efforts to expand Soviet territory and influence to the maximum.

At least part of this attitude reflected the outspoken concern of the British. Churchill, seeing the specter of Soviet power replacing the German threat on the Continent as the Soviet armies rolled westward through Eastern Europe, persistently sought to settle his grievances with the Soviet Union before the war had ended and before United States troops might be withdrawn from Europe. Frequently through the early days of Truman's administration, the Prime Minister bombarded the new President with warnings about the post-war Soviet menace. He argued that matters with the Soviet Union in Europe had progressed about as far as they possibly could by correspondence, and on May 6 he suggested that a meeting of the three heads of government should be held as soon as possible to iron out their differences by direct consultation.[85] Truman agreed on May 9 that a conference should be held; but he felt that the Soviets should be maneuvered into requesting it and indicated that he would not be able to get away from Washington until the end of the fiscal year, at the earliest.[86]

Churchill became more persistent. He doubted that Stalin would propose such a conference, but he thought that the Soviet Premier would respond to an invitation from either the United States or Great Britain or from both. He urged that United States forces should not retreat from military positions they had taken in Europe to the occupational lines in Germany agreed to at Yalta.[87]

After the Potsdam Conference had been arranged as a result of Hopkins' visit with Stalin in late May and early June, 1945, Churchill suggested that United States forces be maintained in Europe as a bargaining factor to be used at the forthcoming meeting. He knew that pressures would be strong on Truman to withdraw troops for duty against Japan as well as to appease those who wanted the United States to play no more than a minor role in postwar Europe.

The Prime Minister believed that powerful forces in the United States Government were at work on Truman to convince him that the United States should act as mediator between Great Britain and Russia in order to create a viable peace in Europe and to permit the redeployment of United States troops to the Far Eastern theater.[88]

To offset the possibility that Britain, weakened by a long war, would be left practically alone to oppose Russian expansion westward, Churchill persistently painted a picture of Russian menace. Thus, in a telegram to Truman on May 11, he vividly described the Russian expansion in Eastern Europe:

This constitutes an event in the history of Europe to which there has been no parallel and which has not been faced by the Allies in their long and hazardous struggle. The Russian demands on Germany for reparations alone will be such as to enable her to prolong the occupation indefinitely . . . during which time Poland will sink with many other states into the vast zone of Russian-controlled Europe. . . .[89]

Churchill's most vigorous plea was included in a message to Truman the next day. He first expressed dismay over the possibility of the withdrawal of United States and Canadian forces from Europe and over the growing weakness of the British and the French. Then he mentioned his anxiety about Soviet moves in Poland, in the Balkans, and in Austria. Somewhat plaintively he asked:

What will be the position in a year or two, when the British and American armies have melted and the French has not yet been formed. . . , when we may have a handful of divisions mostly French, and when Russia may choose to keep two or three hundred on active service?[90]

He went on:

. . . 3. An iron curtain is drawn down upon their Russian front. We do not know what is going on behind. . . . All kinds of arrangements will have to be made by . . . Eisenhower to prevent another immense flight of the German population westward as this enormous Muscovite advance into the centre of Europe takes place. And then the curtain will descend again. . . . Thus a broad band of many hundreds of miles of Russian-occupied territory will isolate Poland.

4. Meanwhile the attention of our peoples will be occupied in inflicting severities upon Germany, which is ruined and prostrate, and it would be open to the Russians in a very short time to advance if they chose to the waters of the North Sea and the Atlantic. . . . To sum up, this issue of a settlement with Russia before our strength has gone seems to me to dwarf all others.[91]

The Prime Minister forcefully expressed himself again on this matter during a session with President Truman's special emissary, Joseph E. Davies, on May 26. Davies opened the conversation by indicating that Truman had sent Hopkins to Moscow to arrange for a tripartite meeting; that the President intended that every agreement made by Roosevelt would be scrupulously supported; that Truman's paramount objective was to maintain peace after victory; and that, since Truman had never met Stalin, he intended to see the Russian Premier prior to the three-power conference. Churchill, who had invited Truman to visit London before he went to Potsdam, apparently became quite bitter at these remarks. He spoke very strongly against the withdrawal of United States troops from Europe, and of the "steel curtain" of the Soviets being clamped down on liberated Eastern Europe.[92]

On the next day Churchill summarized his position in a note for President Truman. After demanding that Great Britain be treated as an equal of the United States and the Soviet Union at the coming conference, he went on to sketch the tripartite relationship as he saw it developing. First, he used the ideological argument:

. . . Britain and the United States are united . . . upon the same ideologies, namely, freedom, and the principles set out in the American Constitution and . . . in the Atlantic Charter. The Soviet Government have a different philosophy, namely communism, and use to the full the methods of police government, which they are applying to every state which has fallen a victim to their liberating arms. The Prime Minister cannot readily . . . accept the idea that Britain and . . . Russia are just two foreign Powers, six of one and half a dozen of the other, with whom the troubles of the late war have to be adjusted. Except in so far as force is concerned, there is no equality between right and wrong. The great causes and principles for which the British and the United States have suffered and triumphed are not mere matters of the balance of power. They . . . involve the salvation of the world.[93]

Here, the Prime Minister, pleading for unity with the United States against the Russian threat from the Continent, was in reality attempting to maintain a balance of power which he on paper was rejecting. Truman was puzzled by Churchill's attitude. He at no time had meant to infer that he would see Stalin at a separate conference. His major objective was to use his meeting with Stalin and Churchill to maintain the unity which had existed during the war. "Unity was even more important to keep the peace." [94] He was concerned with Russian excesses in Europe and expected to back Churchill firmly in his opposition to them. And yet he still had a major war in the Far East on his hands; and his military was still indicating, although not so strongly as they had to Roosevelt, that Russian participation was desirable. Allied unity was necessary to satisfy their objective.

The British Foreign Minister, Anthony Eden, who was in the United States that spring for the United Nations Conference at San Francisco, provided further evidence of Churchill's distrust of the Russians. Following a stag dinner for Eden at the British Embassy on April 16, Stimson wrote that ". . . the English are very pessimistic over Russia and from some of the things that Eden told me it would look rather as if there is good reason for it." [95] Eden persistently transmitted not only Churchill's concern over Russian actions in Europe, but also his belief in the necessity of coping with them rapidly if outstanding issues were to be settled.[96]

Warnings of Russian intransigence also came from the United States Ambassador to Russia, W. Averell Harriman, who, following Roosevelt's death, had returned to the United States to stay until the Hopkins mission to Moscow in late May. Soon after he arrived he met with Truman, Grew, and Bohlen at the White House on April 20. At that time he expressed his doubts about Soviet intentions. The Soviets had two basic policies, he thought. One involved cooperation with the United States and Great Britain and the other required Soviet control over their neighboring states. He continued by saying that the Western Allies:

. . . were faced with a "barbarian invasion of Europe." He was convinced that Soviet control over any foreign country meant not only that their influence would be paramount in that country's foreign relations, but also the Soviet system with its secret police and its extinction of freedom of speech would prevail. . . . He added that he . . . felt that it was possible . . . to arrive at a workable basis with the Russians. He believed that this would require . . . the abandonment of any illusion that the Soviet government was likely soon to act in accordance with the principles to which the rest of the world held in international affairs.[97]

As the meeting broke up, Harriman drew Truman aside to tell him that one of the reasons he had returned to Washington was to help Truman understand, as Roosevelt had understood, that the Russians were breaking their agreements.[98] Truman was apparently much impressed by Harriman's warnings. At one point he asserted ". . . that we intended to be firm with the Russians and make no concessions from American principles or traditions in order to win their favor." [99]

On May 15 Harriman again expressed his position clearly during a meeting with Truman, Grew, and Bohlen:

. . . the problem of our relations with Russia is the number one problem affecting the future of the world and the fact was that at the present moment we were getting farther and farther apart. . . . He said he felt that the . . . longer the tri-partite meeting was delayed the worse the situation would get, and that while he assumed . . . that we were not prepared to use our troops in Europe for political bargaining nevertheless if the meeting could take place before we were in a large measure out of Europe he felt the atmosphere of the meeting would be more favorable and the chances of success increased. . . .[100]

The Ambassador, while expecting trouble, still hoped that a settlement might be negotiated at a high-level conference.

Within this atmosphere of warnings from abroad, top-policy advisers to President Truman developed their own doubts of Russian intentions in Europe and the Far East. Some became particularly doubtful of the United States policy of involving Russia in the war in the Far East. Their various opinions were stated to the President at a White House meeting on April 23.[101] Although Poland was the major item of discussion, the conversation covered the general Russian problem. Stettinius mentioned the virtual impasse in Russian-Western relations concerning Poland. Stimson then took the some-what more realistic point of view, that Russian interests and goals in Poland should be carefully weighed in view of their past relations with that nation, and indicated that any split with the Soviets would be extremely serious. Forrestal, however, assumed a more critical stance against the Russian position. He believed that:

. . . this difficulty over Poland could not be treated as an isolated incident—that there had been many evidences of the Soviet desire to dominate adjacent coun-tries and to disregard the wishes of her allies. It was his belief that for some time the Russians had been under the impression that we would not object if they took over all of Eastern Europe, and he said it was his profound conviction that if the Russians were to be rigid in their attitude we had better have a showdown with them now rather than later.[102]

The major concern of all was to avoid a break with the Russians; for such an event might eliminate a settlement in Europe, might wreck plans for establishing the United Nations, and might worsen the situation in the Far East. General Marshall emphasized the importance of this latter problem. After professing unfamiliarity with the Polish political situation, he went on to say that:

. . . from the military point of view the situation in Europe was secure but that he hoped for Soviet participation in the war against Japan at a time when it would be useful for us. The Russians . . . might delay their entry into the . . . war until we had done all the dirty work. He was inclined to agree with Mr. Stimson that . . . a break with Russia was very serious.[103]

Deane responded to Marshall's statement by expressing his opinion that the Soviet Union would enter the war as soon as it could, regardless of its position elsewhere.

This meeting reflected the seriousness with which the United States Government viewed its relations with Russia that April. It illustrated the basic dilemma—even as relations with the Soviets were deteriorating in Europe their collaboration in the Far East was still desired.

During the review of military plans against Japan which took place in April, Marshall continued to state that Russia's participation in the war would be a prerequisite to the planned invasion of Japan.[104] On April 14, the Joint Staff Planners (JPS) reviewed the war situation for the JCS. They stated a somewhat different position from that of Marshall:

> Because of our ability to interdict Japanese movement between the Asiatic mainland and Japan. . . , early Russian entry into the war against Japan and attendant containing of the Kwantung army is no longer necessary to make invasion feasible.
>
> It should be noted that the Cairo declaration included provision that Manchuria be returned to China and that Russia has not yet subscribed to the principles of this declaration. If Russia enters the war her forces will probably be the first into Manchuria. This will raise the question of introducing at least token U. S. forces into China.[105]

Apparently the JPS had not seen the United States–Soviet agreement on the Far East, negotiated at Yalta, in which Stalin had accepted Nationalist Chinese sovereignty over Manchuria. Their paper, however, revealed their doubts as to the need for Soviet intervention, their anticipations that the Soviets would act, and their concern over the postwar Soviet position in Manchuria.

Similar doubts were being expressed at the political level. The general question of Russia's position in the Far East was raised by Forrestal at a State-War-Navy meeting on May 1. The Secretary of the Navy posed, among other questions, the following: (1) How thoroughly should Japan be defeated? (2) Was Japan to be readmitted to the "society of nations after demilitarization?" (3) What was the United States policy toward Russian influence in the Far East? Did the United States wish to counter that influence with either China or Japan after the war? [106]

As a result of a meeting on the morning of May 12, Grew posed certain questions of his own in a memorandum to Stimson and Forrestal. The Acting Secretary of State had long been seriously worried about the general Russian position and about Soviet plans in the Far East. His general attitude was expressed in a memorandum to himself on May 19. He believed that the war had achieved only one purpose for the United States: protection from the power of Germany and Japan. It was in no sense a war to bring lasting peace because the result would be ". . . merely the transfer of totalitarian dictatorship and power . . . to Soviet Russia which . . . would constitute in the future as grave a danger to us as did the Axis." [107] The United Nations would be unable to maintain peace because of the veto for the permanent members of the Security Council. Already the Soviet Union was demonstrating the type of world it wanted. He expected eventual Russian control of Europe, and, if the United States did not take steps to stop it, ". . . once Russia is in the war against Japan, then Mongolia, Manchuria, and Korea . . . would gradually slip into Russia's orbit, to be followed in due course by China and eventually Japan . . ." [108] He concluded with these dire predictions of what might occur unless the United States opposed such developments:

A future war with Soviet Russia is as certain as anything in this world can be certain. It may come within a very few years. We shall therefore do well to keep up our fighting strength and to do everything in our power to strengthen our relations with the free world.

Meanwhile we should insist upon the control of strategic air and naval bases. The most fatal thing we can do is to place any confidence whatever in Russia's sincerity, knowing without question that she will take every opportunity to profit by our clinging to our own ethical international standards. She regards and will continue to regard our ethical behavior as a weakness to us and an asset to her.

As soon as the San Francisco Conference is over, our policy toward Soviet Russia should immediately stiffen, all along the line. . . .[109]

The question which Grew asked Forrestal and Stimson reflected the feelings he had expressed to himself in the above memorandum. They were as follows:

1. Is entry of the Soviet Union into the Pacific War at the earliest possible moment of such vital interest to the United States as to preclude any attempt by the United States to obtain Soviet agreement to certain desirable political objectives in the Far East prior to such entry?
2. Should the Yalta decision in regard to Soviet political desires in the Far East be reconsidered or carried into effect in whole or in part?
3. Should a Soviet demand, if made, for participation in the military occupation of the Japanese home islands be granted or would such occupation adversely effect our long term policy for the future treatment of Japan?[110]

Grew went on to outline for his colleagues the State Department's opinion as to what political commitments might be sought from the Soviet Union prior to United States fulfillment of the Yalta agreement. The State Department desired, first, that the Soviet Government exert its influence to unify China under the Nationalist Government; second, that the Russians adhere unequivocally to the Cairo Declaration in regard to Manchuria and Korea; third, that the Soviet Union support a four-power trusteeship of Korea; and, fourth, that the Soviets agree to provide landing rights in the Kuriles for commercial planes from the United States prior to United States acceptance of Soviet annexation of those islands.[111]

Stimson replied for the War Department on May 21. His position was somewhat different. His opinions again reflected consultation with General Marshall. First, the War Department believed that the political actions of the United States would not materially affect the Soviet Union's entry into the war which would be undertaken to satisfy its own military and political needs. The military still felt that Russian participation would shorten the war and, thus, save American lives. Second, it estimated that the concessions made to Russia at Yalta involved territories which, with the possible exception of the Kuriles, the Russians had the power to obtain regardless of United States military action short of war. And, third, it considered the question of Russian participation in the military occupation of Japan to be a political question which involved possible advantages and disadvantages to the military. The Department concurred ". . . in the desirability of obtaining the four commitments and clarifications desired of the Soviet Government by the Department of State.[112] On the same day, Forrestal wrote to Grew that he agreed with the position taken by Stimson.[113]

There the matter was apparently shelved, at least insofar as any direct action was involved. It is doubtful that Truman saw either of the above documents.[114] But Stimson at least gave these matters considerable thought and increasingly recognized their connection with the possible use of the atomic bombs on Japan. His *Diary* entries, recorded during the period he was preparing his answer to Grew's letter, indicated the nature of his thinking. On May 3, after listing Grew's three questions, he wrote, "The questions cut very deep and in my opinion are powerfully connected with our success with S-1." [115] The next day he mentioned discussing the Grew question first with Marshall and then with McCloy:

I told him (McCloy) that my own opinion was that the time now and the method now to deal with Russia was to keep our mouths shut and to let our actions speak for words. The Russians will understand them better than anything else. It is a case where we have got to regain the lead and perhaps do it in a pretty rough and realistic way. They have rather taken it away from us because we have talked too much and have been too lavish with our beneficences to them. I told him this was a place where we really held all the cards. I called it a royal straight flush and we musn't [sic] be a fool about the way we play it. They can't get along without our help and industries and we have coming into action a weapon which will be unique. . . .[116]

On May 15 Stimson reported a "pretty red hot session" over Grew's questions of the State-War-Navy Committee meeting. He felt that, at the time, the questions were somewhat premature since the three Secretaries were not in a position to answer them. They might, perhaps, be considered at the coming meeting of the heads of government in July. He then again referred to the atomic weapons:

Over any such tangled wave of problems the S-1 secret would be dominant and yet we will not know until after that time probably, until after that meeting, whether this is a weapon in our hands or not. We think it will be shortly afterwards, but it is a terrible thing to gamble with such big stakes in diplomacy without having your mastercard in hand.[117]

In considering Chinese Foreign Minister T. V. Soong's suggestion that the United States fight the Japanese on the Chinese mainland, Stimson wrote later that day:

. . . that . . . [he] was resolved that we shall not do so unless it is over my dead body. . . . The Japanese campaign involves . . . too great uncertainties; first, whether Russia will come in though we think that will be all right; and second, when and how S-1 will resolve itself.[118]

Because of his control of the atomic bomb program, Stimson's approach to the Far Eastern situation and to Russia was of some importance. The Secretary of War was a realist. He recognized that the Soviet Union had political interests in the areas along the periphery of its territory which it would attempt to satisfy if it had the power to do so. Soviet strategic needs in Manchuria, Korea, Sakhalin, the Kuriles, and Japan would probably lead to their military intervention against Japan. The United States, now somewhat cool to such a development, had throughout the war consistently sought Soviet action in the Far East and was not presently in the military position to stop it. The Soviets, therefore, might at the termination of hostilities, particularly if they were prolonged, occupy an extended area in Eastern Asia. Aside from the redefinition of the unconditional surrender formula, which seemed unlikely, the one imponderable—the force which might not only end the war before an invasion and the resultant loss of American lives became necessary, but also before the Soviets could exert their power in the area—was S-1. The atom bomb was Stimson's ace in the hole.

Whether Truman thought along these lines is doubtful. Overburdened with a number of complex problems, he was still operating at a relatively superficial level in connection with the Russian situation in the Far East. He recognized that he had to be firm with the Russians and at the same time maintain allied unity. He wanted to end the war quickly to save American lives. Yet he was unwilling to risk the popular dissatisfaction resulting from a modification of unconditional surrender so as to preserve the Emperor, the one conciliatory act that might have quickly terminated hostilities. He would sanction blockade, air attack, and invasion of Japan. To ease the difficulty of invasion, to shorten the war and save lives, he would explore the possibilities of implementing Roosevelt's policy of involving Russia in the war with Japan.

To this end, he dispatched an ailing Harry Hopkins to Moscow on his last mission for the United States. One of Hopkins' primary responsibilities was to ascertain whether or not Stalin intended to fight Japan. Hopkins discussed the Far Eastern question at length with Stalin on May 28. Stalin said at that time that the Soviet Armies would be sufficiently prepared to attack by August 8, 1945. The actual date of operations, however, would depend on the implementation of the Yalta agreements. If China would give assent to those agreements, the Soviets would be ready to act in August. He concurred with Hopkins that the matter should be raised with the Chinese Foreign Minister, T. V. Soong, during his anticipated visit to Moscow after he finished his duties at the United Nations Conference in San Francisco.[119]

Stalin informed Hopkins that it would be necessary to hold serious discussions regarding the zones of operations in the Far East and the areas of occupation in Japan. He then said that he favored unconditional surrender for Japan and the elimination of the Emperor. But he was cold-bloodedly realistic about the bitter fighting which the Japanese might use to oppose the allied effort to force unconditional surrender and suggested a possible alternative. He remarked that

. . . war such as the present could only happen once in a hundred years and it was better to take advantage of it and utterly defeat Japan and . . . in that manner assure fifty or sixty years of peace. . . . He said there was one other possibility and that would be to accept a conditional surrender and then subsequently to impose in stages successively harsher terms which would cope with the Japanese military potential. In other words unconditional surrender in stages. He . . . did not exclude this latter possibility.[120]

Stalin, at the same time, made a number of statements to Hopkins which were to reassure Truman about Russian ambitions in the Far East after the war. He mentioned that he favored Chinese unity under Chiang Kai-shek who was the best of the Chinese leaders. The Soviet Union, he said, had no territorial claims in regard to China. Furthermore, in any area of China where Soviet troops were operating, Chinese administration might be set up under Chiang. Stalin also accepted the idea of a four-power trusteeship for Korea and emphasized that ". . . the United States must play the largest part in helping China to get on their [sic] feet; the Soviet Union with its own internal reconstruction and Great Britain would be occupied elsewhere." [121]

The Hopkins conversations with Stalin were very encouraging to Truman. Apparently the Soviet Union was accepting the United States position in the Far East. Truman, who probably had not heard of Grew's reservations, was prepared to implement the Yalta agreement by facilitating the negotiation of a treaty by the Chinese and the Russians which would guarantee the relationship, conditionally negotiated at Yalta by Roosevelt and Stalin, between China and Russia. The President "was reassured to learn . . . that Stalin had confirmed the understanding reached at Yalta about Russia's entry into the war against Japan . . . . Russian entry into the war against Japan was highly important to us." [122] The United States continued its policy of promoting Russian entrance into the war in the Far East despite a growing distrust of Soviet intentions on the part of both the British and of some within the higher levels of the government in Washington. In preparation for the Potsdam Conference, Truman called a meeting of his top military advisers on June 18.[123] At that time Marshall had reaffirmed the Joint Chiefs of Staff support for Russian participation. He stated that ". . . if the Japanese are ever willing to capitulate short of complete military defeat in the field they will do it when faced by . . . (1) . . . air bombardment and sea blockade, . . . (2) a landing on Japan . . . , and also perhaps coupled with (3) the entry or threat of entry of Russia into the war . . . our objectives were to get the Russians to deal with the Japs in Manchuria (and Korea if necessary) and to vitalize the Chinese to a point where, with assistance of American air power and some supplies, they can mop out their own country." [124] He went on to say that "an important point about Russian participation in the war is that the impact of Russian entry on the already helpless Japanese may well be the decisive action levering them into capitulation at that time or shortly thereafter if we land in Japan. To substantiate his position he read from a telegram from MacArthur in which the General had indicated that the hazard and losses from invasion would ". . . be greatly lessened if an attack is launched from Siberia sufficiently ahead of our target date to commit the enemy to major combat." [125]

Admiral King and General Eaker, sitting in for General Arnold, supported this position generally. But King later emphasized that ". . . regardless of the desirability of the Russians entering the war, they were not indispensable and he did not think we should go so far as to beg them to come in. While the cost of defeating Japan would be no greater there was no question . . . but that we could handle it alone. He thought that the realization of this fact should greatly strengthen the President's hand in the forthcoming conference." [126] Only Admiral Leahy expressed a "jaundiced view" of the need for Soviet participation.[127]

Truman once more accepted the conclusions of his military. He announced to them that ". . . one of his objectives in connection with the coming conference would be to get from Russia all the assistance in the war that was possible." [128] This was to be his position at Potsdam despite the fact that by the middle of July conversations in Moscow among Stalin, Molotov, Harriman, and Soong on the implementation of the Yalta agreement regarding Russian-Chinese relations in Outer Mongolia and Manchuria had reached an impasse which was not to be resolved until after the Potsdam Conference. Knowing full well that Stalin had tied his entrance into the Japanese war to successful negotiation of a Sino-Soviet treaty which would provide the Soviet Union a more advantageous position along its border areas with China, Truman informed the Chinese on July 23 that he did not expect them to make concessions beyond those outlined in the Yalta agreement.[129] He was willing to deviate that far from his purpose of involving Russia in the war. On the other hand, the President has recorded the objectives of his trip to Potsdam quite specifically:

As our forces in the Pacific were pushing ahead, paying a heavy toll in lives, the urgency of getting Russia into the war became more compelling. Russia's entry into the war could mean the saving of hundreds of thousands of American casualties.

That was one of the compelling reasons that would take me out of the country to a meeting with Stalin and Churchill. And this is why we were urging the Chinese and the Russians to conclude an accord on the basis of the . . . agreement at Yalta.[130]

And again:

In preparation for the conference with Churchill and Stalin, I was going over in my mind the purposes for which I was traveling to Potsdam. Of course my immediate purpose was to get the Russians into the war against Japan as soon as possible, but my main objective was to come out with a working relationship to prevent another world catastrophe.[131]

And finally:

There were many reasons for my going to Potsdam, but the most urgent to my mind was to get from Stalin a personal reaffirmation of Russia's entry into the war against Japan, a matter which our military chiefs were most anxious to clinch. . . .[132]

Thus, despite doubts concerning the need for Russian intervention and questions about Russian intentions which were expressed by some of his military and political advisers, Truman accepted the Army version of the need for Russian support as expounded by Marshall.

Grew, Forrestal, and Stimson, all of whom would have liked to have seen the war against Japan end without Russian intervention, were not men to remain silent. And yet after their exchanges in May, there is little evidence that they exerted much effort to convince Truman to change his stand. It seems that they had all accepted Stimson's belief that Russia would enter the war against Japan whatever the United States did. In view of the need for harmony among the Allies, it was unwise to create difficulties by withdrawing the request for Russian intervention when the United States had little capability to effect that action one way or the other. The Secretary of War was, at the same time, developing another force against Russian expansion. Truman might ask the Russians to enter the war, or they might enter without a request to satisfy their own interests. Stimson hoped soon to have S-1 to neutralize any political advantage they might gain.

Even as the Secretary of War was envisaging the atomic weapon as a major power factor in wartime and postwar politics, certain scientists within the Manhattan Engineer District continued their attempts to persuade the government to choose an alternative other than that of dropping the powerful weapons on Japan. As indicated earlier, the Franck Report had had little if any effect on the decisions of the Interim Committee. The actions of others seeking the same ends were to be no more successful.

On July 3, Leo Szilard, who earlier in March and May had unsuccessfully attempted to warn Roosevelt and then Truman of the danger to the United States which might result from a postwar atomic weapons race following United States use of the atomic bombs on Japan, circulated among his fellow scientists at the Metallurgical Laboratory at Chicago a draft petition to the President for their consideration.[133] Szilard's petition was opposed to the use of the atomic bomb. He now believed that such action was not only inexpedient but also immoral.

> Once they were introduced as an instrument of war it would be difficult to resist the temptation of putting them to . . . use. . . . Thus a nation which sets the precedent of using these newly liberated forces of nature for purposes of destruction may have to bear the responsibility of opening the door to an era of devastation on an unimaginable scale.[134]

Szilard had requested permission from Compton to circulate his petition. In answer to Compton's request on Szilard's behalf, Groves informed Compton on July 7 that he had no objection to Szilard's circulating his petition provided that it was classified; that it was shown only to those possessing the extent of information possessed by Szilard and who knew as much information as was included in the petition; and that it was forwarded to the highest political and military channels.[135] Since Szilard's petition in its original form overlooked a number of considerations including that of the additional United States military losses which might result if the war was prolonged because of an unwillingness to use the bombs, it found insufficient support among the scientific community at Chicago and was, therefore, redrafted.[136]

The new draft, "Petition to the President of the United States," was ready on July 17.[137] It was signed by seventy scientists including Szilard.[138] As had the earlier draft, it suggested a demonstration of the weapon to the Japanese which would provide them an opportunity to consider the consequences of a refusal to surrender.

The earlier Szilard petition and his later draft stimulated considerable opposition as well as support among his colleagues. Following General Groves' suggestion, Compton, who was troubled by the apparent strength of opinion at Chicago against the decision to use the bomb, had already called on Farrington Daniels, the director of the Metallurgical Laboratory, to conduct a poll in order to sample scientific opinion.[139] The poll was taken on June 12, and the results were transmitted to Compton on the next day. It listed five procedures for use of the bomb and asked which came closest to the method each of those polled would choose in using the weapon against Japan.[140] Of the nearly 150 scientists who responded, ". . . 15 per cent favored its limited use, 26 per cent favored an experimental demonstration before military use, and 13 per cent preferred to avoid any military use whatever." [141] The questions which were posed by Daniels were so vague that they elicited responses which only in a very general way indicated opinion at Chicago. And yet Compton has written of the results of the poll. ". . . There were a few who preferred not to use the bomb at all, but 87 per cent voted for its military use, at least if after other means were tried this was found necessary to bring surrender." [142] He neglected to mention that many indicated by their votes that they preferred using a variety of other means first. He also implied that, in addition to support for use from the Interim Committee and from the scientists who were polled, ". . . mechanics in our shops who were working long hours in fabricating the bomb or in building instruments concerned with its development" also favored employing the weapon on Japan.[143] Other than the possibility that some of the 150 who were polled were mechanics, no evidence has been found to indicate that such technicians were consulted.[144]

Another group that had not signed Szilard's petition circulated its own on July 13. This petition signed by eighteen scientists favored use, particularly against cities, but only after the Japanese had been afforded an opportunity to surrender on terms assuring their peaceful development; after convincing warnings had been transmitted to Japan that its refusal to surrender would be followed by the use of the new weapon; and after responsibility for use of the bomb had been shared with the allies of the United States.[145] Compton indicated that this group was suggesting a policy on use which was practically identical to that accepted by Truman and Stimson. In the warning to be included in the Potsdam Declaration, however, nothing was said about a new weapon, and the responsibility for use was hardly shared with Russia.[146]

Several letters from individual scientists strongly favoring use of the weapons were also sent to Compton. One from a George W. Parker to Compton on July 16 favored the use of the bombs to save the lives of United States fighting men. It also expressed the opinion that

. . . An impressive victory over Japan with an impressive weapon should inspire American diplomacy and world opinion to effectively tame the present hard-booted Russian ego which is now an embarrassing threat to the plans for world security.[147]

Another such letter which was sent by Evan J. Young to Martin D. Whitaker of the Metallurgical Laboratory on July 14 read, in part:

. . . Therefore, with no strings attached, let the War Department use this weapon at the earliest and most expeditious moment, in whatever manner will produce optimum results in the way of shortening the war and saving American lives.[1148]

The evidence indicates, therefore, that scientific opinion at Chicago was at best divided. Most who expressed an opinion, however, favored some sort of demonstration followed by a warning in which the threat from the new weapon would be emphasized.

This division of opinion explained Compton's dilemma when on July 23 he was asked by Colonel K. D. Nichols, district engineer of the Manhattan Engineer District, to report the results of the opinion polls on the use of the bomb to Washington. Compton ". . . accordingly wrote out a message summarizing the results as objectively as [he] could and handed it to the Colonel." [149] An hour later Nichols informed Compton that Washington wanted to know what he himself thought. Compton's reaction, as he recalled it later, was interesting:

What a question to answer! Having been in the very midst of these discussions, it seemed to me that a firm negative stand on my part might still prevent an atomic attack on Japan. . . . I knew all too well the destruction and human agony the bombs would cause. I knew the danger they held in the hands of some future tyrant. These facts I had been living with for four years. But I wanted the war to end. I wanted life to become normal again. I saw a chance for an enduring peace that would be demanded by the very destructiveness of these weapons. I hoped that by use of the bombs many fine young men I knew might be released at once from the demands of war and thus be given a chance to live and not to die.[150]

Compton, then, supported use of the atomic weapon. It seemed to him that the bomb should be used, but as humanely as possible. Nichols sent his message to Washington.

Compton assumed too much when he reasoned that there was an immediate connection between his action and the resultant use of the bombs. "Washington" was apparently General Groves. On July 25 Nichols sent Groves a memorandum to which was attached Compton's letter of July 24 transmitting the various petitions, poll results, and letters mentioned above. In that letter, Compton had indicated that the procedure most favored by all informed groups was ". . . a military demonstration in Japan, to be followed by a renewed opportunity for surrender before full use of the weapon [was] employed." [151] This, as he knew from his participation as one of its members, was somewhat different from the recommendation of the Interim Committee that the weapons be used on military-civilian targets.[152] Nichols' covering memorandum recommended that the materials be forwarded to the President with the proper comments. Apparently the "proper comments" included his accompanying opinion:

It is believed that by such action and example (sending the items to the President) it will be more nearly possible to control the individual activities of the various scientists who have ideas regarding the political and social implications concerning use of the weapons and to confine their activities to proper channels where security for the project will not be jeopardized. Contrary to the hopes of Mr. Leo Szilard who started the original petition, thereby precipitating the other petitions, it is believed that these collective papers generally support the present plans for the use of the weapon.[153]

Thus, Nichols' interpretation of the scientists' opinions was that they generally supported the existing plans.

Groves, however, apparently never showed these indications of scientific opinion to the President. On August 1, after the final authorization to use the atomic weapons had been made, Groves took Nichols' memorandum and its attached papers to Stimson's office. Stimson and Harrison seemed to consider these further statements of scientific opinion irrelevant. Top scientists involved in MED had already stated their opinions on use to the Interim Committee. Stimson and the President and the others involved in policymaking at the highest level had made their decision. Truman was still out of the country, and it would serve no purpose to transmit the materials to him. "Harrison merely deposited them in his S-1 files." [154] Thus, it is very unlikely that the President was informed of these later scientific suggestions as to the use of the bomb until it was too late.[155] Yet another line of action suggesting modification of the policy of use died, this time within the War Department.

Insofar as consideration by those at the Potsdam Conference was concerned, then, efforts to modify the situation in such a way that the atomic bombs would not need to be used had failed. The change in unconditional surrender so as to provide for the possibility that the Japanese might retain their Emperor was dying at the hands of Secretary of State Byrnes. The effort to offset the political effects of anticipated Russian entrance into the Far Eastern war was promoting the bomb's rapid use. And the last, futile attempts of some scientists to influence the President through the administrative apparatus of the MED had ended, buried in its files, too late to have had any effect. The bombs would soon be ready; the planes and the men were well trained; future military plans envisioned horrible losses in men and equipment. The stage was set for Potsdam and for the President's final sanction to the decision to use the atomic bomb.

NOTES TO CHAPTER 8

1 See pp. 81–95.

2 Jesse F. Steiner, "Shall We Bomb Hirohito's Palace?" *The New York Times Magazine*, March 11, 1945, pp. 8, 45, 46.

3 A good summary of Japanese attitudes toward the Emperor during World War II appears in Otto D. Tolischus, *Through Japanese Eyes* (New York: Reynal and Hitchcock, 1945), pp. 22–55.

[4] Alexander H. Leighton, *Human Relations in A Changing World* (New York: E. P. Dutton and Company, Inc., 1949), p. 91.

[5] Kase Toshikazu, *Eclipse of the Rising Sun* (London: Jonathan Cape, 1951), p. 234.

[6] Kato Masuo, *The Lost War: A Japanese Reporter's Inside Story* (New York: Alfred A. Knopf, Inc., 1946), pp. 229–30.

[7] Leighton, *Human Relations in a Changing World*, p. 93.

[8] The complete text of the report appears in Leighton, *Human Relations in a Changing World*, Appendix B, pp. 227–89.

[9] *Ibid.*, p. 60.

[10] *Ibid.*, p. 229, 253.

[11] *Ibid.*, pp. 71–72.

[12] Leighton, *Human Relations in a Changing World*, p. 260.

[13] Roger Burlingame, *Don't Let Them Scare You: The Life and Times of Elmer Davis* (Philadelphia; J. B. Lippincott Company, 1961), p. 251.

[14] *IPR Hearings*, Testimony of Eugene H. Dooman, p. 729. Davis did, however, strongly support the work of Admiral Ellis Zacharias and Naval Intelligence unit OP-16-W in their efforts to moderate the unconditional surrender policy. This could possibly indicate his desire to change the policy; or, in view of the other fragmentary evidence, it might reflect his desire to trap the Japanese into unconditional surrender and the elimination of the Emperor by propaganda indicating United States moderation. See Zacharias, *Secret Missions*, pp. 341, 346.

[15] Ellis M. Zacharias, *Secret Missions: The Story of an Intelligence Officer* (New York: G. P. Putnam's Sons, 1946), p. 366.

[16] *Ibid.*, pp. 366–67.

[17] *Ibid.*, p. 371.

[18] *Ibid.*, pp. 399–424, which includes the texts of the broadcasts.

[19] Important passages of Zacharias' letter to the *Post* are quoted in Zacharias, *Secret Missions*, pp. 370–71.

[20] Zacharias, *Secret Missions*, pp. 420–24.

[21] *Ibid.*, pp. 372–73.

[22] *Ibid.*, pp. 341–45.

[23] Walter Millis (ed.), *The Forrestal Diaries* (New York: The Viking Press, Inc., 1951), p. 53. See pp. 419, ff.

[24] *Ibid.*, p. 55.

[25] Ray S. Cline, *Washington Command Post: The Operations Division* (Washington: U. S. Government Printing Office, 1951), p. 343, text, and fn. 36.

[26] See, p. 177.

[27] U. S. Department of Defense, *The Entry of the Soviet Union into the War Against Japan* (Washington: 1955), p. 63.

[28] Cline, *Washington Command Post*, p. 344.

[29] *Ibid.*, p. 345.

[30] Stimson, *Diary*, June 26, 1945. S-1 was the War Department's code designator for the atomic bomb.

[31] Secretary of State Stettinius was involved in efforts to negotiate the Charter of the United Nations at San Francisco and did not participate in this State Department action, although he was kept informed and did not oppose it.

[32] *Public Papers of the Presidents of the United States: Harry S. Truman, 1945* (Washington: U. S. Government Printing Office, 1961), p. 2.

[33] *Ibid.*, p. 50. See also Truman, *Memoirs*, I, 207 and Zacharias, *Secret Missions*, pp. 346–50. Zacharias reports that this document had its origins in OP-16-W and the

OWI. Before Roosevelt's death, they had drawn up a proposed declaration by the President to clarify unconditional surrender to the Japanese. The proposal had been presented to Roosevelt during his last few weeks at Hyde Park by Elmer Davis. Roosevelt's death delayed the public announcement, and in the days immediately following nothing could be done to bring it to Truman's attention. Zacharias, however, heard indirectly through one of Truman's secretaries, Matthew J. Connelly, that the paper containing the proposed declaration was on Truman's desk and would receive his attention. Zacharias next heard of it on May 8 after it had been released by Truman.

34 Joseph C. Grew, *Turbulent Era: A Diplomatic Record of Forty Years, 1904–1945* (Boston: Houghton Mifflin Company, 1952), II, 1421.

35 Truman, *Memoirs*, I, 209–10.

36 Grew, *Turbulent Era*, II, 1420.

37 *Ibid.*, pp. 1414–15.

38 Cordell Hull, *Memoirs* (New York: The Macmillan Company, 1948). II, 1591–93.

39 *IPR Hearings*, Part 3, p. 704. Grew, *Turbulent Era*, p. 1422. Dooman had been counselor of the United States Embassy in Tokyo under Grew.

40 *IPR Hearings*, Part 3, p. 728. Dooman's testimony was given in 1951. He does not specify when the intercepts were made but his implication is that they occurred in April and May, 1945, prior to the later messages between Togo and Sato in July and August, 1945.

41 *Ibid.*, pp. 728–29. Dooman, on whose account this relies, was not present at the meeting but was informed about the Policy Committee's reactions immediately after the meeting by Grew.

42 *Grew Papers*, one file titled "Odd Papers Belonging to Stimson's Correspondence." This file contains loose copies of letters and memoranda. The above quotation was from a Memorandum of Conversation with President made by Grew after he had met Truman on May 28. Judge Samuel Rosenman was also present.

43 Truman, *Memoirs*, I, 416–17.

44 Grew, *Turbulent Era*, II, 1423. See also fn. 10 for Grew's refutation of Forrestal's diary entry which indicated that Truman had not been in accord with Grew's view. The weight of evidence supports the Forrestal citation. Although, as Grew contends, Truman favored Grew's statements on May 28, by June 18 he had apparently changed his position, at least insofar as Grew from his talks with Truman on July 15 and July 16 interpreted it. See Millis (ed.), *The Forrestal Diaries*, p. 69. Although the evidence is flimsy, there is a possibility that Truman's ultimate decision not to modify the unconditional surrender formula as Grew suggested was in part motivated by a distrust of Grew which resulted from Grew's part in the abrupt termination of lend-lease to Russia in a manner Truman had not approved. Truman, *Memoirs*, I, 28.

45 *Grew Papers*, "Odd Papers Belonging to Stimson's Correspondence," Memorandum of Conversation in Stimson's Office, May 29, 1945. Grew mentions that Admiral King was absent and that Elmer Davis, Judge Rosenman, and Dooman also attended. See also Stimson, *Diary*, May 29. 1945. Stimson reports that Major Mathias Correa, Forrestal's legal adviser, Assistant Secretary of State John I. McCloy, and Assistant Secretary of State James Dunn attended as well as those mentioned by Grew.

46 See *IPR Hearings*, Part 3, p. 729, for Dooman's account in which he mentioned that Elmer Davis was much opposed to the suggested change. Dooman's May, 1945, "Draft of a Proclamation by the Heads of State of the U.S.—U.K.—[U.S.S.R.] China" appears to be the first draft of what later became the Potsdam Declaration. For a clarification of the nature of this draft, see below, p. 228, fn. 66. U.S.S.R. was placed in brackets to be deleted in case Russia was not yet at war with Japan when the Proclamation was issued. Grew, *Turbulent Era*, II, 1428–34.

47 *Grew Papers,* "Conversations with the President," Vol. I. This volume includes carbons and photocopies of State Department Memoranda of these conversations listed by date. Truman recalled that Grew did not report this consensus to him until a later meeting on June 18. Truman, *Memoirs,* I, 417.

48 *Public Papers of Harry S. Truman,* p. 98.

49 Millis (ed.), *The Forrestal Diaries,* pp. 68–69.

50 Although Grew does not specifically say so, this is probably the same draft that came out of the State Department in May.

51 *Grew Papers,* "Conversations with the President," June 15, 1945.

52 *Ibid.,* June 16, 1945.

53 Grew, *Turbulent Era,* II, 1435–36.

54 *Grew Papers,* "Conversations with the President," June 18, 1945. Grew, *Turbulent Era,* II, 1437. Truman, *Memoirs,* I, 417.

55 *Potsdam Papers,* I, 908–909. Stimson, *Diary,* June 18, 1945.

56 *Potsdam Papers,* I, 909. For slightly varying statements of Leahy's position, see Leahy, *I Was There,* pp. 384–85 and Leahy, *Diaries,* XI, 98–99, June 18, 1945.

57 *Potsdam Papers,* p. 909.

58 Millis (ed.), *The Forrestal Diaries,* pp. 70–71. This *Diary* entry describes a meeting between McCloy and Forrestal on March 8, 1947, at which McCloy recalled taking this position. Forrestal's memory was faulty, for he indicated that neither he nor Stimson were present.

59 John J. McCloy, *The Challenge to American Foreign Policy* (Cambridge: Harvard University Press, 1953), p. 42. In view of Truman's statement recorded in the minutes of the meeting as indicated above, p. 204. McCloy's recollection of Presidential support for his proposal seems inaccurate. No record of the latter stages of the conversation is recorded in the minutes except that the concluding statement, "The President and the Chiefs of Staff then discussed certain other matters," may cover such remarks. *Potsdam Papers,* I, 910.

60 Millis (ed.), *The Forrestal Diaries,* p. 69.

61 *Ibid.,* pp. 69–70.

62 Stimson, *Diary,* June 19, 1945.

63 Stimson's proposal was possibly similar to Dooman's draft of May 24. However, the editors of the *Potsdam Papers* state that Dooman had introduced a variant draft of Stimson's paper as the alleged State Department draft of May 24 which they claim is in reality considerably different from Stimson's. They do not mention the nature of the difference. *Potsdam Papers,* I, 897, fn. 1. See also F. C. Jones, Hugh Borton, and B. R. Pearn, *The Far East, 1942–1946* (London: Royal Institute of International Affairs, Oxford University Press, 1955), p. 310, fn. 3, for Borton's statement that the State-War-Navy Committee had previously drafted and approved such a document which had been prepared the previous summer (1944) by Dr. George H. Blakeslee and Borton. Stimson had, it is alleged, presented a paper which had originated in the State Department and had been approved interdepartmentally. The text of the draft ultimately delivered by Stimson to Truman on July 2 appears in *Potsdam Papers,* I, 893–94. See also Cline, *Washington Command Post,* p. 345, in which the author states that the document was the work of Stimson, McCloy, representatives of the State Department, the Navy Department, the Army Air Forces, G-2 (Military Intelligence Section), the Civil Affairs Division, and the Operations Division.

64 *Potsdam Papers,* I, 887–88. Stimson, *Diary,* June 26, 1945. Millis (ed.), *The Forrestal Papers,* pp. 71–72. See *Stimson Papers,* two loose-leaf files of letters and memoranda, one "to Stimson" and the other "from Stimson," for McCloy's memorandum.

65 *Stimson Papers,* June 30, 1945.

[66] *Potsdam Papers*, I, 893, fn. 4.

[67] Henry L. Stimson, "The Decision to Use the Atomic Bomb," *Harper's Magazine*, CXCIV (February, 1947), 102–4, contains the complete text of Stimson's "Memorandum for the President." See also *Potsdam Papers*, I, 889–92 for the text, and pp. 893–94 for the draft of the warning. Henry L. Stimson and McGeorge Bundy, *On Active Service in Peace and War* (New York: Harper and Brothers, 1947), pp. 620–24.

[68] This is a paraphrase of Stimson's memorandum. *Potsdam Papers*, I, 892.

[69] Stimson, *Diary*, July 2, 1945.

[70] *Ibid.*, July 2 ,1945.

[71] *Potsdam Papers*, I, 884–87.

[72] James F. Byrnes, *All in One Lifetime* (New York: Harper and Brothers, 1958), p. 296. James F. Byrnes, *Speaking Frankly* (New York: Harper and Brothers, 1947), p. 206.

[73] *Potsdam Papers*, II, 4.

[74] Hull, *Memoirs*, II, 1594.

[75] Grew, *Turbulent Era*, II, 1424.

[76] Millis (ed.), *The Forrestal Diaries*, pp. 73–74. This refers to Charles E. Bohlen who served as one of Truman's State Department advisers and as translator.

[77] *Potsdam Papers*, I, 895–97, includes the text of the MacLeish memorandum.

[78] *Ibid.*, p. 897. There is no indication as to what effect this letter had on Byrnes.

[79] *Potsdam Papers*, I, 900.

[80] *Ibid.*, p. 901.

[81] Grew, *Turbulent Era*, II, 1424, On July 8 the Combined Intelligence Committee of the CCS issued an estimate of the Japanese situation which indicated that the Japanese might well be ready to surrender completely if only the institution of the Emperor were retained; see U. S. Department of Defense, *The Entry of the Soviet Union into the War Against Japan*, pp. 85–88. This report was discussed during the first meeting of the Combined Chiefs of Staff at Potsdam on July 16. *Potsdam Papers*, II, 36.

[82] Grew Papers, "Letters, 1945," 6 vols., arranged alphabetically by name of addressee. Items are carbons of letters, unsigned, but often with typed or stamped signatures. *Potsdam Papers*, I, 902–3.

[83] *Potsdam Papers*, I, 1267. Italics are added.

[84] *Ibid.*, I, 1268. *Grew Papers*, "Grew Conversations, 1945," 3 vols., July 17, 1945.

[85] *Ibid.*, I, 3.

[86] *Ibid.*, p. 4.

[87] *Ibid.*, p. 5.

[88] Winston S. Churchill, *The Second World War: Triumph and Tragedy* (Boston: Houghton Mifflin Company, 1953), VI, 570.

[89] *Potsdam Papers*, I, 6–7.

[90] *Ibid.*, I, 8–9. Churchill, *Triumph and Tragedy*, pp. 572–74, for a slightly edited version of this cable.

[91] *Potsdam Papers*, I, 9. Churchill, *Triumph and Tragedy*, pp. 573–74.

[92] *Potsdam Papers*, I, 64–67. Complete text of Davies' report is included, pp. 64–78.

[93] Churchill, *Triumph and Tragedy*, p. 579.

[94] Truman, *Memoirs*, I, 260.

[95] Stimson, *Diary*, April 16, 1945.

[96] Millis (ed.), *The Forrestal Diaries*, p. 48.

[97] Truman, *Memoirs*, I, 70–71.

[98] *Ibid.*, p. 72.

[99] *Ibid.*, p. 71.

[100] *Potsdam Papers*, I, 13.

[101] Those present included Stettinius, Stimson, Forrestal, Leahy, Marshall, King, Assistant Secretary of State Dunn, Harriman, General Deane, and Bohlen. See Truman, *Memoirs*, I, 77.

[102] *Ibid.*, p. 78.

[103] *Ibid.*, p. 79.

[104] U. S. Department of Defense, *The Entry of the Soviet Union into the War Against Japan*, p. 54.

[105] U. S. Department of Defense, *The Entry of the Soviet Union into the War Against Japan*, p. 67. The Cairo Declaration was negotiated on December 1, 1943; for text, see U. S. Department of State, *Bulletin*, IX (December 4, 1945), 393.

[106] Millis (ed.), *The Forrestal Diaries*, p. 52.

[107] The text of this memorandum, which Grew later that morning read to Harriman and Bohlen, was locked in his private dispatch box and left there for two or three years. No one else saw it; so it could not have had much effect except as it reflected Grew's thoughts which, presumably, colored his later actions. See Grew, *Turbulent Era*, II, 1445–46.

[108] *Ibid.*, p. 1446.

[109] *Ibid.*, Grew's word is accepted for the fact that this was written in May, 1945, although the term *free world* might indicate the contrary. Grew's efforts to modify the policy of unconditional surrender and limit Russian participation in the war in the Far East should be considered in the light of this memorandum.

[110] *Grew Papers*, "Letters, 1945," 6 vols. The copy in Grew's Papers is addressed to Forrestal. The text in Grew, *Turbulent Era*, II, 1456–57 is addressed to Stimson. For drafts of the Yalta agreement concerning Soviet entry into the war in the Far East, see *Yalta Papers*, pp. 896–97.

[111] *Grew Papers*, "Letters, 1945"; Grew, *Turbulent Era*, II, 1456–57.

[112] Grew, *Turbulent Era*, II, 1457–59, which contains the text of this document.

[113] U. S. Department of Defense, *The Entry of the Soviet Union into the War Against Japan*, p. 71, fn. 31. This work also includes Grew's memorandum and Stimson's answering letter.

[114] So far as can be ascertained, Truman fails to mention either in his *Memoirs*.

[115] Stimson. *Diary*, May 13, 1945.

[116] *Ibid.*, May 14, 1945.

[117] *Ibid.*, May 15, 1945.

[118] *Ibid.*, May 15, 1945.

[119] *Potsdam Papers*, I, 41–52, includes the Bohlen memorandum of the conversations of May 28. Hopkins transmitted reports on the conversations directly to Truman and the State Department. Sherwood, *Roosevelt and Hopkins*, p. 902. Sherwood includes a record of the Hopkins-Stalin talks, pp. 887–912. See also Truman, *Memoirs*, I, 262–70.

[120] *Potsdam Papers*, I, 42.

[121] *Ibid.*, pp. 45–47. The above is a paraphrased account of the conversation.

[122] Truman, *Memoirs*, I, 265.

[123] See pp. 203–4.

[124] *Potsdam Papers*, I, 904–5.

[125] *Potsdam Papers*, I, 905–906.

[126] *Ibid.*, p. 910. King was willing to go along with United States invasion of Japan and promotion of Russian entrance into the war, but only half-heartedly. See King and Whitehill, *Fleet Admiral King*, pp. 591, 598, 621; see also U. S. Congress, Senate, Committee on Armed Services and Committee on Foreign Relations, *Hearings on the Military Situation in the Far East*, 82nd Cong., 1st Sess. (Washington: 1951), pp. 3055–56.

127 Leahy, *I Was There*, p. 385.

128 *Potsdam Papers*, I, 909.

129 Truman, *Memoirs*, I, 320.

130 Truman, *Memoirs*, I, 314–15.

131 *Ibid.*, pp. 322–23.

132 *Ibid.*, p. 411.

133 Photostat of the petition included in *MED Files: Harrison-Bundy Series*, Folder #76, "S-1 Interim Committee—Scientific Panel."

134 Arthur H. Compton, *Atomic Quest: A Personal Narrative* (New York: Oxford University Press, Inc., 1956), p. 242.

135 *MED Files: Harrison-Bundy Series*, Folder #76, "S-1 Interim Committee—Scientific Panel."

136 *Ibid.*, p. 242, Compton writes that the petition ". . . found almost no support." On the other hand, Szilard recalls that it was signed by about fifty-five of his colleagues; see Alice K. Smith, "Behind the Decision to Use the Atomic Bomb: Chicago 1944–45," *Bulletin of the Atomic Scientists*, XIV (October, 1958), p. 303.

137 The original of this petition is included in *MED Files: Harrison-Bundy Series*, Folder #76, "S-1 Interim Committee-Scientific Panel."

138 *MED Files: Harrison-Bundy Series*, Folder #76. Seventy signatures appear on the original petition. There seems to be some confusion as to the number who signed. At the time he turned it over to Compton, Szilard told him it contained sixty-seven signatures of scientists residing at Chicago; see Compton, *Atomic Quest*, p. 242. On the other hand ,in 1958 Szilard recalled that it contained only sixty-three; see Smith, "Behind the Decision to Use the Atomic Bomb," p. 303. Further confusion may result from a reference to the petition in a covering letter transmitting a copy to Groves which indicates it was signed by sixty-seven scientific personnel at Clinton Laboratories. This introduces the unlikely possibility that there might have been another petition from Clinton on the same date. No other evidence exists to substantiate that conclusion, and since the Metallurgical Laboratory worked closely with the Clinton works, the "two" petitions are assumed to be the same. *MED Files: Harrison-Bundy Series*, Folder #76, "S-1 Interim Committee—Scientific Panel."

139 Compton, *Atomic Quest*, p. 243.

140 Arthur H. Compton and Farrington Daniels, "A Poll of Scientists at Chicago, July, 1945", *Bulletin of the Atomic Scientists*, IV (February, 1948), 44, 63.

141 *Ibid.*, p. 63. See also Smith, "Behind the Decision to use the Atomic Bomb," pp. 304–5, which contains a most incisive criticism of the poll as a gauge of scientific opinion at Chicago.

142 Compton, *Atomic Quest*, p. 244.

143 *Ibid.*, p. 244.

144 Smith, "Behind the Decision to Use the Atomic Bomb," p. 305.

145 Photostat of this petition appears in *Med Files: Harrison-Bundy Series*, Folder #76, "S-1 Interim Committee—Scientific Panel." See also Compton, *Atomic Quest*, p. 242.

146 See, pp. 241–43, 246–47.

147 Photostat of this letter appears in *MED Files: Harrison-Bundy Series*, Folder #76, "S-1 Interim Committee—Scientific Panel."

148 Photostat of this letter appears in *MED Files: Harrison-Bundy Series*, Folder #76, "S-1 Interim Committee—Scientific Panel."

149 Compton, *Atomic Quest*, p. 246.

150 *Ibid.*, p. 247.

151 Photostat of Nichols' memorandum of July 25 and Compton's letter of July 24 are included in *MED Files: Harrison-Bundy Series*, Folder #76, "S-1 Interim Committee—Scientific Panel."

152 See p. 135.

153 *MED Files: Harrison-Bundy Series*, Folder #76, "S-1 Interim Committee—Scientific Panel."

154 See Hewlett and Anderson, *The New World, 1939/1946*, p. 400, and fn. 115, p. 697, on which this account is based. No evidence was discovered in the MED Files to substantiate this account. Some of the files were not, however, available. Hewlett and Anderson cite as their source for the above account *MED Files* including notes for possible use of Secretary Patterson in talking to Mr. Charles Ross, undated. Ross was Truman's Press Secretary. From Hewlett and Anderson's account, it is uncertain that Stimson saw the materials himself. They were delivered to his "office" and Harrison disposed of them. Stimson makes no reference to them in his *Diary* on August 1 or on any other date. Perhaps, neither the President nor the Secretary of War saw these materials.

155 Lewis L. Strauss, *Men and Decisions* (Garden City: Doubleday and Company, Inc., 1962), p. 194, indicates that Szilard's petition apparently reached the White House on August 17.

CHAPTER **9**

POTSDAM AND PEACE?

AT THE Potsdam Conference which lasted officially from July 17 until August 1, 1945, the United States, the United Kingdom, and the Soviet Union attempted to arrange a basis for future mutually suitable relations in areas where the war had already ended. Already, before the war with Japan was over, they were jockeying for advantageous political positions during the peace to follow. There, also, each planned for the defeat of Japan in such a way as to satisfy its existing and anticipated needs. The United Kingdom and the Soviet Union sought to reestablish in some measure their war-weakened positions in an area where the introduction of massive United States power loomed as a new factor. The United States, heavily involved in its war against Japan, attempted to negotiate arrangements which would not only quickly end hostilities but which would also provide it with the leverage to continue to develop its influence in the Far East.

The original participants at the Potsdam Conference were Prime Minister Churchill, President Truman, and Premier Stalin. During the conference a new Prime Minister, Clement R. Attlee, replaced Churchill whose party lost in the British election of July 26. The conference was recessed on July 26 and 27 following Churchill's departure for Great Britain and awaiting Attlee's arrival at Potsdam on July 28. Each of the heads of government brought with him a considerable retinue. It was to be the last full-dress conference of World War II. Most of Truman's top-level military and civilian aides attended. Significantly, the President relied heavily on his new Secretary of State, James F. Byrnes, who traveled both to and from Potsdam in the President's party. Under Secretary Joseph C. Grew and those who had supported the modification of the surrender formula were notably absent.[1] Although the Joint Chiefs of Staff and Admiral Leahy were on hand to provide military advice, Truman seems to have gone to very little trouble to invite his two service secretaries. Forrestal was not invited. During the conference, however, he flew to Berlin on his own initiative to make sure Truman had seen the complete exchange of telegrams between the Japanese Foreign Minister, Togo, and his Ambassador in Moscow, Sato.[2] He arrived too late to participate directly in the President's decisions. Stimson, on the other hand, had been invited to attend, but only in a backhanded fashion. At the White House meeting with Truman, on July 2, at which he had presented his "Memorandum Outlining a Proposed Program for Japan," the Secretary of War had urgently requested that he accompany the President to Potsdam. Truman had originally demurred because of Stimson's health but had put off his decision until the next day.[3] During an afternoon meeting with the Secretary of War on July 3, Truman ". . . told [Stimson] that he would like to have [him] to be somewhere near where [he] could help out in the coming conference. [Stimson] told him that meant that he should have to be in Berlin and that [he] should bring McCloy with [him]. He (Truman) said, 'All right'. . . ." [4]

Stimson's position at the conference was an unusual one. He was part of the President's party and yet was separate from it. On July 6 Stimson, McCloy, and H. H. Bundy, Special Assistant to the Secretary of War, sailed on the S. S. *Brazil* for Gibraltar and from there flew to Berlin on July 15. Stimson stayed at Potsdam until July 25. He was not an official member of the conference and did not attend its meetings. His function was to give general advice to the President.[5] The Secretary of War's relations with Byrnes were cordial but apparently distant. A passage from Stimson's *Diary* reflected the nature of the relationship. On July 19, Stimson complained to Byrnes that he was not getting information as to what was occurring at the conference. The Secretary of State's response is unrecorded, but Stimson went on:

He (Byrnes) gives me the impression that he is hugging matters in this Conference pretty close to his bosom, and that my assistance, while generally welcome, was strictly limited in the matters in which it should be given.[6]

One of the matters on which Stimson's advice was vital was that concerning the development of the atomic bomb. He was, in fact, to be the major source of information on the bomb's progress for the United States delegation. Before he left for Potsdam he ". . . had set up a special channel of communication between himself and Groves when he designated George L. Harrison as his representative in Washington to cover atomic affairs." [7] Although Stimson was to be unsuccessful at Potsdam in modifying the unconditional surrender policy so as to indicate to the Japanese the possibility of retaining their Emperor, he played the important role of carrying most of the information concerning the preparation of the atomic bomb to Truman and the other participants.

The order of procedure followed at Potsdam generally provided that the Joint Chiefs of Staff and the Foreign Ministers meet separately during the mornings. At afternoon meetings the Combined Chiefs of Staff gathered to discuss the morning decisions of the Joint Chiefs of Staff. Later in the afternoons and during the evenings the heads of government would meet in plenary sessions.[8]

Although the conferees discussed a great variety of matters involving their interests in Europe and Asia, their handling of the war against Japan was of immediate concern. In making decisions in this area they, in fact, established conditions which were conducive to the use of the atomic bombs. At Potsdam they did not significantly modify the situation which prior to the conference had led to the rapid development of the weapons. The United States and Great Britain continued, if perhaps half-heartedly, to suggest Russian involvement in Manchuria against Japan. The policy of unconditional surrender, although redefined during the conference to imply greater leniency to Japan, was not changed significantly in specifying possible retention of the Emperor. And the military plans for the defeat of Japan, the plans that raised the specter of great numbers of Allied casualties, were accepted practically unchanged from the general form in which they had been presented to Truman on June 18 at the White House.[9]

Except in regard to relatively minor details, there seems to have been little discussion at Potsdam on the overall plans for the defeat of Japan. Prior to the Potsdam Conference on June 29, the Joint Chiefs of Staff had prepared a "Memorandum on the Development of Operations in the Pacific," outlining United States proposals for military action against Japan for the approval of the Combined Chiefs of Staff. The paper described the general operations as follows:

1. In conformity with the overall objective to bring about the *unconditional surrender* of Japan at the earliest possible date, the United States Chiefs of Staff have adopted the following concept of operations for the main effort in the Pacific:
   a. From bases in Okinawa, Iwo Jima, Marianas, and the Philippines to intensify the blockade and air bombardment of Japan in order to create a situation favorable to—
   b. An assault on Kyushu . . . in order to establish a tactical condition favorable to—
   c. The decisive invasion of the industrial heart of Japan through the Tokyo Plain. . . .[10]

The date for the invasion of Kyushu was to be November 1, 1945. The Tokyo Plain was to be attacked on March 1, 1946. In another memorandum of July 7, the Joint Chiefs of Staff had recommended to the Combined Chiefs of Staff:

a. That for the purpose of planning production and for the allocation of manpower, the planning date for the end of organized resistance by Japan be 15 November, 1946; that this date be readjusted periodically to conform to the course of the war.[11]

At Potsdam on July 16, the Combined Chiefs of Staff noted the June 29 memorandum of the Joint Chiefs of Staff without discussion.[12] On July 19, they agreed that the planning date for the end of Japanese resistance should be November 15, 1946.

For some time prior to the Potsdam Conference the British Chiefs of Staff had been studying the June 14 memorandum of the Joint Chiefs of Staff which had included their recommendations as to the basic objectives, strategy, and policies which should be followed toward Japan. This memorandum had been the basis for discussions between Truman and the Joint Chiefs of Staff on June 18 and had provided the framework within which the June 29 memorandum on operations had been developed. Now, at Potsdam, on July 20, the British Chiefs of Staff suggested only minor changes in the terms of the June 14 memorandum. The overall objective remained unconditional surrender. The overall strategic concept for the prosecution of the war was unchanged.

3. In cooperation with other Allies to bring about at the earliest possible date the defeat of Japan by: lowering Japanese ability and will to resist by establishing sea and air blockades, conducting intensive air bombardment, and destroying Japanese air and naval strength; invading and seizing objectives in the Japanese home islands as the main effort; . . . establishing absolute military control of Japan; and liberating Japanese-occupied territory if required.[13]

This objective was unchanged in successive meetings.

Although further drafts reflected reaction to British changes, the basic objective remained the same. It appeared in a "Redraft of Basic Objectives" by the Joint Chiefs of Staff on July 21.[14] At their meeting of July 23, the Joint Chiefs of Staff approved this redraft.[15] That afternoon it received the approval of the Combined Chiefs of Staff for submission to the President and the Prime Minister.[16] At 11:30 A.M. on July 24, the Combined Chiefs of Staff met with Truman and Churchill to consider basic policy toward Japan. During the discussion nothing was said about changing the basic objectives. The two heads of government accepted and approved the strategy which had remained unchanged since June 14. It would continue to be the basis for Allied military policy toward Japan until its surrender.[17] Thus, the President was reasonably anticipating a prolonged war involving considerable casualties following blockade, bombardment, and invasion of Japan.

The modification of the unconditional surrender formula in a warning to Japan, was one means which might eliminate the necessity for anticipated military operations. At Potsdam, much of the pressure for clarifying the surrender policy so as to at least assure the Japanese that they might retain their imperial system came from Secretary of War Stimson. He was partially supported by Churchill. And although Stalin was not directly involved in the relevant discussions, he had already implied that he favored at least a public clarification of unconditional surrender to lure the Japanese into capitulation. In addition, the United States and British military leadership favored a change on military grounds. Apparently Secretary of State Byrnes and President Truman were the major obstacles to the suggested redefinition in the warning to Japan. Significantly, given the primary role which the United States was playing in the fight against Japan and given their positions within the United States Government, they were able to prevail. The Potsdam Declaration, the last public description of the policy of unconditional surrender, included no specific statement regarding the Emperor.

The draft of the Potsdam Declaration which Byrnes carried to Potsdam included the same significant reference to the Emperor as had the earlier draft which Stimson had submitted to Truman on July 2 and on which this new version was based.[18] The general form was the same and was to remain unchanged. It first asserted that the overwhelming power of the forces allied against Japan made it foolhardy for the Japanese to resist. Then it enumerated the terms for which there were no alternatives, from which there would be no deviation, and in the acceptance of which there could be no delay. The key articles possibly affecting the position of the Emperor were as follows:

(6) There must be eliminated for all time the authority and influence of those who have deceived and misled the people of Japan into embarking on world conquest, for we insist that a new order of peace, security, and

justice will be impossible until irresponsible militarism is driven from the world. . . .

(10) We do not intend that the Japanese shall be enslaved as a race or destroyed as a nation, but stern justice shall be meted out to all war criminals. . . .

(12) The occupying forces of the Allies shall be withdrawn from Japan as soon as these objectives have been accomplished and there has been established beyond doubt a peacefully inclined, responsible government of a character representative of the Japanese people. *This may include a constitutional monarchy under the present dynasty* if the peace-loving nations can be convinced of a genuine determination of such a government to follow policies of peace. . . .

(13) We call upon the Japanese people and those in authority in Japan to proclaim now the *unconditional surrender* of all the Japanese armed forces. . . . The alternative for Japan is prompt and utter destruction.[19]

If articles (6) and (10) were read without the assurances of article (12), the declaration seemed to imply the elimination of the imperial government and the possibility that the Emperor might be tried as a war criminal. These were two conditions the Japanese consistently refused to consider. On the other hand, if the provisions regarding "the present dynasty" were included, there was reasonable assurance given to the Japanese that the position of the Emperor would not be affected under articles (6) and (10). Article (13) further indicated leniency toward the government of Japan by apparently limiting the application of unconditional surrender to the armed forces. In view of the generally moderate definition which was thus given to unconditional surrender, it was felt by those who favored changing the policy that the words specifically relating to the Emperor might lead the Japanese to surrender.

Support for issuing the moderate form of the document continued through the early days of the Potsdam Conference until the declaration was issued on July 26. Stimson went to work on Truman and Byrnes even before the first formal sessions. On July 16 he sent Truman and Byrnes another of his memoranda on the conduct of the war with Japan. In it he again urged that ". . . warnings be delivered to Japan, designed to bring about her capitulation as quickly as possible." The recent news he had received of ". . . attempted approaches on the part of Japan to Russia [impelled him] to urge prompt delivery of [the] warning. [He] would therefore urge that we formulate a warning to Japan to be delivered during the course of this Conference, and rather earlier than later, along the lines of the draft prepared by the War Department and now approved . . . by both the State and Navy Department." [20] In the meantime, he favored the continuation of present military action, and a possibly stronger warning at a time when atomic weapons and Russian force might come into action. The Secretary of War was already campaigning for his moderate warning.

Support for his general position also developed that day within the Combined Chiefs of Staff. At their meeting during the afternoon of July 16, Field-Marshal Sir Alan Brooke

. . . asked whether the United States Chiefs of Staff had given any thought to the question of the interpretation of the term "unconditional surrender." From the military point of view it seemed to the British Chiefs of Staff that there might be some advantage in trying to explain this term to the Japanese in a manner which would ensure that the war was not unduly prolonged in outlying areas. If, for instance, an interpretation could be found and communicated to the Japanese which did not involve the dissolution of the Imperial institution, the Emperor would be in a position to order the cease-fire. . . . If an interpretation on these lines could be found an opportune moment to make it clear to the Japanese might be shortly after a Russian entry into the war.[21]

Here the Field-Marshal was thinking of changing the surrender policy for far more limited military ends than the hope of a rapid general capitulation by the Japanese.

The United States Chiefs of Staff informed Brooke that much thought had already been devoted to the matter on the political level. Admiral Leahy suggested that, since the problem was predominantly a political one, it might be useful for Churchill to explain to Truman British views as to how unconditional surrender should be clarified for the Japanese. As a result the British Chiefs were invited ". . . to consider the possibility of asking the Prime Minister to raise with the President the matter of unconditional surrender of Japan." [22]

Unfortunately for those who sought to modify the surrender policy in regard to the Emperor, former Secretary of State Hull was cabling Byrnes on the same day to appeal to him not only to refuse to include the reference to the Emperor in the forthcoming warning, but also to delay the warning itself until its success was assured by the ". . . climax of allied bombing and Russia's entrance to the war." [23] This appeal found favor with Byrnes and probably killed any chance for a significant revision. Byrnes cabled Hull the next day with his assurances that the declaration should be delayed and, when issued, should not include the reference to the Emperor.[24]

These messages, however, were not apparently available to those who sought change. Early in the morning of July 17 Stimson again conferred with Byrnes at the Little White House, the President's residence at Potsdam. It was at this meeting that Byrnes asserted himself on the issue and in effect discouraged the Secretary of War from future direct approaches. Stimson recorded on that evening that

Byrnes was opposed to a prompt and early warning to Japan which I had first suggested. He outlined a time-table on the subject warning which apparently has been agreed to by the President, so I pressed it no further. . . .[25]

From then on, although he would continue to fight, Stimson's effort was to be a compensatory action, based on the least objectionable compromise.

Later, on the morning of July 17 at a meeting of the Joint Chiefs of Staff, Admiral Leahy suggested that, in his opinion, it was suitable for them to comment on the proposed warning from a military point of view and recommended a change in wording in the paragraph relating to the Emperor. Marshall then stated that the ". . . attitude of the Joint Chiefs of Staff should be that nothing should be done prior to the termination of hostilities that would indicate the removal of the Emperor of Japan, since his removal might influence the cessation of hostilities in areas outside of Japan proper." He suggested that the Joint Chiefs of Staff send a memorandum to the President which, along with other suggestions, would ". . . also include the views he had previously expressed in regard to doing nothing to indicate that the Emperor might be removed from office upon unconditional surrender." [26] The memorandum was prepared and sent to the President the following day.

Meanwhile, on July 17, the British military were initiating an approach to Truman through Churchill. Lord Ismay, in a "Minute to the Prime Minister," suggested that it might be appropriate for him to raise the question with Truman of redefining unconditional surrender so as to provide for the retention of the Emperor. The British Chiefs favored such a move on the military grounds of reducing fighting in the outlying areas of the Japanese Empire after a Japanese surrender through the device of an imperial order to Japanese forces to cease hostilities. Despite their recognition of Churchill's possible reluctance to bring up such a matter concerning a military area in which the United States was predominant, the British Chiefs of Staff forwarded this point of view to the Prime Minister.[27] Churchill discussed the problem with Truman the next day.

On the morning of July 18, the Joint Chiefs of Staff approved and forwarded their memorandum on unconditional surrender to the President. In it they suggested the omission of the phraseology in article (12) referring to the Emperor. Although they felt, as Marshall had pointed out the day before, that nothing should be done to indicate that the Emperor would be removed after unconditional surrender, they opposed with apparent inconsistency the only specific statement providing for the possibility of the Emperor's retention. Their reasoning in proposing the change in article (12) of the proposed proclamation followed this line:

To some of the extreme devotees of the Emperor, the phrase, "This may include a constitutional monarchy under the present dynasty," may be misconstrued as a commitment by the United Nations to depose or execute the present Emperor and install some other member of the Imperial family. To the radical elements in Japan, the phrase may be construed as a commitment to continue the institution of the Emperor and Emperor worship.[28]

Their memorandum then recommended that Article (12) of the declaration should read:

The occupying forces of the Allies shall be withdrawn from Japan as soon as our objectives are accomplished and there has been established beyond doubt a peacefully inclined, responsible government of a character representative of the Japanese people . . . *subject to suitable guarantees against further acts of aggression, the Japanese people will be free to choose their own form of government.*[29]

Thus, specific reference to the Emperor would be omitted. There seemed to be little recognition that the Japanese might interpret this suggested provision to be a threat to the Emperor's position. His authority might be permanently eliminated under article (6) and he might be tried as a war criminal under article (10).[30] Despite the fact that in the last paragraph of their memorandum, the Joint Chiefs considered ". . . it inadvisable to make any statement or take any action at the present time that would make it difficult or impossible to utilize the authority of the Emperor to direct a surrender of the Japanese forces in the outlying areas as well as in Japan proper," they had, in effect, recommended the omission of the only phrase relating directly to the Emperor that had within it the possibility of inducing Japanese surrender.[31] They were primarily interested in changing unconditional surrender to alleviate possible postsurrender difficulties. They failed to understand that the changes they suggested in article (12) might well delay that surrender. Their action, although perhaps seeking the same immediate objective as Stimson's, in effect supported the position of Byrnes and Truman and probably lessened the Secretary of War's chances of changing the surrender policy.

That afternoon at luncheon, Churchill followed Ismay's suggestion and discussed the matter with Truman. He indicated that the Japanese might surrender sooner than expected, but that neither he nor Stalin wanted to give the President the idea that they were trying to influence him to seek peace. Churchill recorded the conversation later:

In the same way I would abstain from saying anything that would indicate that we were . . . reluctant to go on with the war against Japan as long as the United States thought fit. However, I dwelt upon the tremendous cost in American life . . . which would be involved in forcing "unconditional surrender" upon the Japanese. It was for him to consider whether this might not be expressed in some other way, so that we got all the essentials for future peace and security, and yet left the Japanese some show of saving their military honour and some assurance of their national existence after they had complied with all safeguards necessary for the conqueror. The President countered by saying that he did not think the Japanese had any honour after Pearl Harbour. . . . My own impression is that there is no question of a rigid insistence upon . . . "unconditional surrender," apart from essentials necessary for world peace and future security, and for the punishment of a guilty and treacherous nation. It has been evident to me in my conversations with Mr. Stimson, General Marshall, and now with the President that they are searching their hearts on this subject, and that we have no need to press it.[32]

Churchill hit fairly close to the mark in his analysis of Truman's position. The President had accepted the basic terminology of the draft declaration. But the national need for revenge for Pearl Harbor and the widespread belief in the United States that the Emperor had been responsible for that action, led him to oppose any leniency toward the hated institution. There would be no rigid insistence on unconditional surrender ". . . apart from the essentials necessary . . .for the punishment of a guilty and treacherous nation . . ." and for a guilty and treacherous Emperor.[33]

Strangely enough, Acting Secretary of State Grew cabled Byrnes on July 19 to request permission to issue a strong statement reaffirming unconditional surrender on the basis of Truman's definitions of May 8 and June 1.[34] He was afraid that the public rumors suggesting a change in the surrender policy which were circulating widely in the American press might lead the Japanese to believe that the United States position was weakening. Now, as he tried to forestall the unfortunate effects of such a conclusion by the Japanese, he apparently acted contrary to the position he had long taken. And yet this was, at least in part, only an appearance. For although his proposed release did not mention the Emperor, it contained language that implied a relatively lenient United States line toward Japan, provided it surrendered quickly.

Stimson partially capitulated to the Byrnes position on July 20. In a memorandum to Truman on that date, he accepted the Joint Chiefs of Staff revisions of article (12) which eliminated the specific reference to the Emperor. On the other hand, he suggested a revision of the last words of article (2), ". . . a determination of all the Allied nations to prosecute the war against Japan until her unconditional capitulation" by replacing "unconditional capitulation" with "until she ceases to resist." [35] He felt that the contradiction between "unconditional" and "capitulation" might, in translation, tend to defeat the objective of the message.

On July 23, Byrnes called Stimson to inquire when the first atomic bomb would be ready. Later that morning, in a similar vein, Truman informed Stimson

. . . that he had the warning message which we prepared on his desk, and had accepted our most recent changes in it, and that he proposed to shoot it out as soon as he heard the definite day of the operation.[36]

The timing for issuing the Potsdam Declaration and the readiness of the atomic bomb had, it seems, become interrelated. Apparently Truman and Byrnes had decided to wait until the new weapons were nearly ready to be used as additional sanctions to impose on the Japanese the terms of the declaration. At the same time everyone, even Stimson, had accepted the revision of the declaration which would make it extremely difficult for the Japanese to assent to its terms.

Truman presented his draft declaration to Churchill on July 24.[37] Although the wording of article (12) had been changed from that proposed by the Joint Chiefs of Staff, their recommendation had generally been accepted. The draft included no reference to the Emperor. This new version was probably the work of Byrnes, approved by Truman. Byrnes indicated that he ". . . finished drafting the warning." [38] The British made changes in the terminology of the document but not in its substance. After their revisions were accepted, Churchill signified his willingness to sign the declaration on July 25.

On July 24, the text of the declaration had also been transmitted to the Chinese. Through Patrick J. Hurley, the United States Ambassador to China, Chiang Kai-Shek was informed that the United States intended to issue the declaration and that his concurrence was requested without delay.[39]

The rapid availability of the atomic bombs and the imminent possibility of a Russian attack on Manchuria led to the necessity for speed. The Japanese must have time to consider the warning if it was to appear that in their possible rejection of this warning lay the basis for atomic attack. Shortly afterward on the same day, Stimson gave Truman the news that the first atomic bomb might be ready for use on Japan by August 1.[40] Truman was delighted and said that the news ". . . gave him the cue for his warning." [41] The President informed Stimson that he had sent the declaration to Chiang and that as soon as the Generalissimo cleared it he ". . . would release the warning and that would fit right in time with the program of the atom bombs . . ." [42] Stimson then interjected a statement which, although consistent with his effort to reassure the Japanese, seemed out of line with his acceptance of the current version of article (12). He emphasized the importance of including the item on the Emperor in the warning; but he had

. . . heard from Byrnes that they preferred not to put it in, and that now such a change was made impossible by the sending of the message to Chiang. [He] hoped that the President would watch carefully so that the Japanese might be reassured verbally through diplomatic channels if it was found that they were hanging fire on that one point. He (Truman) said that he had that in mind, and that he would take care of it."[43]

Stimson, it seems, despite his earlier compromise, was making a last effort to give the Japanese assurances in regard to their Emperor. There is no evidence that Truman later attempted to use diplomacy to reassure the Japanese Government on this point.

In fact, the President became impatient as word of Chiang's concurrence failed to materialize quickly. On July 25, the White House Map Room wired

Hurley that Truman wanted an immediate reply from Chiang. In fact, if an answer was not received within twenty-four hours, the President and Prime Minister would release the declaration, presumably without Chiang's approval. Hurley's answer, with apologies for Chiang's absence from Chungking and for the inefficiencies of the Chinese system of communications, arrived in Potsdam on July 26.[44]

The declaration was finally issued by Truman at 9:20 P.M. on July 26 from Berlin.[45] It contained no specific reference to the Emperor. Article (12) read:

The occupying forces of the Allies shall be withdrawn from Japan as soon as these objectives have been accomplished and there has been established in accordance with the freely expressed will of the Japanese people a peacefully inclined and responsible government.[46]

Now only Japanese capitulation could forestall use of the atomic bomb and the Russian attack.

The Japanese had been seeking Russian mediation since July 13 when Ambassador Sato had indicated to the Soviet Deputy, Foreign Minister S. A. Lozovsky, that the Emperor wished to send Prince Konoye as his special emissary to Moscow. Lozovsky had indicated that, since Molotov and Stalin were preparing for their journey to Potsdam, it was doubtful that a Soviet answer to the Japanese request could be delivered prior to their departure.[47]

Throughout the Potsdam Conference, the Soviet Government delayed answering the Japanese Ambassador. As the conference ran on, the efforts of the Japanese Government to obtain such Russian mediation became progressively more desperate. The growing anxiety of the Japanese was readily apparent in the exchange of wires between Foreign Minister Togo and Ambassador Sato.

On July 17 Togo warned Sato that if word of the negotiations between Japan and the Soviet Union ever leaked out, ". . . the results would be most dire. . . ."[48] He was thinking primarily of possible violent reaction from the Japanese military if any but the top officers on the Supreme Council for the Direction of the War discovered the mediation attempt. Later that day he again emphasized to Sato Japan's desperate situation. Somewhat plaintively he wired:

. . . Not only our High Command but also our Government firmly believes that even now our war potential is still sufficient to deal the enemy a severe blow, but against an enemy who can make repeated attacks we cannot always be completely free from anxiety. In such times, we continue to maintain our war strength; *if only the United States and Great Britain would recognize Japan's honor and existence we would terminate the war* and would like to save mankind from the ravages of war, but if the enemy insists on unconditional surrender to the very end, then our country and His Majesty would unanimously resolve to fight a war of resistance to the bitter end. Therefore, inviting the Soviet Union to mediate fairly does not include unconditional surrender. . . ."[49]

Sato assured Togo the next day that his previous suggestions that the Japanese accept a solution similar to unconditional surrender did not include giving up the fundamental character or form of the Japanese Government. That should be Japan's only necessary condition in accepting unconditional surrender.[50] Both the Japanese Foreign Minister and his Ambassador wished to salvage their imperial system and were, apparently, ready to negotiate surrender on that condition alone.

On July 19 Sato informed Togo that during the previous evening Lozovsky had handed him a note in which the Soviet Government had indicated it could not reply to the Japanese request for the reception of Konoye's mission because it was worded in general terms and contained no specific proposal. "The Mission of Prince Konoye . . . [was] also not clear to the Government of the U.S.S.R." [51] Sato followed this information with a long, urgent message to Togo on July 20. He vigorously suggested that the Japanese Government accept all of the conditions demanded by the enemy except one which would eliminate the "national polity" or the "fundamental character of our form of government." [52] The Ambassador was, in effect, asking that the mission of Konoye be described to the Soviet Government as one which might negotiate Japan's surrender on the irreducible terms of preserving the imperial institution.

When Togo heard of the Russian delay in accepting Konoye's mission, he quickly sent Sato more definite proposals for the Prince's mission in order to satisfy the Soviet demands. Konoye was to seek Russian assistance in terminating the war; he was to explain the "concrete intentions" of the Japanese in regard to that matter; and he was to negotiate a basis for greater cooperation between Japan and the Soviet Union both during and after the war. Unconditional surrender was impossible. But Japan was ready to present specific conditions for peace through Konoye. Togo emphasized that because of internal conditions in Tokyo it was presently impossible and to Japan's disadvantage to openly announce such conditions prior to the hoped-for conversations between Konoye and the Russians.

On July 25 the Foreign Minister urged Sato again to lose no time in discovering Soviet intentions. He referred to Admiral Zacharias' broadcast from the United States on July 21 in which the Admiral, professing to be a spokesman for the United States Government, indicated that Japan might accept unconditional surrender on the basis of the Atlantic Charter. Although Togo considered Zacharias' action as ". . . simple propaganda strategy," he went on to state that the Japanese Government, although it was impossible to accept unconditional surrender, would ". . . like to communicate to the other party through appropriate channels that . . . it would have no objection to a peace based on the Atlantic Charter. The difficult point is the attitude of the enemy, who continues to insist on the formality of unconditional surrender. . . . Also it is necessary to have them understand that we are trying to end hostilities by asking for very reasonable terms in order to secure and maintain our nation's existence and honor." [53]

In line with Togo's orders, Sato once more arranged a conference with Lozovsky on July 25. At that time, as before, Lozovsky said that he would transmit the new Japanese proposal to his government and that he would inform Sato as soon as he had received his government's instructions.[54] This was the last effort prior to the Potsdam Declaration that the Japanese were to make to arrange mediation by the Soviet Union. But the Sato-Togo messages seemed to indicate the willingness of the Japanese Government to accept surrender provided the imperial institution was maintained.

Before Truman issued the Potsdam Declaration, the United States Government in Washington had had access to the messages between Togo and Sato.[55] Whether Truman or the others in the United States delegation saw the more recent exchanges which indicated a Japanese willingness to surrender provided the Emperor was retained is questionable. In Washington, Forrestal saw them as they came into the Naval communications center.[56] Stimson recorded his receipt of an ". . . important paper in re Japanese maneuverings for peace" on July 16.[57] Although he failed to mention the nature of the paper, his reference next day to ". . . the recent news of attempted approaches on the part of Japan to Russia" indicates that it probably concerned the early Togo-Sato exchange.[58] Another entry in his *Diary* on June 20 noted a visit from Allen Dulles with ". . . something which had recently come into him with regard to Japan," presumably views of the informal feelers through Switzerland.[59] No other notation concerning Stimson's knowledge of additional Japanese overtures to Russia has been found.

Apparently Forrestal sent the Togo-Sato messages to Admiral Leahy as quickly as they were received in Washington.[60] If so, Leahy probably passed the information on to Truman and the Joint Chiefs of Staff.[61] Only Truman, however, later mentioned that he had known about Japanese peace feelers prior to the occasion at Potsdam when Stalin mentioned the Japanese efforts to him.[62] If the above information is accurate, Truman probably had read the texts of the Togo-Sato telegrams following their transmission to Leahy at Potsdam.

In any case the President was informed by Stalin, both directly and indirectly, of the Japanese request for mediation prior to the transmission of the Potsdam Declaration. Stalin had first informed Churchill during the evening of July 17 of the Japanese offer of mediation on July 13. Churchill, in turn, had given the information to Truman at luncheon the following day. Apparently Stalin's account had been both factual and accurate, but he had told

Churchill that he had not wanted to notify Truman personally because he had not wished the President to get the idea that the Soviet Government planned to act as an intermediary between the United States and Japan. However, during Truman's courtesy call on Stalin at 3:00 P.M. on July 18, the Soviet Premier had handed Truman a copy of one of Sato's wires. Stalin had inquired of Truman as to whether he should answer it, and the President had answered in a noncommittal fashion that he had no respect for Japanese good faith. Stalin then had said that, perhaps, a general nonspecific answer pointing out that the purpose of the Konoye mission was unclear might be sent to lull the Japanese to sleep in view of the pending Soviet attack on Manchuria. Truman thought that might be a satisfactory course of action. He was, therefore, not only informed about the Togo-Sato messages; but he was also consulted by Stalin in determining the response the Soviet Union would make to the proffered Konoye mission.[63]

The information was also brought to Byrnes' attention during the conference, both at this meeting and at a later session. Stalin left Byrnes with the impression that the Japanese would ". . . fight to the death rather than accept unconditional surrender." [64] Whether Truman had this impression on July 26 is hard to determine. He, at any rate, had apparently had the opportunity to consult the texts of the Japanese exchanges and, perhaps, unless the Soviet Union had also broken the Japanese code, had more information than the Russians.

Truman, therefore, was familiar with the Japanese efforts to obtain Russian mediation before he issued the Potsdam Declaration. Given that information he did not seek either to promote such negotiations or to use diplomatic channels to initiate a possible surrender. Nor did he change article (12) of the declaration. Japan would have to accept unconditional surrender as defined, despite its qualms about the future of the Emperor, or suffer the force of an atomic explosion. The Potsdam Declaration included no mention of this new and powerful sanction to unconditional surrender.

The formulation of the Potsdam Declaration had been handled without consulting the Russians. On July 26, the day it was issued, Byrnes sent a copy of the declaration to Molotov for his information with a notice that it had already been given to the press for publication on the morning of July 27.[65] The Russians seemed to be furious; for the declaration, along with the atomic bomb, might possibly be used by the United States to end the war with Japan before Russian military action could provide the basis for a more favorable Russian position in the Far East. Molotov, through his interpreter, telephoned Byrnes' office that evening to request that the declaration be held up for a few days. He seemed much disturbed when he was told that it had already been released.[66]

The next evening the matter came up again at a meeting between Byrnes and Molotov. Byrnes informed Molotov that the news of his phone call the previous evening had only reached him in the morning when it was too late to stop the release. Molotov said he had phoned as soon as he had received Byrnes' notice on the previous evening. Byrnes replied that even then it had been too late. "He explained that the President for political reasons had considered it all important to issue an immediate appeal to the Japanese to surrender." [67] Byrnes indicated that the declaration had been cleared with the British and the Chinese. This must have rubbed salt in Molotov's wounds. He remarked that the Russians had not been informed until after the release. Byrnes pointed out that the Soviet Government had not been consulted because it was not yet at war with Japan, and the United States did not desire to embarrass it as a neutral. Although Molotov then terminated the conversation, he left the impression that the matter might be brought up again by Stalin. [68]

Stalin raised the point offhandedly at the plenary session on July 28. In announcing that the Russian delegation had received new proposals from Japan for Soviet mediation, he said that, "Although the Soviet Delegation had not been informed when the document was drawn up against Japan they, nevertheless, were informing the other countries of this approach." [69] His interpreter then read an account of Sato's note to Lozovsky of July 25 in which the Japanese Ambassador had requested further Soviet attention to Prince Konoye's proposed mission on terms laid down by Togo. [70] Stalin mentioned that ". . . there was nothing new in this except that it was more definite than the previous approach and that it would receive a more definite answer than was the case the last time, and that the answer would be in the negative." [71] Even as the President thanked Stalin for the information, he quite likely was already fully informed about the Japanese actions.

Not only had Truman very likely seen the earlier Togo-Sato messages, but it seems that he also received confirmation of them from Forrestal who arrived in Potsdam on July 28 carrying all of the Japanese telegrams sent by July 25. Forrestal, who believed that the Togo-Sato wires indicated that Grew and he had been correct in their attempts to include in the Potsdam Declaration the item on the Emperor, had flown uninvited to Potsdam. On his arrival he saw both Byrnes and Truman. [72] For the first time, according to Byrnes, the Secretary of State saw the texts of the messages in detail. His preoccupation with European affairs at Potsdam and the short time he had been in office precluded wide knowledge of the details of the Japanese phase of the war on which he had expected little discussion at Potsdam. [73] Again, it seems unlikely that the messages had completely escaped Byrnes' and Truman's attention, for they had been coming in to Leahy throughout the conference.

On July 28, the President awaited news of Japan's reaction to the Potsdam Declaration. Despite the fact that he had not made specific reference in it to the possible retention of the Emperor, he presumably had reason to hope that its terms, which must have seemed lenient to him, might be acceptable to the Japanese. This hope, however, reflected a misunderstanding of the relation of the Emperor to the Japanese polity, a possible misinterpretation of the plea in the Togo-Sato wires, and an understandable uncertainty about the internal situation in Japan and its impact on the policies of the Japanese Government. Or, perhaps, there was no longer need for hope, for within a few days his new weapon would be launched as he had already ordered. If it failed, the Russians would soon enter the war. These new factors in a power equation already disastrous to Japan would, perhaps, make Japanese acceptance of the Potsdam Declaration academic. So with a growing predominance of military power in the Far East, with an atomic weapon soon ready to go, with an anticipation of Russian participation later in August, he could await the results of Japanese deliberation of his declaration with the confidence born of power.

The Japanese reaction to the Potsdam Declaration was somewhat to be expected. Foreign Minister Togo, in the SCDW meeting which was called on July 27 to consider the declaration, expressed his belief that the declaration did not demand unconditional surrender and that the Emperor's wishes for peace had reached the United States through Moscow and had resulted in a moderation of its terms. He felt, however, that some of its terms were unclear. He, therefore, thought it advisable to enter negotiations with the allies in order to obtain clarification and revision of the document. He particularly feared the consequences to Japan if the allies were to get the impression that it had rejected the declaration.[74]

Admiral Toyoda, supported by General Anami and General Umezu, believed that the declaration should be released to the press along with a strong statement from the government condemning it.[75] Despite such military opposition, Togo was able to obtain agreement from both the SCDW and, later in the day, from the Cabinet that Japan should wait for additional developments before answering the declaration and should continue to seek a clarification of the intentions of the Soviet Union. The Japanese Government also decided to publish the declaration, so edited as to remove some of its most lenient sections, as straight news without the strong accompanying statement which the military desired.[76]

On the morning of July 28, however, when the Japanese papers published the edited draft of the proclamation they also printed a statement that the Japanese Government had decided to *mokusatsu* the declaration, to kill it with silence.[77] Apparently Premier Suzuki, who favored Togo's point of view, had come under considerable military pressure during the previous evening and had used the word *mokusatsu* in a sense as a compromise, as an ambiguous bridge between the two factions in the SCDW, hoping that it would be interpreted to indicate that the ". . . cabinet was withholding comment on the Declaration, that a decision was not yet to be announced." [78] Instead *Domei,* the semiofficial news agency of Japan, translated *mokusatsu* to mean "ignore," and thus created a false impression of the Cabinet's decision the previous day. Despite the deplorable situation the statement could not be withdrawn, for Radio Tokyo had already beamed it to the United States.[79] The next morning the military demanded a stronger statement to eliminate the confusion as to what the ambiguous *mokusatsu* meant. Premier Suzuki partially gave in to their demands at a press conference held at 3:00 P.M. that afternoon. In answer to the planted question as to ". . . the Premier's view regarding the Joint Proclamation by the three countries," Suzuki replied:

I consider the joint declaration of the three powers to be a rehash of the Cairo Declaration. The government does not regard it as a thing of any great value; the government will just ignore (*mokusatsu*) it. We will press forward resolutely to carry the war to a successful conclusion.[80]

Suzuki had thus gone beyond simply ignoring the declaration. He had publicly proclaimed it to be of little value. But he still used the ambiguous term *mokusatsu,* perhaps hoping for an interpretation abroad more in line with the wishes of the peace group.

Whatever his desires, the result was disastrous from the point of view of those in the SCDW seeking peace. The Japanese action was treated in the United States as a rejection, as a dismissal of the declaration with a contemptuous gesture.[81] Thus, on the day when Stalin was informing Truman for the second time of the Japanese overtures to the Soviet Union, United States radio monitors were reporting to Truman that ". . . Radio Tokyo had reaffirmed the Japanese Government's determination to fight. Our proclamation had been referred to as 'unworthy of consideration,' 'absurd,' and 'presumptuous.' " [82]

The following days must have been terrible ones for Sato in Moscow. He was at a loss to explain his government's response to the Potsdam Declaration in view of the fact that Togo still sought Russian mediation to end the war. On July 28 after asking Tokyo for clarification of the B.B.C. announcement that the Japanese Government would "ignore" the statement of July 26, he advised that the desired meeting with Molotov could not take place unless ". . . a special, concrete, and definite proposal for termination of the war is presented by . . . Japan." [83] Two days later on July 30 he reported that, in his opinion, ". . . Stalin feels there is absolutely no necessity for making a voluntary agreement with Japan." [84] At 5:00 P.M. that afternoon he again met Lozovsky. Again he urgently requested an answer to Japan's request for Soviet mediation. Again Lozovsky pointed out that Molotov and Stalin were in Berlin; again there would be a delay in delivering the Soviet reply. And, thus, Sato's efforts ended as they had begun. He and Japan were asked to wait for the Soviet answer. When it came on August 8, it would be Russia's declaration of war.

In this way political efforts to arrange a basis for peace during the days of the Potsdam Conference ended in failure. The movement to modify unconditional surrender significantly in the Potsdam Declaration had failed, and the declaration had been "rejected" by the Japanese. Diplomatic overtures by the Japanese Government in search of Soviet mediation to end the war had proved to be futile before the Russian tactic of delay, used to forward Stalin's intention of capitalizing on Japan's growing weakness in the Far East. Peace seemed beyond the limits of United States diplomacy. The military plans for invasion indicated a long war. And looming on the eastern horizon was the once-desired promise of a Russian attack on Manchuria.

Even as the United States Government at Potsdam vacillated in modifying the policy of unconditional surrender, it followed a doubtful course toward continued promotion of Soviet participation in the war against Japan. Truman went to Potsdam with the intention of involving the Soviet Union militarily in the Far East. Events during the period of the conference led to increased doubts in the minds of some concerning the need for Soviet support. And yet the Soviet intervention had long been sought. Now that it appeared imminent, it not only was hardly needed, it could not be stopped. At Potsdam, therefore, although the United States was increasingly cool toward Soviet military action against Japan, it continued to formally solicit Soviet support because it had long done so and because it would now be useless to do otherwise. The Russians could not be kept out.

Particularly after the successful test of an atom bomb on July 16, some of Truman's highest advisers believed that Soviet intervention was no longer needed to force a Japanese surrender. Secretary of State Byrnes was one who not only believed that the Russians were not necessary but also that their entrance should be avoided if possible by forcing a rapid end to the war. He has written that

. . . in view of what we knew of Soviet actions in Eastern Germany and the violations of the Yalta agreements in Poland, Rumania and Bulgaria, I would have been satisfied had they determined not to enter the war. Notwithstanding Japan's persistent refusal to surrender unconditionally, I believed the atomic bomb would be successful and would force the Japanese to accept surrender on our terms. I feared what would happen when the Red Army entered Manchuria.[85]

When the agreement arranging Russian intervention had been made at Yalta, the military and political situations had been entirely different. Now, although there was little need for Russian assistance, Byrnes believed that since an agreement had been made the United States should stand by it. Aside from the moral consideration there might be political advantages to such a course.

There was no need to give the Russians additional excuse for evading their obligations in Europe. There was a need for collaboration with the Soviets if the postwar political situation was to be orderly. Nevertheless, Byrnes hoped for a rapid end to the war to forestall the expansion of Russian power into Manchuria; and he relied on the atomic bomb to force surrender before the inevitable Russian invasion. His remarks to Forrestal on July 28 indicated that attitude. He mentioned, at that time, that it was not his intention to get the Russians into the war although he believed they could not be kept out. He went on to say that ". . . he was most anxious to get the Japanese affair over with before the Russians got in, with particular reference to Dairen and Port Arthur. Once in there . . . it would not be easy to get them out." [86]

Very much like the Secretary of State, Truman's two service Secretaries also were doubtful of the need for Soviet intervention. Although Forrestal exercised little influence at Potsdam, his views were expressed at least to Byrnes and, perhaps, to Truman on July 28. As Secretary of the Navy he had long accepted the Navy viewpoint that, given time, the war could be ended by bombardment and blockade without Russian aid. At Potsdam, he agreed with Byrnes that it would now be difficult to stop a Russian move into Manchuria.[87]

Secretary of War Stimson had long opposed the entrance of the Soviet Union into the war in the Far East. He had not favored the Yalta arrangements and their acceptance of the expansion of Russian influence into Manchuria.[88] On July 16 he had sent a memorandum to the President which indicated his concern with the consequences of Russian action. He, first, had suggested that informing the Russians about the proposed Potsdam Declaration should hinge on whether or not an agreement satisfactory to the United States on the terms of Russian entry into the war had been negotiated. Second, he had believed that the Yalta agreements should not cause the United States concern from a security point of view, provided they interpreted consistently with the traditional "Open Door' policy toward China. And, third, he had felt that the Russians should, perhaps, be accorded a token occupation force in Japan as long as it was weaker than that of the United States and provided their contribution to the conquest of Japan had been creditable.[89]

That same day Stimson received news of the success of the atomic bomb test which changed his attitude considerably. His approach was also affected by his growing dismay at the evidence of Russian authoritarianism in the occupation of Berlin.[90] By July 23 he had come to the conclusion along with General Marshall that ". . . with our new weapon we would not need the assistance of the Russians to conquer Japan." [91] The next day he reported to Truman that he and Marshall believed that Russian force was no longer necessary to defeat Japan. Stimson also now hoped that the atomic bombs would end the war before the Soviet armies moved on Manchuria.

These attitudes of Truman's top civilian advisers were supported by the positions of the President's Chief of Staff and of the Joint Chiefs of Staff. Admiral Leahy, despite his lack of confidence in the atomic bomb, believed that the United States and the British could defeat Japan without the Russians and advised the President that there was no need to make concessions to entice the Soviets into the war.[92]

The Joint Chiefs of Staff, who were directly responsible for military success in the war, were apt to take a more conservative point of view. They looked on any increment of power, even if it came from the Soviet Union, as an added means to victory. General Marshall had consistently supported Soviet participation. On the morning of July 23, Truman had requested Stimson to discover if there had been any change in the General's thinking. Stimson arranged a meeting after lunch with Marshall, Arnold, McCloy, and Bundy. It was there that Marshall, somewhat indirectly modified his position. He pointed out that the original objective of Russian intervention, the neutralizing of the Japanese Kwantung Army in Manchuria, had been accomplished by the massing of Russian armies along the Manchurian border. He thought, however, that even if the United States could now defeat Japan without Russian support, the Russians would nevertheless move into Manchuria and take whatever they wanted, since they would no longer be limited by the Yalta agreements. Marshall also suggested that the United States should try to discover Russian intentions during the Potsdam Conference. From the indefinite survey of Marshall's opinion, Stimson came to the conclusion that the General believed with him that the atomic weapon eliminated the need for a Soviet attack on the Japanese.[93]

Arnold's comments, if any, were unrecorded by Stimson. He generally believed, however, that Japan was ". . . already on the verge of collapse." [94] Japan's sudden surrender, he wrote later, was something of a surprise; for it had been estimated that capitulation would take about four atomic bombs. Nevertheless, despite his feeling that Russia would be the future enemy of the United States, Arnold was pleased when Stalin announced at dinner on July 23 that he hoped their next meeting would be in Tokyo. For Arnold, this was the first time Stalin had openly talked about declaring war on Japan. The General of the Army Air Forces evaluated Stalin's move mostly in terms of available air bases closer to Japan.[95]

Other military leaders, although not very influential at Potsdam, had similar ideas. Admiral King who attended the conference, apparently went along with the decisions taken earlier by the Joint Chiefs of Staff which supported Russian invasion. He seems to have taken no strong position on the issue. General Eisenhower, who was not directly involved with the conference but who visited the President at Berlin, urged that Truman make no concessions to attract the Russians into the war. They were eager to intervene particularly since ". . . Japan was already thoroughly beaten." [96] He foresaw many difficulties which would arise following Soviet involvement and advised against it.[97]

This weight of opinion reflecting a reconsideration of the United States desire for a Soviet attack on Japan had its effect on Truman. He has written that throughout the conference his most important immediate goal was to obtain a commitment of Russian participation because of the demands from his military.[98] And yet, although this may have reflected the military opinion in view of the impossibility of blocking Russian entrance, most of those whom Truman consulted believed that the Soviets were no longer necessary to achieve victory. Churchill has also indicated that the climate of opinion had changed after July 16 and that it had influenced Truman. He has written, "The President and I no longer felt that we needed his (Stalin's) aid to conquer Japan . . . In our opinion [Russian troops in the Far East] were not likely to be needed. . . ." [99] Again, following a meeting with Byrnes in which the Secretary of State had told him that the United States was advising the Chinese against making additional concessions in their negotiation of a Far Eastern settlement with the Russians, Churchill noted, "It is quite clear that the United States do not at the present time desire Russian participation in the war against Japan." [100] And yet despite the changing military situation and the resultant shift in opinion among those within the United States group at Potsdam, Truman did not openly oppose Russian intervention. At the same time his growing coolness to such a move might have been demonstrated by the fact that he did little to promote Soviet action. He had apparently accepted the prevailing line: the Russians were not needed; but the United States had an agreement with them concerning their participation in the Far East and should observe it; this was particularly so since there was little if anything the United States could do to stop them; it was, therefore, wise, given their possible utility to the United States if plans concerning use of the atomic bomb and other military actions were ineffective in defeating Japan, at least not to oppose their intervention.

The course of events relating to this matter during the Potsdam Conference, when considered within the changing evaluation of the need for Russian intervention on the part of the United States delegation, seems to bear out the above analysis. As a part of every draft of the planned "Basic Undertakings and Policies for the Prosecution of the War," including the final one approved by Churchill and Stalin, there was listed first among . . . "tasks [which] will be undertaken in order to assist in the execution of the over-all strategic concept: a. Encourage Russian entry into the war against Japan. Provide such aid to her war-making capacity as may be necessary and practicable in connection therewith." [101] There was no official deviation from this announced policy.

DECISION OF DESTINY

Furthermore, at a meeting of the Combined Chiefs of Staff on July 24, General A. I. Antonov announced that the Soviet Union would be ready to commence operations during the last half of August. The actual date would depend on the completion of negotiations with the Chinese.[102] During the remainder of this meeting and the one which convened the following day involving both the Joint Chiefs of Staff and the Soviet Chiefs of Staff, efforts were made to arrange tactical cooperation between the Russian forces, on the one hand, and the British and the United States forces, on the other. The obvious implication to be derived from these talks was that everyone involved accepted, at least formally, the certainty of Soviet involvement.[103]

In addition to military preparations for Soviet entry into the war, assurances were also given by Stalin to Truman that Russia would fight Japan. During their first meeting prior to a luncheon on July 17, the Soviet leader twice brought the matter up. He ". . . told the President that the Soviets would be ready for such entry by the middle of August, but said prior to acting they would need to complete their negotiations and reach agreement with the Chinese." [104] Later during the conversation, Stalin repeated that the Russians would attack in mid-August.

The matter arose one final time. At the end of a meeting with Truman and Byrnes on July 29, Molotov mentioned that Stalin, who was absent, wished him to bring up the matter of Soviet entry into the war. He suggested that the Allies who were fighting Japan address a formal request to the Soviet Union asking for its entry into the war. Molotov said that this request could be based on Japan's refusal to accept the recent ultimatum to surrender as well as on the basis of shortening the war and saving lives. He pointed out again that agreement with the Chinese would be necessary before the Soviets would move into Manchuria.[105]

Truman promised to examine the Soviet request carefully. He handed the problem of solving the dilemma thus posed to Byrnes. The Secretary of State knew that the Russo-Japanese Neutrality Pact would be in effect until April, 1946. It was true that the United States had been consistently requesting the Soviet intervention which would violate this pact. But the military necessity which had occasioned that policy no longer existed. Japan was expected to be defeated without Russian help. Although the United States did not wish to violate its agreement with Russia by withdrawing its support for Soviet participation, it, at the same time, did not feel a need to hasten Soviet entry. On the other hand, to refuse Molotov's request might threaten the pattern of Soviet-American relations. Byrnes, on the suggestion of his Special Assistant, Benjamin V. Cohen, decided to make the United States request on the basis of the recently signed, but as yet unratified, Charter of the United Nations. The result was Truman's unsigned letter, drafted by Byrnes, which was transmitted to Stalin on July 31.[106]

Truman's letter mentioned three bases for Soviet action: the first, paragraph 5 of the Moscow Declaration of October 30, 1943, signed by the United States, the Soviet Union, the United Kingdom, and China provided that ". . . for the purpose of maintaining international peace and security . . . they will consult with one another and . . . with other members of the United Nations with a view to action on behalf of the community of nations."

The second, Article 106 of the proposed Charter of the United Nations, stated that: "Pending the coming into force of such special agreements referred to in Article 43 . . . the parties of the Four-Nation Declaration, signed at Moscow . . . and France shall in accordance of the provisions of paragraph 5 . . . consult with one another . . . with a view to such joint action on behalf of the Organization as may be necessary for the purpose of maintaining international peace and security." And finally, the third, Article 103 of the Charter, which asserted that "In the event of a conflict between the obligations of the Members . . . under the . . . Charter and their obligations under any international agreement their obligations under the . . . Charter shall prevail." [107]

The first paragraph of Truman's letter read: "It seems to me that under the terms of the Moscow Declaration and the provisions of the Charter, . . . it would be proper for the Soviet Army to indicate its willingness to consult and cooperate with other great powers now at war with Japan with a view to joint actions on behalf of the community of nations to permit peace and security.[108]

The letter reflected Byrnes' and Truman's attempt to satisfy the immediate needs of the Russian relationship, while providing the Soviets with nothing concrete on which to base action. There was no direct request for Russian intervention, only a suggestion of consultation and cooperation. And, of course, the letter was not signed.

By the end of the Potsdam Conference it was fairly well understood in the United States delegation that the Russians would enter the war sometime after the middle of August. In fact, despite Stalin's repeated reference to a Russo-Chinese agreement, Byrnes and Truman both felt as early as July 17 that ". . . Stalin would enter the war whether or not such Chinese concessions are made, and will thereafter satisfy Soviet demands regardless of what the Chinese attitude may be." [109] Leahy also was sure of Russia's intentions. He noted on July 28, after mentioning Stalin's revelations of Japan's efforts to seek Russian mediation, that it was ". . . clearly evident that Stalin is determined to enter the war against Japan which is plainly to the advantage of Russia now that Japan is certain to be defeated by the Allies." [110] And on July 31, in reference to Truman's letter suggesting consultation, he wrote, "The President did not ask the Soviets to join with us in the war against Japan, which I am sure Stalin will in his own interest do in any event." [111]

Thus, the anticipations concerning the war against Japan which had existed prior to Potsdam were not officially changed at the conference. All obstacles to Russian involvement in the war in the Far East had apparently been eliminated. The Soviets were expected to declare war on Japan sometime around the middle of August. The unconditional surrender policy had been liberally defined in the Potsdam Declaration, but not so liberally as to bring a rapid Japanese acceptance of its terms. It was likely that the Japanese would fight on. To overcome this last-ditch Japanese resistance the President and Prime Minister had approved military operations promising the defeat of Japan, but only after a long war involving a costly invasion. Into this nexus of political and military circumstances, the new weapon, the atomic bomb, was introduced on July 16, at the time of the opening sessions of the Potsdam Conference.

It remains, therefore, necessary to trace the events which led to the dropping of the atomic weapons on Japan. At no time during that history does there appear any deviation from the policy of the Interim Committee, the policy which was essentially that of the War Department, to use the weapons as soon as they were ready and as soon as the weather permitted. In a formal sense, President Truman made the decision to use the weapons either at the Potsdam Conference or shortly thereafter. He certainly had the authority to stop the operation. And yet it seems that, in effect, conditions being what they were he could not reasonably have done so. The immediate decisions involved in military use of the bomb were being made for him. In line with the policy suggested in early June, General Groves was rapidly preparing the bomb for utilization. Marshall, Stimson, and Truman did nothing to delay the process.

The event which promised the opportunity to use the nuclear weapons was the successful test of Fat Man, in the desert at Alamogordo, New Mexico, at 5:30 A.M. on July 16, 1945.[112] The test was a complete success, and Groves telephoned the information through his office to Harrison at 7:30 that morning.[113] Harrison, in turn, sent the news to Stimson in a prearranged code: "Operated on this morning. Diagnosis not yet complete but results seem satisfactory and already exceed expectations. Local press release necessary as interest extends great distance. Dr. Groves pleased. He returns tomorrow, I will keep you posted."[114] The Secretary of War received the message at 7:30 P.M., Berlin time. Here was good news, indeed. The long and costly effort had paid off. After sending through Harrison his ". . . warmest congratulations to the Doctor and his consultants," Stimson hurried with the message to the Little White House, where he told the news to Truman and Byrnes.[115] The President and Secretary of State were ". . . greatly interested, although the information was still in very general terms."[116] There is no evidence that the discussion involved the use of the atomic bombs.[117] After luncheon that afternoon with Churchill, Attlee, and others, Stimson told

Churchill of Harrison's message. As Stimson recalled the Prime Minister's reactions: "He had not heard from his own people about the matter. He was intensely interested and greatly cheered up, but was strongly inclined against any disclosure. . . ." [118] Churchill had not been informed that the test was to take place, and he received the new with considerable enthusiasm.[119]

That afternoon in Washington Groves and Harrison drafted their second message to the Secretary of War: "Doctor has just returned most enthusiastic and confident that Little Boy is as husky as his big brother. The light in his eyes discernible from here to Highhold and I could have heard his screams from here to my farm." [120]

Stimson received Harrison's second message on July 18. He immediately took it to Truman ". . . who was highly delighted . . . [and] evidently very greatly reinforced over the message . . . and said he was very glad [Stimson] had come to the meeting." [121]

Truman lunched with Churchill that day about 1:30 P.M. Although no official record of the conversation at the luncheon exists, Truman apparently discussed with the Prime Minister the problem of telling the Russians about the atomic bombs. Churchill took the position, with Truman's concurrence, that if Stalin was informed about the successful test of the new weapons, he should not be given any particulars of its development.[122] There was no indication of a discussion of use.

During that afternoon and evening in Washington, Groves was drafting an extended account of the Alamogordo test. It was ready to go with the regular courier who left at 2:00 A.M. for Potsdam. The report was written to inform Stimson of those details of the test which could not be sent by telegram. Harrison cabled Stimson that the "Doctor [would] send detailed report by courier leaving tomorrow." [123]

Very little occurred at Potsdam on Thursday, July 19, in reference to the nuclear weapons. At noon Stimson talked over some of the problems of S-1 with Lord Cherwell, Churchill's scientific adviser, and Bundy. The Secretary of War's account is the only record of the conversation: "At twelve o'clock Lord Cherwell called and he and Bundy and I sat out under the trees and talked over S-1. He was very reasonable, on the subject of notification to the Russians, feeling about as doubtful as we. He reported Churchill as being pleased with our luncheon together . . . and much cheered by the talk." [124] That same day Stimson sent a long memorandum to Truman expressing his distrust of the Russians, his doubts as to the compatibility of the Soviet and American systems, and his belief that

. . . *no* world organization containing as one of its dominant members a nation whose people are not possessed of free speech but whose governmental action is controlled by autocratic machinery of a secret political police, [can] give effective control of this new agency (S-1) with its devastating possibilities.

. . . before we share our new discovery with Russia we should consider carefully whether we can do so safely under any system of control until Russia puts into effective action [a free constitution.][125]

That evening the Secretary confided to his *Diary*, in reference to the difficulty of a democratic nation attempting to get along permanently with an authoritarian one: "The question is very important just now, and the development of S-1 is bringing it to focus. I am beginning to feel that our committee which met in Washington on this subject and was so set upon opening communications with the Russians on the subject may have been thinking in a vacuum." [126] Truman's reaction to Stimson's sentiments has not been recorded. But his subsequent approach to Stalin to inform him of S-1 seems to indicate general agreement.[127] No further official consideration was given to the atomic bombs on July 18. And, in fact, there was, it seems, no discussion of their use. That question was awaiting arrival of Groves' account of the test.

The courier carrying Groves' report arrived at Potsdam by 11:30 A.M. on Saturday, July 21. Stimson and Bundy read the report enthusiastically and made an appointment at 3:30 P.M. to show it to the President. On the way to see Truman, Stimson took the report to Marshall. At the Little White House soon afterward, he read it to Truman and Byrnes. "They were immensely pleased. The President was tremendously pepped up by it and spoke to me of it again and again when I saw him. He said it gave him an entirely new feeling of confidence. . ." [128] Later that day, after he had shown the report to Churchill, Stimson cabled his congratulations to Groves and mentioned that he had referred Groves' report to the Joint Chiefs of Staff who also were "much encouraged." [129]

Other problems concerning the employment of the nuclear weapons arose on July 21. Harrison wired the Secretary of War: "All our local military advisors engaged in preparation favor your pet city and would like to feel free to use it as first choice if those on the ride select it out of four possible spots in the light of local conditions at the time." [130] Stimson wired back that he was aware of no new factors to change his decision in regard to Kyoto and that, on the contrary, the situation at Potsdam tended ". . . to confirm it." [131] Later during the day Harrison again cabled Stimson, this time to inform him of the readiness of the bombs. "Patient progressing rapidly and will be ready for final operations first good break in August. Complicated preparations for use are proceeding so fast we should know not later than July 25 if any change in plans." [132] The weapons were fast approaching completion as Groves' men prepared them for use. But on July 21, at least, there seems to have been no discussion of the question as to whether they should be used.

On July 22, Stimson called on Truman at 9:20 in the morning to discuss Harrison's two most recent cables. Truman ". . . was intensely pleased by the accelerated timetable. As to the matter of the special target which [Stimson] had refused to permit, [Truman] strongly confirmed Stimson's view and said he felt the same way. . . ." [133]

Later that morning, at 10:40, Stimson and Bundy talked with Churchill and Lord Cherwell for over an hour. Stimson later described the session:

Churchill read Groves' report in full. He told me that he had noticed at the meeting of the Three yesterday that Truman was evidently much fortified by something that had happened and that he stood up to the Russians in a most emphatic and decisive manner, telling them as to certain demands that they absolutely could not have and that the United States was entirely against them. When he got to the meeting after having read this report he was a changed man. . . . Churchill said he now understood how this pepping up had taken place and that he felt the same way. His own attitude confirmed this admission. He now not only was not worried about giving the Russians information on the matter but was rather inclined to use it as an argument in our favor in the negotiations. The sentiment of the four of us was unanimous in thinking that it was advisable to tell the Russians at least that we were working on that subject and *intended to use it if and when it was successfully finished.*[134]

Churchill again was very enthusiastic. He saw in the use of the bomb ". . . a speedy end to the Second World War, and perhaps to much else besides." [135] Bundy has reported that the Prime Minister exclaimed, "Stimson, what was gun powder? Trivial. What was electricity? Meaningless. This atomic bomb is the Second Coming in Wrath." [136] And it must be emphasized that all favored telling the Russians they were going to use it.

Immediately following this conference, Churchill was invited to visit Truman. With Truman were Leahy and Marshall. Churchill described how he, and presumably the Americans, saw the atomic bombs as a means of ending the war quickly, without invasion and without Russian participation. Significantly he wrote:

. . . *there never was a moment's discussion as to whether the atomic bomb should be used or not.* To avert a vast, indefinite butchery, to bring the war to an end, to give peace to the world, to lay healing hands upon its tortured peoples by a manifestation of overwhelming power at the cost of a few explosions, seemed after all our toils and perils, a miracle of deliverance.

. . . The final decision now lay in the main with President Truman, who had the weapon; but I never doubted what it would be, nor have I ever doubted since that he was right. The historic fact remains . . . that *the decision whether or not to use the atomic bomb to compel the surrender of Japan was never even an issue.* There was unanimous, automatic, unquestioned agreement around our table; nor did I ever hear the slightest suggestion that we should do otherwise.[137]

Truman, in turn, has recorded the following (although, perhaps, not in specific reference to this meeting):

The final decision of where and when to use the atomic bomb was up to me. Let there be no mistake about it. I regarded the bomb as a military weapon and *never had any doubt that it should be used.* The top military advisers to the President recommended its use, and when I talked to Churchill he unhesitatingly told me that he favored the use of the atomic bomb if it might aid to end the war.[138]

Certainly Churchill did not oppose the use of the weapon. Presumably since the Americans had the bomb and since he, therefore, could do little about its use, he saw no need to oppose an event which might provide a counterforce with which the United States could oppose the threat of Russian expansion. The British had already formally given their consent to the use of the weapon at a meeting of the Combined Chiefs of Staff on July 4. At that time, Field Marshal Sir Henry Maitland Wilson had ". . . stated that the British Government concurred in the use of the T.A. weapon against Japan. He added that the Prime Minister might wish to discuss the matter with the President at the forthcoming meeting in Berlin." [139] Now the Prime Minister had discussed the matter with the President. The question of use was apparently a foregone conclusion.

Despite Truman's assertion that "the top military advisers to the President recommended its use," apparently some were only minimally consulted. It certainly seems doubtful that Admiral King and Admiral Leahy favored use of the bomb despite the President's recollection that he had consulted them.[140] The matter was not discussed in meetings of either the Joint Chiefs of Staff or the British Chiefs of Staff.[141] It seems more reasonable to assume that the advice had come from Stimson, Marshall, Arnold, and Groves who was going ahead as if the decision had long ago been made, as indeed it had.

About the time that Truman and Churchill were conferring on the atomic bomb on July 22, Stimson called in General Arnold and showed him Harrison's messages and Groves' report. Arnold apparently assumed that the bomb would be used. He concerned himself only with the targets to be attacked. He confirmed Stimson's decision to eliminate Kyoto as a target and suggested that General Carl A. Spaatz, who was to take command of the Strategic Air Force in the Pacific, have tactical control of specific target selection, after coordinating his decision with Groves.[142] Arnold also informed the Secretary of War that ". . . it would take considerable hard work to organize the operations [sic] now that it was to move forward." [143]

That same day Marshall cabled General Thomas T. Handy, his Acting Chief of Staff, that he was sending Colonel John N. Stone, Arnold's courier, to Washington with orders to Handy, Groves, and Spaatz to prepare a tentative directive to Spaatz covering use of the bomb. The tentative directive was to be submitted to Marshall and Stimson for approval; but Spaatz was to be given a copy, for it was not necessary for him to have the final directive prior to his imminent departure for the Pacific. Any changes in the tentative directive might be sent to him later.[144] Spaatz was, in effect, receiving on July 22 his orders to use the bomb.

The next day's events indicated more conclusively the likelihood that the decision to use the atomic bomb had already been made. At Potsdam, Byrnes called on Stimson at 10:30 A.M. to try to pin down more definitely the timing of the use of S-1.[145] As a result Stimson sent Harrison the following message:

We are greatly pleased with apparent improvement in timing of patients [*sic*] progress. We assume operation may be anytime after the first of August. Whenever it is possible to give us more definite date please immediately advise us here where information is greatly needed. Also give name of place or alternate places, always excluding the particular place against which I have decided. My decision has been confirmed by highest authority.[146]

Harrison answered in three separate cables to Stimson. In the first he listed the targets as Hiroshima, Kokura, and Niigata in that order. In the second he stated: "Operation may be possible anytime from August 1 depending on state of preparation of patient and condition of atmosphere. From point of view of patient only, some chance August 1 to 3, good chance August 4 to 5, and barring unexpected relapse almost certain before August 10." [147] Harrison's third cable indicated Groves' anticipations of future deliveries of atomic weapons. The first Fat Man would be ready by August 6 and the second by August 24. Three bombs of both types were expected to be ready in September and others would be supplied at an accelerating monthly rate until seven might be produced in December. The increased rate reflected a change in design approved by Groves.[148] Thus, by the end of the day Stimson had reason to expect that the bombs would be ready early in August and that others would be produced with increasing frequency.

Meanwhile, at 11:00 A.M. Stimson again spoke to Truman about coordinating the warning to Japan with the use of the weapons. Truman told him ". . . that he had the warning message we had prepared on his desk . . . and that he proposed to shoot it out as soon as he heard the definite day of operations." [149] Apparently Truman, too, was merely waiting for news from the field as to when the bomb would be used.

After lunch on July 23, Stimson discussed the S-1 development with Marshall, Arnold, Bundy, and McCloy. They ". . . talked about the killing of women and children; [*sic*] the destruction of surrounding communities, the effect on other nations, and the psychological reaction of the Japanese themselves." [150] Arnold suggested testing the explosive effect of the atomic bomb by dropping it in a harbor, but his plan was not accepted. Finally, Stimson asked Marshall's opinion on Russian intervention now that the bomb existed. He was not surprised that the General now believed that they would not now need Russian participation.[152] The question of use seems not to have been considered. Back in Washington, Groves was drafting the directive ordering Spaatz to provide for the bombing of Japan.[153]

On July 24, Handy sent Marshall a copy of the directive to Spaatz for the approval of Stimson and Marshall. Groves also transmitted a long memorandum to Marshall to obtain his ". . . final approval of [the] plan of operation." [154] In it he mentioned that the first gun-type bomb would be ready between August 1 and August 10 and that it would be delivered on Hiroshima, Kokura, and Nagasaki. Harrison had already cabled to Stimson:

"I personally feel it is most important that [the] Directive . . . which Handy is sending Marshall . . . be approved tomorrow, Wednesday, if possible even if it is necessary to modify it later." [155]

While Washington pressed for action, Stimson was seeing Truman to deliver the news Harrison had sent giving the anticipated dates of the operation. Truman's response was that ". . . that was just what he wanted, that he was highly delighted and that it gave him his cue for his warning." [156] The new sanction to the Potsdam Declaration now seemed to be ready.

That afternoon after the plenary session, Truman took the opportunity to tell Stalin personally that the United States had a new weapon. There had been considerable thought given to this action by the Interim Committee, by Stimson, and by Churchill as well as by the President; all had agreed that Stalin only be informed that the weapon was to be used, but that he should not be told about the details of development or the nature of the bombs.[157] The different versions of the revelation are interesting. Truman records the following: "On July 24 I casually mentioned to Stalin that we had a new weapon of unusual destructive force. The Russian Premier showed no special interest. All he said was that he was glad to hear it and hoped we would make 'good use of it against the Japanese.' " [158]

Byrnes has written two accounts of this conversation which are substantially the same:

At the close of the meeting of the Big Three on the afternoon of July 24, the President walked around the larger circular table to talk to Stalin. After a brief conversation the President rejoined me and we rode back to the "Little White House" together. He said he had told Stalin that, after long experimentation, we had developed a new bomb far more destructive than any other known bomb, and that we planned to use it very soon unless Japan surrendered. Stalin's only reply was to say that he was glad to hear of the bomb and that he hoped we would use it.[159]

Two other eyewitness reports exist. One, by Leahy, records the following:

At the plenary session of July 24, Truman walked around to Stalin and told him quietly that we had developed a powerful weapon, more potent than anything yet seen in the war. The President said later that Stalin's reply indicated no special interest and that the Generalissimo did not seem to have any conception of what Truman was talking about. It was simply another weapon and he hoped we would use it effectively.[160]

Churchill's version is more graphic if less informative:

Next day, July 24, after our plenary meeting had ended. . . . I saw the President go up to Stalin, and the two conversed alone with only their interpreters. I was perhaps five yards away, and I watched with the closest attention the momentous talk. I knew what the President was going to do. What was vital to measure was its effect on Stalin. . . . He seemed to be delighted. . . . As we were going to our cars I found myself near Truman, "How did it go?" I asked. "He never asked a question," he replied.[161]

It now seems that this meeting was far less momentous than Churchill believed. It is almost certain that Stalin had heard about the atomic bomb at least a month before the Potsdam Conference and, perhaps, long before that. Before and during the early years of World War II, Russian scientists had already developed the theoretical knowledge upon which a bomb might be built. As early as the spring of 1940 a "Special Committee for the Problem of Uranium" had been established under the Presidium of the Academy of Sciences.[162] On October 12, 1941, a prominent Soviet scientist, Peter L. Kapitsa, had mentioned to an audience of scientists the feasibility of manufacturing atom bombs.[163] At this time, "exploration of methods of separating uranium isotopes" had been progressing at about the same rate in the Soviet Union as in the United States, and in the "theoretical explanation of some of these methods" the Russians may have been somewhat in the lead.[164] After the German invasion of Russia in June, 1941, however, the exigencies of war had caused the Soviet Union to curtail its program sharply just about the time that the United States and Great Britain were accelerating theirs.[165] The Soviet program had later been reactivated after 1943 as the Germans retreated. The war, therefore, delayed the progress of Soviet nuclear development seriously. But during the latter years of the war Soviet scientists were accumulating the knowledge upon which an atomic bomb could be built.

There is some evidence that Stalin knew of such developments. Certainly he had opportunity to review the work of the Academy of Sciences. It has also been reported by a former Soviet official that in the Soviet Government it was an ". . . open secret that atomic research was being pushed hard under Stalin's own direction." [166] Near the end of 1942, this same official heard rumors that Stalin had met with Academician Kapitsa in a special conference devoted to atomic energy.[167] Despite the doubtful quality of this evidence, it is generally supported by the record of another defecting Soviet officer, Ivan Krylov. In a conversation with the secretary to Anastas Mikoyan, one Poyarsky, Krylov reported the secretary as saying that ". . . already they (the Kremlin) are talking about the next conflict. We have reliable information to the effect that the U. S. Government is going all out to manufacture a secret weapon: the atomic bomb." [168] And further Poyarsky asserted that he feared that the United States would be tempted to use the weapon against the Soviets; that the Russians would ". . . ask the Americans to give [them] all the necessary information about its manufacture [and if] they refuse [the Soviets would] know what to think"; that he hoped that the Soviet Union would obtain the secret ". . . whether the U. S. Government [was] prepared to give it to [them] voluntarily or not"; and that he expected to obtain it through ". . . [their] network of agents in the United States." [169] The conversations, of course, only indicate a probability that Stalin knew not only about nuclear research in the Soviet Union but also through his espionage net about developments in the United States.

This is not the place to review the activities of Soviet atomic espionage in the United States during World War II. Suffice it to say that widespread activities were underway at Berkeley; at Los Alamos, where the leading source was Klaus Fuchs, a German-born British scientist; at the Russian embassy in Ottawa through another British scientific contact, Alan Nunn May; and at Chicago and other points throughout the United States.[170]

Perhaps, the activities of Klaus Fuchs indicate most conclusively the probability that Stalin by the time of Potsdam had considerable information concerning the new United States weapon. Certainly Fuchs had sufficient knowledge to have passed on revealing information to his contact, Harry Gold, who acted as courier for Anatoli A. Yakovlev, the Russian vice-consul in New York.[171] General Groves has recently written that Fuchs ". . . knew the general progress of atomic development up until the fall of 1942, when we stopped the almost complete interchange of information. He knew the general design of the gaseous diffusion plant at Oak Ridge and many of its details. He knew the details of design for both types of atomic weapons, the gun type and the implosion type. He knew our thinking about how these could be improved. . . ."[172] Through 1944 and 1945, Fuchs contacted Gold at least five times. In the early summer of 1944 he delivered to Gold information about the actual plans for the design of the uranium bomb and about the principles and details of the gaseous diffusion plant at Oak Ridge. He also indicated the scale and timing of the United States program. Fuchs was sent to Los Alamos, probably in July, 1944. At a later meeting with Gold early in 1945 in Cambridge, Massachusetts, Fuchs turned over the details of the plutonium bomb (Fat Man), described its design and method of construction, and indicated that plutonium was being produced at Hanford, Washington. He also gave Gold a description of the detonating device of Fat Man. At another meeting with Gold in New Mexico, Fuchs indicated that the ". . . first atomic explosion would take place in the New Mexican desert near Alamogordo, during the following months."[173] Gold probably transmitted this information to Yakovlev in June, 1945. It seems, therefore, that by the time of Potsdam, Stalin's ". . . director of intelligence in Moscow had then a full account of the making of the bomb. . . ."[174]

Assuming that Fuchs turned over the information he had to Gold; that Gold, in turn, transmitted it to Yakovlev; that the Russian vice-consul cabled it to Moscow; and that the intelligence apparatus in Moscow carried it to Stalin, it seems likely that the Soviet Premier knew of the atomic bomb at least a month before Potsdam. Given the likelihood of his prior knowledge of Russian nuclear research, he probably was able to evaluate the information he received. Therefore, given the general reactions of the eyewitnesses to

Stalin's disinterested response to Truman's mention of the weapon after the July 24 plenary session, it seems apparent that the Soviet Premier was covering a considerable knowledge with a bland indifference.

And, furthermore, it is just possible that Truman had some prior indication that Stalin might have previously known about the weapon. Certainly the MED security staff and Groves had early indications of Soviet espionage activities.[175] Late in 1944, Groves had presented Roosevelt a paper on the matter which Roosevelt read in the General's presence.[176] On December 31, 1944, Stimson also had informed Roosevelt of Soviet espionage. He had told the President that he knew the Russians were spying on S-1 work but that he had no detailed knowledge of their activities.[177] Of course, because of the minimal contact between Roosevelt and Truman between December, 1944, and the former's death, it is unlikely that any of the information had been passed to Truman. But Groves has further testified that the matter was brought to Truman's attention during his April 25 conference with Stimson and Groves.[178] And, of course, Stimson might have been kept informed, although his *Diary* indicates that he gave the matter little if any attention. It is possible therefore, that Truman already knew that Stalin had obtained specific information about the weapon when he announced its existence to the Soviet leader on July 24.

Meanwhile, orders to use the weapon were quickly processed. Marshall's message to Handy giving the Secretary of War's approval to the directive to Spaatz was transmitted to Washington on July 25. In effect, from then until Hiroshima, the decision to use the weapons lay in the hands of the military. It is true that Truman could have stopped the operation. This he apparently never seriously considered. Yet he later recalled, it was ". . . necessary to set the military wheels in motion, as these orders did, but the final decision was in my hands. . . ."[179]

The orders to General Spaatz contained four paragraphs. In the first the 509th Composite Group was directed to deliver its ". . . first special bomb as soon as weather will permit visual bombing after *about* 3 August, 1945, on one of the targets: Hiroshima, Kokura, Niigata and Nagasaki. . . ."[180] Insofar as the approved earliest time of delivery was concerned, the word "about" was of some significance. Groves and Harrison had indicated that Little Boy would be ready by August 1.[181] Why then delay the bombing until August 3? Groves' explanation clarifies the situation. He points out that August 1 had always been considered by him as the target date, but that long-range predictions indicated that the weather would not be suitable until August 3. Nevertheless, since Little Boy was expected to be ready by August 1 and since the weather might clear earlier than August 3, the word "about" was inserted. As Groves explains it: ". . . the word 'about' is thoroughly understood in the American Army. Official travel regulations of that period defined 'about' as normally including a period of four days before and four days after the specific date cited. Everyone understood this. . . ." [182] Of course this directive was not an official travel order. But apparently the word "about" made the date August 3 sufficiently flexible so as to include possible use on August 1, weather permitting.

The second paragraph of the order indicated that ". . . additional bombs will be delivered on the above targets as soon as made ready. . . ." [183] Provision was thus made for the possibility that the Japanese might not surrender. The concluding paragraphs centralized publicity control in Washington and instructed Spaatz to transmit copies of his directive to MacArthur and Nimitz. And thus the die was cast.

On July 26 the Potsdam Declaration was issued by the heads of government. It did not include reference to the Emperor, and at 3:00 P.M. on July 28, Tokyo time, Premier Suzuki announced to a press conference that he would ignore it. His statement was taken as rejection. The machinery developing the product to be delivered on Hiroshima ground on.

During the following days little activity concerning the atomic bombing of Japan occurred at the higher levels of the United States Government. By July 28, Stimson and his aides were back in the United States, receiving reports that S-1 was doing well.[184] On July 30 the Secretary of War along with Harrison, Page, Groves, and Bundy worked on the draft of the Presidential announcement to be made after the first atomic drop. During the day Groves received a report from his deputy on Tinian, Brigadier General Thomas F. Farrell. It indicated that the first bomb would be ready by 11:00 P.M. July 31 and that both he and General LeMay interpreted August 1 as falling ". . . within the intent of the directive." [185] Those in the field, it seemed, interpreted "about 3 August" as flexibly as Groves had expected. Stimson transmitted the news to Truman, still at Potsdam:

The time schedule on Groves' project is progressing so rapidly that it is now essential that statement for release by you be available not later than Wednesday, 1 August. . . .

While I am planning to start a copy by special courier tomorrow in the hope you can be reached, nevertheless, in the event he doesn't reach you in time, I will appreciate having your authority to have White House release revised statement as soon as necessary.[186]

The Secretary expected the bombs to go anytime after August 1. Only the weather and a military decision now intervened.

On July 31, Pacific time, the gun-type bomb was operational, and the 509th was ready. The Secretary of War informed Truman that he was sending him the draft of his message on the atomic bomb by courier. He again appended the warning that the weapon might be dropped by August 1, Pacific time, which was hours ahead of Washington time.[187]

The President quickly cabled back that Stimson was to release the message when ready but not before August 2.[188] The requested delay until August 2 in releasing the message is difficult to explain. On that date Truman was leaving Potsdam to fly to England where he would board the U.S.S. *Augusta*, at anchor in Plymouth Roads. That afternoon at 3:55, British time, the *Augusta* got underway for the United States. There seems to be no reasonable connection between the President's situation or his political needs, and the possible delay in making his announcement, had the first bomb been dropped on August 1.

Meanwhile on July 28, the new British Prime Minister Clement Attlee arrived in Potsdam with his Foreign Minister Ernest Bevin. On August 1, Truman handwrote a note to Attlee informing him of the atomic test.[189] The news required no decision by Attlee, since Churchill had already given British consent to the bomb's use. Attlee agreed with the former Prime Minister. Except in the negative sense of refusing to disagree with the combined decisions to use the bomb, he played no part in sanctioning the final operation.[190]

On August 2, the release of the scientific paper describing, after its use, the development of the bomb was authorized by Stimson largely on Groves' recommendation.[191] Despite British doubts, most of the scientists involved believed that it contained nothing which could be used by possible competitors. Here again Groves' importance was demonstrated. Additionally he has stated that he in reality initiated the orders for the operation. The ". . . . orders for our operation against Japan would originate with me, be approved by him (Marshall), and be issued to Spaatz over Arnold's signature." [192] This was apparently the line of action which initiated the atomic operation against Japan. Only in the negative sense, that he did not stop the operation, did Truman participate in the final decision.

And yet Truman has written that ". . . the final decision was in his hands, and was not made until we were returning from Potsdam." [193] This was, of course, a recollection written nearly eight years later in 1953. No evidence has been found to substantiate the President's contention. It is possible that Truman, without confiding in anyone, was weighing the possibilities of calling off the bombing. As President, he certainly had the authority to countermand the operations already begun. But there is no indication that he wished to do so. Only, it seems, in this general, negative way was the decision to use the atomic weapons made during the trip from Plymouth to Newport News.

Stimson kept Truman informed of the developments in regard to S-1 during the President's voyage home. On Thursday, August 2, he radioed that, depending on the weather, Groves' operation was scheduled to begin on Friday. He messaged again on August 3 that the weapons had been ready since August 1 and that on Tinian they were awaiting the first favorable opportunity to deliver them.[194] Stimson noted in his *Diary* on August 4 that the operation had been postponed from Friday until Saturday or Sunday.[195] Finally on Sunday, August 5, the prediction indicated clearing weather. Since it took twenty four hours to ready the weapons, take-off would have to come the next day. At 2:45 A.M. on August 6, Pacific time, Colonel Paul W. Tibbets, the pilot, lifted the B-29 *Enola Gay* with Little Boy aboard off of North Field, Tinian, enroute to Hiroshima. Just after 8:15 A.M., Japanese time, Little Boy was dropped on Japan. The decision to launch the atomic bomb had been consummated. There is no evidence that anyone, from the President down, suggested reconsideration during these last few days.

Events moved rapidly following the atomic bombing of Hiroshima. Within three days the Japanese Government suffered three tremendous blows. Hiroshima was attacked on August 6. On August 8 at 5:00 P.M., Moscow time, Ambassador Sato finally received his long-sought interview with Molotov. But the Foreign Minister had not called Sato in to transmit the Russian answer to the Japanese request for mediation. He announced the Russian declaration of war on Japan. Two hours later Russian troops were attacking the Japanese in Manchuria. The Japanese Government received the shocking news on August 9 through a Soviet radio broadcast. Sato's cable informing Togo of the results of his meeting with Molotov had never cleared Moscow. Later that morning at 10:58 Japanese time the second atomic bomb, this time Fat Man carried in the B-29 *Bock's Car* piloted by Major Charles W. Sweeney, dropped on Nagasaki. The Japanese Supreme Council for the Direction of the War (SCDW) was at the time locked in futile debate between those members led by Foreign Minister Togo who favored acceptance of the Potsdam Declaration and the group led by War Minister Anami who wanted to fight on to obtain better terms.

The SCDW faced an impossible situation. Although the military had restricted dissemination of information about the atomic bombing of Hiroshima, news of President Truman's broadcast threatening future destruction from this revolutionary weapon had spread to Japan by air and by leaflet. More important, the Council was faced with the wreck of its hopes for a mediated peace by the Soviet Union. The Cabinet had met during the afternoon of August 7. But no action had been taken pending an investigation of the Hiroshima incident by the Army. On August 8, Togo met in audience with the Emperor and pleaded that because of the atomic bombing it was all the more important to end the war. The Emperor agreed that the atomic bombing could provide an excuse for surrender without seeking further concessions. Premier Suzuki called a most urgent meeting of the SCDW for 11:00 A.M., August 9. All present agreed that the Potsdam Declaration should be accepted provided it was interpreted to include the preservation of the national polity as an indispensable condition. The military led by Anami demanded three additional conditions: that Japan should not be occupied unless it was necessary, and if so on a minimal scale; that disarmament should be a Japanese responsibility; and that war criminals should be tried by Japan.[196] They believed that Japan could fight one last battle to inflict serious losses on an enemy beachhead. Togo pointed out the futility of such a suggestion and advocated surrender on the condition that the Emperor be maintained. The SCDW adjourned at 1:00 P.M., undecided.

The matter was debated in the Cabinet inconclusively that evening. Finally Suzuki requested an Imperial Conference shortly before midnight on August 9. The Emperor heard both positions stated respectively by Togo and Anami. Neither side would give. Finally Suzuki requested that the Emperor resolve the division at about 2:00 A.M., August 10. The Emperor quietly and sadly supported Togo, and the conference ended. By 3:00 A.M. the Cabinet had endorsed the imperial decision. At 7:00 A.M. August 10 the Japanese message of acceptance of the Potsdam Declaration was transmitted through Switzerland to the United States and through Sweden to the United Kingdom and to the Soviet Union.[197] It was addressed to Secretary of State Byrnes. Its key paragraphs read:

The Japanese Government are ready to accept the terms enumerated in the joint declaration which was issued at Potsdam on July 26th, 1945, . . . with the understanding that the said declaration does not comprise any demand which prejudices the prerogatives of his Majesty as a Sovereign Ruler.

The Japanese Government sincerely hope that this understanding is warranted and desire keenly that an explicit indication to that effect will be speedily forthcoming.[198]

The Japanese thus accepted the Potsdam Declaration but only with the provision regarding the Emperor which had been struck out of article (12).

During those three days following Hiroshima the United States government had waited for a Japanese reaction while keeping the pressure on Japan. The President's statement announcing the bombing of Hiroshima, originally worked on by the Interim Committee and finally drafted in the War Department on July 30, was approved by Truman for release from Washington following the first bombing. It contained an ominous threat written with the intention of convincing Japan to surrender. The President announced:

We are now prepared to obliterate more rapidly and completely every productive enterprise the Japanese have above ground in any city. We shall destroy their docks, their factories, and their communications. Let there be no mistake; we shall completely destroy Japan's power to make war.

It was to spare the Japanese people from utter destruction that the ultimatum of July 26 was issued at Potsdam. Their leaders promptly rejected that ultimatum. If they do not now accept our terms they may expect a rain of ruin from the air, the like of which has never been seen on earth. Behind this air attack will follow sea and land forces in such numbers and power as they have not yet seen and with the fighting skill of which they are already aware.[199]

At the same time that the President's announcement was issued, Stimson released a statement outlining the development of the atomic bomb project. The War Department and the administration was demonstrating their ingenuity and foresight to the world.

On August 8, Truman announced to a press conference, "*Russia has declared war on Japan. That is all!*"[200] The President had returned to Washington just before midnight on August 7. He had received news of the Russian action early in the afternoon of August 8 from Harriman. Since Chinese-Russian negotiations seemed far from agreement, the Russian declaration was unexpected. And yet the President has written that, "This move did not surprise us. Our dropping of the atomic bomb on Japan had forced Russia to reconsider her position in the Far East."[201] Certainly the Russian move had come earlier than anticipated. Although Stalin had informed Hopkins as early as May 28 that Soviet troops would be in position to attack by August 8, he, then as later, had tied the date of attack to successful Sino-Soviet negotiations implementing the Yalta agreement on the Far East. At Potsdam he had left the impression that the attack would come late in August. Apparently influenced by the lenient terms offered to Japan in the Potsdam Declaration, by the American possession of the atomic bomb, and by the obvious American air and naval superiority in and around the Japanese home islands, Stalin stepped up his plans for attacking Manchuria.[202]

On August 9 the second bomb was dropped on Nagasaki, two days early because of anticipated poor weather. Truman states that the delay of five days had been planned in order to give the Japanese time to consider surrender but that weather had intervened.[203] If the original objective for delaying the attack was political, it seems somewhat contradictory to modify the plan for tactical reasons. And yet the further objective of convincing the Japanese that the United States had a number of bombs, perhaps, justified moving up the attack on Nagasaki. At any rate, the decision had been made in reality long before. The original drop-date for Fat Man, August 11, had been chosen because it had been the earliest date when sufficient materials were expected to be ready. General Groves who had been convinced by Admiral William R. E. Purnell that ". . . the second blow [should] follow the first one quickly, so that the Japanese would not have time to recover their balance," decided to take the chance of the introduction of "a considerable measure of uncertainty" by ordering the bomb readied by August 8.[204] The Nagasaki strike, therefore, more likely represented the convictions of General Groves, rushing to demonstrate the atomic superiority of the United States to hasten Japanese surrender, rather than any high-level decision to give the

Japanese time to consider capitulation. It is interesting to conjecture whether the imperial decision would have been made on August 10 without the added blow on Nagasaki.

Early in the morning of August 10, United States monitoring devices picked up a broadcast from Radio Tokyo transmitting the Japanese offer to accept conditionally the Potsdam Declaration. Anticipating that an official message would soon follow, Truman assembled Leahy, Byrnes, Stimson, and Forrestal to consider a United States response.[205]

After his advisors had arrived, Truman posed the question. It was one about which they had long been arguing since, in fact, that meeting on May 29 when Grew had raised the issue of defining unconditional surrender so as to provide the Japanese the possibility of retaining their imperial system.[206]

Truman asked:

Were we to treat this message from Tokyo as an acceptance of the Potsdam Declaration? There had been many in this country who felt that the Emperor was an integral part of the Japanese system which we were pledged to destroy. Could we continue the Emperor and yet expect to eliminate the warlike spirit of Japan? Could we even consider a message with so large a "but" as to the kind of unconditional surrender we had fought for?[207]

Stimson answered first. For the past few days before the Japanese offer, he had been suggesting a lenient policy toward a defeated Japan. On August 8 he had seen Truman to record his support for issuing the scientific report on the development of the atomic bombs and had, incidentally, recommended kindness and tact in handling the Japanese surrender.[208] The next day he had spoken to Byrnes following a White House meeting at which Truman had decided to issue the scientific report. Stimson had urged the Secretary of State to deal sympathetically with the Japanese in arranging surrender. Apparently, he had met with doubtful success; for, although he believed Byrnes and Truman were in sympathy with his suggestion, he wrote, "The difficult thing is to get negotiators together and I urged very strongly on Byrnes that he should make it as easy as possible for the Japanese." [209] Now the Secretary of War reaffirmed his position. He explained that it would be to the advantage of the United States to retain the Emperor, the only authority which all Japanese acknowledged.[210] He believed that the United States should accept the Japanese note and stop the bombing.[211]

Admiral Leahy supported Stimson. He suggested that the Emperor should be retained, if only to use him in implementing the terms of surrender.[212] Leahy believed that the question of retaining the Emperor was a minor matter as compared to the possible delay of United States victory which might follow a rejection of the Japanese offer.[213]

Byrnes presented the case against Stimson and Leahy. He has stated his position in two accounts. The first indicated his unwillingness to ". . . retreat from our demand for unconditional surrender. That demand was presented to Japan before the use of the bomb and before the Soviet Union was a belligerent. If any conditions are to be accepted he wanted Japan and not the United States to state the conditions." [214] In his second account he added another argument for his position. Since both the British and the Russians had accepted the Potsdam Declaration including unconditional surrender, any retreat from that position might incur delay in obtaining their required acceptance of the United States response to the Japanese note.[215] Byrnes also pointed out the possible unfortunate domestic political results in accepting the Japanese offer. He believed that the government might be severely criticized for refusing to require unconditional surrender. He was troubled about accepting the Japanese note in view of the strong antagonism to the Emperor in the United States as a result of repeated condemnatory statements by Presidents Roosevelt and Truman. Stimson, recognizing this situation, somewhat poignantly remarked later in his *Diary*, "Now they have come to plague us." [216]

It was apparently Forrestal who suggested the compromise. The United States might accept the Japanese note, but it should state the acceptance in such terms that the intent of the Potsdam Declaration would not be violated.[217]

Truman then directed Byrnes to draft an answer which ". . . might convey such an understanding." [218] Byrnes returned with the official note from the Japanese and the answer he had drafted. Both were presented to the Cabinet at 2:00 P.M. The Cabinet approved Byrnes' note which stated in reference to the general position of the Emperor:

With regard to the Japanese Government's message accepting the terms of the Potsdam proclamation, but containing the statement, "with the understanding that the said declaration does not comprise any demand which prejudices the prerogatives of His Majesty as a sovereign ruler," our position is as follows:

From the moment of surrender the authority of the Emperor and the Japanese Government to rule the state shall be subject to the Supreme Commander of the Allied powers who will take such steps as he deems proper to effectuate the surrender terms. . . .

The ultimate form of government of Japan shall, in accordance with the Potsdam Declaration, be established by the freely expressed will of the Japanese people.[219]

Here, Byrnes had neatly straddled the issue. The implication that the Emperor might remain presumably might satisfy the Japanese. On the other hand, his control by the Supreme Commander of the Allied powers was, it was hoped, sufficient to satisfy those in the United States who opposed any concession regarding the retention of the Emperor.[220] The United States reply was transmitted to the British, Russian, and Chinese Governments for approval. The British quickly accepted it with one minor change. Chiang Kai-shek signified his concurrence on August 11 at 7:35 A.M. Although Foreign Minister Molotov for the Soviet Union attempted to delay the United States answer to the Japanese, first, by stating that it deviated from unconditional surrender, and, second, when that failed, by trying to attach delaying conditions, he ultimately accepted it on August 11. On that day it was transmitted to Japan.

In the intervening days strategic bombing and naval strikes on Japan continued. Another atomic bomb was scheduled to be dropped. General Groves, not wanting ". . . to provide any basis for later claims that we had wantonly dropped a third bomb when it was obvious the war was over," had gone to Marshall on August 9 for instructions as to the disposition of the materials for the next bomb which ". . . would be ready for delivery to the field momentarily." [221] At that time he and Marshall had decided that if there was no surrender by August 13, shipments for the third bomb would be resumed. Inasmuch as no surrender was announced and he was unable to contact Marshall or Stimson on August 13, Groves himself decided to hold up deliveries for the next bomb. Thus, as in so many instances, it was General Groves who made the immediate decisions, formerly in developing the bomb for use, now to stop its further use on Japan.[222]

The United States note of August 11 nearly led the Japanese to take action which would have prolonged hostilities. Foreign Minister Togo was informed of the broadcast version just after midnight, Japanese time, on August 12. The official text arrived from Switzerland early on August 12 but announcement of its coming was apparently held up by the Foreign Office to provide time to build its supplementary arguments.[223] In the interim at 3:00 P.M. on August 12, the Cabinet discussed the question of accepting the United States offer. Again, opposition arose because of the equivocal statements regarding the Emperor's position after surrender. Generally, the group which favored continuation of the war refused to accept the provision that placed the Emperor under the Supreme Commander of the Allied Powers during the occupation as well as the provision which indicated that the future Japanese Government be established by the will of the people.[224] The Cabinet adjourned determined to take no action until the official text had arrived. Togo was busy lining up support for acceptance from the Emperor, the Lord Privy Seal Kido, and Premier Suzuki who was undecided.

After the official reception of the United States note on August 13, the SCDW met in the air-raid shelter of the Premier's residence. The Council was divided as on August 9, three favoring acceptance and three against. After the meeting had dissolved without decision, Togo again went to the Emperor who agreed that the note should be accepted. The question was how to engineer acceptance, given the dangerous opposition of the three military representatives. An attempt in a Cabinet meeting that afternoon failed to reach the required unanimity.

On August 14, at Suzuki's instigation a joint meeting of the Cabinet and the Imperial Command met in Imperial Conference. After Suzuki outlined to the Emperor the difference which had led to their indecision the

Emperor signified in a short speech that he desired them to accept the United States offer. He concluded his remarks with these words:

I agree with the Foreign Minister that it is not intended to subvert the national polity of Japan; but unless the war be brought to an end at this moment, I fear that the national polity will be destroyed, and the nation annihilated. It is therefore my wish that we bear the unbearable and accept the Allied reply, thus to preserve the state as a state and spare my subjects further suffering. I wish you all to act in that intention. . . . I desire that the services also be made to comprehend my wishes.[225]

Late during the night of August 14, the Japanese reply was transmitted to the Allied governments. The Japanese accepted the terms proposed by the United States in its note of August 11.

To a news conference called at 7:00 P.M., Washington time, on August 14, Truman read the Japanese note announcing capitulation. He stated that General MacArthur had been named Supreme Commander to receive the Japanese surrender and that arrangements were being made to sign the surrender at the earliest opportunity. All offensive action had been suspended. The final act was played out with the signature of the surrender document by the Foreign Minister of the new Japanese Government, Shigemitsu Mamoru, at 9:04 A.M., September 2, on the battleship U.S.S. *Missouri* in Tokyo Bay. At 10:00 A.M. in Washington Truman proclaimed September 2, 1945, as V-J Day. The war with Japan was over.

NOTES TO CHAPTER 9

[1] *Potsdam Papers*, I, 142–43, includes the complete list of State Department personnel who assisted Truman.

[2] Walter Millis (ed.), *The Forrestal Diaries* (New York: The Viking Press, Inc., 1951), pp. 76–78. Lewis L. Strauss, *Men and Decisions* (Garden City: Doubleday and Company, Inc., 1962), pp. 188–89. See p. 247.

[3] Stimson, *Diary*, July 2, 1945.

[4] *Ibid.*, July 3, 1945.

[5] *Ibid.*, July 6 and July 15, 1945.

[6] *Ibid.*, July 19, 1945.

[7] Leslie R. Groves, *Now It Can Be Told* (New York: Harper and Brothers, Publishers, 1962), p. 302. See also *MED Files: Harrison-Bundy Series*, Folder #64, "S-1 Interim Committee—Potsdam Cables," which includes a handwritten note of July 6 by Harrison to himself: "Wants me to be in complete charge 'stand in my stead' and act wholly on my own during his absence." This was a note of a telephone call from Stimson on July 6.

[8] *Potsdam Papers*, II, pp. v–viii.

[9] See pp. 179–180.

[10] *Potsdam Papers*, I, 910–11. Italics are supplied.

[11] *Ibid.*, p. 915.

[12] *Ibid.*, II, 38.

[13] *Ibid.*, pp. 1299–1304; this includes the original text of the Joint Chiefs of Staff June 14 memorandum as well as changes suggested by the British.

[14] For text of redraft, *Ibid.*, pp. 1307–8.

[15] *Ibid.*, p. 272.

[16] *Ibid.*, p. 299.

[17] The minutes of this meeting are included in *Potsdam Papers*, II, 339–44. The text of the Combined Chiefs of Staff "Report to the President and the Prime Minister of the Agreed Summary of Conclusions Reached by the Combined Chiefs of Staff at the 'Terminal' Conference" appears on pp. 1462–73.

[18] See pp. 205–6. The text of the revised draft appears in the *Potsdam Papers*, I, 897–99. It is undated, and may not be the draft given to Byrnes on July 6 before he left for Potsdam.

[19] *Ibid.*, pp. 898–99. Italics are added.

[20] *Ibid.*, II, 1265–67. Stimson, *Diary*, July 16, 1945.

[21] *Potsdam Papers*, II, 36.

[22] *Ibid.*, p. 37.

[23] *Ibid.*, p. 1267.

[24] *Ibid.*, p. 1268. See pp. 206–8.

[25] Stimson, *Diary*, July 17, 1945.

[26] *Potsdam Papers*, II, 40.

[27] John Ehrman, *Grand Strategy* (London: Her Majesty's Stationery Office, 1956), VI, 291, includes the text of this minute.

[28] *Potsdam Papers*, II, 1286–69.

[29] *Ibid.*, p. 1269. Italics are those of the Joint Chiefs of Staff.

[30] See pp. 236–37.

[31] *Potsdam Papers*, II, 1269. See Leahy, *I Was There*, pp. 418–19, which indicates that the general feeling of the military was that ". . . it would be helpful and wise to explain to Tokyo that unconditional surrender did not mean the complete destruction of the Japanese Government. We were certain that the Mikado could stop the war with a royal word. This declaration was an attempt to get the Emperor on our side and to tell the Japanese that capitulation did not necessarily mean the destruction of their empire." This statement does not seem to be consistent with the Joint Chiefs' change of article (12) which was transmitted by Leahy.

[32] This is a quotation from Churchill's notes; see Ehrman, *Grand Strategy*, VI, 302–03. Parts of the citation are found in *Potsdam Papers*, II, 81. For an edited account see Churchill, *Triumph and Tragedy*, pp. 641–42. Truman only implies that the conversation took place. Truman, *Memoirs*, I, 387.

[33] See pp. 193–95.

[34] *Potsdam Papers*, II, 1270–71.

[35] *Ibid.*, pp. 1271–72.

[36] Stimson, *Diary*, July 23, 1945. "Operation" refers to the day when the first atomic bomb would be ready.

[37] Truman, *Memoirs*, I, 387. *Potsdam Papers*, II, 1275.

[38] Byrnes, *All in One Lifetime*, p. 296. Byrnes, *Speaking Frankly*, p. 206.

[39] *Potsdam Papers*, II, 1278.

[40] See pp. 261–62.

[41] Stimson, *Diary*, July 24, 1945.

[42] *Ibid.*

[43] *Ibid.* See also Grew, *Turbulent Era*, II, 1424–25, where the Acting Secretary of State later wrote of Stimson's activities: "Mr. Stimson did take energetic steps at Potsdam to secure the decision by the President and Mr. Churchill to issue the proclamation. In fact, the opinion was expressed to me by one American already in Potsdam, that if it had not been for Mr. Stimson's wholehearted initiative, the Potsdam Conference would have ended without any proclamation to Japan being issued at all. But even Mr. Stimson was unable to have included within the proclamation a categorical undertaking that unconditional surrender would not mean the elimination of the dynasty if the Japanese people desired its retention."

[44] *Potsdam Papers*, II, 1282–83.

[45] Truman, *Memoirs*, I, 390. The routine followed in handling the declaration's dissemination is included in *Potsdam Papers*, II, 1290.

[46] *Potsdam Papers*, II, 1474–76, which includes the final text.

[47] See pp. 168–69.

[48] *Potsdam Papers*, II, 1248.

[49] *Ibid.*, p. 1249. Italics are added.

[50] *Ibid.*

[51] *Ibid.*, pp. 1250–51.

[52] *Ibid.*, pp. 1253–57.

[53] *Ibid.*, pp. 1260–62.

[54] *Ibid.*, pp. 1262–64.

[55] See p. 23.

[56] Millis (ed.), *The Forrestal Diaries*, pp. 74–77; *Diary* entries July 13, 15, 24, 1945.

[57] Stimson, *Diary*, July 16, 1945.

[58] *Potsdam Papers*, II, 1266.

[59] Stimson, *Diary*, July 20, 1945.

[60] Strauss, *Men and Decisions*, p. 188.

[61] Herbert Feis, *Japan Subdued* (Princeton: Princeton University Press, 1961), p. 57, fn. 10; p. 58.

[62] See *Potsdam Papers*, I, 873, where the editors admit they are uncertain as to ". . . precise extent to which the United States Delegation at the Berlin Conference was aware of the contents . . ." of the Togo-Sato cables. They mention Truman's assertion as stemming from conversations between the President and State Department historians on January 24, 1956. No way has been found to check the President's recollection.

[63] Ehrman, *Grand Strategy*, p. 302. *Potsdam Papers*, II, 81. Churchill, *Triumph and Tragedy*, pp. 641–42. For the Stalin-Truman conversation of July 18, see *Potsdam Papers*, II, 86–87, 1587–78. The first citation includes a copy of longhand notes Bohlen made of the meeting. The second includes a memorandum which provides a reconstruction by Bohlen of his notes. The memorandum is dated March 28, 1960.

[64] Byrnes, *Speaking Frankly*, pp. 205, 262.

[65] *Potsdam Papers*, II, 1284.

[66] Byrnes, *Speaking Frankly*, p. 207, and Byrnes, *All in One Lifetime*, p. 297, offer two slightly different accounts. Apparently neither Byrnes nor Molotov were personally involved in this phone conversation.

[67] *Potsdam Papers*, II, 449 ff., contains the minutes of this meeting.

[68] *Potsdam Papers*, II, 449–50. See also Truman, *Memoirs*, I, 387. Truman's account indicates that Stalin could not be a party to the declaration ". . . since he was still at peace with Japan." It does not explain why Stalin was not consulted previous to its announcement. Truman says that he considered it desirable to inform Stalin of the decision to issue the declaration and that he ". . . spoke to him privately about this in the course of the conference meeting." The President fails to mention the date of

the meeting or to indicate Stalin's reaction. Both Stalin's and Molotov's later reactions would indicate they had not been informed. No other record has been found of Truman's conversation with Stalin; but since it was private, it is unlikely that any such account exists. Truman. at any rate, had reason to believe from the conversation between Hopkins and Stalin on May 28, 1945, that Stalin would not oppose a public modification of unconditional surrender.

[69] *Potsdam Papers*, II, 460.

[70] See pp. 244–45.

[71] *Potsdam Papers*, II, 460.

[72] Mills (ed.), *The Forrestal Diaries*, pp. 76–78.

[73] Forrestal does not specify in his *Diaries* that he showed these messages to Byrnes and Truman. Perhaps, since the Potsdam Declaration had already been issued, he felt it useless to bring up additional arguments in favor of the original form of the article referring to the Emperor. See Byrnes, *All in One Lifetime*, p. 297, for Byrnes' statement of his meeting with Forrestal. Also see Strauss, *Men and Decisions*, pp. 189 and 437, fn. 10, for a copy of Byrnes' letter to Strauss, which indicates the reasons for Byrnes' ignorance of the details of the Togo-Sato messages.

[74] Togo, *The Cause of Japan*, pp. 313–14.

[75] Many accounts of Japanese "rejection" of the Potsdam Declaration already exist. The most useful ones are the following: Butow, *Japan's Decision to Surrender*, pp. 142–49; Kase, *Eclipse of the Rising Sun*, pp. 207–11; Togo, *The Cause of Japan*, pp. 311–14. See also William J. Coughlin, "The Great Mokusatsu Mistake," *Harper's Magazine*, CCVI (March, 1953), pp. 31–40; Hasegawa Saiji, "*Review of Japan's Decission to Surrender* by Robert J. C. Butow," *Japan Quarterly*, III (January–March, 1956), 123–24. Hasegawa who was, at the war's end, head of the overseas section of *Domei*, the semi-official news agency of Japan, differs with Butow's conclusion that Suzuki's use of "mokusatsu" was the cause of the Allied assumption that Japan had rejected the Potsdam Declaration. He claims that the United States and Great Britain did not intend that Japan should accept the declaration. If this was their desire, he reasons, why didn't they deliver the proclamation through neutral diplomatic channels intead of radioing its "high-handed" words around the world so that the Japanese Government found it difficult to comply? He feels that it was the intention of the three Allies to continue the war.

[76] Butow, *Japan's Decision to Surrender*, pp. 144–45. Togo, *The Cause of Japan*, pp. 312–13. Kase, *Eclipse of the Rising Sun*, pp. 210–11.

[77] The word *mokusatsu* means literally to kill with silence. It could be variously interpreted: to take no notice; to treat with silent contempt; to ignore; to withhold comment.

[78] Coughlin, "The Great Mokusatsu Mistake," *Harper's Magazine*, CCVI, 32. This version is based on the statement of Kawai Kazuro, editor of the *Nippon Times*, an influential Japanese newspaper and semiofficial organ of the Foreign Office; it relies on his diary and his recollections of July 27 and 28.

[79] Togo, *The Cause of Japan*, p. 314.

[80] Butow, *Japan's Decision to Surrender*, p. 148. This is a translation from the Tokyo *Asahi Shimbun* of July 30, 1945. For a slightly different version, see *Potsdam Papers*, II, 1293.

[81] Butow, *Japan's Decision to Surrender*, pp. 148–49. Butow feels that, whatever Suzuki's intentions, the impact of his statement both within Japan and around the world was that Japan refused to accept the Potsdam Declaration. His ambiguity was not considered ambiguously.

[82] Truman, *Memoirs*, I, 397.

[83] *Potsdam Papers*, II, 1294–95. In Sato's wire the word "not" before "take place" was omitted, apparently in error.

[84] *Potsdam Papers*, II, 1297.

[85] Byrnes, *Speaking Frankly*, p. 208.

[86] Millis (ed.), *The Forrestal Diaries*, p. 78. Byrnes, *All in One Lifetime*, p. 297. For a somewhat different point of view, see *The Forrestal Diaries*, p. 70, which includes a later entry of March 8, 1947, describing a conversation with McCloy who stated that at Potsdam, Truman had been ". . . under the pressure of Secretary Byrnes [when] he stated his principal mission would be to get the Russians into the war against the Japs. . . ." The evidence seems to contradict this statement.

[87] Millis (ed.), *The Forrestal Diaries*, p. 78. Byrnes, *All in One Lifetime*, p. 297.

[88] Stimson and Bundy, *On Active Service in Peace and War*, p. 637.

[89] *Potsdam Papers*, II, 1322–33. This account is a paraphrase of Stimson's recommendations.

[90] Stimson, *Diary*, July 19, 1945.

[91] *Ibid.*, July 23, 1945. *Potsdam Papers*, II, 1324.

[92] Stimson, *Diary*, July 4, 1945. *Potsdam Papers*, II, 1324.

[93] Stimson, *Diary*, July 23, 1945. Some doubt of this conclusion by Stimson might arise from later statements attributed to Marshall in 1954 and 1955 by an editor of *U. S. News and World Report* who interviewed Marshall. Marshall is reported to have said that he had doubts as to the efficacy of the atomic bombs, which might lead one to conclude that he felt their possible failure might be backstopped by a Russian attack. In another vein, he is reported to have said that the Joint Chiefs of Staff had planned to use nine atomic bombs in the initial invasion of Japan. Other more reliable evidence indicates that the planning for the invasion of Japan involved no consideration of the use of the new weapons. John P. Sutherland, "The Story Gen. Marshall Told Me," *U. S. News and World Report*, XLVII (November, 1959), 50–56.

[94] Arnold, *Global Mission*, p. 598.

[95] *Ibid.*, pp. 586, 590, 598.

[96] Millis (ed.), *The Forrestal Diaries*, pp. 78–79.

[97] Eisenhower, *Crusade In Europe*, pp. 441–42.

[98] Truman, *Memoirs*, I, 411.

[98] Churchill, *Triumph and Tragedy*, p. 640.

[100] Ehrman, *Grand Strategy*, p. 292. *Potsdam Papers*, II, 276.

[101] *Potsdam Papers*, II, 1463.

[102] *Ibid.*, pp. 344–53 and 408–17, includes respectively the minutes of each of these meetings.

[103] *Ibid.*, p. 1585. The memorandum from which this has been quoted was prepared by Charles E. Bohlen in March, 1960, from longhand notes he had prepared of the original conference. Other than Bohlen's notes, no other official record of the conference exists. *Potsdam Papers*, II, 43–46.

[104] *Ibid.*, p. 1586. See also Hillman, *Mr. President*, p. 123, for Truman's *Diary* entry of July 19, 1945, on this meeting. Leahy was apparently not at the luncheon. Byrnes, *Speaking Frankly*, pp. 205–68. Byrnes, *All in One Lifetime*, p. 209.

[105] *Potsdam Papers*, II, 466.

[106] Byrnes, *Speaking Frankly*, pp. 208–9. Byrnes, *All in One Lifetime*, p. 298. Leahy, *I Was There*, p. 422, and Leahy, *Diaries*, XI, July 29, 1945, which indicate Leahy's opposition to this move. He wrote: "I do not believe that the President should place us under a permanent obligation that would be attached to such a request. The British and ourselves are fully capable of defeating Japan without assistance."

107 Text of Truman's letter appears in *Potsdam Papers*, II, 1333–34; see also Truman, *Memoirs*, I, 402–4. Truman claims that after consultations with the British and his advisers he felt there was no question that the Russians would enter the war under these provisions whether requested to do so or not.

108 *Potsdam Papers*, II, 1334.

109 Leahy, *Diaries*, XI, July 17, 1945.

110 *Ibid.*, July 28, 1945.

111 *Ibid.*, July 31, 1945.

112 A number of accounts of the Trinity test of Fat Man at Alamogordo are available. The most useful are included in Herbert Feis, "The Secret that Traveled to Potsdam," *Foreign Affairs*, Vol. XXXVIII (January, 1960), 300–17, which includes a copy of Groves' July 18 memorandum; Groves, *Now It Can Be Told*, pp. 288–304; Richard G. Hewlett and Oscar E. Anderson, Jr., *The New World, 1939/1946* (University Park: The Pennsylvania State University Press, 1962), pp. 376–80; William L. Laurence, *Dawn Over Zero: The Story of the Atomic Bomb* (New York: Alfred A. Knopf, Inc., 1946), pp. 179–95; William L. Laurence, *Men and Atoms* (New York: Simon and Schuster, Inc., 1959), pp. 123–33; *Potsdam Papers*, II, "Grove's Memorandum for the Secretary of War," July 18, 1945, 1361–68; and *Thoughts by E. O. Lawrence*, pp. 1369–70.

113 *MED Files: Harrison-Bundy Series*, Folder #98, "Interim Committee Log."

114 *MED Files: Harrison Bundy Series*, Folder #64, "S-1 Interim Committee—Potsdam Cables." The file contains copies of this and following messages. *Potsdam Papers*, II, 1360.

115 *MED Files: Harrison-Bundy Series*, "S-1 Interim Committee—Potsdam Cables." See also Harvey H. Bundy, "Remembered Words," *The Atlantic Monthly*, CXCIX (March, 1957), 57, in which Bundy reports that Stimson remarked to McCloy and him after he had heard of the test at Alamogordo: "Well I have been responsible for spending two billions of dollars on this atomic venture. Now that it is successful I shall not be sent to prison in Fort Leavenworth."

116 Stimson, *Diary*, July 16, 1945. *Potsdam Papers*, II, 1360, fn. 2. William Hillman, *Mr. President*, p. 284, quotes Truman to the effect that he ". . . went into immediate conversation with Byrnes, Stimson, Leahy, General Marshall, General Arnold, General Eisenhower, and Admiral King. [He] asked for their opinion whether the bomb should be used. The consensus of opinion was that the bomb should be used." The log of the President's trip contains no notice of such a meeting on July 16; see *Potsdam Papers*, II, 10–11. See also Truman, *Memoirs*, I, 415, where the President recalls that Stimson flew to Potsdam the next day to bring him the details, and that he then called in Byrnes, Leahy, Marshall, Arnold, and King to consider use of the weapon. Eisenhower is not mentioned in this account. No mention is made of the meeting in Dwight D. Eisenhower, *Crusade in Europe*, p. 443, which indicates that Eisenhower had no part in the decision. No reference to this meeting appears in the Leahy *Diaries* or in Leahy, *I Was There*. See also Byrnes, *Speaking Frankly*, p. 262, in which the Secretary of State indicates that he cannot recall the circumstances under which Stimson brought the news; and Byrnes, *All in One Lifetime*, where no mention is made of these events. In Arnold, *Global Mission*, p. 584, the General recalls a dinner party on July 16 attended by Stimson, Byrnes, the JCS, and Truman, which lasted from 7:30 P.M. to 9:30 P.M. He does not mention a discussion of use of the atomic bomb. On the other hand the log of the President's trip fails to mention the dinner party that evening, but does indicate that Truman ate with Stimson, Marshall, King, and Arnold the next evening. Craven and Cate (eds.), *The Army Air Forces in World War II*, V, between

pp. 712 and 713, includes a photocopy of a letter from Truman to the authors written on January 12, 1953, in which he outlines the steps in his decision. He mentions that a meeting including Byrnes, Stimson, Leahy, Marshall, Eisenhower, King, "and some others" was called, but he does not indicate its date. See also King and Whitehill, *Fleet Admiral King: A Naval Record*, p. 621, where it is indicated that Marshall and Arnold were called to Stimson's villa on July 16 as soon as Stimson had received word of the test. The Admiral does not mention his participation. Finally, see Compton, *Atomic Quest*, p. 245, where Truman recalled to Compton that "when the full account reached him" several days after July 16 he called a meeting of the JCS to give his assent to use. From this mass of confusing evidence it has been concluded that such a meeting was called at a later date, but that it probably did not include Eisenhower, and, perhaps, neither King nor Leahy.

117 Stimson, *Diary*, July 17, 1945. *Potsdam Papers*, II, 1266.

118 Stimson, *Diary*, July 17, 1945. Churchill's argument against disclosure referred to disseminating information, not to disclosing the weapon through its use. Apparently Attlee was not told of the successful test until Truman informed him on August 1; see *Potsdam Papers*, II, 1375, and Lord Attlee, "The Hiroshima Choice," *The Observer*, September 6, 1959, p. 16.

119 Churchill, *Triumph and Tragedy*, pp. 637–38. Churchill writes that Stimson laid before him a sheet of paper on which was written, "Babies satisfactorily born." This phraseology has not been discovered in any of Harrison's messages. Apparently it originated with Stimson.

120 *MED Files: Harrison-Bundy Series*, Folder #64, "S-1 Interim Committee—Potsdam Cables." *Potsdam Papers*, II, 1360–61. Highhold was the name of Stimson's home on Long Island; and Harrison's farm was located in Upperville, Virginia.

121 Stimson, *Diary*, July 18, 1945. *Potsdam Papers*, II, 1361. The "meeting" mentioned here is probably the Potsdam Conference rather than a specific hearing.

122 Churchill, *Triumph and Tragedy*, pp. 640–41; see also *Potsdam Papers*, II, 79–82.

123 *MED Files: Harrison-Bundy Series*, Folder #64, "S-1 Interim Committee—Potsdam Cables." See also Groves, *Now It Can Be Told*, p. 303.

124 *Potsdam Papers*, II, 111.

125 *Ibid.*, pp. 1155–57, which includes the text of this document entitled, "Reflections on the Basic Problems Which Confront Us."

126 Stimson, *Diary*, July 19, 1945.

127 See pp. 262–63.

128 Stimson, *Diary*, July 21, 1945.

129 *MED Files: Harrison-Bundy Series*, Folder #64, "S-1 Interim Committee—Potsdam Cables." Stimson, *Diary*, July 21, 1945.

130 *MED Files: Harrison-Bundy Series*, Folder #64, "S-1 Interim Committee—Potsdam Cables." *Potsdam Papers*, II, 1372. Stimson's "pet city" was Kyoto.

131 *MED Files: Harrison-Bundy Series*, Folder #64, "S-1 Interim Committee—Potsdam Cables." *Potsdam Papers*, II, 1372.

132 *MED Files: Harrison-Bundy Series*, Folder #64, "S-1 Interim Committee—Potsdam Cables." *Potsdam Papers*, II, 1372.

133 Stimson, *Diary*, July 22, 1963. *Potsdam Papers*, II, 1373.

134 Stimson, *Diary*, July 22, 1945. *Potsdam Papers*, II, 225. Italics are supplied.

135 Churchill, *Triumph and Tragedy*, p. 638.

136 Harvey H. Bundy, "Remembered Words," *The Atlantic Monthly*, CXCIX (March, 1957), 57.

137 Churchill's is the only account of this meeting. Italics are supplied; Churchill, *Triumph and Tragedy*, pp. 638–39. Leahy and Marshall may not have been present. The

log of the President's trip indicates that only Churchill and Truman participated in the discussion. *Potsdam Papers*, II, 17.

138 Truman, *Memoirs*, I, 419. Italics are supplied.

139 *Potsdam Papers*, I, 941–42.

140 King and Whitehill, *Fleet Admiral King: A Naval Record,* p. 621. Leahy, *I Was There*, p. 441.

141 King and Whitehill, *Fleet Admiral King: A Naval Record*, p. 621. Arthur Bryant, *Triumph in The West* (Garden City: Doubleday and Company, Inc., 1959), p. 368. This latter account is based on the *Diaries* of Field-Marshal Lord Alanbrooke, Chief of the Imperial General Staff. It is Alanbrooke's contention that the British Chiefs of Staff were not consulted.

142 Arnold, *Global Mission*, p. 589.

143 Stimson, *Diary*, July 22, 1945.

144 *MED Files: Harrison-Bundy Series*, Folder #64, "S-1 Interim Committee—Potsdam Cables." See also Fletcher Knebel and Charles W. Bailey, II, *No High Ground* (New York: Harper and Brothers, Publishers, 1960), pp. 95–96, in which the authors indicate that Spaatz himself originated the final directive to use the bombs by refusing to do so without written authorization. No other evidence has been found to substantiate this allegation.

145 Stimson, *Diary*, July 23, 1945.

146 *MED Files: Harrison-Bundy Series*, Folder #64, "S-1 Interim Committee—Potsdam Cables." *Potsdam Papers*, II, 1373.

147 Both of these cables appear in *MED Files: Harrison-Bundy Series*, Folder #64, and *Potsdam Papers*, II, 1372.

148 *Ibid.*, p. 1372.

149 Stimson, *Diary*, July 23, 1945.

150 Arnold, *Global Mission*, p. 589.

151 Arnold, *Global Mission*, p. 590.

152 Stimson, *Diary*, July 23, 1945.

153 Groves, *Now It Can Be Told*, pp. 308–9. Complete text included.

154 *Ibid.*, p. 309. Groves' cable also is included in *MED Files*, Folder #27 , 5a, tab c.

155 *MED Files: Harrison-Bundy Series*, Folder #64. "S-1 Interim Committee—Potsdam Cables."

156 Stimson, *Diary*, July 24, 1945.

157 Herbert Feis, "The Secret That Travelled To Potsdam," *Foreign Affairs*, pp. 300–17.

158 Truman, *Memoirs*, I, 416.

159 Byrnes, *Speaking Frankly*, p. 263. Byrnes, *All in One Lifetime*, p. 300, includes a slightly different account. In this work, Byrnes mentions that Truman was accompanied by Bohlen, Truman's interpreter, and that he had apparently heard Truman say substantially, "You may be interested to know that we have developed a new and powerful weapon and within a few days intend to use it against Japan." Byrnes also records that he watched Stalin's expression as Truman's statement was being interpreted and that he ". . . was surprised that he smiled blandly and said only a few words." Later in the car Truman told Byrnes that Stalin had said that he hoped Truman would ". . . make good use of it against the Japanese." Later, in 1956, Truman also recalled that Bohlen had been with him when he informed Stalin of the bomb. When questioned about the matter in 1960, Bohlen denied he had been a party to the conversation. See *Potsdam Papers*, II, 378, fn. 2.

160 Leahy, *I Was There*, p. 429.

161 Churchill, *Triumph and Tragedy*, p. 669–70.

[162] M. J. Ruggles and A. Kramish, *The Soviet Union and the Atom: The Early Years* (Santa Monica: The Rand Corporation, 1956), p. 21. This work is a detailed study of the development of nuclear energy research in the Soviet Union.

[163] *Ibid.*, p. v.

[164] *Ibid.*, p. 29.

[165] *Ibid.*, pp. 30–31.

[166] Victor Kravchenko, *I Chose Freedom* (New York: Charles Scribner's Sons, 1946), p. 426. Kravchenko was an official of the Soviet Purchasing Commission in Washington who defected to the United States on April 3, 1944.

[167] *Ibid.*, p. 426.

[168] Ivan Krylov, *Soviet Staff Officer* (London: The Falcon Press, 1951), p. 267.

[169] *Ibid.*, pp. 267–68.

[170] A number of works have been concerned with this activity. Perhaps, the most valuable are: David J. Dallin, *Soviet Espionage* (New Haven: Yale University Press, 1955), pp. 453–70; Alan Moorehead, "Traitor Klaus Fuchs: He Gave Stalin the A-Bomb," *The Saturday Evening Post*, CCXXIV (May 24, 31; June 7, 14, 1952); Francis Noel-Baker, *The Spy Web: A Study of Communist Espionage* (London, The Batchworth Press, 1954); *The Report of the Royal Commission to Investigate the Facts Relating to and the Circumstances Surrounding the Communication, by Public Officials and Other Persons in Positions of Trust of Secret and Confidential Information to Agents of a Foreign Power* (Ottawa: Edmond Cloutier, Printer to the King's Most Excellent Majesty, Controller of Stationery, 1946); U. S. Congress, House, Committee on Un-American Activities, *Report on Soviet Espionage Activities in Connection with the Atomic Bomb*, 80th Cong., 2d sess., (Washington: 1948); and U. S. Congress, Senate, Committee on the Judiciary, *Testimony of Former Russian Code Clerk Relating to the Internal Security of the United States* (Washington: 1955). Despite its somewhat lurid title, Moorehead's article seems to be a careful review of Fuch's activities.

[171] Moorehead, "Traitor Klaus Fuchs," *The Saturday Evening Post*, May 31, 1952, p. 70.

[172] Groves, *Now It Can Be Told*, pp. 144–45.

[173] Moorhead, "Traitor Klaus Fuchs," *The Saturday Evening Post*, pp. 70, 72.

[174] *Ibid.*, p. 72. Moorehead provides no source for this information. Other accounts which corroborate various details of this general review appear in: "The Case of the World's Greatest Secret," *Life Magazine*, XXIV, (April 16, 1951), 53-6; *The New York Times*, February 5, 11, March 2; "Spies in U. S. Told Russia All," *U. S. News and World Report*, XXX (April 6, 1951).

[175] Groves, *Now It Can Be Told*, p. 141.

[176] U. S. Congress, House, Committee on Un-American Activities, *Report on Soviet Espionage Activities in Connection with the Atomic Bomb*, p. 163. This was Groves' testimony.

[177] *Stimson Papers*. This memorandum of the conference was found in one of two loose-leaf files of letters and memoranda.

[178] U. S. Congress, House, Committee on Un-American Activities, *Report on Soviet Espionage Activities in Connection with the Atomic Bomb*, p. 163.

[179] Craven and Cate (eds.), *The Army Air Forces, in World War II*, V, 712–13. Truman's letter of January 12, 1953 to Professor Cate is the source of this quotation.

[180] *Ibid.*, pp. 696–97. Between these pages there is a photocopy of the directive from Hardy to Spaatz. Italics are supplied.

[181] See p. 261.

[182] Groves, *Now It Can Be Told*, pp. 311–12.

[183] Craven and Cate (eds.), *The Army Air Forces in World War II*, V, 696–97.

184 Stimson, *Diary*, July 28, 1945.

185 Groves, *Now It Can Be Told*, p. 311. This cable was sent on July 31, Tinian time.

186 *Potsdam Papers*, II, 1375. *MED Files: Harrison-Bundy Series*, Folder #64, "S-1 Interim Committee—Potsdam Cables."

187 *MED Files: Harrison-Bundy Series*, Folder #74.

188 *Ibid.*, Folder #64, "S-1 Interim Committee—Potsdam Cables."

189 *Potsdam Papers*, II, 1375, fn. 1.

190 Lord Attlee, "The Hiroshima Choice," *The Observer*, September 6, 1959.

191 Stimson, *Diary*, August 2, 1945.

192 Groves, *Now It Can Be Told*, pp. 310–11. See also *MED Files: Harrison-Bundy Series*, Folder #64, "S-1 Interim Committee—Potsdam Cables," which includes possible corroborating evidence in the form of an undated, unsigned, and undirected memorandum attached to a cable from Marshall to MacArthur on August 12, 1945, informing him that General Groves had ordered scientific groups to investigate results of bombing of Hiroshima and Nagasaki. The covering memorandum was printed in pencil, probably by Groves, on a memorandum form that went into use after June 1, 1946. It reads: "This message from Marshall to MacArthur clearly indicates that Gen. [*sic*] Groves made the decisions regarding the bomb and Gen. [*sic*]. Marshall effectuated them." Since Groves had custody of these files for a considerable period of time after World War II, this memorandum seems to be Groves' later comment on his own function.

193 Craven and Cate (eds.), *The Army Air Forces in World War II*, V, 712–13.

194 *MED Files: Harrison-Bundy Series*, Folder #64, "S-1 Interim Committee—Potsdam Cables."

195 Stimson, *Diary*, August 4, 1945.

196 Togo, *The Cause of Japan*, p. 317.

197 This account is based on Butow, *Japan's Decision to Surrender*, pp. 150–78; Kase, *Eclipse of the Rising Sun*, pp. 222–39; and Togo, *The Cause of Japan*, 314–21.

198 Text appears in Butow, *Japan's Decision to Surrender*, p. 244.

199 Text appears in *Public Papers of the Presidents of the United States: Harry S. Truman, 1945*, pp. 197–200.

200 *Public Papers of the Presidents of the United States: Harry S. Truman, 1945*, p. 200.

201 Truman, *Memoirs*, I, 425.

202 See William Hardy McNeill, *America, Britain, and Russia: Their Cooperation and Conflict, 1941–1946* (London: Oxford University Press, 1953), p. 637, fn. 2, where McNeill cites a work by Kalinov, *Les Maréchaux soviétiques vous parlent*, pp. 245–46, to indicate that ". . . the Russian invasion of Manchuria was accelerated on orders from Moscow, received 3 August, giving warning of the impending Japanese surrender." See also Deane, *Strange Alliance*, pp. 276–77, for his opinion that the atom bomb hastened Soviet action. He also makes interesting comments on the lack of interest the Russian people showed toward the war against Japan. It obviously was not a "national" war, but one quickly entered to secure additional political positions in the Far East before Japan surrendered.

203 Truman, *Memoirs*, I, 426. See Craven and Cate (eds.), *The Army Air Forces in World War II*, V, 718.

204 Groves, *Now It Can Be Told*, pp. 341–42.

205 Truman, *Memoirs*, I, 427–28. See also Millis (ed.), *The Forrestal Diaries*, p. 83, where Forrestal indicates in his *Diary* citation of August 10 that, in addition to those mentioned by Truman, the Director of the Office of War Mobilization, John Snyder; Captain James K. Vardaman, Jr., the President's Naval Aide; and Major General Harry H. Vaughn, Truman's Military Aide, also attended.

206 See p. 202.

207 Truman, *Memoirs*, I, 428.

208 Stimson, *Diary*, "Memo of Conference with Pres.," August 8, 1945.

209 *Ibid.*, August 9, 1954.

210 Truman, *Memoirs*, I, 428.

211 Stimson, *Diary*, August 10, 1945; Millis (ed.), *The Forrestal Diaries*, p. 83.

212 Truman, *Memoirs*, I, 428.

213 Stimson, *Diary*, August 10, 1945.

214 Byrnes, *Speaking Frankly*, p. 209. Byrnes had been presented with a statement of Grew's opinion on this matter on August 7. Grew, of course, had taken a line similar to that of Leahy and Stimson; see Grew, *Turbulent Era*, II, 1438–40.

215 Byrnes, *All in One Lifetime*, p. 305.

216 Byrnes does not emphasize this latter point. However, see Millis (ed.), *The Forrestal Diaries*, p. 83, and Stimson, *Diary*, August 10, 1945.

217 Millis (ed.), *The Forrestal Diaries*, p. 83; Truman, *Memoirs*, I, 428.

218 Truman, *Memoirs*, I, 428.

219 Text appears in Butow, *Japan's Decision to Surrender*, p. 245.

220 Among those who took this stronger view against the retention of the Emperor were Archibald MacLeish, Dean Acheson, and Harry Hopkins; Stimson, *Diary*, August 10, 1945. Also Hanson Baldwin, Fiorella La Guardia, Carlos Romulo, Senators McMahon, Russell, Fulbright, McClellan, Taylor, and White, and General Claire Chennault, among others, see *IPR Hearings*, Part 9, pp. 3069–70.

221 Groves, *Now It Can Be Told*, pp. 352–53.

222 *Ibid.*, p. 353.

223 Butow, *Japan's Decision to Surrender*, p. 193. Kase, *Eclipse of the Rising Sun*, p. 241, and Togo, *The Cause of Japan*, pp. 323, claim the note arrived on August 13.

224 Togo, *The Cause of Japan*, p. 327. Butow, *Japan's Decision to Surrender*, pp. 193–208. Kase, *Eclipse of the Rising Sun*, pp. 240–58.

225 This is, in part, Togo's version; see Togo, *The Cause of Japan*, p. 334. A different and extended version based on other accounts appears in Butow, *Japan's Decision to Surrender*, pp. 207–8. No transcript has been available.

CHAPTER 10

INTERNATIONAL POLITICS, MORALITY AND NUCLEAR WEAPONS

THE atomic bombs had exploded, the Soviet Union had entered the war, Japan had capitulated, and World War II had ended. In analyzing the significance of the decision of the United States Government to use the atomic bombs, it is necessary to consider the milieu in which the action was taken, not only in its specifics but also in its generalities. First, the decision was made within the framework of the political pressures of the international system of states. Second, the decision reflected the, perhaps, unique approach to that system by the United States. Third, the decision resulted from a number of uncertainties within the United States Government about the immediate international situation within which the United States operated. And fourth, but by no means least, the decision to use the bombs reflected the characteristics of the decision-making process within that complex administrative structure of the United States Government during the latter months of World War II. Each of these elements of the political situation of the summer of 1945 contributed to the decision to use the nuclear weapons.

In August, 1945, the United States Government acted within the international system of states. That system was characterized by the sovereign independence of its components, a legalism which reflected the fact that men emotionally identified primarily with the nation-states within which they lived. The focus of human loyalty was the nation-state. Throughout its existence the system had witnessed the growth of a variety of firmly held national creeds. Such nationalisms frequently projected their ethical, legal, and political opinions and practices to the world as examples of the universally right and desirable. Nationalism was not only the emotional basis for internal union but also, at times, the intellectual rationalization for imperial expansion. Each such creed in each such sovereign state tended to develop among its faithful both the conviction of its intrinsic rightness and the self-satisfying assurance of the wrongness of conflicting nationalisms. Thus, the world was politically organized into a number of units with different capabilities and with different national value systems, but with similar beliefs in the moral superiority of their respective systems.

The decentralized nature of this political system carried with it the threat of violence and, as the weapons men used became more efficiently deadly, of annihilation. Each government in each state depended upon itself or its allies for its continued existence. Since that existence was the basis for satisfying the interests of its individual citizens and groups, it was of greatest importance to each that the state be preserved. Death for the individual was preferable to the elimination of the state. No higher entity with sufficient power existed to preserve the state. Only by maximizing its power within the limits of its capabilities, considered in the broadest sense, could a government reasonably insure the continuity of its state, the highest goal of most of its people.

As governments continuously tried to satisfy the needs of their peoples against threats from without, some, more dynamic than others, inevitably followed policies of expansion into the territories of states from which there was a potential threat. Widespread support developed in such governments for the concepts that it was safer than not to attack the possible enemy before it could strike and that it frequently was necessary to expand into the areas of states of lesser power in order to satisfy strategic needs reflecting the threat from potential enemies, either real or imagined. Thus, either in a global sense or in a more limited geographical sense, states found their enemies in other states with conflicting interests. As each maximized its power to offset such threats, it became a potential threat to the others. There was no protective international organization with the power to obviate the threat. The United States Government in 1945 was operating in a world of international semianarchy.

Certain factors tended to reduce this anarchy among states. With the growth of technological knowledge, the improvement of communication and transportation, and the increase in international social and economic relationships, there developed a growing interdependence as individuals, groups, and governments recognized that some of their interests transcended national lines. And yet, particularly during times when national survival was threatened, this international interdependence became less the basis for a developing cosmopolitanism than the symbol of a foreign corruption of the purity of the national creed and, therefore, a threat to the national entity.

As such international contacts, nevertheless, increased during periods of relaxed political tension, it became convenient for governments to accept rules of international law based frequently on assumed international ethical standards, but more usually upon the practice of states. Such rules, sanctioned by the implicit or actual consent of the governments of the various states, were generally followed because it was convenient from the standpoint of national interest to do so. However, the objectives of the international system of law and the ends of international ethics, when filtered through the screen of national interpretation, became the preservation of the nation-state rather than the maintenance of either the law or the ethical norm. In fact, quite regularly, the rules of international law and the norms of international morality were utilized as the rationalizations under which governments, either sincerely or insincerely, justified the political moves they felt called upon to make in order to achieve their highest goals, the preservation or enhancement of the nation-states they represented.

Among the conventional and customary rules of international law were those which outlawed certain of the more inhumane weapons which the ingenuity of men placed at the service of governments. Dumdum bullets and poison gas were outlawed; and certain techniques of land, sea, and aerial warfare were generally considered to be impermissible. The major premise upon which such conventions rested was one which had been stated in the Hague Convention of 1907 to the effect that, "The right of belligerents to adopt means of injuring the enemy is not unlimited." [1] Possibly from this general principle and from the various conventional and customary rules either banning use of specific weapons or limiting specific acts of war, it might be asserted that the use of nuclear weapons was illegal. Since the effects of these weapons were indiscriminate in their application to all within a relatively large blast area, and since their intent, if they were to be widely used, was to destroy enough of the enemy population to cause its surrender, the employment of such weapons presumably was not "unlimited" in the general sense of the Hague Convention.

Despite, however, the apparent legal reassurance to be derived from such reasoning, the international situation in the summer of 1945 followed years of massive bombardment from the air. The rules of warfare, although followed when convenient, were frequently violated by all parties when the exigencies of their military situations demanded it. Each government still extolled the rules of international law, utilized the law's provisions to justify the military actions it felt called upon to undertake, and did what it felt had to be done to preserve the national entity. The highest goal of governmental action was the preservation of the nation-state. If the rules of international law promoted that end, they would be followed. If the norms of international morality furthered that goal, they would be accepted.

Such was the ingenuity of men and the ambiguity of the law and the norms of morality, that acts undertaken solely to enhance the political situation of a state were readily and, perhaps, sincerely described as moral and legal. In their own eyes, most men who governed judged the means they used to preserve the state as justified. There were no immoral or illegal governments acting during World War II, at least as each judged its own actions.

In the final analysis, the choices of action that were made during the war were not made for humanity; and they were not made to preserve the populations of enemy states. They were made for the preservation of each state itself during a period of intense danger when the continuity of the state was seriously threatened. This is not to say that certain men did not rebel on moral grounds against choosing what to them were immoral alternatives in certain situations. Most, however, were able to justify even an obviously inhumane act on the grounds that the destructiveness and horror of war must be ended and that humanity as a whole, both the defeated and the victorious, would benefit from the success of the victor. The evaluation of the moral quality of the resultant political situation remained the function of the victorious government.

This, then, was the nature of the international political situation within which the United States Government acted to utilize the nuclear weapons against Japan. The Japanese had, in the view of the United States, participated in a number of immoral and illegal actions from the time of Pearl Harbor throughout the war. Now, in the summer of 1945, under an authoritarian praetorianism it was persistently fighting on, attempting to arrange a negotiated peace which might maintain the foundations upon which it could again build a military power with which it might threaten the interests of the United States. The symbol of that authoritarianism was the Emperor, the god-human, whose position was maintained by means of a political-religious myth spread among the Japanese people by Japan's warlords to satisfy their own ends. It would be doing a service to the Japanese people to eliminate the Emperor and to introduce some sort of a popularly chosen regime. It would be doing a service to humanity to end the present war, despite the fact that some

Japanese might be killed in the effort. It would be satisfying the demands of international law and morality to promote quickly and by all possible means an Allied victory.

Such rationalizations did not necessarily indicate hypocrisy. They reflected, however, the requirements of the United States, as its government interpreted them, in the international system of states. They reflected the need to guarantee the security of the United States in a world where only this country's power might do so. It, therefore, seems somewhat superfluous and irrelevant to either condemn or to praise the use of the atomic bombs in terms of the norms of international morality or the rules of international law. These were generally supported only at times when the security of the United States was not endangered, at times other than those reflecting the uncertainties and dangers of World War II.

The decision to use the atomic bombs by the United States Government not only reflected the nature of the international system of states, it also resulted, in part, from the characteristic, if not unique, manner in which the United States had generally envisioned that system. Its approach had frequently been both moralistic and utopian.

The United States Government moralized throughout World War II as it generally had in its international relationships of war or peace. It tended to see the political antagonist or the military enemy as intrinsically bad, and its government was not above preaching to such foes in terms of the conventional United States political morality. Since other states reflected different political cultures they frequently failed to measure up to United States ideals. During peace, therefore, when the antagonist was presumed to represent an immoral, unprincipled force, the United States Government found it difficult to accept compromises. During war, the enemy, widely thought to be evil and deadly, must be stamped out as a political force. It must be forced to unconditional surrender.

The policy of unconditional surrender followed toward Germany and Japan during World War II was, in fact, a manifestation of such moralizing. Despite possible military and political advantages that might be gained from modifying its application against Japan, it proved to be very difficult to change significantly. Too long had the United States Government proclaimed the evils of the Japanese. They would be forced to surrender for their own good, without compromise. The Emperor, the symbol of an untrustworthy, hated government, must go. Many in the United States thought his retention would be a negation of the very objectives for which the United States had fought. It was significant that both in the Potsdam Declaration and in the United States note of August 11, the terms included the promise that following the war a government would be established in Japan which would reflect the "freely expressed will of the Japanese people." [2] Almost universally within the United States Government it was assumed that this method of selection by the Japanese would suit their political and cultural needs and, thus, be attractive. This was, however, the provision that created most hesitancy within the Japanese Government before it decided to surrender. To those in that government, and probably to most Japanese, the fear that this technique might be the excuse for the establishment of a republic to replace the divine monarchy made it difficult to accept. And yet the United States Government, moralizing from its own experience, presumed that a system similar to its own might be similarly attractive to the Japanese.

This tendency on the part of the United States to moralize in considering international relations was accompanied by an inclination to accept somewhat utopian solutions to international problems. Wars were widely considered to be aberrations in the orderly course of international politics. When they occurred, they were fought by the United States for objectives which, in practice, were hardly accomplishable. Wars were fought to bring peace, to save the world for democracy, or to establish a world peace under international organization. The assumption was frequently accepted that all that was required was to eliminate the threat from authoritarians, whether they were the monarchs of the Central Powers during World War I or the dictators and Emperor of the Axis Powers during World War II, in order to bring a lasting peace among the victorious "democracies." This feeling was at least publicly strong among those high in the United States Government who had had considerable experience in formulating its foreign policy. Little recognition was given to the historic fact that wartime coalitions of states tended to split apart following wars as the victorious allies found new threats in each other. This was particularly so when they obliterated the power of the wartime enemy. In the power vacuum thus created one or both of the allies quickly exerted power in the search for a new defensive or offensive position against its present danger, the former ally. This was, of course, occurring in Europe and the Middle East during the summer of 1945 and was soon to occur in East Asia. Ultimately unconditional surrender was to require of the United States that it extend its power to Japan and to certain of the offshore islands of Asia, as well as to the Asiatic mainland in Korea and North China, in order to forestall possible Russian expansion into those areas. Peace was not to be established in the absolute sense. The result would rather be a readjustment of political relationships reflecting the postwar distribution of power.

Another characteristic of the United States approach to international politics during World War II was its emphasis on the role of the military in policymaking. Somewhat to Churchill's dismay, this United States approach lasted long after he felt there was any doubt as to ultimate Allied victory. Often when he suggested political considerations which might delay military success, he was accused of obstruction at best and, at worst, of unjustified efforts to reestablish the British Empire. The military approach was obvious in Roosevelt's efforts to delay a political settlement in Europe until after the war had been won. There seemed to be little recognition of the probability that the distribution of military force at the end of the war would roughly reflect, in areas of strategic interest to the victorious Allies, the pattern of power on which a *de facto* if not a *de jure* settlement would be based.

The reliance on the military approach in conducting United States foreign policy also created a certain inflexibility in the choice of possible alternatives of action. The final criterion for judging a suggested policy was usually stated in terms of the question: will this action help to win the war quickly? It was left to the period after the enemy had surrendered to answer the question: what political goals should be sought? The end of action was victory. What was to occur after that would be decided during the period of peace. An illustrative statement of this position has been written to describe Stimson's point of view at the time the bomb was used:

Stimson believed, both at that time and later, that the dominant fact of 1945 was war, and that therefore, necessarily, the dominant objective was victory. If victory could be speeded by using the bomb, it should be used; if victory must be delayed in order to use the bomb, it should *not* be used. So far as he knew, this general view was fully shared by the President and all his associates. The bomb was thus not treated as a separate subject, except to determine whether it should be used at all; once that decision had been made, the timing and method of the use of the bomb were wholly subordinated to the objective of victory; no effort was made, and none was seriously considered, to achieve surrender merely in order not to have to use the bomb. Surrender was a goal sufficient in itself, wholly transcending the use or nonuse of the bomb.[3]

It seems worth pointing out that both the tactical decision as to the timing and method of using the bombs and the decision as to whether they should be used at all were based on military considerations. It might also be asked why was surrender "a goal sufficient in itself?" Would not the use of the atomic bombs possibly generate political repercussions of even greater importance than a surrender which, within varying estimates of time, was practically a foregone conclusion? Although such questions were considered, they fell beneath the weight of the predisposition to accept the military concept that the end of war is victory. Decisions generally failed to reflect the consideration that victory would merely signify a new international political relationship.

The military approach caused the United States Government to concentrate on relatively short-range rather than long-range goals. The military dealt with today rather than with tomorrow. This is not to say that there was no long-range military planning, for there was. But such plans were limited by their logical termination—the end of the war. Plans for the military defeat of Japan did not progress beyond the anticipated date for Japan's surrender. It was reasonable that military planners looked primarily to the immediate problems of battle; for if these were not solved, there would be neither the need nor the chance to solve the political problems likely to occur later. It was understandable that the military approach was essentially conservative, that it depended on weapons it had rather than on those it hoped to have, and that it doubted the possibility of achieving surrender of the enemy until it had achieved complete military victory. A curious concomitant of these characteristics seemed to be the predisposition to believe that the long-range plans, developed over a considerable period of time, at various levels of military authority, had almost a predictive quality. Thus, what was planned for the future became part of the framework for determining what might be done in the present as if the plans represented not merely estimates of the future but reality itself. When policy was formulated within the straitjacket of planning, it reflected the choice of one of a limited number of alternatives within the vision of the planner. The elements of the plan became the criteria for reality and the limitations on policy. What *might* happen became what was *likely* to happen or what would happen and determined what *should* happen.

Add to its moralizing, to its utopianism, to its reliance on the military approach in time of war, the essential and general belief of the United States that it was intrinsically right. This feeling of rightness was, perhaps, the outgrowth of the feeling of uniqueness arising from the geographic separation from Europe which, among other things, so long permitted the United States to act almost unrestricted by European power; from the puritanical sense of moral superiority to the societies so recently left behind; and from the belief, reflecting a preoccupation with internal affairs and minimal contact with other states of the world, that the hypocrisies and subterfuges of international politics were not for the United States. At times these attitudes led the United States to believe that it might withdraw from international politics to escape defilement. Usually such attitudes produced an equation between the line of policy the United States was following and the will of God. This latter relationship, of course, cannot be disproved. But the tendency was to assume it rather than to demonstrate a rational basis for the presumption. Military actions of the United States were frequently seen as the instruments of the Creator which He utilized to bring peace through United States victory. Even in war, it was felt, the people of the United States were intrinsically peace-loving. Even when dropping an atomic bomb the United States government was proving its desire for peace.

These general attitudes of the United States toward the international system of states, toward the character of peace and war, and toward the United States' relationship with other states, strongly conditioned the decision to use the atomic weapons. United States victory would bring a new and better life to Japan and a lasting peace under the United Nations, as well as an end to the slaughter of Japanese people. Anything that might be done, therefore, to hasten such victory was desirable. Nuclear weapons were to be used to save the Japanese nation and the Allied soldiers from the horrors that had been planned for them from conventional bombardment and invasion. To win the war was to rid the world of a major danger to peace by eliminating the unprincipled military regime in Japan. If the war was to be won quickly, the bombs must be used. And yet underlying this reasoning, well recognized among the top policymakers but not widely publicized among the people, was a certain realism, a certain response to the anticipated postwar political situation. For the use of the bombs to hasten the end of the war would also provide an opportunity for the flow of United States power into the vacuum left in Japan before the Soviet Union could expand the power it might develop from potential military successes. Expansion of Russia's power might be cut off almost before it began. United States policy was, thus, characterized by a blend of realism in action and idealism in exposition.

So, in part, the decision to use the atomic bombs reflected the requirements of the United States in the international system and, in part, it reflected the characteristic United States approach to the requirements of that system. It also reflected the specific evaluation of the United States Government of the military and political situation it found itself in with respect to Japan and the Soviet Union in the Far East.

This evaluation was based on a variety of uncertain and in some ways erroneous assumptions in regard to Japan. The major and overriding assumption was that the Japanese were likely to resist to national obliteration before accepting Allied terms of surrender. While it was true that some Japanese were so prepared to act and that others were being conditioned by their government to act similarly, it was also true, and even recognized by some in the United States, that Japanese morale was low, that the Japanese had, in the past, been known to surrender when the fight no longer seemed worth the effort, and that the Japanese were disillusioned with their wartime leadership. Although censorship and propaganda used by his government made it difficult for the average Japanese to know how the war was developing, the spring and summer of 1945, which brought incendiary bombs, attacks by carrier aircraft, and a tightening naval blockade, generally demonstrated the decline of Japanese military capability to resist. The general United States acceptance, however, of the propaganda which the Japanese Government issued to demonstrate the willingness of the Japanese to resist to the death created the general impression that conventional weapons would successfully bring surrender only after a long and costly war.

In addition to the misunderstanding involved in the overestimation of the Japanese will to resist, the United States also imperfectly understood the needs of the peace group within the Japanese Government. When United States spokesmen called for unconditional surrender and when they promised the obliteration of the Japanese polity, they strengthened the group in the

Japanese Government which wished to resist. As a result of many public pronouncements from the United States, this faction found ready-made evidence that the United States intended to obliterate Japan. Under this persuasion many Japanese *would* resist to the death. Under this persuasion, efforts by the peace group to seek a settlement looked like treason and might become the justification for their assassination or incarceration.

United States attitudes toward Russia were also based on imponderables. During the war the United States had been allied with the Soviet Union— which continued to follow a hated and dynamic ideology—against Germany, a state which had produced an even more hated and more immediately threatening ideology. Reactions to this wartime alliance differed among those in the United States Government. Some still considered the Soviet Army, despite the alliance of necessity, to be the spearhead of a menacing communism and thought every move of the Soviet Union outward along its borders to be evidence of its effort to communize the world. Some, at the other extreme, looked on Soviet-American cooperation during the alliance, such as it was, as the forerunner of a brighter future between the Soviet Union and its Allies. They wished to trust the good faith of the Soviet Union, to do nothing during the war to disturb the amicable relationship that existed, and to ensure cooperation in the creation of a postwar international organization. Apparently few, like Stimson, considered the Soviet Government to be motivated, at least in the short run, by considerations of power and thus amenable to persuasion and compromise. Even he, however, believed that ultimately democratic and authoritarian societies would prove to be basically incompatible; and he had little hope for a fruitful postwar association with the Soviet Union.

Then, as now, the difficulties involved in determining the motivation of Russia's policy plagued the United States Government. At that time the Soviet Union had expanded its power into Eastern Europe and was negotiating with Nationalist China for the acquisition of certain political rights in Manchuria. The United States Government was uncertain as to whether such expansion represented a Soviet effort to acquire limited strategic positions primarily necessary for the defense of Russia, on the one hand, or on the other hand, to promote the communization, first, of Western Europe and the Far East and then of the world. The insecurities of the nation-state system as well as the ideological pretensions of the Soviet Government led the United States to assume the worst and to conclude that the primary motivation of Soviet action lay in the dictates of communism. Thus, even while the United States, to encourage Soviet participation in the war against Japan, was following through with the Yalta agreements which promised Soviet concessions in Manchuria, Sakhalin, and the Kuriles, it did so with growing concern about future Soviet expansion which might threaten both the traditional United States policy of the Open Door and the maintenance of a favorable distribution of power in East Asia. These uncertainties concerning Soviet intentions when coupled with the difficulties of determining the response of Japan influenced the United States Government's decision to use the atomic bombs. The United States attempted to resolve these immediate political difficulties within the requirements of its security in the nation-state system as it interpreted its role in that system. The most attractive alternative was to attend to first things first when faced with a variety of future perplexities. The most attractive alternative was to win the war, to achieve a satisfying victory quickly, and to resolve such political problems later.

Within its general security requirements, within its traditional approach to foreign policy, and within its uncertainty as to the existing political-military situation, the United States Government reached the decision to use the atomic bombs on Japan. But that decision was affected more, perhaps, by certain characteristics of the United States political system itself. The governmental structure rested, first, on a large and complicated administrative apparatus which had grown somewhat unpredictably and inconsistently during the war. Second, it was characterized by a somewhat irrelevant method of choosing a Vice-President. Third, it provided no suitable means of assuring that the Vice-President would be prepared to assume the office of President. And, fourth, even during a war in which the powers of the President had been used extensively, it provided for a legislative-executive relationship which strongly conditioned the development of its policy. Each of these characteristics was to affect the decision to drop the atomic bomb.

During World War II, governmental agencies mushroomed in Washington. Many traditional agencies like the Department of State, the Department of War, and the Department of the Navy grew to such a size that their subdivisions were scattered among a number of widely separated buildings. A number of new organizations such as the Office of Price Administration, the Office of War Information, the Office of Strategic Services, the Office of War Mobilization, and the Office of Defense Transportation, to name but a few, had been established to fill specific wartime needs, sometimes with little clear definition of their relationship to the traditional agencies.

The governmental structure that Harry S. Truman took over as President suffered many of the administrative difficulties of large size and unplanned organization. Frequently there was a breakdown in communications horizontally within the governmental structure itself and vertically from it to the President. The structure suffered from an inertia produced by the need for complex interdepartmental consultations. There was the additional problem of coordinating the activities of the many operating agencies. This was particularly so during the spring of 1945. Roosevelt, at best an artist as an administrator, had never been much interested in administrative detail. He had relied on his somewhat formidable personal capacity and the advice of a few advisers to handle the diplomacy of the war; and frequently he had operated somewhat out of touch with key agencies, particularly with the Department of State. Interested in greater problems, he had left the difficulties of administration—except in the personal or political sense—to be solved by others or not at all. Now, however, Roosevelt was dead, and Truman was President. Immediately there was a jockeying for position close to the new President both by those within the administration who wished to improve their situations or promote their ideas and by those, not formerly part of the government, who now envisioned opportunities resulting from real or imagined past relationships with Truman. The President consequently operated within a general administrative confusion. But all within the government was not confusion; one agency, the Manhattan Engineer District, under able administration, continued to fulfill its function efficiently. It had developed its own built-in momentum; it was guided by expert hands.

Perhaps one of the gravest difficulties the new President faced was in obtaining adequate information upon which to base his decisions, particularly those involving foreign and military affairs. Soon after he had taken office, Truman was informed by Secretary of State Stettinius that Roosevelt had regularly received a two-page daily summary of important diplomatic developments. Truman asked Stettinius to continue the practice and to send him:

. . . an outline of the background and the present status of the principal problems confronting this government in its relations with other countries. These written reports, along with material from other departments and the Joint Chiefs of Staff . . . were immensely helpful in filling gaps in [his] information. In fact, they were indispensable as aids in dealing with many issues, and from the first [he] studied them with the greatest care.[4]

In this way he received information from the Department of State, from the Joint Chiefs of Staff, and from certain other departments. But, quite naturally, most of this information reflected generally accepted points of view and led to a continuation of Roosevelt's policies. Information suggesting changes in direction frequently failed to reach him. Information, for instance, suggesting the changing conditions in Japan existed within the administration. It is questionable that it reached the President.

Here, of course, one is dealing in areas of probability. And yet the evidence indicates that much information concerning the conditions within which the atomic bombs were used never or, at best, seldom reached the President or those at the top who advised him.

There seems to be no doubt, for instance, that the President, Byrnes, and Stimson knew of the exchanges between Foreign Minister Togo and Sato, the Japanese Ambassador to Moscow, in which the two diplomats attempted to arrange for Russian mediation. And yet it is unclear as to whether any of the three had seen all of the messages at least until Forrestal showed them to Byrnes on July 28. It is significant that Byrnes was so new in office and so preoccupied with problems in Europe that he only reviewed these exchanges in detail at that time. Whether later Sato-Togo messages were seen by Truman and Byrnes has not been determined. At any rate, given the predisposition of the United States Government to believe in a prolonged Japanese struggle, it was reasonable, even if the messages were seen, to give greater emphasis to Togo's frequent refusal of unconditional surrender than to his search for some sort of settlement which would approximate unconditional surrender.

It also seems doubtful that the work of the Foreign Morale Analysis Division, which outlined with detailed accuracy the disillusionment and reduced morale among the Japanese civilian population, ever got beyond the Office of War Information to which it was sent. This work would have substantiated the conclusion of Naval Intelligence that the Japanese were looking for an acceptable means of surrender. And yet it is unclear as to whether such conclusions were ever transmitted beyond Forrestal to Truman. That the recommendations of many of the scientists at the Metallurgical Laboratory at the University of Chicago were sent from Stimson's office either to the Interim Committee or to Truman in time to influence their decisions seems highly doubtful. And the disposition of a variety of studies by the Office of Strategic Services, which indicated among other things the growing difficulties of the Japanese economy and the advantages of associating the Emperor with a move for peace, is unclear.[5] No indication has been found that Truman ever saw such information. And one has the feeling that much of the information available at various levels in the government which portrayed a far more realistic view of the Japanese situation than that held at the top never reached those responsible for the decision to use the nuclear weapons. Of course, Grew's point of view regarding the Emperor was presented to the President from time to time both by the Acting Secretary of State and by Stimson. If it had been substantiated by other supporting intelligence, it might have prevailed. Again, however, one lapses into conjecture.

It seems generally conclusive, however, that considerable information relevant to the decision to use the atomic bomb never reached Truman, largely because of the nature of the United States governmental apparatus. He, himself, has commented cogently on the administrative situation within which he operated:

Strange as it may seem, the President . . . was not completely informed as to what was taking place in the world. Messages that came to the different departments of the executive branch often were not relayed to him because some official did not think it was necessary to inform the President. The President did not see many useful cables and telegrams that came from different American representatives abroad.[6]

Even as such information failed to reach the President in the spring and summer of 1945, General Groves was going ahead as he had been ordered, producing his new weapon for use.

In addition to certain problems of administrative size and organization, the decision to use the bombs resulted, in part, from the method by which the United States nominated its Vice-Presidents and from the relationship that frequently developed between the President and the Vice-President. As was customary and politically expedient, the Vice-Presidential candidate was chosen by the Democratic convention of 1944 primarily to balance the ticket, to give it a broader appeal than it would otherwise have had, and to appease contesting factions within the party. Other more knowledgeable, more experienced candidates than Truman were ready to accept the position. It is true that the Vice-Presidency did not usually attract such hopefuls since, barring the President's death, it had frequently been a dead end for politicians. And yet in 1944, various personal estimates of Roosevelt's possibly failing health led to a spirited contest. These other candidates were not, however, thought by the party leadership to be so generally acceptable as Truman. The Senator from Missouri, therefore, became the candidate. With all due regard for Mr. Truman, it cannot be said that he was prepared for the Presidency, particularly for the handling of foreign affairs. His previous activities had generally involved domestic politics at the national and state levels. On becoming President he was forced to deal with a variety of complicated and delicate problems concerning foreign affairs for which he had had little experience.

His inexperience, at least in part, reflected the general relationship which usually developed between the President and Vice-President in the United States system of government. The influence and activities of the Vice-President depended almost completely on the actions of the President. In this case, Roosevelt did not consult Truman on matters of foreign or military policy and helped to create a situation where his sudden death left the handling of United States policy to an inexperienced and relatively ignorant man. It must be stated, however, that Truman made every effort to eliminate that ignorance. But burdened by a number of more immediate political problems, it is doubtful that he was able to devote much time to what to him appeared primarily a military and technological problem, the use of the atomic bombs.

The relationship between the administration and the Congress also influenced, although uncertainly, the decision to drop the bombs. Particularly sensitive to congressional disapproval if it resulted in a reduction in appropriations, the administration acted as diligently as possible to justify the expenditures it incurred. The construction of the bombs and the production of their fissionable material had been accomplished only as a result of considerable unexplained costs. The technique of obtaining appropriations on these terms had been highly irregular and had required secrecy both from officials in the administration and from leaders of the Congress. The political imagination of certain administrators involved in the project was reasonably staggered by the possibility that the physicists might be incorrect in their anticipations. If it had proved to be impossible to construct a bomb despite the tremendous amounts devoted to the program, the halls of Congress might very well have echoed and reechoed with angry denunciations of the war's greatest boondoggle. One need not make too much of this. It hardly seems likely that the bombs were used merely to justify an expenditure. And yet this was probably a consideration in quickly testing and using them. Their successful use turned what might have been a political liability into what was undoubtedly a great political asset. What a demonstration of administrative foresight that, as a result of conducting a large and novel program throughout the war, atomic bombs had been produced just in time to effect the surrender of Japan! The timing could hardly have been more fortuitous.

Mr. Truman, therefore, acted under a number of general and specific conditions in finally sanctioning the use of the weapons. That decision represented the influence of the system of nation-states, the United States role in that system, its government's evaluation of the Japanese and Russian imponderables, and the very nature of the government itself and the President's position within it.

Within this milieu, a number of more specific forces immediately influenced President Truman's decision. Among these were factors affecting Truman's position at the Potsdam Conference. He had just heard that an atomic weapon had been successfully exploded and that two others would be ready by early August. Although he had known nothing about the Manhattan Engineer District prior to becoming President, he now knew something of the magnitude of its plant, of the expenditure that had been made for its efforts, and of the numbers and importance of the men who had been involved. Throughout the war, stimulated by the fear of prior German success, these men had devoted a considerable part of their lives to develop an atomic weapon. At least from the time the program came under the control of the War Department, the weapon had been developed for use. All activities of the Manhattan Engineer District had aimed at building it for use. And a squadron of specially modified bombers had been prepared to carry it to Japan. Now, following this tremendous effort, bombs had been built, the planes were ready, and the targets had been chosen. All of these actions were taken within the War

Department by Stimson, Marshall, or Arnold, and frequently initiated by Groves. There was no need for Truman to make positive decisions to ready the weapon. These decisions were rapidly and efficiently made for him.

Bear in mind, also, the nature and position of the President when he came to power. Relatively new to national politics and completely new to administrative responsibilities at the national level, he had been abruptly elevated from a position of some prestige and little influence to what was probably the most powerful, complicated administrative position in the world. Moderate, considerate, humble, and intelligent, he had recognized his limitations and had decided to rely on those who had worked with Roosevelt to continue Roosevelt's policies for winning the war. Roosevelt's aides were men of considerable stature, force of character, and prestige. It would have been extremely difficult for Truman to have opposed their recommendations, even if he had known what they had been doing and even if he had wanted to do so. It seems unlikely that either of these conditions existed. He had been predisposed to follow Roosevelt's policies. He had been reasonably inclined to follow the advice of the men who had worked to implement those policies. There had been, therefore, no change in the Manhattan Engineer District's general directive after Truman had become President even though the threat of Germany had soon been eliminated. The bombs, when developed, were still to be used.

Consider, next, that Truman had been advised by the Interim Committee, a group of eminent scientists and government officials, to use the weapon on a military-civilian target as soon as possible. This recommendation undoubtedly had considerable influence on Truman's ultimate decision. The Interim Committee's advice, however, must be considered in terms of the committee's character and its actions. It was true that it was an interdepartmental committee with representation from the Navy Department, from the State Department, and from the Department of War. But it operated under the Secretary of War who had hand-chosen its members. All of them except William L. Clayton from the Department of State and Ralph A. Bard from the Navy Department had been personally connected with the development of the weapon. Scientists were represented, but with the exception of Fermi, who with Szilard had been instrumental in developing the first chain reaction, those on the committee were scientists responsible for the administration of the program. Furthermore, it seems that the discussion in the committee of use of the weapons was initiated almost accidentally. The item had not appeared on its agenda and was given very little of the committee's time. Among other responsibilities it had what was considered to be a more important obligation, the development of a method to administer the program after the war had ended. The committee was in a real sense the Secretary of War's committee. It advised him to use the weapon. Inasmuch as he had come to this conclusion separately, he informed the President of both his and the committee's recommendations. More realistically, however, Stimson chose individuals for the committee who were not apt to oppose use of the weapon. Furthermore, they were advised by Marshall who maintained a conservative view as to how long the war with Japan would last and by Groves who was building the weapon. They received no advice from the more optimistic officers of the Navy or Air Force. Even as the committee sat, the War Department was going ahead with preparations for the weapon's use.

Consider also the policies which the United States had followed toward Russia and Japan in the Far East through most of the war. For years this government had sought Russian entrance into the war against Japan. Such an agreement had been negotiated at Yalta in February, 1945. Only shortly after Truman became President had doubts begun to grow concerning the need for Russian help. Despite such uncertainties, which by late July, 1945, were widely held, most of the United States delegation at Potsdam felt that Russia would enter the war whether or not the United States withdrew its request. Furthermore, a withdrawal might be looked upon by the Soviet Union as a means of evading the obligations accepted at Yalta and might provoke the unrestricted advance of Russian power beyond the limits of its concessions. It might also undercut the bargaining position of the United States vis-à-vis the Soviet Union in Europe; for already the United States was accusing Stalin, intent on solidifying his control of Eastern Europe, of violating the agreements he had made at Yalta. On the surface then the United States continued to support Russian intervention which was accepted as an inevitability; and yet it does not follow that this country desired the Russians to intervene. In massing their troops on the Siberian border, they were already fulfilling the military task assigned to them, that of neutralizing the Japanese forces in Manchuria. And yet, recognizing that a Russian move was almost inevitable, it still made sense to use the nuclear weapon in an attempt to end the war with sufficient speed in order to minimize the expansion of Soviet influence in Korea, North China, and the Japanese Islands.

Not only was Truman saddled with a practically defunct Russian policy in the Far East, but he was also restricted by the emotionally charged, well-propagandized policy of requiring Japan to surrender unconditionally. Despite the fact that even at the higher levels of the United States government some believed that Japan would capitulate on conditions favorable to the United States, the Japanese steadfastly refused to consider a forced change in their imperial system. This created a serious obstacle to a change in unconditional surrender, for the Emperor was widely considered in the United States as a symbol of expansionary Japanese militarism which the United States had committed itself to eradicate. Moreover, since Japan was considered to have started the war by the attack on Pearl Harbor, it did not satisfy a widespread desire for revenge to treat Japan more leniently than Germany which had been eliminated as a power factor in Europe. Finally, conditional surrender did not satisfy the military's desire for victory. In the opinion of many, it would provide Japan with the opportunity to rise again as a threat to the United States. Therefore, although Truman might have hoped, as did some, that clarifying unconditional surrender in the Potsdam Declaration might bring about a rapid Japanese surrender, he was unwilling to specify concessions regarding the Emperor, both because of the resultant antagonism which could be expected from the United States people and from his government, and also because of his evaluation of the position of the Emperor in the Japanese system.

Consider, additionally, the military evaluation of the state of the war against Japan. It might very well last through most of 1946. It would very likely result in considerable casualties and much expense. And it might result in the obliteration of much of what was Japan. Accepting these serious predictions, it made sense from a humanitarian point of view to use the atomic weapons now available in two swift blows which might be expected to stop the bloodshed. It was true that a considerable number of Japanese would be killed, but their lives might be reasonably sacrificed to the cause of peace.

As important, perhaps, as any of these factors was the fact that the bombs existed. Their use had long been planned. The products which had taken so much effort were now available to be tested in battle against a hated enemy representing much that was considered evil. Their use would be a demonstration of the success of the program. Their testing would be done under conditions best calculated to evaluate the impact of blast. Already a team of experts was being readied to send into Japan to evaluate their effects.

The weapons were ready; the planes and crews were prepared. Japan refused to surrender unconditionally, and the long, bloody war seemed likely to continue. The Soviet Union, increasingly intractable in Europe, was about to enter the war in the Far East where its prolonged involvement against a shrinking Japanese Empire might provide it a new and dangerous position of strength. All those who advised the President supported the Interim Committee's recommendation which favored the bomb's use. And there was Harry S. Truman, a Missouri politician, farmer, and onetime businessman, steeped in many of the traditional oversimplifications of the United States approach to international politics, a new and uncertain President, a humble man, by most accounts a moral man, a man who wanted to be a strong President. He did not have to give the order to drop the bombs; that had already been done. He could have ordered the operation stopped. To him, there was no reason to do so. The bombs were dropped.

This action by the United States has been criticized on both moral and political grounds. It is difficult to accept the reasonableness of the moral criticisms. Among these, perhaps, the most frequently asserted is that the use of the bombs on urban communities where they killed indiscriminately was inhumane. And yet, the previously accepted and frequently used mass conventional bombings over Japan and Germany had caused a similar result. They had merely been less efficient. By that late period of World War II such actions were common. They were also planned for future operations against Japan. Within that frame of reference, as unfortunate as it might have been, and within the theoretical uncertainties as to the level of destruction which might be expected from the atomic bombs, it probably seemed no serious moral deviation to use the weapons. With the well-developed understanding that the productivity of a nation was directly connected with its ability to resist, and with the knowledge that particularly in Japan the pattern of productivity was spread widely among small private producers in urban communities, the rationale for mass bombing had been developed.[7] The distinction between civilian and military targets had approached the vanishing point as war became total. Certainly the distinction was no longer understood by Truman who wrote:

> In deciding to use this bomb I wanted to make sure that it would be used as a weapon of war prescribed by the laws of war. That meant that I wanted it dropped on a military target. I had told Stimson that the bomb should be dropped as nearly as possible upon a war production center of prime military importance.[8]

The Interim Committee suggested that the targets purposefully be dual targets including military and civilian establishments. From the expected shock to the civilian population, the Japanese Government might be led to accept unconditional surrender to avoid a reapplication of the horror. It was expected to understand the futility of resistance. Of course, the United States also had its moral argument—that the immediate destruction of lives and property would, in the long run, save lives by shortening the war. Although there may be some doubt that such would be the result, no one could prove the contrary. On the other hand, that reasoning was built on the assumption that the predicted fact which was never to happen would inevitably have been the fact if the bombs had not been dropped. This, too, was beyond demonstration.

Truman and Stimson and others involved in the decision were humane individuals. They had humanity's interests at heart in describing their actions, and yet except in a very general sense their accounts evaded the major point. Those who participated in making this decision were operating near the end of the world's greatest war neither in the interests of humanity as a whole nor of Japanese humanity specifically. They acted primarily for the humanity of the United States. It was frequently said and widely believed that for them any number of enemy dead was preferable to the death of one United States citizen. They were operating in the interests of the United States and only incidentally in the interests of humanity when the two could be served by the same action. This is not to say that their action was morally justified under existing ethical norms. It does indicate that, perhaps, quite sincerely they found moral rationalizations for their actions in terms of the national value system which they were acting to preserve.

Closely associated with this moral complaint is another criticism frequently stated that, granting the justification for the bombing of Hiroshima, there was no moral basis for so quickly attacking Nagasaki before the Japanese Government had time to react. Again this criticism overlooks the rationale under which the bombs were dropped. They were used to end the war quickly by convincing the Japanese that resistance was futile. Two were dropped in close temporal proximity to create the illusion that the United States had a stockpile of such weapons. Such action was morally justifiable since it aimed to save lives by shortening the war. The fact is, the use of the two bombs was looked upon as one operation; and only tactical considerations involved in preparing the bombs and in assuring suitable weather governed the timing of the second drop. The moral justification for the first covered the moral requirements for the second.

A third moral criticism which verges on the political asserts that the use of the atomic weapons was completely unnecessary as the Japanese Government was prepared to surrender before the bombs were dropped; and the United States Government knew it. It seems likely that Truman, Byrnes, and Stimson had heard of Japanese efforts to negotiate peace. Because of their unofficial nature, in the case of attempts through Sweden and Switzerland, and because of the ambiguity of the language of the Togo-Sato exchanges, the United States Government did not think that these efforts were either representative of the Japanese Government or indicative of Japan's willingness to accept unconditional surrender.

Certainly there was a recognizable split in the Japanese Government between the peace group and the group desiring to carry on the war. Certainly the Emperor had aligned himself unofficially with the former. And yet, to bring about the final capitulation, a catalyst was necessary to eliminate the resultant indecision by providing the Emperor with the justification for action. That catalyst may have been the atomic bombs. As Butow has written:

The atomic bombing of Hiroshima and Nagasaki and the Soviet Union's declaration of war did not produce Japan's decision to surrender, for that decision —in embryo—had long been taking shape. What these events did do was to create that unusual atmosphere in which the theretofore static factor of the Emperor could be made active in such an extraordinary way as to work what was virtually a political miracle.[9]

On the other hand, it may have been Russian intervention marking the end of Togo's efforts to obtain Russian mediation that caused Japan to surrender.

It must be remarked, however, that, even if Japan had surrendered following Russian involvement and a war of perhaps greater duration, the postwar political position of the United States in the Far East might have been worsened by a possible expansion of Soviet power. Again, the decision to drop the atomic bombs was essentially political or tactical, despite the moral terms in which it has been described. Evidences of possible Japanese capitulation, such as they were, were interpreted in terms of the military evaluation of the state of war, in terms of anticipated postwar political relationships, and in terms of the needs of the developing atomic bomb program and the administration's domestic situation.

The most telling criticism of United States policy toward Japan was that which objected to the inflexible interpretation of the policy of unconditional surrender. That policy was based on the military concept of complete victory. Barring total annihilation of the enemy, however, it was recognized that surrender always occurred on conditions established by the victor. The public pronouncement of such a policy to a nation as strong in its nationalism as Japan might very well prolong the war. Despite the fact that many officials, both in the military and in the government, recognized this situation, the policy had been so strongly enunciated that it proved to be difficult to modify. Any change in its interpretation, it was feared, might bring unfortunate political repercussions for the administration.

But more than this, the cause of unconditional surrender was believed in by many who wanted to eliminate Japan as a threat to United States interests in the Far East and by others who believed with some feeling that Japan was representative of evil and that the power behind that evil should be stamped out. Any modification of unconditional surrender, particularly in regard to the Emperor, was considered by many to be tantamount to a compromise with evil, to an abrogation of right principle, and to a surrender of the very object for which the United States had been fighting. There is no guarantee that the Japanese would have surrendered conditionally. And yet the evidence that exists indicates that, had the unconditional surrender formula been modified significantly, it is very likely that Japan would have surrendered, perhaps before the atomic weapons were used, on terms which would have been advantageous to the United States.

The political consequences of utilizing the atomic bombs are difficult to evaluate because this action was not the only cause of the developing postwar antagonism. Some have said that the use of the bombs, in effect, was the first act in the cold war since their purpose was to obtain for the United States a political position in the Far East to offset possible Russian threats.[10] It seems certain that the desire to counteract the expansion of Soviet power in the Far East was an element of the motivation for using the atomic weapons. But it seems to be too simple to call their use either the first act or the cause of the cold war. For, as a matter of fact, the antagonism between the

Soviet Union and the Western Powers had already begun to develop before the bombs were used. Just as the United States, in this case, was maneuvering for position in the Far East, so the Soviet Union had already obtained positions of strength in Eastern Europe. The contest to develop respective positions of strength for the postwar political struggle was quite recognizable before August of 1945. The bombs' use was only one among many actions which led to the postwar confrontation between the United States and the Soviet Union.

The current nuclear armaments race has been attributed to the demonstration of the power of the atomic weapons on Hiroshima and Nagasaki. This position, it seems, rests on the erroneous assumption that the Soviet Government had practically no knowledge of the potentialities of the weapons at that time, and that it was forced to speed up its efforts to develop comparable weapons once it recognized that the bomb was available. The evidence seems to indicate, however, that Soviet scientists had already acquired much, if not all, of the theoretical knowledge necessary for developing a weapon and that Stalin probably knew of the nature of the United States weapon before it was used. Given the tenets of the communist ideology, given the emerging conflict of interest between the Soviet Union, on the one hand, and the United States and Great Britain, on the other, it seems reasonable to believe that the Soviet Government would have exerted considerable energy to develop a similar weapon whether or not the bombs had been dropped.

Similarly the argument that the use of the bombs, insofar as this act threatened the mutual trust which existed among the Allies, undercut the chances of effective postwar international organization seems inconclusive. This approach, in effect, condemns the use of the atomic weapons for their destructive impact on a changing international political pattern which was leading to world order. It seems, however, that the United Nations had never been based on mutual trust and that it was essentially a device within which the techniques of nationalism were expected to be practiced in the interests of the states which were members of the organization. It is true that some foresaw the development of world peace through the international organization. But practicing statesmen were not generally among this group. They were intent on satisfying more immediate national aspirations. It does not seem that the promotion of a successful United Nations would have been changed materially one way or the other had the bombs not been dropped.

Only symbolically can the use of the atomic bombs be said to have caused definable moral consequences. The morality of total war had already been sanctioned by the requirements of national security. The use of the atomic weapons symbolized the acceptance of total war and provided the precedent for their possible use by other governments. Given the insecurities inherent in the international system of states, given the apparently overriding concern of men to preserve their nations' existence, it seems that no precedent would be needed for the future use of nuclear weapons. Their magnitude presently has become so overwhelming, their ownership so distributed, that they have introduced an element of stability into relationships among states possessing such weapons. And yet this element of stability has only placed limits on the degree of international antagonism. And such limits are not absolutely restrictive. Nuclear weapons may again be used.

The decision to use the atomic bombs, then, reflected a complex of domestic and international political forces affecting the United States Government. It was based on political rather than moral grounds, although the action was described sincerely, perhaps, in moral terms. Their use symbolized as, perhaps, no other act has, the bankruptcy of the nation-state system which justifies with national morality the moral abomination of total war. And yet men in nations hold most dearly their national myths. Men in nations react violently to changes in national prerogatives. And men in nations appear resolved to live in such units within the foreseeable future. The key to peace lies in establishing the basis for accommodation among the interests of the various states. It does not lie in unconditional surrender for a national enemy. It does not lie in total war and the use of nuclear weapons.

NOTES TO CHAPTER 10

[1] Nagendra Singh, *Nuclear Weapons and International Law* (London: Stevens and Sons, Ltd., 1959), p. 147.

[2] Robert J. C. Butow, *Japan's Decision to Surrender* (Stanford: Stanford University Press, 1954) pp. 243–45.

[3] Henry L. Stimson and McGeorge Bundy, *On Active Service in Peace and War* (New York: Harper and Brothers, 1948) 629–30.

[4] Harry S. Truman, *Memoirs* (Garden City: Doubleday and Company, Inc., 1955), I, 14.

[5] U. S. Office of Strategic Services, R. and A. Branch: *Japan: Winter 1944–1945,* Current Intelligence Study Number 19, (Washington: May 18, 1945); and *Japan— Conflicting Political Views,* Number 3216, (Washington: July 23, 1945). The originals of these and other OSS studies are now available in the Library of Congress.

[6] William Hillman, *Mr. President* (New York: Farrar, Straus and Young, 1952), p. 14.

[7] Robert C. Batchelder; *The Irreversible Decision, 1939–1950* (Boston: Houghton Mifflin Company, 1962), pp. 170–89, contains a clear exposition of the development of the technique of mass bombing.

[8] Truman, *Memoirs,* I, 420.

[9] Butow, *Japan's Decision to Surrender,* p. 31.

[10] P. M. S. Blackett, *Fear, War and the Bomb: Military and Political Consequences of Atomic Energy* (New York: McGraw-Hill Book Company, Inc., 1949), pp. 127–43. Norman Cousins and Thomas K. Finletter, "A Beginning for Sanity," *The Saturday Review of Literature,* XXIX (June 15, 1946), 5–9, 38–40.

Bibliography

ARTICLES

Atkinson, Brooks. "The Vast Job in the Vast Pacific." *The New York Times Magazine* (May 13, 1945).

"Atomic Bombs and the Postwar Position of the U. S. in the World." *Bulletin of the Atomic Scientists,* Vol. III (December, 1947).

Attlee, Lord. "The Hiroshima Choice." *The Observer* (September 6, 1959).

Baldwin, Hanson W. "This is the Army We Have to Defeat." *The New York Times Magazine* (July 29, 1945).

"Before Hiroshima." *Bulletin of the Atomic Scientists,* Vol. I (May 1, 1946).

Brukes, Austin M. "With the Atomic Bomb Casualty Commission in Japan." *Bulletin of the Atomic Scientists,* Vol. III (June, 1947).

Bundy, Harvey H. "Remembered Words." *The Atlantic Monthly,* Vol. CXCIX (March, 1957).

"The Case of the World's Greatest Secret." *Life,* Vol. XXIV (April 16, 1951).

Chamberlain, John. "Washington in June," *Life,* Vol. XVIII (June 11, 1945).

Compton, Arthur H., and Daniels, Farrington. "A Poll of Scientists at Chicago, July 1945." *Bulletin of the Atomic Scientists,* Vol. IV (February, 1948).

Compton, Karl T. "If the Atomic Bomb Had Not Been Used." *The Atlantic Monthly,* Vol. XLXXVIII (December, 1946).

Contemporary Japan. Vol. XIV (January-December, 1945).

Coox, Alvin. "The Myth of the Kwantung Army." *Marine Corps' Gazette,* Vol. XLII (July, 1958).

Coughlin, William J. "The Great Mokusatsu Mistake." *Harper's Magazine,* Vol. CCVI (March, 1953).

Cousins, Norman, and Finletter, Thomas K. "A Beginning for Sanity." *The Saturday Review of Literature,* Vol. XXIX (June 15, 1946).

Feis, Herbert. "The Secret That Traveled to Potsdam." *Foreign Affairs,* Vol. XXXVIII (January, 1960).

Frisch, O. R. "Physical Evidence for the Division of Heavy Nuclei under Neutron Bombardment." *Nature Supplement,* CXLIII (February 18, 1939).

Goudsmit, S. A. "How Germany Lost the Race." *Bulletin of the Atomic Scientists,* Vol. I (March 15, 1946).

Hasegawa, Saiji. "Review of Japan's Decision to Surrender by Robert J. C. Butow." *Japan Quarterly,* Vol. III (January-March, 1956).

Laurence, William L. "The Atom Gives Up." *The Saturday Evening Post Treasury.* (New York, Simon and Schuster, 1954.)

Moorehead, Alan. "Traitor Klaus Fuchs: He Gave Stalin the A-Bomb." *The Saturday Evening Post,* Vol. CCXXIV (May 24, 31; June 7, 14, 1952).

Morison, Samuel Eliot. "Why Japan Surrendered." *The Atlantic Monthly,* Vol. CCVI (October, 1960).

Morton, Louis. "National Policy and Military Strategy." *The Virginia Quarterly Review,* Vol. XXXVI (Winter, 1960).

———. "Soviet Intervention in the War with Japan." *Foreign Affairs,* Vol. XL (July, 1962).

———. "The Decision to Use the Atomic Bomb." *Foreign Affairs,* Vol. XXXV (January, 1957). This article appears also as Chapter 23 in Greenfield, Kent Roberts, ed., *Command Decisions.* Washington, Office of the Chief of Military History, Department of the Army, 1960.

"Russia and the Atomic Bomb." *Bulletin of the Atomic Scientists,* Vol. I (February 15, 1946).

Smith, Alice Kimball. "Behind the Decision to Use the Atomic Bomb: Chicago, 1944-45." *Bulletin of the Atomic Scientists,* Vol. XIV (October, 1958).

"Spies in U. S. Told Russia All." *U. S. News and World Report,* Vol. XXX (April 6, 1951).

Steiner, Jesse F. "Can Japan's Millions Take It Till the End?" *The New York Times Magazine* (July 15, 1945).

————. "Shall We Bomb Hirohito's Palace?" *The New York Times Magazine* (March 11, 1945).

Stimson, Henry L. "The Decision to Use the Atomic Bomb." *Harper's Magazine*, Vol. CXCIV (February, 1947).

Sutherland, John P. "The Story Gen. Marshall Told Me." *U.S. News and World Report*, Vol. XLVII (November 2, 1959).

Szilard, Leo and Walter H. Zinn, "Instantaneous Emission of Fast Neutrons in the Interaction of Slow Neutrons with Uranium." *Physical Review*, LV (April 15, 1939). *New York Times*, January, 1945—August 15, 1945.

Zinn, Howard. "A Mess of Death and Documents." *Columbia University Forum*, Vol. V (Winter, 1962).

BOOKS

Allen, James S. *Atomic Imperialism*. New York: International Publishers, 1952. Allen is the pen name for Sol Auerbach.

Alperovitz, Gar. *Atomic Diplomacy: Hiroshima and Potsdam*. New York: Simon and Schuster, Inc., 1965.

Amrine, Michael. *The Great Decision: The Secret History of the Atomic Bomb*. New York: G. P. Putnam's Sons, 1959.

Armstrong, Anne. *Unconditional Surrender: The Impact of the Casablanca Policy upon World War II*. New Brunswick: Rutgers University Press, 1961.

Arnold, H. H. *Global Mission*. London: Hutchinson and Co., Ltd, 1951.

Asbell, Bernard, Global Mission Inc., *When F.D.R. Died*. New York: Holt, Rinehart and Winston, Inc., 1961.

Atomic Energy. London: Royal Institute of International Affairs, 1948.

Barkley, Alben W. *That Reminds Me*. Garden City: Doubleday and Co., Inc., 1954.

Batchelder, Robert C. *The Irreversible Decision, 1939-1950*. Boston: Houghton Mifflin Co., 1962.

Baxter, James Phinney, 3rd. *Scientists Against Time*. Boston: Little, Brown and Co., 1947.

Beloff, Max. *Soviet Policy in the Far East*. London: Oxford University Press, 1953.

Blackett, P. M. S. *Fear, War, and the Bomb: Military and Political Consequences of Atomic Energy*. New York: McGraw-Hill Book Co., Inc., 1949.

Braunbek, Werner. *The Drama of the Atom*. Edinburgh: Oliver and Boyd, 1958.

Broad, Lewis. *The War That Churchill Waged*. London: Hutchinson, 1960.

Brodie, Bernard, ed. *The Absolute Weapon: Atomic Power and World Order*. New York: Harcourt, Brace and Co., Inc., 1946.

Bryant, Arthur. *The Turn of the Tide*. Garden City: Doubleday and Co., Inc., 1957.

————. *Triumph in the West*. Garden City: Doubleday and Co., Inc., 1959.

Burlingame, Roger. *Don't Let Them Scare You: The Life and Times of Elmer Davis*. Philadelphia: J. B. Lippincott Co., 1961.

Butcher, Harry C. *My Three Years with Eisenhower*. New York: Simon and Schuster, Inc., 1946.

Butow, Robert J. C. *Japan's Decision to Surrender*. Stanford: Stanford University Press, 1954.

Byrnes, James F. *All in One Lifetime*. New York: Harper and Brothers, Publishers, 1958.

———. *Speaking Frankly*. New York: Harper and Brothers, Publishers, 1947.

Cantril, Hadley, ed. *Public Opinion*, 1935-1946. Princeton: Princeton University Press, 1951.

Carroll, Wallace. *Persuade or Perish*. Boston: Houghton Mifflin Co., 1948.

Chamberlin, William Henry. *America's Second Crusade*. Chicago: Henry Regnery, 1950.

Churchill, Winston S. *The Second World War, Vol. IV, The Hinge of Fate*. Boston: Houghton Mifflin Co., 1950.

———. *The Second World War, Vol. V, Closing the Ring*. Boston: Houghton Mifflin Co., 1951.

———. *The Second World War, Vol. VI, Triumph and Tragedy*. Boston: Houghton Mifflin Co., 1953.

Clark, Ronald W. *The Birth of the Bomb*. New York: Horizon Press, 1961.

Cline, Ray S. *Washington Command Post: The Operations Division*. Washington, Office of the Chief of Military History, Department of the Army, 1951.

Compton, Arthur H. *Atomic Quest: A Personal Narrative*. New York: Oxford University Press, Inc., 1956.

Craig, William. *The Fall of Japan*. New York: The Dial Press, Inc., 1967.

Craven, Wesley Frank, and Cate, James Lea, eds. *The Army Air Forces in World War II, Vol. V, The Pacific: Matterhorn to Nagasaki, June 1944 to August 1945*. Chicago: University of Chicago Press, 1953.

Current, Richard N. *Secretary Stimson: A Study in State Craft*. New Brunswick: Rutgers University Press, 1954.

Dallin, David J. *Soviet Espionage*. New Haven: Yale University Press, 1955.

Daniels, Jonathan. *The Man of Independence*. Philadelphia: J. B. Lippincott Co., 1950.

Deane, John R. *The Strange Alliance*. New York: The Viking Press, Inc., 1947.

Delbars, Yves. *The Real Stalin*. London: George Allen and Unwin, Ltd., 1953.

Ehrman, John. *Grand Strategy*, Vols. V, VI. London: Her Majesty's Stationery Office, 1956.

Eisenhower, Dwight D. *Crusade in Europe*. Garden City: Doubleday and Co., Inc., 1948.

Evans, Medford. *The Secret War for the A-Bomb*. Chicago: Henry Regnery Co., 1953.

Farley, James A. *Jim Farley's Story: The Roosevelt Years*. New York: McGraw-Hill Book Co., Inc., 1948.

Feis, Herbert. *Between War and Peace: The Potsdam Conference*. Princeton: Princeton University Press, 1960.

————. *Churchill, Roosevelt, Stalin: The War They Waged and the Peace They Sought*. Princeton: Princeton University Press, 1957.

————. *Japan Subdued: The Atomic Bomb and the End of the War in the Pacific*. Princeton: Princeton University Press, 1961.

————. *The Atomic Bomb and the End of World War II*. Princeton: Princeton University Press, 1966.

————. *The China Tangle*. Princeton: Princeton University Press, 1953.

Fermi, Laura. *Atoms in the Family*. Chicago: The University of Chicago Press, 1954.

Fleming, Denna Frank. *The Cold War and Its Origins*, Vols. I, II. Garden City: Doubleday and Co., Inc., 1961.

Flynn, Edward J. *You're the Boss*. New York: The Viking Press, Inc., 1947.

Fogelman, Edwin, ed. *Hiroshima: The Decision to Use the A-Bomb*. New York: Charles Scribner's Sons, 1964.

Gideonese, Harry D.; Fosdick, Raymond B.; Ogburn, William F.; and Schuman, Frederick L. *The Politics of Atomic Energy*. New York: Woodrow Wilson Foundation, 1946.

Giovannitti, Len, and Freed, Fred. *The Decision to Drop the Bomb*. New York: Coward-McCann, Inc., 1965.

Goudsmit, Samuel A. *ALSOS*. New York: Henry Schuman, Inc., 1947.

Gowing, Margaret. *Britain and Atomic Energy*. New York: St. Martin's Press, Inc., 1964.

Grew, Joseph C. *Turbulent Era: A Diplomatic Record of Forty Years, 1904-1945*, Vol. II. Boston: Houghton Mifflin Co., 1952.

Greueff, Stephane. *Manhattan Project: The Untold Story of the Making of the Atomic Bomb*. Boston: Little, Brown and Co., 1967.

Groves, Leslie R. *Now It Can Be Told: The Story of the Manhattan Project*. New York: Harper and Brothers, Publishers, 1962.

Gunther, John. *Roosevelt in Retrospect*. New York: Harper and Brothers, Publishers, 1950.

Hanayarna, Shinso. *The Way of Deliverance: Three Years with the Condemned War Criminals*. New York: Charles Scribner's Sons, 1950.

Hankey, Lord. *Politics: Trials and Errors*. Chicago: Henry Regnery, 1950.

Hart, B. H. Liddell. *The Defense of the West*. New York: Morrow, 1950.

Hashimoto, Mochitsura. *Sunk: The Story of the Japanese Submarine Fleet, 1942-1945*. London: Cassell and Co., Ltd., 1954.

Hassett, William D. *Off the Record with F. D. R., 1942-1945*. New Brunswick: Rutgers University Press, 1958.

Hewlett, Richard G., and Anderson, Oscar E., Jr. *A History of the United States Atomic Energy Commission: The New World, 1939/1946*. University Park: The Pennsylvania State University Press, 1962.

Hillman, William. *Mr. President*. New York: Farrar, Straus and Young, 1952.

Hull, Cordell. *Memoirs*, Vol. II. New York: The Macmillan Company, 1948.

Hunt, Frazier. *The Untold Story of General MacArthur.* New York: The Devin-Adair Co., 1954.

Irving, David. *The German Atomic Bomb: The History of Nuclear Research in Nazi Germany.* New York: Simon and Schuster, Inc., 1967.

Ismay, Lord. *Memoirs.* New York: The Viking Press, Inc., 1960.

James, David H. *The Rise and Fall of the Japanese Empire.* London: George Allen and Unwin, Ltd., 1951.

Jones, Francis Clifford. *Japan's New Order in East Asia: Its Rise and Fall, 1937-45.* London: Oxford University Press, 1954.

Jones, F. C., Borton, Hugh, and Pearn, B. R. *The Far East, 1942–1946.* London: Royal Institute of International Affairs, Oxford University Press, 1955.

Josephson, Matthew. *Sidney Hillman, Statesman of American Labor.* Garden City: Doubleday and Co., Inc., 1952.

Jungk, Robert. *Brighter Than a Thousand Suns: A Personal History of the Atomic Scientists.* New York: Harcourt, Brace and Co., Inc., 1958.

Karig, Walter; Harris, Russell L.; and Manson, Frank A. *Battle Report: Victory in the Pacific,* Vol. V. New York: Rinehart and Co., Inc., 1949.

Kase Toshikazu. *Eclipse of the Rising Sun.* London: Jonathan Cape, 1951. Published in the United States as *Journey to the Missouri.* New Haven, Yale University Press, 1950.

Kato Masuo. *The Lost War: A Japanese Reporter's Inside Story.* New York: Alfred A. Knopf, Inc., 1946.

Kecskemeti, Paul. *Strategic Surrender: The Politics of Victory and Defeat.* Stanford: Stanford University Press, 1958.

King, E. J., and Whitehill, W. M., *Fleet Admiral King: A Naval Record.* New York: W. W. Norton & Co., Inc., 1952.

Knebel, Fletcher, and Bailey, Charles W. II. *No High Ground.* New York: Harper and Brothers, 1960.

Kravchenko, Victor A. *I Chose Freedom.* New York: Charles Scribner's Sons, 1946.

Krylov, Ivan. *Soviet Staff Officer.* London: The Falcon Press, 1951.

Lamont, Lansing. *Day of Trinity.* New York: Atheneum Publishers, 1965.

Lang, Daniel. *Early Tales of the Atomic Age.* Garden City: Doubleday and Co., Inc., 1948.

———. *From Hiroshima to the Moon: Chronicles of Life in the Atomic Age.* New York: Simon and Schuster, Inc., 1959.

Lapp, Ralph E. *Atoms and People.* New York: Harper and Brothers, Publishers, 1956.

———. *The New Force: The Story of Atoms and People.* New York: Harper and Brothers, Publishers, 1953.

Laurence, William L. *Dawn Over Zero: The Story of the Atomic Bomb.* New York: Alfred A. Knopf, Inc., 1946.

———. *The Discovery, the Uses and the Future of Atomic Energy. Men and Atoms.* New York: Simon and Schuster, Inc., 1959.

Leahy, William D. *I Was There.* New York: McGraw-Hill Book Co., Inc., 1950.

Le Bourdais, D. M. *Canada and the Atomic Revolution.* McClelland and Stewart Co., Ltd., 1959.

Leighton, Alexander H. *Human Relations in a Changing World.* New York: E. P. Dutton and Co., Inc., 1949.

Lord, Russell. *The Wallaces of Iowa.* Boston: Houghton Mifflin Co., 1947.

McCloy, John J. *The Challenge to American Foreign Policy.* Cambridge: Harvard University Press, 1953.

McNeill, William Hardy. *America, Britain, and Russia: Their Cooperation and Conflict, 1941-1946.* London: Oxford University Press, 1953.

Martin, Joe. *My First Fifty Years in Politics.* New York: McGraw Hill Book Co., Inc., 1960.

Maxon, Yale Candee. *Control of Japanese Foreign Policy: A Study of Civil-Military Rivalry, 1930-1945.* Berkeley: University of California Press, 1957.

Millett, John D. *The Organization and Role of the Army Service Forces.* Washington: Office of the Chief of Military History, Department of the Army, 1954.

Millis, Walter, ed. *The Forrestal Diaries.* New York: The Viking Press, Inc., 1951.

Moorehead, Alan. *The Traitors.* London: Hamish Hamilton, 1952.

Morison, Elting E. *Turmoil and Tradition: A Study of the Life and Times of Henry L. Stimson.* Boston: Houghton Mifflin Co., 1960.

Morison, Samuel Eliot. *History of United States Naval Operations in World War II, Vol. XIV, Victory in the Pacific: 1945.* Boston: Little, Brown and Co., 1960.
———. *Strategy and Compromise.* Boston: Little Brown and Co., 1958.

Nathan, Otto and Norden, Heinz. *Einstein on Peace.* New York: Simon and Schuster, Inc., 1960.

Newcomb, Richard F. *Abandon Ship! Death of the U. S. S. Indianapolis.* New York: Henry Holt and Co., 1958.

Newman, Bernard. *Soviet Atomic Spies.* London: Robert Hale, Ltd. 1952.

Noel-Baker, Francis. *The Spy Web: A Study of Communist Espionage.* London: The Batchworth Press, 1954.

Public Papers of the Presidents of the United States: Harry S. Truman, 1945. Washington: United States Government Printing Office, 1961.

Rigdon, William M. *White House Sailor.* Garden City: Doubleday and Co., Inc., 1962.

Robinson, Edgar Eugene. *The Roosevelt Leadership, 1933-1945.* Philadelphia: J. B. Lippincott Co., 1955.

Roosevelt, Elliott. *As He Saw It.* New York: Duell, Sloan and Pearce, 1946.

Roper, Elmer. *You and Your Leaders: Their Actions and Your Reactions, 1936-1956.* New York: William Morrow and Co., Inc., 1957.

Rosenman, Samuel I., comp. *The Public Papers and Addresses of Franklin D. Roosevelt: The Call to Battle Stations, 1941; Humanity on the Defensive, 1942; The Tide Turns, 1943; Victory and the Threshold of Peace, 1944-45.* New York: Harper and Brothers, Publishers, 1950.

————. *Working With Roosevelt.* New York: Harper and Brothers, Publishers, 1952.

Roskill, S. W. *The War at Sea, 1939-1945,* 3 Vols. London: Her Majesty's Stationery Office, 1961.

Ruggles, M. J., and Kramish, A. *The Soviet Union and the Atom: The Early Years.* Santa Monica: The Rand Corporation, 1956.

Sherwood, Robert E. *Roosevelt and Hopkins: An Intimate History.* New York: Harper and Brothers, Publishers, 1948.

Shigemitsu Mamoru. *Japan and Her Destiny: My Struggle for Peace.* New York: E. P. Dutton and Co., Inc., 1958.

Singh, Nagendra. *Nuclear Weapons and International Law.* London: Stevens and Sons, Ltd., 1959.

Slessor, Sir John. *The Central Blue.* New York: Praeger, 1957.

Smith, Alice Kimball. *A Peril and a Hope.* Chicago: University of Chicago Press, 1965.

Smyth, Henry De Wolf. *Atomic Energy for Military Purposes: The Official Report on the Development of the Atomic Bomb under the Auspices of the United States Government, 1940-1945.* Princeton: Princeton University Press, 1945.

Soviet Foreign Policy During the Patriotic War: Documents and Materials. London, no date.

Spaight, James Maloney. *The Atomic Problem.* London: Arthur Barron, Ltd., 1948.

Stettinius, Edward R., Jr. *Roosevelt and the Russians: The Yalta Conference.* Garden City: Doubleday and Co., Inc., 1949.

Stimson, Henry L. and McGeorge Bundy. *On Active Service in Peace and War.* New York: Harper and Brothers, 1947.

Strauss, Lewis L. *Men and Decisions.* Garden City: Doubleday and Co., Inc., 1962.

Teller, Edward. *The Legacy of Hiroshima.* Garden City: Doubleday and Co., Inc., 1962.

The Pacific War Research Society, comp. *Japan's Longest Day.* Tokyo: Kodansha International, Ltd., 1965.

The War Reports of General of the Army George C. Marshall, General of the Army H. H. Arnold, Fleet Admiral Ernest J. King. Philadelphia: J. B. Lippincott Co., 1947.

Togo Shigenori. *The Cause of Japan.* New York: Simon and Schuster, Inc., 1956.

Tolischus, Otto D. *Through Japanese Eyes.* New York: Reynal and Hitchcock, 1945.

Truman, Harry S. *Memoirs, Vol. I, Year of Decisions.* Garden City: Doubleday and Co., Inc., 1955.

Tugwell, Rexford G. *A Chronicle of Jeopardy, 1945-55.* Chicago: University of Chicago Press, 1955.

————. *The Democratic Roosevelt.* Garden City: Doubleday and Co., Inc., 1957.

Tully, Grace. *F. D. R. My Boss.* New York: Charles Scribner's Sons, 1949.

Vandenberg, Arthur H., Jr. *The Private Papers of Senator Vandenberg.* Boston: Houghton Mifflin Co., 1952.

Wedemeyer, Albert C. *Wedemeyer Report.* New York: Henry Holt and Co., 1958.

Welles, Sumner. *Seven Decisions That Shaped History.* New York: Harper and Brothers, Publishers, 1950.

White, William S. *Majesty and Mischief: A Mixed Tribute to F. D. R.* New York: McGraw-Hill Book Co., Inc., 1961.

Whitney, Courtney. *MacArthur: His Rendezvous with History.* New York: Alfred A. Knopf, Inc., 1956.

Williams, Mary H. comp., *United States Army In World War II, Special Studies: Chronology, 1941–1945.* Washington: Office of the Chief of Military History, Department of the Army, 1960.

Willoughby, Charles A., and Chamberlain, John. *MacArthur 1941–1951.* New York: McGraw-Hill Book Co., Inc., 1954.

Woodward, Llewellyn. *British Foreign Policy in the Second World War.* London: Her Majesty's Stationery Office, 1962.

Yoshida Shigeru. *The Yoshida Memoirs: The Story of Japan in Crisis.* London: William Heinemann, Ltd., 1961.

Young, Roland. *Congressional Politics in the Second World War.* New York: Columbia University Press, 1956.

Zacharias, Ellis M. *Secret Missions: The Story of an Intelligence Officer.* New York: G. P. Putnam's Sons, 1946.

DOCUMENTS

Documents on American Foreign Relations. Vols. IV–VII. World Peace Foundation, 1941-1945.

Great Britain, Ministry of Information. *Economic Developments in Japan and Japanese-controlled Territory from September 1944 to the Time of Her Collapse,* 2 Parts. London, 1945.

Parliamentary Debates, House of Commons, Fifth Series Vols. CCCLXXXVI, CCCXCVII. London, 1943, 1944.

The Report of the Royal Commission to Investigate the Facts Relating to and the Circumstances Surrounding the Communication, by Public Officials and Other Persons in Positions of Trust of Secret and Confidential Information to Agents of a Foreign Power. Edmond Cloutier, Printer to the King's Most Excellent Majesty, Controller of Stationery. Ottawa, 1946.

U. S. Atomic Energy Commission, *In the Matter of J. Robert Oppenheimer: Transcript of Hearing Before Personnel Security Board.* Washington, 1954.

U. S. Congress, House, Committee on Military Affairs. *Hearings On an Act for the Development and Control of Atomic Energy,* 79th Cong., 1st sess., Serial No. 8403. Washington, 1945.

U. S. Congress, House, Committee on Un-American Activities. *Hearings Regarding Communist Infiltration of Radiation Laboratory and Atomic Bomb Project at the University of California, Berkeley, Calif.,* 81st Cong., 1st sess., 3 Parts, Serial Nos. 92914 and 76878. Washington, 1949, 1950, 1951.

U. S. Congress, House, Committee on Un-American Activities, *Hearings Regarding Shipment of Atomic Material to the Soviet Union During World War II,* 81st Cong., 1st and 2nd sessions, Serial No. 99334. Washington, 1950.

U. S. Congress, House, Committee on Un-American Activities. *Hearings Regarding Steve Nelson,* 81st Cong., 1st sess., Serial No. 92080. Washington, 1949.

U. S. Congress, House, Committee on Un-American Activities. *Report on Soviet Espionage Activities in Connection with the Atomic Bomb,* 80th Cong., 2nd sess. Washington, 1948.

U. S. Congress, Senate, Committee on Armed Services and Committee on Foreign Relations. *Hearings on the Military Situation in the Far East,* 82nd Cong., 1st sess. 5 Parts, Serial No. 83797. Washington, 1951.

U. S. Congress, Senate, Committee on Foreign Relations. *A Decade of American Foreign Policy: Basic Documents, 1941–49,* 81st Cong., 1st sess., Senate Document No. 123, Serial No. 98756. Washington, 1950.

U. S. Congress, Senate, Committee on the Judiciary. *Hearings on the Institute of Pacific Relations,* 82nd Cong., 1st and 2nd sessions, 15 Parts, Serial No. 88348. Washington, 1951-53.

U. S. Congress, Senate, Committee on the Judiciary. *Testimony of Former Russian Code Clerk Relating to the Internal Security of the United States.* Washington, 1955.

U. S. Congress, Senate, Special Committee on Atomic Energy. *Hearings on Atomic Energy,* 79th Cong., 1st sess. 5 Parts, Serial No. 79879. Washington, 1945, 1946.

U. S. Congress, Senate, Special Committee on Atomic Energy. *Hearings on Atomic Energy Act of 1946,* 79th Cong., 2nd sess., 5 Parts, Serial No. 81930. Washington, 1946.

U. S. Congress, Senate, *Surrender of Italy, Germany, and Japan,* 79th Cong., 1st sess., Senate Document No. 91, Washington, 1946.

U. S. Department of the Army, The Manhattan Engineer District. *The Atomic Bombings of Hiroshima and Nagasaki.* Washington, 1946.

U. S. Department of the Army. *Manhattan Engineer District Files: Harrison-Bundy Series.* World War II Records Division, National Archives, General Services Administration.

U. S. Department of Defense. *The Entry of the Soviet Union into the War Against Japan: Military Plans 1941–1945.* Washington, 1955.

U. S. Department of War. *Biennial Report of the Chief of Staff of the United States Army to the Secretary of War,* July 1, 1943, to June 30, 1945. Washington, 1945. *Supplement: Atlas of the World Battle Fronts in Semimonthly Phases to August 15, 1945.* Washington, 1945.

U. S. Department of State. *Bulletin,* Vols. IX and XIII. Washington, December 4, 1945 and August 12, 1945.

U. S. Department of State. *Foreign Relations of the United States, Diplomatic Papers: The Conferences at Cairo and Tehran, 1943.* Washington, 1961.

U. S. Department of State. *Foreign Relations of the United States, Diplomatic Papers: The Conferences at Malta and Yalta, 1945.* Washington, 1955.

U. S. Department of State. *Foreign Relations of the United States, Diplomatic Papers: The Conference of Berlin (The Potsdam Conference, 1945).* Vols. I, II. Washington, 1960.

U. S. Department of State. *The International Control of Atomic Energy.* Washington, 1947.

U. S. Department of State. *U. S. Relations with China.* Washington, 1949. Annex 43.

U. S. Office of Strategic Services. *Crisis in Japan,* Current Intelligence Study No. 13. Washington, April 20, 1945. Library of Congress.

U. S. Office of Strategic Services. *Developments in Japanese Reactions to Surrender.* Washington, August 31, 1945. Library of Congress.

U. S. Office of Strategic Services. *Japan–Conflicting Political Views,* No. 3216. Washington, July 23, 1945. Library of Congress.

U. S. Office of Strategic Services. *Japan: Winter 1944–1945,* Current Intelligence Study No. 19. Washington, May 18, 1945. Library of Congress.

U. S. Office of Strategic Services. *The Japanese Emperor and the War.* Washington, September 8, 1944. Library of Congress.

U. S. Office of Strategic Services. *Working Outline for Analysis of Policy Issues Regarding Japan,* No. 3034. Washington, May 16, 1945. Library of Congress.

U. S. Strategic Bombing Survey. *Japan's Decision to End the War.* Washington, 1946.

U. S. Strategic Bombing Survey. *The Effects of Atomic Bombs on Hiroshima and Nagasaki.* Washington, 1946.

U. S. Strategic Bombing Survey (Pacific), Naval Analysis Division. *Interrogations of Japanese Officials,* OPNAV-P-03-100, Vols. I, II. Washington, 1946.

U. S. Strategic Bombing Survey (Pacific), Naval Analysis Division. *The Campaigns of the Pacific War.* Washington, 1946.

U. S. S. R. Ministry of Foreign Affairs. *Stalin's Correspondence with Churchill, Attlee, Roosevelt and Truman, 1941–45,* Vols. I, II. New York, E. P. Dutton and Company, Inc., 1958.

Personal Correspondence

Ralph A. Bard	August 4, 1958
Styles Bridges	August 12, 1958
Vannevar Bush	August 8, 1960
James F. Byrnes	August 11, 1958
Joseph G. Grew	August 14, 1958
Leslie R. Groves	August 21, 1958
George L. Harrison	February 14, 1955
Mrs. Gertrude G. Harrison	August 17, 1960

Francis H. Heller   July 2, 1958
Alexander Leighton   July 15, 1958
Mrs. George C. Marshall   July 29, 1960
Louis Morton   August 11, 1958
J. R. Oppenheimer   August 15, 1960
Harry S. Truman   August 8, 1958
Henry A. Wallace   August 9, 1958

Personal Papers

Grew, Joseph C., *Papers*. Houghton Library, Harvard University.
Hopkins, Harry L. *Papers*. Franklin D. Roosevelt Library.
Leahy, William D., *Diaries*, 15 Vols. Library of Congress, Vols. 8–11.
Roosevelt, Franklin D. *Papers*. Franklin D. Roosevelt Library.
Stimson, Henry L. *Diary*, 3 Vols. Yale University Library.
Stimson, Henry L. *Papers*. Yale University Library.

Personal Interview

Groves, Leslie R., September 8, 1960. Stamford, Connecticut.

Index